THE ZOLLVEREIN

THE ZOLLVEREIN

W. O. HENDERSON

FRANK CASS & CO. LTD.

1968

Published by
FRANK CASS AND COMPANY LIMITED
67 Great Russell Street, London WC1

First published in the series
Cambridge Studies in Economic History

First edition	1939
Second edition	1959
New impression	1968

Printed in Great Britain by
Thomas Nelson (Printers) Ltd., London and Edinburgh

To
My Wife

PREFACE TO THE FIRST EDITION.

It is in no way necessary for an Editor writing in October 1938 to explain the significance of any study of how nineteenth-century Germany came together out of a loose bundle of states, each with its own economy and fiscal policy, into Bismarck's "Second Reich". The story of the unification, and of the part that the Zollverein took in its attainment, are in general very familiar: no historian has neglected them. There have also been close studies in English of various episodes in Zollverein history; but we have no connected and fully documented account of that history as a whole. This is what Mr Henderson offers.

The material available is almost overwhelming. It is not the least merit of Mr Henderson's study that an—at first sight—unwieldy mass of German work has been mastered and put in order. German archives had already been pretty thoroughly ransacked by his German predecessors; but he has been able to make important contributions to the story of Zollverein—and anti-Zollverein—planning and diplomacy from the archives of Vienna and London. More useful still, he has placed the actors and actions of his story against a lightly but clearly drawn background of nineteenth-century German agriculture, industry and commerce in evolution.

To-day it looks as though the welding of Germany, at least of old Germany, into an economic whole were all but complete, But very recently traces of the old divisions and their imperfect welding were visible. Throughout a great part of Mr. Henderson's narrative, for example, Hamburg the Free City, Harburg its Hanoverian neighbour, and Altona the port of Holstein appear as rivals. The last traces of rivalry based on distinct trade policies disappeared just fifty years ago. But the three towns were only united quite recently, by the present German Government, into the one greater Hamburg of a "Third Reich".

J. H. CLAPHAM

INTRODUCTION TO THE SECOND EDITION

This book was written when a number of German scholars were engaged in research on various aspects of the history of the Zollverein. At that time interest in the rise and expansion of the German customs union had been stimulated by the celebration of the centenary of the founding of the Zollverein. Three important volumes of documents concerning the negotiations which led to the establishment of the customs union were edited by Eisenhart Rothe and Ritthaler and numerous monographs and articles appeared which investigated both the origin and the development of the Zollverein.

My purpose was to provide English readers with a concise account of the history of the German customs union based not only upon these—and earlier—inquiries but also upon my own researches in the archives of London and Vienna. In the last twenty years little new material on the Zollverein has become available. A survey by Rogge of List's attitude to the Zollverein appeared in 1939.[1] The abortive negotiations at Stuttgart and Darmstadt in the early 1820s have been examined by Arnold H. Price. He has shown that although these discussions did not lead to the establishment of even a regional union some of the plans considered at that time were later embodied in the treaty by which Prussia and Hesse-Darmstadt formed a customs union in 1828.[2] The commercial policy of the Thuringian States between 1825 and 1833 has been examined by H. Patze.[3] Anglo-German commercial negotiations in the 1830s and early 1840s are discussed in Lucy Brown, *The Board of Trade and the Free Trade Movement 1830-42* (1958).

My account of the Zollverein endeavoured to show that the establishment of the customs union—and other economic developments—helped to prepare the way for the subsequent political unification of Germany and that it would be a mistake to describe the founding of the Reich purely in terms of the diplomatic skill

[1] H. Rogge, *England, Friedrich List und der deutsche Zollverein* (1939).
[2] Arnold H. Price, *The Evolution of the Zollverein* (University of Michigan Press, 1949).
[3] H. Patze, *Die Zollpolitik der thüringischen Staaten, 1825–1833* (University of Jena dissertation, 1945) and article in the *Vierteljahrschrift für Sozial- und Wirtschafts-Geschichte*, Vol. 40 (1953).

of Bismarck and the military achievements of Moltke. The statesmen who made and developed the customs union—men like Motz, Pommer Esche and Delbrück—should also be numbered among the founders of the united Germany of 1871. Moreover the Zollverein was a factor of great importance in promoting the economic expansion of Germany in the middle of the nineteenth century. It was not merely after 1871 that coal and steel, cotton and wool, chemicals and electricity, shipbuilding and shipping, banking and insurance expanded rapidly in Germany. Earlier progress in the days of the Zollverein also contributed to making Germany the leading industrial state on the Continent. The work of industrialists such as Harkort, Krupp and Mulvany and of statesmen and officials like Beuth, Rother and von der Heydt had laid the foundations of the future economic greatness of Germany some time before political unification was achieved.

Today a study of the history of the establishment and growth of the Zollverein has a new significance. In the middle of the twentieth century Western Europe is trying to do what Germany accomplished over a hundred years ago. It is widely appreciated that high tariffs, rigid quotas and exchange restrictions seriously impede international trade and that the establishment of a customs union would actively promote the expansion of the European economy. Having successfully set up the European Coal and Steel Community in 1952 Western Germany, France, Italy, Holland, Belgium and Luxemburg have proceeded to found a Common Market.

In the circumstances there is something to be learned from an examination of the only large customs union between independent states which worked satisfactorily in the nineteenth century. A survey of the way in which numerous German states, diverse in size, character and material interests came together and established a customs union may throw some light on the problems that face the European Common Market of our own day. The difficulties which German statesmen had to overcome in the 1830s when they set up the Zollverein are in some respects similar to those which the founders of the modern Common Market will have to overcome.

Some aspects of the history of the Zollverein, which are relevant to the establishment of the Common Market, may be mentioned. Germany's experience in the nineteenth century shows that the successful working of a customs union does not require

Member States to be of approximately equal size or to have reached the same stage of economic development. The Zollverein included large States, such as Prussia, and tiny States such as the Anhalt duchies. It included territories whose modern manufactures were already developing such as the Rhineland, Westphalia and Saxony—and regions which still had purely agrarian economies. Defective administrative arrangements are no insuperable obstacle to the success of a customs union. The existence of the veto might have made it impossible to carry on the business of the Zollverein. In fact, negotiations prior to Council meetings enabled difficulties to be settled which might otherwise have led to unfortunate public disputes between member States. German experience too suggests that a customs union stimulates technical progress and promotes industrial expansion. It was no accident that the early railway age in Germany coincided with the formative years of the Zollverein. The Germans discovered that with the development of the Zollverein further economic integration was inevitable. In transport, monetary affairs, commercial law and many other aspects of economic life the German States co-operated much more closely in the 1860s than they had in the 1830s. And this was, in no small measure, due to the existence of the Zollverein. On the other hand the optimistic view that the economic integration of independent States necessarily leads to political integration as well is untenable since twenty years of economic co-operation in Germany did not prevent the outbreak of civil war in 1866.

In writing the history of the Zollverein it has naturally been necessary to refer to various aspects of the growth of the German economy between 1815 and 1871. But the discussion of such topics as the increase in population, the building of roads, railways and canals, the expansion of the mining and textile industries, the rise of great manufacturing regions and the extension of the overseas trade of Hamburg and Bremen must necessarily be very brief. I have described in outline the salient features of the economic history of Germany in the nineteenth century in the second volume of the Admiralty's Geographical Handbook on Germany (1944), and this account has been reprinted in E. J. Passant, *A Short History of Germany, 1815–1945*. Certain topics which throw light on the development of the German customs union are discussed in my studies of *Britain and Industrial Europe* (1954) and *The State and the Industrial Revolution in Prussia*

(1958). The first of these books examines the contribution of English capitalists, entrepreneurs and skilled workers to the genesis of the industrial revolution in Germany while the second includes accounts of the rise of Upper Silesia, the Ruhr, and the Saar as well as a survey of the achievements of Motz who played so important a part in the founding of the Zollverein.

University of Manchester.

W. O. HENDERSON

CONTENTS

LIST OF TABLES

LIST OF MAPS

ABBREVIATIONS

Beiträge...	*Beiträge zur Beurteilung der Zollvereinsfrage* (1852).
B.T.	Board of Trade papers in the Public Record Office.
E.H.R.	*English Historical Review.*
Ec.H.R.	*Economic History Review.*
F.O.	Foreign Office Papers in the Public Record Office.
M.Ch.C.	MS Proceedings of the Manchester Chamber of Commerce.
P.P.	Parliamentary Papers.
Stenographische Berichte	*Stenographische Berichte über die Verhandlungen des...deutschen Zollparlaments* (1868–70).
Verhandlungen	*Verhandlungen der General-Konferenz in Zollvereinsangelegenheiten* (15 volumes, 1836–63).
Vienna Archives	Wiener Haus- Hof- und Staats- Archiv.
V.S.W.	*Vierteljahrschrift für Sozial- und Wirtschaftsgeschichte.*

ACKNOWLEDGEMENTS

I desire to thank Dr J. H. Clapham for many valuable suggestions in preparing the manuscript for publication and in seeing the proofs through the press; my brother (Dr G. B. Henderson of the University of Glasgow) for criticising the book chapter by chapter as it was written; my father and mother for assistance in translating German documents, in compiling the index and in correcting proofs; Mr E. Raymond Streat for permission to examine the manuscript records of the Manchester Chamber of Commerce; and Mr H. Butterfield for permission to examine the papers of Mr John Ward in the Perne Library, Peterhouse.

W. O. H.

November, 1938

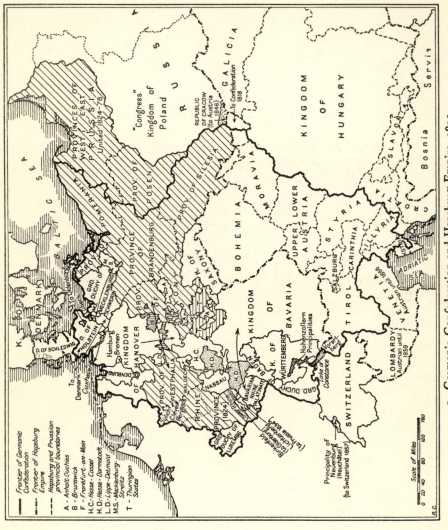

I. Germanic Confederation and Hapsburg Empire, 1815

Chapter I

GERMANY IN 1815

(1) POLITICAL DIVISIONS[1]

Almost the only form of unity which Germans possessed in the eighteenth century was that of language and culture, and even this was no strong bond. It was not an easy matter for Germans to understand each other's dialects. Since Luther's day the written language had been more stable. Lessing may perhaps be regarded as the first of the modern German dramatists and critics, and by 1790 Germany was on the eve of her great age of literary achievement. The influence of French culture in Germany was very strong in the eighteenth century. Frederick the Great himself normally spoke and wrote in French. He was proud to have Voltaire at his court. His palace and grounds at Sans Souci were modelled on Versailles. Germany had no religious unity such as Catholic France and Protestant England possessed, for North Germany was Protestant; Austria, South Germany, the Rhineland and Silesia were predominantly Catholic.

Politically, too, there was little unity. In the eighteenth century Germany was divided into over three hundred States—Kingdoms, Electorates, Duchies, Imperial Cities, ecclesiastical territories, estates of Imperial Knights and many more. They varied in size from Great Powers like the Hapsburg Empire and Prussia to insignificant Principalities like Reuss-Greiz, Reuss-Schleitz, Reuss-Gera and Reuss-Lobenstein. Their territories were scattered. Thus Prussia only succeeded in joining East Prussia to Brandenburg and Pomerania in 1772 and Austria had territories on the Danube, the upper Rhine[2] and in the Nether-

---

[1] See map 1.   [2] The Breisgau on the right bank of the upper Rhine.

lands.[1] It was common for States to enclose completely territories belonging to other sovereigns. The confusion was worst in Central Germany and in the valleys of the Rhine and Danube. In theory this motley collection of States did not enjoy complete independence, their rulers owing allegiance to the Holy Roman Emperor. But by the end of the eighteenth century this had become little more than a formality. The German States in fact acted as sovereign States. The Holy Roman Empire was a mere shadow—a weak and ridiculous institution, flouted on every hand and fit only for the gibes of Voltaire.

During the Revolutionary and Napoleonic Wars Germany was overrun by the French and her antiquated political and social institutions were swept aside sometimes by the conquerors and sometimes by the Germans themselves. The Holy Roman Empire came to an end. The lands of the Imperial Knights, the Imperial Cities and the Church were absorbed by other States. Under Napoleon's influence Germany was organised in three parts. In the north-east was Prussia, ruthlessly reduced in size by the loss of all her territories lying west of the Elbe and of her share of the second and third partitions of Poland. In the south, Austria was less harshly treated but she lost her possessions in the Netherlands, on the Rhine and Danube and also Tirol and Vorarlberg. The other German States, nominally independent but actually under French control, were united in the Confederation of the Rhine (*Rheinbund*). The southern members—Bavaria, Württemberg and Baden— had their possessions increased and were much more compact than before. The northern members were, to a great extent, new States like Westphalia and Berg, set up by Napoleon.

After the defeat of Napoleon in 1814 and 1815, Germany's political structure was again reorganised. It was, of course, impossible to reintroduce the chaotic conditions of the eighteenth

---

[1] The Austrian Netherlands covered much of the territory now held by Belgium and Luxemburg but were divided into two parts by the territories of the Bishop of Liége which stretched from the Dutch frontier across the Meuse to the French frontier at Givet.

century. The German States now numbered only thirty-eight.[1] The Holy Roman Empire was not set up again but its place was taken by the Germanic Confederation (*Deutscher Bund*). Only four of the free cities were revived—Frankfurt-am-Main and the three Hansa towns (Hamburg, Bremen and Lübeck). No restoration of the ecclesiastical States was made. The three southern States were not reduced to their previous limits, though Bavaria had to return Vorarlberg and Tirol to Austria. This is significant, for the southern States—especially when supported by Austria—proved to be a barrier to the attainment of German unity under Prussian leadership. It should be observed, too, that many of Napoleon's valuable social and legal reforms in the Rhineland and South Germany remained.

In other respects Napoleon's work was swept aside. French expansion eastwards was checked. France had annexed all German lands west of the Rhine and north of a line drawn from the junction of the Rhine and Lippe to Travemünde on the Baltic. All this was lost in 1814. Saarbrücken, Saarlouis and Landau, which France had been allowed to retain, were taken from her in November 1815 after the Hundred Days. The States that Napoleon had set up in the north of Germany dis-

---

[1] Thirty-eight in 1815; thirty-nine in 1817 when Hesse-Homburg became a member of the Confederation. Between 1817 and the dissolution of the Confederation in 1866 the number of members was reduced to thirty-three:

1825–26. When the Sachse-Gotha line died out its territories were divided between the Duke of Sachse-Coburg (thereafter Duke of Sachse-Coburg-Gotha), the Duke of Sachse-Meiningen (thereafter Duke of Sachse-Meiningen-Hildburghausen) and the Duke of Sachse-Hildburghausen (thereafter Duke of Sachse-Altenburg).

1847. Anhalt-Köthen dynasty died out and its territories went to Anhalt-Dessau.

1849. Princes of Hohenzollern-Hechingen and Hohenzollern-Sigmaringen ceded their sovereign rights to Prussia.

1863. Anhalt-Bernburg dynasty died out and its territories went to Anhalt-Dessau.

1886. Hesse-Homburg dynasty died out and its territories went to Hesse-Darmstadt.

appeared. Hanover recovered her independence and had more extensive territories than in the eighteenth century. Prussia secured her old German territories and some Polish lands and added to them substantially.

In 1815 Austria was the most powerful of the German States. The Hapsburg Empire had no racial unity but it did possess a certain measure of economic and geographical unity.[1] It included the whole of the middle Danube basin. Its "natural" frontiers were the Alps, the mountains surrounding the Bohemian Plain, the Carpathians, the Transylvanian Alps and the Dinaric Alps. The Hapsburgs had expanded beyond those limits. From the Alps they had descended to the fertile valley of the Po, from the Carpathians to the upper Vistula. So Austria was interested in Italian, Polish and Balkan problems. She had, however, withdrawn from the Rhine and had left to Prussia the defence of Germany's western frontier. Austria's representative presided over the deliberations of the German Federal Diet at Frankfurt-am-Main and in the years that followed the Napoleonic Wars her policy of repressing Liberal sentiments in Germany triumphed. The South German States and many of the small States of Central Germany looked to Austria as their protector against Prussian aggression. But Prussia, under Frederick William III, was more interested in maintaining "law and order" in Germany in co-operation with Metternich than in attempting to emulate Frederick the Great by challenging Austria's position of supremacy in Germany.

Prussia was, after Austria, the largest and most powerful of the German States. Most of her population were Germans and she was more closely identified with German interests than Austria. It is true that she held the two Polish provinces of Posen and West Prussia and was thus to some extent a Slav State—but not nearly to the same extent as she would have been if she had retained the vast Polish territories that she had

[1] R. Sieger, "Die geographischen Grundlagen der Österreich-ungarischen Monarchie...", in *Geographische Zeitschrift*, XXI (1915), pp. 1–22, 83–105, 121–31.

governed between 1795 and 1806. In the eighteenth century
the Hapsburgs, by their possessions on the Rhine and in the
Netherlands, might have attempted to check French expansion
eastward but they had failed to prevent the loss of Lorraine and
had allied themselves with the French in the hope of defeating
Frederick the Great and so recovering Silesia which he had
seized in 1742. Prussia, under Frederick the Great, had beaten
the French at Rossbach. Under the leadership of Stein and his
successors she had recovered from the crushing defeat of Jena-
Auerstädt and had taken an honourable part in the War of
Liberation. In 1815, by acquiring the provinces of Westphalia
and the Rhineland, Prussia became Germany's chief bulwark
against French aggression. Her territories were rather more
than 100,000 square miles in extent—about half the size of
France—and her population numbered some ten millions. Yet
Prussia failed for many years to take that place in German
affairs to which her history, geographical position, size and
population entitled her. Frederick William III and his
ministers were generally content to follow Metternich's lead.
In economic matters, however, Prussia adopted a policy of her
own which ultimately led to the establishment of a large measure of economic unity in Germany.

Prussia's territories were divided into two parts. Her eastern
possessions stretched from Memel at the mouth of the Vistula
to Mühlhausen at the south of the Harz Mountains. There were
seven provinces in this part of the Prussian dominions—East
Prussia, West Prussia (which were combined into one province
between 1824 and 1878), Posen, Pomerania, Brandenburg,
Saxony and Silesia. Some of these provinces were larger than
they had been in the eighteenth century. Swedish Pomerania
(*Neu Vorpommern*) and the island of Rügen had been added to
Pomerania. Saxon territories annexed in 1815 were divided
among three Prussian provinces. Lower Lausitz was added to
Brandenburg, part of upper Lausitz to Silesia and territories
further west to the new province of Saxony. This province was
not compact but was nearly cut in two by Anhalt.

The western possessions of Prussia stretched from the Dutch frontier to Bingen and from Trier on the Moselle to Minden on the Weser. They were composed partly of Church lands once ruled by the Bishops of Münster, Osnabrück, Paderborn, Cologne and Trier. They included the Ruhr district which was later to become so important an industrial centre. In 1815 these territories were divided into three provinces— Westphalia, the lower Rhine and Jülich-Cleves-Berg—but in 1824 the two last named were joined to form the new Rhineland Province. The eastern and western portions of Prussia were divided by Hesse-Cassel, Brunswick and the southern portion of Hanover.

While in the eighteenth century it had been Prussia's ambition to add to her dominions the Polish "corridor" which divided East Prussia from Brandenburg and Pomerania, in the nineteenth century Prussia wished to join her eastern and western provinces at the expense of States like Hanover and Hesse-Cassel. Economic union was secured in 1831 when Hesse-Cassel joined the Zollverein and was consolidated in 1854 on the adhesion of Hanover. Political union was not achieved until 1866[1] when, after the Seven Weeks War, Prussia annexed not only Schleswig-Holstein but Hanover, Hesse-Cassel, Nassau and Frankfurt-am-Main.

There were several German States of moderate size (the middle states)—Hanover, Saxony, the two Mecklenburgs, Oldenburg, Schleswig and Holstein north of the River Main and Bavaria, Württemberg and Baden south of the Main.

---

[1] Between 1815 and 1866 Prussia's territorial acquisitions were small and did not assist in joining her eastern and western provinces—Lichtenberg (purchased from the Duke of Sachse-Coburg-Gotha, 1834), Hohenzollern-Hechingen and Hohenzollern-Sigmaringen (joined Prussia voluntarily, 1849), Lippstadt (1850), Wilhelmshaven (purchased from Oldenburg, 1854) and Lauenburg (annexed 1865). The connection of the Swiss district of Neuchâtel (Neuenburg) with the Prussian monarchy ceased in 1857.

Hanover, the largest of the North-German middle States, fell into three geographical divisions—the main part of the Kingdom which lay between the North Sea and the Harz Mountains, the territory lying in the valley of the Ems between Emden and Osnabrück,[1] and the district south of the Harz Mountains which was cut off by Brunswick from the rest of the country.

The Kingdom of Saxony was compact. It had lost territory in 1815 but retained the important commercial city of Leipzig and was soon to become the most industrialised of the middle States. Mecklenburg-Schwerin was a small but compact State lying between the Elbe and the Baltic. Mecklenburg-Strelitz was situated on the upper Havel south-east of Mecklenburg-Schwerin.[2] The Duchies of Schleswig and Holstein were joined to the Crown of Denmark by a personal union. Holstein was in the German Confederation but Schleswig was outside. Oldenburg lay to the west of the Weser and stretched from the North Sea nearly as far south as the Prussian province of Westphalia.

South Germany, once a medley of scattered territories, now had only three States of importance—Bavaria, Württemberg and Baden. Bavaria had mountain frontiers in the east (the Bohemian Forest) and south (the Bavarian Alps). To the north it stretched beyond the Main. Separated from the main part of Bavaria was the Bavarian Palatinate which lay on the left bank of the Rhine. Württemberg lay in the upper Neckar valley. It reached to the Lake of Constance in the south and had the hills of the Black Forest as its western frontier. Baden occupied the narrow strip of land between the Rhine and the Black Forest. In the south-west its territories reached the western end of Lake Constance: in the north-east they stretched across the Neckar.[3]

[1] This part of the King of Hanover's dominions was joined to the main portion of the country only by a narrow strip of marshland.

[2] A fragment of Mecklenburg-Strelitz lay adjoining the western frontier of Mecklenburg-Schwerin.

[3] On the upper Danube were the two small Principalities of Hechingen and Sigmaringen which were governed by Catholic Hohenzollern rulers.

In Central Germany there were a number of moderate-sized and small States. Many of them had scattered fragments of territory which were enclaves in other States. Brunswick's territories were thus scattered. Two principal districts may be distinguished. One, in the Harz Mountains, cut off Göttingen from the main part of Hanover. The other district contained the capital and lay east and south of the River Aller, a tributary of the Weser. Lippe-Detmold lay to the west of Brunswick and was surrounded on three sides by Prussian territory.

The three Anhalt Duchies (Dessau, Köthen and Bernburg) stretched across the Elbe and were almost entirely surrounded by Prussian territory. Hesse-Cassel (Electoral Hesse) lay on the upper Weser. Hesse-Darmstadt (Grand Duchy of Hesse) was in two chief parts, one lying north and the other south of the River Main: they were divided by the territory of Frankfurt-am-Main and of Hesse-Cassel. Nassau, though small, was compact and lay on both sides of the River Lahn.

The Thuringian States were on the upper Werra and upper Saale and their territories were mixed up together in a state of almost incredible confusion. They included the territories of the Ernstine line of the Wettin family,[1] the lands of the senior[2] and junior[3] branches of the Reuss family and the Principalities of Schwarzburg-Rudolstadt and Schwarzburg-Sondershausen. They had only two institutions in common—a court of appeal and the University of Jena. But in Karl August of Sachse-Weimar, Thuringia had a ruler who, by calling Goethe and Herder to his court, had made Weimar for a time one of the greatest cultural centres of Germany.

There were also four free cities in Germany—Hamburg, Bremen, Lübeck and Frankfurt-am-Main. Hamburg territory outside the city included several neighbouring villages, the district of Cuxhaven-Ritzebüttel at the mouth of the Elbe and the island of Neuwerk in the North Sea.

[1] Sachse-Weimar, Sachse-Gotha, Sachse-Meiningen, Sachse-Hildburghausen and Sachse-Coburg.   [2] Reuss-Greiz.
[3] Reuss-Lobenstein, Reuss-Schleiz and Reuss-Ebersdorf.

Although the political map of Germany had been much simplified, frontiers were still very confused in some parts of the country, particularly north of the Main between the Rhine and Elbe. Within a few miles of Frankfurt-am-Main, for example, were the territories of five different States, so that the city in which the Diet of the Germanic Confederation met came to be an asylum for "all the rascals of central Germany; anyone who was ejected over the Hesse-Darmstadt frontier entered by another gate after a short walk through Homburg or Nassau...".[1]

In these circumstances it is hardly surprising that Germans themselves were sometimes none too clear about the political geography of the Fatherland. The statesmen assembled at Vienna in 1815 failed to make Hesse-Homburg a member of the Confederation because they forgot all about her. Later, when some of the smaller States of Central Germany were trying to come to an agreement to build new roads it was found, after some months, that one of the frontiers they had been discussing was different from what they had all along assumed.[2] These conditions obviously hampered German commerce. The great rivers and the chief roads generally crossed numerous frontiers where delays occurred and dues had to be paid. Hanover, for example, levied duties at Stade which bore heavily on goods going up the Elbe.

The government of the various German States was, for the most part, in the hands of the princes and the landed aristocracy. Only in the South German States, in some of the smaller States of Central Germany, and in the free cities had parliamentary institutions developed to some extent, and here the middle classes were not without influence in public affairs. In the Hapsburg Empire and in Prussia there were no national parliaments, the only representative assemblies being provincial

[1] H. von Treitschke, *Deutsche Geschichte im neunzehnten Jahrhundert*, II (1927), p. 379.
[2] P. Thimme, *Strassenbau und Strassenpolitik in Deutschland zur Zeit der Gründung des Zollvereins*, 1825–35 (1931), p. 26.

estates. Not until 1847 were the separate Diets of Prussia brought together in a United Diet. Saxony and Hesse-Cassel had medieval estates until 1831 and the two Mecklenburgs preserved them until the end of the Great War!

The German States were united in a Confederation. Prussia's Polish provinces (West Prussia and Posen) and East Prussia as well as most of the Hapsburgs' non-German lands were excluded. The Confederation was a *Staatenbund* and not a *Bundesstaat*—that is to say, it was a union of sovereign States in which unanimity was essential before joint action could be taken and it was not a federation of States in which the members gave up some of their sovereign rights to the central power. The Diet of the Confederation was a meeting of delegates who voted according to their instructions: it was not a parliament in which members voted without consulting their constituencies. The delegates at Frankfurt-am-Main had, indeed, the privileges of ambassadors. It was obviously difficult for an assembly so constituted to work effectively.

(2) ECONOMIC CONDITIONS[1]

The lack of effective political unity in Germany and the strength of the spirit of particularism in 1815 help to explain the economic backwardness of the country in comparison with Britain or France. Voltaire had declared that Germany was condemned to eternal poverty,[2] and conditions after the

[1] See A. Sartorius von Waltershausen, *Deutsche Wirtschaftsgeschichte*, 1815–1914 (1923), part i; Werner Sombart, *Die deutsche Volkswirtschaft im neunzehnten Jahrhundert* (6th edition, 1923), book i; Josef Kulischer, *Allgemeine Wirtschaftsgeschichte...*, II (1929), book iv; J. H. Clapham, *The Economic Development of France and Germany*, 1815–1914 (4th edition, 1936), chs. ii and iii; Pierre Benaerts, *Les Origines de la Grande Industrie allemande* (1932), ch. iii; Carl Brinkmann, "The Place of Germany in the Economic History of the Nineteenth Century", in *Ec.H.R.* IV (April, 1933); and W. O. Henderson, "The Rise of German Industry", *Ec.H.R.* V (April, 1935), pp. 120–4.

[2] H. Feis, *Europe the World's Banker* (1930), p. 60.

Napoleonic Wars seemed to justify his prophecy. German States aimed at economic self-sufficiency, but the resources of the country as a whole remained comparatively undeveloped. Her commerce decayed. Her shipping was insignificant and she had little carrying trade. She had few foreign investments. Little use was made of her coal deposits. The Ruhr district produced only 388,000 tons of coal in 1815. Her industries, with few exceptions, were small. Germany was predominantly an agricultural country and remained so for some time. Three-quarters of her population of 25 millions lived in the country. In Prussia the urban population remained almost stationary in the first half of the nineteenth century: it rose only from 26·4 to 28 per cent of the total population between 1800 and 1849.

Agricultural conditions in Germany were very varied. East of the Elbe the land had once been conquered by Germans from Slavs and both races had left their mark on the agriculture of the region. Some of the villages appear to have retained to a considerable extent their original Slavonic organisation and had been little changed by the German colonists. In these villages the houses were grouped in the form of a circle or an oblong outside of which lay the three open fields divided into irregular strips. Other villages had been founded by German and other settlers. In Mecklenburg, Pomerania and other districts were to be found "marsh colonies" in which there was a large dyke to keep out the water. The houses lay alongside the dyke and had plots of land behind them. "Forest colonies" were common in Silesia and Bohemia. They lay in valleys and consisted of a row of houses along a stream: each house had its own piece of land behind it. Both types of "colonies" had been introduced from Western Germany in the Middle Ages, the "marsh colonies" from Holland and the coast of Frisia, the "forest colonies" from the Black Forest, the Odenwald and the Thuringian Forest.

A more important result of the German conquest and settlement of the Slav territories east of the Elbe was that the land was divided into large estates each under a lord of the manor. The lords, or Junkers, had for the last two centuries been increasing their private domains as much as possible. They seized waste lands, drained marshes and felled forests. They also got rid of small tenants (*Bauernlegen*) and added the land they had cultivated to their own. Attempts of rulers to stop this process had generally been ineffective or had been undertaken too late. In the eighteenth century it was common for domains to be leased to farmers who cultivated on a large scale but in the nineteenth century the tendency was for the Junkers to farm their estates themselves.

Agricultural conditions west of the Elbe and in Schleswig and Holstein were more complicated than in the east. Compact villages with open fields were common in Western Germany. They resembled the existing three-field villages in North-east France and those which were soon to be only a memory in the English Midlands. There were, however, many exceptions to this type of agriculture which are to be accounted for partly by geographical conditions. In forest and hilly regions and in the valleys of the Rhine and its tributaries, where vineyards were common, there were few open fields. Sometimes there were smallholdings farmed by the owner, sometimes—as in the Eiffel—land was still held in common. In some districts the owner might be free to cultivate as he pleased but in other regions communal methods survived. The marshy Frisian coast resembled the coasts of Holland and Flanders and was a district of isolated farmhouses and "marsh colonies". Cleves and Gelders resembled neighbouring parts of Holland where there were scattered farms on which improved methods of working the land were used. Where towns had developed in Western Germany, agricultural conditions had naturally changed in the vicinity. It was necessary to provide food for the town and frequently raw materials for local domestic industries. Agricultural changes in the second half of the eighteenth century had included the general introduction of red clover for fodder, the extension of potato-growing in the sandy plains of the north and of tobacco-culture in the south, and the improvement of the breeding of horses, cattle and sheep.

Generalisations regarding the position of German peasants in 1815 are as difficult to make as those on agricultural conditions. But here, too, the Elbe forms a rough line of division. In the west the most fortunate peasants, though legally subject to a lord, were virtually free: the rent and services they gave were generally nominal. Other peasants had to work regularly for their lord and their freedom was limited since they might be obliged, for example, to grind their corn at the lord's mill. The occupation of much of Western Germany by the French during the Napoleonic Wars improved the position of the peasant so far as his relations with his lord were concerned though he suffered in other ways. In Eastern Germany, on the other hand, the services demanded from the peasants—and particularly from his family—were heavier than in the west. The emancipation of the peasants was a slow process. In the eighteenth century rulers like Frederick the Great, Joseph II and Karl Friedrich of Baden had begun the work. They naturally found it easier to carry out their reforms on their own domains than in other parts of their territories. In Prussia the work was taken up again between 1807 and 1821 when a series of edicts and regulations—of which the best known are those of 1807–8— were issued. Peasants gave up part of their lands to their lords and became full proprietors of the remainder. The change, however, was not completed by the middle of the nineteenth century. The lowest grades of peasants—such as the *Kossäthen*—were untouched by these laws and generally became agricultural labourers pure and simple.

The German town, like the German countryside, retained in 1815 many medieval characteristics. Towns were small and had frequently hardly outgrown their ancient walls. Berlin had less than 200,000 inhabitants, Hamburg had 100,000, Breslau and Munich 60,000 each. The inhabitants were frequently engaged in agricultural work for part of their time. Berlin still had its open fields, cultivated on a communal basis by persons who had no compact plots but a number of scattered strips. Wiesbaden had open fields and scattered strips thirty years later.[1] In other ways, however, the town was sharply divided from the country-side. Until 1806 it was illegal in Prussia for a noble to buy land from a free peasant or for a peasant to buy land in a town. The principles of the old gild system remained in most German States until the 'forties and 'fifties. Industries were run by small men working in their own homes and in direct contact with the consumer. In 1816 there were nearly twice as many "masters" as workmen.[2] As the social prestige and financial prospects of Civil Servants and professional men in Germany were generally better than those of men engaged in business, there was little to attract enterprising young men to industrial or commercial pursuits.

Lack of capital hindered industrial expansion. Such "capitalist" enterprises as were undertaken in Germany in the early nineteenth century were often financed from the profits of agriculture or commerce. There were great landlords in East Germany who set up breweries, distilleries, sugar-refineries, mines and foundries as part of their estates. In other parts of the country such enterprises were financed out of the private resources of their owners. Krupp's first foundry (for cast steel) was set up with 50,000 thalers collected from family resources. Borsig's engineering firm was established with 8000 thalers of personal savings.[3] The technique of German money markets was far behind that of Amsterdam, London or Paris. But there were considerable developments shortly after 1815 owing, first, to the heavy borrowings of many German States after the con-clusion of peace and, secondly, to the decline of the Amsterdam

---

[1] T. C. Banfield, *Industry of the Rhine*, I (1846), p. 170.

[2] There were 258,830 masters and 145,459 men. See the table in G. Schmoller, *Zur Geschichte der deutschen Kleingewerbe im neunzehnten Jahrhundert* (1870), p. 65.

[3] M. M. Postan, "Recent Trends in the Accumulation of Capital", in *Ec.H.R.* VI, no. 1 (October, 1935). Cf. E. Kohn-Bramstedt, *Aristocracy and the Middle-Classes in Germany...*, 1830–1900 (1937), ch. ii.

money market after the occupation of that city by the French.[1]

Most of the raw materials needed by German workers in the towns were to be found at home. Timber from native forests was used by the builder and carpenter. Iron and steel were produced in the Rhineland and upper Silesia. There were nine million sheep in Prussia alone to supply the needs of wool manufacturers. Flax was grown in Silesia, tobacco in South Germany, barley and hops in Bavaria. The chief imports of raw materials were cotton and tobacco from America, and hemp and furs from Russia. Other imports were cane-sugar from the West Indies, spices from the Far East, wines from France, Spain and Portugal, fruits and silks from Italy, and manufactured articles—particularly textiles and hardware—from Britain.

Napoleon's work in Germany had had important effects upon German industries. There was a collapse of certain industries which had been artificially created by rulers in the eighteenth century to produce luxuries for their capitals or a surplus of goods suitable for export to secure a "favourable balance of trade". Industries also suffered in those parts of the country where the French occupation had involved particularly heavy financial sacrifices. But the disappearance of many States, the abolition of internal dues in new States, the opening of the French and Belgian markets to manufactures in those parts of Germany which were incorporated in the French Empire,[2] and the crippling of English competition by the Continental System all favoured the expansion of certain industries. Yet the Conti-

---

[1] R. Ehrenberg, *Capital and Finance in the Age of the Renaissance* (English translation, 1928), pp. 374–5. For the early development of the Berlin market for dealing in foreign Government stock, see B. Brockhage, *Zur Entwicklung des preussisch-deutschen Kapitalexports*, vol. 1, *Berliner Markt für ausländische Staatspapiere*, 1816–40 (1910); cf. H. Stuebel, *Staat und Banken im Preussischen Anleihewesen von 1871–1913* (1935), ch. i, sect. i (development of Prussian national debt, 1820–50).

[2] Thus the iron industry of the region west of the lower Rhine expanded to meet the demands of the armament manufacturers of Liége.

nental System "had not built up industry so firmly as to prevent
a relapse for some years after the close of the blockade; and this
was due to the incapacity of protection to provide for the
adoption of the technical advances that had not been introduced
before the beginning of the blockade".[1]

The German textile industries had flourished in the Middle
Ages, had declined after the Thirty Years War, and had shown
signs of revival in the eighteenth century. The raw materials
of the linen and woollen industries were produced at home but
cotton had to be imported from the Eastern Mediterranean.
At the end of the eighteenth century the manufacture of linen
was flourishing, particularly in Silesia, Saxony and Münster.
"The value of linen manufactures exported from Prussia in
1799 was about £2,000,000 being fully a fourth part of all the
manufactures in that country." The linen cloths of Westphalia
had a world-wide reputation. The Continental System struck
the industry a severe blow and even in the 'sixties it had not
"reached its former very prosperous condition".[2] The ever-
recurring distress of the Silesian handloom linen weavers was
a serious social problem.[3] The chief product of the cotton industry was not a pure cotton cloth but fustian (*Barchent*), a
cloth made from linen warp and cotton weft. Mechanical
spinning was introduced into Saxony in 1782, mechanical
weaving shortly afterwards. But before machinery had had
time to make much progress, the industry received a check
owing to its inability to get American cotton at the time of the
Continental System.[4] The woollen industry was of some im-

[1] E. F. Heckscher, *The Continental System* (1922), p. 306.

[2] A. J. Warden, *The Linen Trade* (1864), pp. 268–71.

[3] For the Silesian linen industry see W. Parschke, *Über den schlesischen
Leinwandhandel* (appeared anonymously, Breslau, 1827); Alfred Zimmermann, *Blüte und Verfall des Leinengewerbes in Schlesien* (Breslau, 1885);
and Christian Meyer, "Die schlesische Leinenindustrie und ihr Notstand",
in *Vierteljahrschrift für Volkswirtschaft, Politik und Kulturgeschichte*,
Jahrgang XXIX, Band CXV (1892), pp. 58–66.

[4] R. M. R. Dehn, *The German Cotton Industry* (1913), pp. 1–4. For a
list of reports, books and articles on the German cotton industry, see

portance. In 1822 a Blackwell Hall factor stated that while the cheaper types of German cloths were not so well manufactured as British cloths, "the Prussian cloths are manufactured with a great deal of address, and I think they are our most powerful rivals".[1] The German silk industry was established in Crefeld and elsewhere but was still in its infancy.

The working of iron and other metals was widespread, particularly in hilly, wooded regions where charcoal was available for smelting and water for power. In the Rhineland, towns specialised in different kinds of iron and steel wares. In the west, Aachen (Aix-la-Chapelle) produced needles and Stolberg brass articles. In the east there were old-established metal—particularly iron and steel—industries in the valleys of the Lenne, Wupper and Sieg. Remscheid produced steel goods, and Solingen cutlery. In the Middle Ages the chief product had been swords and a high standard of workmanship had been attained. Then other articles such as knives and scissors were manufactured. The old gild system came to an end in 1809. "With the breakdown of trade supervision, the efficiency of the workers was undermined and much of the ancient skill was lost. From the standpoint of industrial technique the century 1750 to 1850 was one of steady retrogression.... Cheapness took the place of quality; the mean triumphs of the unscrupulous merchant were substituted for the artistic achievements of the self-reliant craftsman."[2] Some 4700 persons were engaged in the industry in 1800. Large factories using steam power were virtually unknown in the first half of the nineteenth century. In Central Germany, mining and metal working were carried on in the Thuringian and Bohemian Forests. In upper Silesia the demand for armaments during the Napoleonic Wars had enabled some expansion to take

pp. 169–70 of the bibliography in W. O. Henderson, *The Lancashire Cotton Famine*, 1861–65 (1934).

[1] J. Bischoff, *A Comprehensive History of the Woollen and Worsted Manufacture...*, II (1842), pp. 199, 362.

[2] G. I. H. Lloyd, *The Cutlery Trades* (1913), pp. 372–3.

place. At Augsburg articles of high value were made in gold, silver and copper.

The organisation of wholesale and transit trade was concentrated at the ports—particularly the North Sea ports of Hamburg and Bremen—and inland towns with adequate communications to the ports and the chief retail markets. Thus Frankfurt-am-Main was linked by water to the Rhine and by road to Hamburg and the markets of South and Central Germany. Cologne was the centre of a network of roads joining the Ruhr district with Aachen and the valley of the Meuse. Breslau derived its importance from the fact that the River Oder was not navigable above it and consequently goods had to be unloaded there.

The importance of the great German fairs for wholesale trade at the beginning of the nineteenth century may be gathered from Charles Reinhard's description of 1805: "The produce and manufactures of Great Britain exported to Germany, with the exception of consignments to particular mercantile houses, are sold at the great fairs held, at certain seasons of the year, at Frankfurt (-am-Main), Leipzig, Brunswick and Nürnberg. The Easter fair at Leipzig is justly celebrated for the immense quantities of British manufactures sold there. Towards the latter end of March, numberless bales of printed and other coloured cottons, of the finest cambrics, and of the most beautiful muslins, are sent from Glasgow, Paisley, Rutherglen and other manufacturing places to Hamburg...."[1]

The fairs suffered from the dislocation of foreign trade during the Napoleonic Wars but subsequently recovered some of their old importance and again became great centres not merely of German but of international trade. McCulloch wrote in 1847 that at the fairs of Frankfurt-am-Main, Frankfurt-an-der-Oder and Leipzig "the concourse of merchants and the business done...are generally very great. They are copiously

---

[1] Charles Reinhard, *The Present State of the Commerce of Great Britain* (1805), p. 7 n., quoted by Arthur Redford, *Manchester Merchants and Foreign Trade*, 1794–1858 (1934), p. 95.

supplied with the cotton stuffs, twist, cloths and hardware of England; the silks and jewellery of France; the printed cotton of Switzerland and Austria; the raw, manufactured and literary products of Germany; the furs of the North; Turkey carpets; Cashmere shawls, etc.; and there also are to be found merchants of all countries, those of Ispahan negotiating with those of Montreal for the purchase of furs; and Georgians and Servians supplying themselves with the cotton of Manchester and the jewellery of Paris. There in fact, are met the representatives, as it were, of every people in the world, labouring, though without intending it, to promote each other's interests, and to extend and strengthen those ties that bind together the great family of the human race."[1]

Communications were very poor in Germany in the early years of the nineteenth century. The character in one of Jean Paul's novels who took some splints with him when setting out on a journey was only taking a necessary precaution. In winter, travelling was particularly difficult. One traveller wrote that in Thuringia in 1814 his coach was stuck in a hole filled with snow and he had to be rescued by a detachment of Russian soldiers. Two years later another traveller took no less than five hours to go by coach from Weimar to Erfurt, a distance of about twelve miles. In the early 'twenties the post-coach from Berlin to Breslau carried only three passengers and took forty hours for the journey. The fare was 12 thalers. Only those who could afford to secure frequent changes of horses moved with any speed. Some good roads, such as the one from Metz to Mainz and Bremen, were built in those parts of Germany that were under the control of the French but they were exceptional. On the whole, river and canal communications were also inadequate. Poor communications hampered trade and at times of bad harvest some towns suffered considerably owing to the difficulty of bringing food from any distance. It was not easy to bring coal and iron together for purposes of manufacture. As

[1] J. R. McCulloch, *A Dictionary of Commerce*, 1 (edition of 1847), p. 572.

late as 1830 Harkort complained that the Westphalian iron industry could not develop as the coal and iron lay 46 miles apart.[1]

Few could have foreseen in 1815 that Germany with her cumbersome federal constitution, her internal tariff barriers and her comparatively poor natural resources would one day become the leading industrial State on the Continent.

[1] L. C. A. Knowles, *The Industrial and Commercial Revolutions in Great Britain...* (edition of 1930), p. 188.

Chapter II

THE ESTABLISHMENT OF THREE CUSTOMS UNIONS IN GERMANY, 1815–1828

(1) THE FAILURE OF THE GERMANIC CONFEDERATION, 1815–20

As early as the fourteenth century an Englishman had referred to the multiplicity of customs barriers in Germany as *miram Germanorum insaniam*.[1] The comment is equally applicable to the state of affairs in the eighteenth century when over three hundred rulers, virtually unchecked by any central authority, levied such customs and excise as they pleased. It would have been bad enough if all these States had had customs frontiers identical with political frontiers. But duties were levied not at the frontiers but on the roads and rivers, at town gates and at markets. It is estimated that in 1790 there were some eighteen hundred customs frontiers in Germany. "The Germans trade like prisoners behind prison bars", declared a Frenchman.[2] In 1722 Bavaria had over four hundred customs houses. The shipper who took goods on the Rhine from Strassburg to the Dutch frontier, on the Main from Bamberg to Mainz, or on the Weser from Minden to Elsfleth (below Bremen) had to pay over thirty tolls on each of these journeys. Fourteen dues were charged on the Elbe between Magdeburg and Hamburg. The traveller who went from Dresden to Magdeburg had to pass

---

[1] W. Roscher, *Zur Gründungsgeschichte des Zollvereins* (1870), p. 5. Nothing came of sixteenth- and seventeenth-century schemes for the economic unification of Germany. See, for example, Michael Doeberl, "Das Projekt einer Einigung Deutschlands auf wirtschaftliche Grundlagen aus dem Jahre 1665...", in *Forschungen zur Geschichte Bayerns*, VI (1898), pp. 163–205.

[2] Quoted by J. Kulischer, *Allgemeine Wirtschaftsgeschichte...*, II (1929), p. 501.

sixteen customs houses. Tariffs were complicated. Prussia, for example, imposed over sixty different rates of customs and excise.[1]

Napoleon's territorial changes in Germany improved matters somewhat, for the number of States was drastically reduced. Between 1807 and 1812 the three southern States dropped most of their internal dues.[2] The administration of customs in Germany, however, was still confused. Few of the thirty-nine States had customs frontiers of the modern type. Most of them continued to raise revenue by local excise dues of various kinds.

Four of the most serious disadvantages of this state of affairs deserve notice. First, legitimate internal trade was seriously hampered. An influential Union of Merchants (*der Deutsche Handels- und Gewerbsverein*)[3] complained in a petition drawn up by Friedrich List[4] in 1819, that numerous customs barriers

[1] For Prussia's tariff policy in the eighteenth century, see Hermann Freymark, *Zur preussischen Handels- und Zollpolitik von 1648–1818* (Halle-an-der-Saale, 1897: Dissertation). Conditions were little better in some other parts of the Continent at the end of the eighteenth century. Thus the Hapsburg Empire, Switzerland and Italy lacked economic unity.

[2] Bavaria, 1807; Württemberg, 1810; Baden, 1812. Bavaria had made some reforms in her customs system as early as 1765 (J. Kulischer, II, p. 501). But nothing came of suggestions that the Confederation of the Rhine should form a customs union.

[3] For the Union of Merchants see *Friedrich List: Werke* (edited by Beckenrath, Goeser and others; eight volumes, 1927–33), I, pp. 67 ff.; H. W. F. Bauerreis, *Kurzgefasste Geschichte des Deutschen Handels- und Gewerbsvereins vom Jahre 1819* (1838); article by J. M. Elch in the *Allgemeines Organ für Handel und Gewerbe* (Cologne, September 29, 1846); translation of German pamphlet by E. E. Hoffmann enclosed in C. Koch to Lord Palmerston, February 4, 1847 (F.O. 30/101); and Hans-Peter Olshausen, *Friedrich List und der Deutsche Handels- und Gewerbsverein* (1935).

[4] For List see *Friedrich List: Werke* (8 vols. 1927–33); Karl Jentsch, *Friedrich List* (1901); Margaret E. Hirst, *Life of Friedrich List* (1909); Karl Goeser, *Der Junge Friedrich List...* (1914); F. Borckenhagen, *National- und handelspolitische Bestrebungen in Deutschland 1815–1822 und die Anfänge Friedrich Lists* (1915), and F. Lenz, *Friedrich List. Der*

"cripple trade and produce the same effect as ligatures which prevent the free circulation of the blood. The merchants trading between Hamburg and Austria, or Berlin and Switzerland must traverse ten States, must learn ten customs tariffs, must pay ten successive transit dues. Anyone who is so unfortunate as to live on the boundary line between three or four States spends his days among hostile tax-gatherers and customs house officials. He is a man without a country."[1]

Secondly, the multiplicity of customs encouraged contraband traffic and "caused the country to swarm with petty smugglers". Thirdly, "the customs house administration was costly and generally inefficient, from the extent of frontier to be guarded".[2] Fourthly, there were many complaints that owing to low duties imposed by ports like Hamburg and Bremen and by great markets like Frankfurt-am-Main, no adequate protection was afforded to German industry at a time when cheap British goods were flooding continental markets. "All States favour home industries by tariffs: Germany alone fails to protect her children", wrote seventy Rhineland manufacturers in a petition to the King of Prussia in April, 1818.[3] Similar sentiments were expressed in a popular ballad of the period:[4]

Mann und das Werk (1936). For the attitude of the Hanse Towns to List's activities at this time see.E. Baasch, "Die deutschen wirtschaftlichen Einheitsbestrebungen, die Hansestädte und Friedrich List bis zum Jahre 1821", in *Historische Zeitschrift* (CXXII), 3rd series, vol XXVI, 1920, pp. 454–485.

[1] The petition of the Union of Merchants is printed by W. von Eisenhart Rothe and A. Ritthaler, *Vorgeschichte und Begründung des deutschen Zollvereins*, 1815–1834, I (3 vols. 1934), pp. 320–4; and in *Friedrich List: Werke*, I (ii), pp. 492–6: English translation in Margaret E. Hirst, pp. 137–44.

[2] John Bowring, *Report on the Prussian Commercial Union*... (P.P. 1840, XXI), p. 2.

[3] Printed by Eisenhart Rothe and Ritthaler, I, pp. 69–71. The separate German States, of course, protected home industries in varying degrees.

[4] These (and other) verses are printed in the *Geschichte der Handelskammer zu Frankfurt-am-Main* (issued by the Frankfurt Chamber of Commerce 1908), p. 332 n.

Auf Fürsten, auf, macht uns durch Wort und Thaten
  Von diesem Joche frey
Denn drückend ist für alle deutschen Staaten
  Die Handels-Tyranney.

O, wehrt der Noth, der Unthat jener Briten
  Mit ernst und Energie
Vergesst es nicht, wir haben mit gestritten
  Für unsere Industrie.

[Ye Princes rise, let action wise
  From bondage make us free,
No German State but feels the weight
  Of traders' tyranny.

For those in need through British greed
  Be earnest effort made,
Forget it not, we too have fought
  To further German trade.]

There were many suggestions in the years that followed the
Napoleonic Wars for remedying Germany's economic difficulties by forming a German customs union. Supporters of
such a proposal claimed that the establishment of free-trade in
Germany, by abolishing all internal dues and by levying substantial dues on the importation of foreign manufactured goods,
would provide the indispensable basis for the revival and expansion of Germany's industries. The fact that so many have
claimed to be the first to propose the uniting of the whole of
Germany within a single customs frontier suggests that the
advantages of such a plan were already recognised, if not by
the general public, at least by some of the leading statesmen,
publicists and business men.

Before the meeting of the Congress of Vienna and during its
deliberations, suggestions were made for the economic unification of Germany. In 1814, for example, Stein advocated the
abolition of all internal dues and prohibitions. Arndt demanded
the unification of coinage, weights and measures and the

removal of internal dues levied on the roads and rivers. Similar views were expressed by Görres in the *Rheinische Merkur*.[1]

The statesmen assembled at Vienna recognised the need for facilitating commerce in Germany. By Article 19 of the Federal Constitution (June 8, 1815) "the Confederated States reserve to themselves the right of deliberating, at the first meeting of the Diet at Frankfurt, upon the manner of regulating the commerce and navigation from one State to another, according to the principles adopted by the Congress of Vienna".[2] By an agreement of March, 1815, which was subsequently embodied in the Final Act of the Vienna Congress, "the Powers whose States are separated or traversed by the same navigable river, engage to regulate, by common consent, all that regards its navigation". The most important principle to be observed in this regulation was freedom of navigation. "The navigation of the rivers, along their whole course, referred to in the preceding Article, from the point where each of them becomes navigable, to its mouth, shall be entirely free, and shall not, in respect to commerce, be prohibited to any one; it being, however, understood, that the regulations established with regard to the police of this navigation, shall be respected; as they will be framed alike for all, and as favourable as possible to the commerce of all nations."[3] Subsequent clauses repeated this provision with specific reference, first, to the Rhine and, secondly, to the Neckar, Main, Mosel, Meuse and Scheldt. But the German Governments did not undertake promptly the negotiations contemplated in 1815, and, both on the roads and the rivers, commerce continued to be hampered by vexatious dues of various kinds.

In 1817, a year of serious economic distress in Germany and Austria, Württemberg appealed to the Federal Diet to secure the removal of recently imposed restrictions on the export

[1] Eisenhart Rothe and Ritthaler, I, pp. 297–8.
[2] E. Hertslet, *Map of Europe by Treaty*, vol. 1 (1875), no. 26.
[3] *Ibid.* no. 11.

of grain although she herself had added to the difficulties of the Vorarlberg by forbidding its export.[1] The Commission which was set up to examine the question confined its attention to the special circumstances of which Württemberg had complained and did not deal with the wider problem of carrying out Article 19. It drew up a draft treaty for internal freedom of trade in various kinds of food. Austria's hostility to this proposal was increased by Bavaria's suggestion that non-German territories of members of the Confederation should be included in any new economic arrangements. Württemberg raised the matter again in February, 1818, but without result.[2] Shortly afterwards Prussia issued her new tariff of May 26, 1818,[3] which many Germans considered a new obstacle in the way of securing German economic unity.

The failure of the first attempt to use the machinery of the Confederation to break down internal customs barriers led to fresh proposals for the formation of a German customs union. Friedrich List, in the petition of the Union of Merchants to the Federal Diet (April 14, 1819) wrote that "only the remission of the internal customs, and the erection of a general tariff for the whole Federation, can restore national trade and

[1] Adolf Beer, *Die österreichische Handelspolitik im neunzehnten Jahrhundert* (1891), p. 54 and "Österreich und die deutschen Handelsbeziehungen in den Jahren 1817–1820", in *Österreich-ungarische Revue*, III (New Series, 1887), pp. 273–311.

[2] Eisenhart Rothe and Ritthaler, I, pp. 314–16, and L. K. Aegidi, *Aus der Vorzeit des Zollvereins* (1865), p. 14. Equally unsuccessful were the attempts made in 1819 to use the machinery of the Confederation to set up a Federal Post Office and to take common action to protect German merchant ships from attacks by pirates. See C. F. Wurm and F. T. Müller, *Die Aufgabe der Hansestädte gegenüber dem deutschen Zollverein so wie in Bezug auf eine gemeinsame deutsche Handelspolitik* (Commissions-Bericht an die vaterstädtische Section der Hamburgischen Gesellschaft zur Beförderung der Kunst und nützlichen Gewerbe, 1847). For C. F. Wurm, see A. Wohlwill, "Beiträge zu einer Geschichte C. F. Wurms", in *Zeitschrift des Vereins für Hamburgische Geschichte*, XXII (1918), pp. 21–122.

[3] See below, p. 39.

industry or help the working classes".[1] A fortnight later (April 27, 1819) the Rhineland merchants asked the King of Prussia to consider whether "it would not be advisable to encourage a revival of German industry by removing all customs barriers within Germany and by simply levying duties on land frontiers and at ports". Carl Friedrich Nebenius, a Baden official, observed in a private memorandum that "no German State will be able to use the means at its disposal to protect native industry without injuring German neighbours more than foreigners because the points of contact and natural commercial connections between German States are much closer than are those between Germany as a whole and the outside world". He advocated the "complete freedom of trade between all States of the Confederation" and hoped that the founding of a German customs union would be followed by a unification of weights and measures, a common coinage, greater uniformity in commercial legislation, and co-operation in constructing roads and canals.[2]

The Baden Chambers passed resolutions in favour of freedom of trade within Germany. Freiherr von Berstett, the Baden representative at the Carlsbad Conferences, raised the question officially in August, 1819. He pointed out the evils of the existing situation and stressed the need for carrying out Article 19. Metternich was more interested in suppressing revolution in Germany than in reviving her trade and industry and he suggested that the discussion of Article 19 should be postponed to the Ministers' Conferences which were shortly to be held in Vienna.[3] Equally fruitless was Baden's attempt to revive the question at the Federal Diet in September of this year.[4] Before

[1] See also the views expressed in July, 1819, in a petition drawn up by E. W. Arnoldi and signed by over 5000 domestic workers, factory-owners and merchants of Thuringia and neighbouring districts. The petition is summarised by Wurm and Müller, pp. 74–6.

[2] The memorandum was published in 1833 as an appendix to C. F. Nebenius, *Denkschrift für den Beitritt Badens zu dem...Zollverein* (1833).

[3] Eisenhart Rothe and Ritthaler, I, pp. 338–47, and L. K. Aegidi, pp. 17–21.

[4] C. F. Wurm and F. T. Müller, pp. 83–4.

the Vienna meeting took place the small State of Schwarzburg-Sondershausen arranged for that part of its territories which was entirely surrounded by Prussian lands to enter the Prussian customs system (October 25).[1] Some German States were alarmed at this and hoped that it might be possible to reach an agreement at Vienna which would save them from having to come to terms with their powerful neighbour.

Vienna was the scene of important discussions on German economic affairs between the end of November, 1819 and May, 1820, but again no practical results were achieved. The clash of interests between Austria, Prussia and the middle German States was clearly brought to light. Austria had not yet achieved economic unity within her own boundaries for Hungary, Tirol, Vorarlberg and the Italian provinces were still cut off by customs frontiers from the rest of the Hapsburg Empire. Her industries were undeveloped and she was not prepared to modify her prohibitive commercial system. In the circumstances closer economic co-operation with the rest of the Germanic Confederation was out of the question. She would not even agree to free-trade in grain. Prussia, too, was going her own way. She was endeavouring to secure the smooth working of her new tariff. She was negotiating with enclaves in her territory in the hope of reducing smuggling into Prussia. She ignored the loud complaints of some of the German States and rejected firmly every suggestion that she should modify her tariff.

The middle States found that their appeals for the carrying out of Article 19 fell on deaf ears. Equally disappointed were Friedrich List and other representatives of the Union of Merchants who appeared in Vienna in the hope of seeing the work of forming a German customs union taken in hand. The Ministers' Conference referred the question of Article 19 to a committee which solemnly reported that it should be handed over to the Federal Diet at Frankfurt-am-Main. In view of the previous record of the Diet in dealing with economic problems it is hardly surprising that the members of the Vienna Con-

[1] See below, p. 44.

ference burst out laughing when the recommendation of the committee was announced.[1]

The failure of the Vienna Conference marks the end of the early attempts to secure economic unity by simultaneous agreement between all German States. Another method of attaining unity was to form small customs unions between a few neighbouring States in the hope that it would eventually be possible to unite them into a wider Zollverein. Prussia, by her treaty with Schwarzburg-Sondershausen, had already taken the first step towards absorbing enclaves into her customs system and preliminary negotiations for the construction of a South German customs union were started in Vienna at the time of the Ministers' Conferences.

(2) THE EXPANSION OF THE PRUSSIAN CUSTOMS SYSTEM, 1818–1828[2]

Prussia had experienced a period of comparative prosperity between 1795 and 1806. A decade of war, however, brought with it grave economic losses which had to be repaired before new progress could be made. In 1815 her finances were in disorder

---

[1] For documents on the Vienna Conferences, see F. von Weech, *Korrespondenz und Aktenstücke zur Geschichte der Ministerialkonferenzen in Karlsbad und Wien in den Jahren 1819, 1820 und 1834* (1865); and Eisenhart Rothe and Ritthaler, 1, pp. 348–80. Cf. L. K. Aegidi, pp. 22–102, and W. Weber, *Der deutsche Zollverein* (1st edition, 1869), ch. ii.

[2] For Prussian economic affairs in the decade after the Napoleonic Wars, see Wilhelm Treue, *Wirtschaftszustände und Wirtschaftspolitik in Preussen, 1815–25* (1937); for Prussia's financial policy, see Hildegard Thierfelder, "Rother als Finanzpolitiker unter Hardenberg 1778–1822", in *Forschungen zur Brandenburgischen und Preussischen Geschichte*, XLVI, part i (1934), pp. 70–111, and Emil Käding, *Beiträge zur preussischen Finanzpolitik in dem Rheinland während der Jahre 1815–40* (1913); for her commercial policy, see Carl Brinkmann, *Die preussische Handelspolitik vor dem Zollverein* (1922); for the geographical factors influencing her commercial policy, see E. Jäger, "Wirtschaftsgeographische Grundlagen der preussischen Zollvereinspolitik", in *Geographische Zeitschrift*, XXVIII (1912), pp. 297–315.

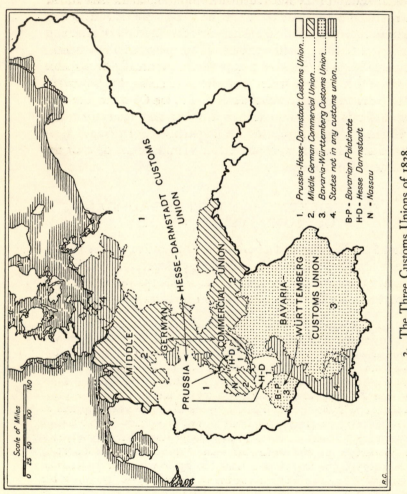

2. The Three Customs Unions of 1828.

(For the position of the Bavarian Palatinate with regard to the South German customs union, see below, p. 63, n. 2.)

owing to contributions extorted by the French and to other war expenses. War expenditure amounted to 206 million thalers between 1806 and 1815 and a further 81 million thalers were added in the next four years. The national debt amounted to 217 million thalers in 1818. Her credit was poor. In 1818 she could raise a loan for £5,000,000 (at 5 per cent interest) in London through Nathan Rothschild only at 72.[1] Further, no general review of Prussia's debts was made. As late as 1820 Motz reported that in the small district of Erfurt the Government was still faced with over two thousand bills dating from the war.[2]

Prussian agriculture and industry suffered from the new tariff walls raised by almost all European States. The collapse of the Continental System was not followed by any attempt to revive trade by keeping import duties at a low level. There was no return in Britain and France to the comparatively enlightened commercial policy of the pre-war generation which had studied the works of Adam Smith and the Physiocrats and had con-

[1] See the dispatches of G. H. Rose and G. S. Douglas to Lord Castlereagh from Berlin—particularly Rose's letters of January 17 (no. 4) and 26 (no. 6), April 26 (no. 11), May 2 (no. 15) and 20 (no. 18), June 6 (no. 27) and July 6 (no. 35) and Douglas's letters of January 31 (no. 1), February 3 (no. 2), 9 (no. 3), 17 (no. 4) and 23 (no. 5), March 21 (no. 10) and April 18 (no. 14) in F.O. 64/113 and 64/115 (all 1818). *The Times* (April 6, 1818) stated that the loan would be issued on the following terms: £2,500,000 at 70, £1,250,000 at 72½, and £1,250,000 at 75. "The loan... never fell below the price of issue, and in 1824 actually touched par. The House of Rothschild, therefore, had every occasion to be pleased with this, the first big State loan which they handled, and they were encouraged to develop this line of business on a large scale." (E. C. Corti, *The Rise of the House of Rothschild* (1928), p. 215.) L. H. Jenks observes that it was "the first unguaranteed foreign loan to make its formal appearance in London, and the first to do homage to the pound sterling" (*The Migration of British Capital to 1875* (1927), p. 38). Cf. R. Ehrenberg, *Die Fugger, Rothschild, Krupp* (1925); B. Brockhage, *Zur Entwicklung des preussisch-deutschen Kapitalexports*, I (1910), pp. 106–10; and H. Stuebel, *Staat und Banken im preussischen Anleihewesen 1871–1913* (1935), ch. i (Introduction).

[2] H. von Treitschke, *Deutsche Geschichte im neunzehnten Jahrhundert*, II (edition of 1927), p. 203.

cluded the famous Anglo-French commercial treaty of 1786. There was unfortunately a revival in these countries of a narrow economic nationalism which found expression in high import duties and prohibitions. Russia, under the guidance of Count Kankrin, favoured the most extreme policy of national self-sufficiency. The Hapsburg dominions, too, reduced their foreign trade to a minimum.

The eastern provinces of Prussia—particularly East and West Prussia, Posen, and Pomerania[1]—found their export of grain and timber hampered by Britain's policy of high protection.[2] European timber which had paid an import duty of 6s. 8d. a load in 1783 was charged 65s. a load in 1813, while colonial timber paid little or nothing. It is hardly surprising that the number of ships engaged in carrying timber from Memel to Britain dropped from between 950 and 1000 before the war to between 200 and 300 afterwards. Equally serious was the effect of the Corn Laws of Britain, Holland and other countries. In Britain, for example, the import duties on wheat in

[1] The economy of these Prussian provinces was based largely upon the production on large estates of grain intended for foreign (mainly British) markets. The other eastern provinces of Prussia—namely Silesia, Brandenburg and Saxony (*Provinz Sachsen*)—had a less one-sided economy. They were more densely populated; they had rather greater capital resources; and they had some manufactures. But in years of good harvest these provinces, too, exported grain.

[2] For a Prussian complaint against the high British import duties on foreign timber see Baron Humboldt to Lord Castlereagh (February 9, 1818). Castlereagh replied on April 24, 1818, that "whilst His Majesty's Government regret that in their opinion the moment is not yet arrived, at which they can recommend that an alteration of the duties on timber should take place, they have great satisfaction in being equally convinced that the operation of them upon the commerce of Prussia is more apparent than real; and that the benefit which is derived from them by His Majesty's subjects in North America is not incompatible with an active, increasing and beneficial intercourse between Great Britain and Prussia". See also Humboldt's memorandum of July 13, 1818, which criticised Britain's commercial policy—particularly her corn laws, timber duties and navigation code—and Bathurst's reply of September 22, 1818 (all in F.O. 64/116).

1791 had been 6*d.* a quarter when the home price was 54*s.* a quarter or over, 2*s.* 6*d.* when the price was between 50*s.* and 54*s.* and 24*s.* 3*d.* when the price was under 50*s.* After the war the Corn Law of 1815 forbade the importation of wheat until the home price rose to 80*s.* a quarter.[1] Consequently, it was only when there was a bad harvest in this country that Danzig —the chief corn port of Northern Europe—could hope to send wheat to Britain. The English market was entirely closed from 1814 to January, 1816, November, 1817 to February, 1818, and February, 1819 to 1822 and was closed to imports from near ports from September to November, 1818. The Silesian linen industry, the chief manufacture of the eastern provinces of Prussia, was seriously hampered by the prohibitive tariffs of Russia and Austria.[2]

While the high duties and prohibitions of Britain, Russia and Austria hit the eastern provinces of Prussia, the tariffs of France and the Netherlands injured the western provinces. During the war industrialists of the Rhineland and Westphalia had, to a great extent, depended upon the markets of France and the Netherlands. Now these markets were virtually closed.[3] Germans complained that it was easier for the camel to pass through the eye of a needle than for the needle itself to pass over the

---

[1] J. R. McCulloch, *Dictionary of Commerce*, II (edition of 1847), p. 1246 (Timber Trade) and I, pp. 394–5 (Corn Laws).

[2] For the Austrian prohibitive system, see Adolf Beer, pp. 1–15 and Karl Hudeczek, *Österreichische Handelspolitik in Vormärz, 1815–48* (1918). For the Russian prohibitive system, see Valentine Wittschewsky, "Die Zoll- und Handelspolitik Russlands...", in *Schriften des Vereins für Sozialpolitik*, XLIX (1892), pp. 363–5. The Russian tariff of 1822 forbade the importation of 301 articles and the export of 22 articles. For the Silesian linen industry, see Alfred Zimmermann, *Blüte und Verfall des Leinengewerbes in Schlesien* (1885).

[3] In a report of June 2, 1814, Sack, the Governor-General of the lower and middle Rhine, referred to local indignation at the new French tariff (Alfred Zimmermann, *Geschichte der preussisch-deutschen Handelspolitik* (1892), p. 8). Cf. W. L. Lindner, "Das Zollgesetz von 1818 und Handel und Industrie am Niederrhein", in *Westdeutsche Zeitschrift für Geschichte und Kunst*, XXX (1911), p. 297.

French frontier. Duties had also to be paid if goods were exported from the new Prussian provinces in the west to the older parts of the Kingdom in the east.

Some compensation for the loss of trade with neighbouring States might have been obtained either in overseas markets or at home. Prussia's overseas commerce, however, was small and was less in her own hands than in those of the merchants of Antwerp, Rotterdam, Amsterdam, Hamburg and Bremen. Her mercantile marine declined from 1102 ships to 722 between 1805 and 1815.[1] Her trade in the Mediterranean was hampered by the Barbary pirates, and she lacked a fleet to repel their attacks. On the great ocean routes to America and India her ships were hardly seen at all. When the Prussian ship *Mentor* returned in 1824 from a voyage round the world with a rich cargo of tea, cotton cloth and raw silk the captain was decorated by the King.

At home the purchasing power of Prussian consumers had been greatly reduced. Only cheap goods could hope to command a sale. Here British manufacturers had an advantage. They had large quantities of manufactured articles, particularly textiles, which had been warehoused for some time since they could not be exported owing to the Continental System. The prohibition on the importation of British goods was raised in various German States in 1813,[2] a year before France opened her ports (April 23, 1814). British goods appeared on German markets at prices with which Prussian manufacturers could not compete. Indeed, British exporters overestimated the capacity of the Continent to absorb their wares—particularly textiles made a few years previously and now out of fashion—and they soon suffered for their error of judgment. Later, better British goods, produced on a large scale by the most efficient machinery of the day, were sent to Germany. The less advanced Prussian

---

[1] Karl Brämer, "Die preussische Rhederei", in *Zeitschrift des Königl. Preussischen Statistischen Bureaus*, x, Heft iv (Oct.-Dec. 1870), pp. 311 ff.

[2] Hamburg, March 19; Prussia, March 20; Saxony, April 14; lower Rhine, November 17, 1813.

manufacturers were again faced with serious competition. Prussian industries were depressed and many complaints were made to the Government.[1]

Prussia endeavoured to foster a revival of her industry and commerce by negotiating treaties with her neighbours and by increasing the efficiency of her methods of production. Little was achieved by the first method. Sack, who was in charge of the newly acquired territories on the Rhine, concluded a commercial treaty with the Belgian provinces in the autumn of 1814. These provinces had recently been freed from French control but their future had not yet been decided. This treaty enabled the manufacturers of the Rhineland and Westphalia to export goods to the Belgian provinces on payment of low duties. It had, however, been concluded by Sack on his own responsibility without consulting his superiors in Berlin. The Prussian Government delayed ratification and the Belgians soon denounced the agreement. Its provisions were acted upon for only a year (November, 1814–November, 1815) and it provided the Rhineland with only a temporary market. In August, 1816, Russia agreed provisionally to allow Prussian cloths to pass through her territory to China. The value of cloths sent through Russia rose from a little over two million roubles in 1817 to nearly six million roubles in the following year. This gave some temporary relief to the Silesian linen-weavers.[2] On the whole, however, Prussia's neighbours showed no signs of making any serious changes in their high tariffs.

[1] See, for example, the petitions of the cotton manufacturers of Reichenbach, April 8, 1815 (Eisenhart Rothe and Ritthaler, I, pp. 23–4), and of the manufacturers of Rheydt, Süchteln, Gladbach and Kaldenkirchen, April 27, 1818 (*ibid.* I, pp. 69–71), and numerous extracts from official reports and newspapers printed by Wilhelm Treue, *Wirtschaftszustände und Wirtschaftspolitik in Preussen*, 1815–25 (1937).

[2] For Russo-Prussian economic relations from the end of the Napoleonic Wars to the founding of the Zollverein, see Alfred Zimmermann, "Die russisch-preussischen Handelsbeziehungen, 1814–1833", in *Jahrbuch für Gesetzgebung, Verwaltung und Volkswirtschaft im Deutschen Reiche*: herausgegeben von Gustav Schmoller, XVI (1892), Heft ii, pp. 1–47.

To increase the efficiency of her manufacturing provinces Prussia attempted to find out what progress had recently been made in other countries. This was no easy task. Britain, for example, still forbade the export of machinery and the emigration of skilled workers. But in those parts of France and the Belgian provinces occupied by allied troops there were opportunities of obtaining information which might be of value to Prussian manufacturers. On February 4, 1814, Sack wrote to Hardenberg, the Prussian Chancellor, suggesting that a secret mission should be sent to these regions. Hardenberg, who had just been complaining of attempts of Russian agents to entice Prussian armourers and steelworkers into Russia, agreed to Sack's proposal. Frank, an architect, and three companions visited Liége, Brussels, Verviers and Sedan as well as various towns in the Rhineland and Westphalia. They tried to secure information of recent technical progress in factories and workshops.[1] Efforts were also made to attract foreign industrialists to Prussia. Thus in 1814 Charles James Cockerill and John Cockerill came to Berlin and, encouraged by the Government, established there a factory for making machinery and another for spinning wool by up-to-date methods. Another way of fostering trade was to improve communications. In 1816 Prussia began to develop her network of roads so as to join Berlin with the principal provinces. Schön in West Prussia and Vincke in Westphalia were particularly active in promoting the construction of roads.[2] Progress, however, was slow at first owing to lack of funds.

The depressed condition of Prussian agriculture, industry and commerce; the hostile tariffs of other European countries and the failure to secure any substantial reduction in those

[1] Wilhelm Treue, "Eine preussische 'technologische' Reise in die besetzten Gebiete im Jahre 1814", in *V.S.W.* xxxviii (1935), pp. 15–40.

[2] P. Simson, "Aus der Zeit von Theodor von Schöns westpreussischem Oberpräsidium", in *Preussische Jahrbücher*, cix (1902), pp. 58–72, and Fritz Sälter, *Entwicklung und Bedeutung des Chaussee- und Wegebaues in der Provinz Westfalen unter ihrem ersten Oberpräsidenten von Vincke* (Marburg, 1917: Dissertation).

tariffs forced Prussia to look for salvation in a reform of her own customs system. She might have been tempted to follow the example of her neighbours and return to the mercantilist traditions of the seventeenth and eighteenth centuries. There were several reasons why such a step was not taken. First, Prussia's economic position was too weak for her to engage in tariff wars such as she had waged against Austria[1] and Saxony between 1755 and 1786. Like the South German States, who had reformed their tariffs between 1807 and 1812, Prussia felt that discretion was the better part of valour. She needed the friendship of Britain and Russia and could not afford to offend them. Secondly, her financial needs made it imperative to increase considerably the revenue from import duties and if the tariff were too high the income derived from it would fall. Thirdly, the Prussian officials who were carrying out the Stein-Hardenberg social and administrative reforms were strongly influenced by the views of liberal writers of the eighteenth century. Many of them had studied at the Universities of Göttingen, Halle, and Königsberg where Liberal ideas—approached sometimes from an economic and sometimes from a philosophical angle—exercised considerable influence.[2] The Civil Servants regarded the new tariff as a necessary step in the reconstruction of Prussia that had followed her defeat at Jena. Some local dues had been abolished in December, 1805, but a more thorough reform was clearly needed.

Those engaged in reforming the Prussian customs system had two main objects in view. On the one hand, they desired to replace the confused mass of national, provincial, local and private dues by a reasonably simple and unified tariff and to remove the collection of import duties from the interior of the

---

[1] See H. Fechner, *Die handelspolitischen Beziehungen Preussens zu Österreich....* 1741–1806 (1886).

[2] See Wilhelm Treue, ch. ii, for details concerning the university careers of the leading Prussian Civil Servants of this period and for a discussion of the importance of English Liberal economic ideas at German universities.

country to the frontiers. On the other hand, they wished to construct a tariff which would be low enough both to make smuggling unprofitable and to avoid giving undue offence to neighbouring countries with whom Prussia was in no position to quarrel. They realised both the advantages and disadvantages of Prussia's geographical position. The Kingdom was divided into two groups of provinces and some financial sacrifice from abolishing internal dues would be necessary if trade between them were to be encouraged. But both parts of the country lay on important European trade routes and transit dues levied on international commerce would not only benefit the Prussian exchequer but would be a useful weapon to use against small German neighbours.

Count von Bülow, the Minister of Finance, had been engaged since 1814 on a general reconstruction of the Prussian system of public finance. In January, 1817, he submitted a draft of the proposed financial reforms, including the new tariff, to the King, with a report indicating clearly the urgent need for a thorough revision of the existing customs system and the reasons for adopting moderate rather than prohibitive duties.[1] The King declined to accept the reforms at once and asked the newly appointed Council of State to examine them. A committee of the Council was appointed to do so. Two influential members —"the real parents and defenders" of the new tariff[2]–were Karl Georg Maassen, an official in the Ministry of Finance, and Johann Gottfried Hoffmann, an eminent statistician. The committee held twenty-six meetings between April 5 and June 3, 1817. Bülow's schemes were subjected to severe criticisms and the proposed reform of the excise on goods produced and consumed at home was rejected.[3] Even the tariff was not accepted without serious opposition.

---

[1] The report is printed by Eisenhart Rothe and Ritthaler, 1, pp. 35–45.

[2] Gustav Schmoller, Das preussische Handels- und Zollgesetz vom 26. Mai 1818 (1898), p. 37.

[3] The reform of the Prussian excise and direct taxation was carried out in 1819–20.

Three main objections to it were raised. First, there was Wilhelm von Humboldt's criticism that the tariff should not become law until it had been considered by a representative assembly. No such body existed in Prussia at the moment but it was hoped that the King would soon grant a constitution. Secondly, there was opposition from certain provinces which feared that their local liberties would be curtailed by the centralised administration of the customs under the new law. Ludwig von Vincke, the able President of the province of Westphalia, took this view. Thirdly, the Protectionists, led by von Heydebreck (President of the province of Brandenburg) and Ladenberg, loudly complained that the proposed duties were too low. On the other hand, this criticism was counterbalanced by petitions which asserted that any return to a prohibitive system would seriously hamper a revival of trade. Eventually the committee accepted the proposed tariff by twenty-one votes to two and the Council of State endorsed this decision.[1] There were, however, further difficulties to be overcome. Bülow resigned his position as Minister of Finance[2] as a protest against the rejection of his proposals for the revision of indirect taxation and the attempt to introduce his financial reforms piecemeal instead of together. His successor, von Klewiz, was a less enthusiastic reformer and arrangements for carrying out the new tariff were made very slowly.

The new Tariff Law was promulgated by the King on May 26, 1818.[3] Two tariffs were introduced—one for the eastern

[1] See the documents in Eisenhart Rothe and Ritthaler, 1, pp. 46–68.

[2] Bülow took charge of the newly founded Ministry of Commerce (*Handelsministerium*). It was abolished in 1825. In 1844 a Board of Trade (*Handelsamt*) was set up again. It was expanded into a Ministry of Commerce in 1848. See below, pp. 185, 194.

[3] The Prussian Tariff Law of May 26, 1818, is printed by Eisenhart Rothe and Ritthaler, 1, pp. 71–8. Copies of the Law of May 26, 1818, and of five Prussian administrative orders concerning customs and excise (of the same date) were sent by G. H. Rose to Lord Castlereagh as an enclosure to no. 56, September 5, 1818 (F.O. 64/114, Prussia: August–December, 1818). See also Hoffmann, "Preussens neues Zollsystem im

provinces, which came into force on September 5, 1818, and one for the western provinces, which came into force on January 1, 1819. The eastern tariff was somewhat higher than the western.

Internal dues and export and import prohibitions were abolished. There were, however, exceptions. Thus, internal dues for which services were rendered—such as tolls on bridges— were retained and special regulations were made to maintain the State monopoly on playing-cards and salt. Foreign raw materials were normally admitted free of duty. Both import duty (*Einfuhrzoll*) and consumption duty (*Verbrauchssteuer*) were levied on goods imported for consumption in Prussia. These duties amounted to about 10 per cent. of the value of manufactured articles and from 20 to 30 per cent of the value of the products of tropical and sub-tropical countries (*Kolonialwaren*). No consumption duty was charged on foreign goods crossing Prussian territory and not consumed in Prussia: they paid transit dues consisting of the import duty and (in exceptional cases) an export duty as well. Transit duties amounted usually to half a thaler (1s. 6d.) a Prussian hundredweight, though dues that were either higher or lower than the normal were payable on certain goods and on traffic on certain routes.[1]

In 1821 the two tariffs were replaced by a single tariff for the

Verhältnis zu den deutschen Nachbarstaaten", in *Preussische Staatszeitung* (February 6, 1819); Erwin Nasse, "Das preussische Zollgesetz vom 26. Mai 1818", in *Kölnische Zeitung* (August 11 and 12, 1879); E. Cremer, *Bedeutung des preussischen Zollgesetzes vom 26. Mai 1818 für die Entwicklung Preussens und den deutschen Zollverein* (1891); Gustav Schmoller, *Das preussische Handels- und Zollgesetz vom 26. Mai 1818* (1898); H. Freymark, *Die Reform der preussischen Handels- und Zollpolitik von 1800–21 und ihre Bedeutung* (1898); W. Menn, "Das preussische Zollgesetz vom 26. Mai 1818, seine Bedeutung für Preussen und den deutschen Zollverein", in *Die Grenzboten*, LXXVII (May 17, 1918), p. 175; Wilhelm Treue, *Wirtschaftszustände und Wirtschaftspolitik in Preussen, 1815–25* (1937), ch. ii; R. Grabower, *Preussens Steuern vor und nach den Befreiungskriegen* (1932), ch. iv; and the article by W. E. Lindner cited above (p. 33, note 3).

[1] See paragraph 14 of the Tariff Law of May 26, 1818.

whole Kingdom, import and consumption duties were combined and transit dues were somewhat reduced and were included in a separate schedule.[1]

Maassen had thus made an ingenious attempt to use the new tariff to further a number of objects not all of which were compatible. It was hoped that the abolition of internal dues would encourage trade between the various provinces. The fact that many raw materials were on the free list would assist manufacturers and farmers. The duties on manufactured goods were low enough to discourage smuggling to some extent but would bring in some revenue and would afford a modest protection to home manufacturers. The higher duties on colonial goods were regarded as revenue duties. The transit dues would also produce a revenue and could be used to influence the direction of commerce on some of the great North European trade routes. But, as Dr Bowring wrote in 1840, "the transit system of the Zollverein is somewhat complicated and inconsistent with the general and simple character of the legislation".[2] To simplify collection, duties were *specific*—that is to say, they were levied on weight and quantity and not by value. Articles of low value generally bore a heavier tax in proportion to their value than more valuable goods of less bulk. The price of certain manufactured articles fell in the 'twenties so that some of them were soon paying as much as 80 per cent *ad valorem*.

The Prussian tariff of 1818 had to face severe criticisms both at home and abroad. In Prussia itself the protectionists complained that the duties were too low, the free-traders that they were too high. The strict control exercised on the frontiers led to considerable opposition. Several border towns, such as Saarbrücken, asked if they might be left outside the new customs frontier. In other German States, particularly those with enclaves in Prussian territory, the tariff was attacked on three main grounds. First, the Prussian market was, to some extent,

---

[1] See J. C. H. Hesse and E. Klein, *Königlich-Preussischer Zoll-Tarif für die Jahre 1825 bis 1827* (1825).

[2] John Bowring, p. 15.

lost. Hanoverian manufacturers, for example, complained that their export of metal wares, woollen goods and paper to Prussia was restricted.[1] Secondly, the Prussian transit dues hampered German commerce. Thirdly, the Maassen tariff appeared to block the way to a general German customs union. These criticisms were made in the petition to the Federal Assembly drawn up by List for the Union of German Merchants and Manufacturers (April 14, 1819). Foreign critics feared that the new transit dues would seriously interfere with the trade of Central Europe.

Many of these criticisms were the complaints of interested persons who feared some temporary loss or inconvenience from the carrying out of the new law. The tariff should be judged not from this narrow point of view but in relation to other administrative changes of the Stein-Hardenberg era.[2] The reorganisation of the customs system brought to an end an intolerable state of affairs. It increased the Prussian revenue, gradually reduced smuggling and helped to draw closer together the scattered provinces of the Kingdom. But the depressed condition of Prussia's economic life was not immediately alleviated by the new tariff. Poor trade continued for some years and in 1825 there was an economic crisis.

Prussia's moderate duties stood out in sharp contrast to the

[1] G. von Gülich, *Noch ein Wort über Handel und Gewerbe des Königreichs Hannover....* (1832), p. 7.

[2] Wilhelm Treue, in his *Wirtschaftszustände und Wirtschaftspolitik in Preussen, 1815–25* (1937), criticises the Prussian tariff law of 1818 on the ground that it did not give Prussian agriculture or industry protection against foreign—particularly British—competition. He argues that the tariff was a failure since there was no improvement in the deplorable economic position of Prussia between 1818 and 1825 and he considers that this failure was reluctantly recognised and to some extent remedied by increasing certain import duties in the late 'twenties and 'thirties. On the other hand, it should be remembered that Prussia's depressed economic condition was due not so much to lack of high import duties as to lack of capital, poor technical equipment, bad communications and so forth. It was necessary to remove these disabilities before Prussia's agriculture and industry could advance. See review of Dr Treue's book in *Ec.H.R.*, IX, i (November, 1938), pp. 93–4.

high tariffs and prohibitions of her neighbours.[1] Huskisson praised the Prussian tariff in a speech in the House of Commons in 1827 and commented: "I trust that the time will come when we can say as much for the tariff of this country."[2]

The tariff, somewhat modified by fifteen years' experience, was adopted by the Zollverein in 1834. Maassen and his colleagues, of course, could not look as far ahead as this. They tackled the immediate economic and fiscal problems of Prussia in 1818 and they tackled them with a considerable measure of success.[3]

One of the difficulties which had to be faced in carrying out the new tariff law concerned the position of enclaves of other German States in Prussian territory. In the eastern provinces there were nine enclaves with an estimated population of 166,000. The Government had to decide whether these districts should be treated as Prussian or as foreign lands. If an enclave were treated as Prussian territory there would be no change in the regulations governing trade in agricultural or manufactured products originating either in Prussia or the enclave. But foreign goods destined for the enclave would pay the same import duty as if they were to be consumed in Prussia itself. On the other hand, if an enclave were treated as foreign territory its commerce with countries other than Prussia would be subject to Prussian transit dues. Goods produced in the enclave but consumed in Prussia would pay import duty. Either arrangement would raise the price of certain articles in the enclave but the second plan would be more burdensome than the first. States which had only part of their frontier in common with Prussia might attempt to avoid the new transit dues by using

[1] Professor J. H. Clapham considers that Prussia had "immeasurably the wisest and most scientific tariff then existing among the great powers" (*The Economic Development of France and Germany*, 1815–1914 (1936), p. 97).

[2] *The Speeches of the Right Honourable William Huskisson*, III (1831), p. 131.

[3] For a discussion of the judgments of historians and economists on the tariff of 1818, see W. Treue, pp. 154–9.

routes that did not go through Prussian territory but this was impossible for the enclaves. Two courses were open to the States concerned. They might enter the Prussian customs system and secure a share of the joint customs revenue or they might try to obtain support from other German Powers, particularly Austria, and so put pressure on Prussia to allow the enclaves complete freedom of trade with the outside world.

Prussia decided to treat the enclaves in the same way as her own territory and to levy her import duties on foreign goods crossing her frontiers on the way to these districts. The first protest came in January, 1819, from the small Thuringian principality of Schwarzburg-Sondershausen. Two-thirds of the country were entirely surrounded by Prussian territory. The district in question—the *Unterherrschaft* (Lower Lordship)—had 30,000 inhabitants. It included the royal residence and the Prince was particularly annoyed at having to pay Prussian import duties on purchases of foreign goods made for his own court. After some hesitation both parties decided to negotiate on the question in dispute. On October 25, 1819, a treaty was signed by which the Schwarzburg-Sondershausen enclaves entered the Prussian customs system.[1]

The first article stated that the payment to be made to the Prince of Schwarzburg-Sondershausen as his share of the joint customs revenue was to be arranged every three years. "This agreement shall be based upon the revenue raised by duties during the preceding three years by the customs administration of the seven Eastern Provinces of Prussia. The share thereof payable to the Prince of Schwarzburg-Sondershausen shall be in the ratio of the population of the Schwarzburg-Sondershausen enclaves to that of the population of the seven Eastern Prussian Provinces." Since the new Prussian Tariff had only recently come into operation, no such calculation could be made

---

[1] Documents on the negotiations are printed by Eisenhart Rothe and Ritthaler, I, pp. 83–91, 106–16. Eisenhart Rothe states (I, p. 8 n.) that he can find no evidence to support Treitschke's suggestion (II, p. 624) that the Prince of Schwarzburg-Sondershausen came to terms with Prussia in order to raise money to build a national theatre.

for the first period of three years, and between January 1, 1819 and December 31, 1821, Schwarzburg-Sondershausen was to receive an annual payment of 15,000 thalers. By the third article it was agreed that "in respect of goods certified as being for the use of the household of the Prince of Schwarzburg-Sondershausen duty will not be charged at the frontier if the certificates so require, but the duty will be deducted from the next quarterly cash payment made to the Prince". The Prince of Schwarzburg-Sondershausen agreed to co-operate with Prussia in suppressing smuggling—particularly the smuggling of salt from the Frankenhausen salt works.[1]

This treaty is important not because of the interests involved —which were trifling—but because of the precedent it created. The principles upon which it was based were maintained in subsequent treaties by which all enclaves in Prussia joined the Prussian customs system within the next few years.[2] The States or parts of States concerned, adopted the Prussian tariff and

[1] The treaty between Prussia and Schwarzburg-Sondershausen is printed in full by Eisenhart Rothe and Ritthaler, 1, pp. 116–19.

[2] The following small districts (enclaves and districts partly surrounded by Prussian territory) were added to the Prussian customs system between 1819 and 1831:

1819. The Lower Lordship (*Unterherrschaft*) of the Principality of Schwarzburg-Sondershausen.

1822. The district of Frankenhausen (belonging to Schwarzburg-Rudolstadt).

1823. The districts of Allstedt and Oldisleben (belonging to Sachse-Weimar): the Upper Duchy (*oberes Herzogtum*) of Anhalt-Bernburg and the district of Mühlingen (belonging to Anhalt-Bernburg).

1826. Lipperode, Cappel and Grävenhagen (belonging to Lippe-Detmold): the Lower Duchy (*unteres Herzogtum*) of Anhalt-Bernburg: the villages of Netzeband, Rossow and Schöneberg (belonging to Mecklenburg-Schwerin).

1828. The Duchy of Anhalt-Köthen and the Duchy of Anhalt-Dessau.

1829. The three Reuss Principalities: The Principality of Lichtenberg and the district of Volkenrode (both belonging to Sachse-Coburg-Gotha), and the district of Meissenheim (belonging to Hesse-Homburg).

1830. The Principality of Birkenfeld (belonging to Oldenburg).

1831. The Principality of Waldeck (but not its isolated County of Lippe-Pyrmont).

received a share of the joint revenue calculated not upon what they had themselves collected but upon the ratio of their population to that of the eastern provinces of Prussia. Their rights as sovereign States were carefully observed. Thus it was agreed that although Prussian customs officials might pursue smugglers into Schwarzburg-Sondershausen territory they might not carry out domiciliary visits there. If these principles were accepted, Prussia was prepared to make concessions on minor matters. This was shown, for example, by the arrangements made with regard to goods purchased by the Court of Schwarzburg-Sondershausen.

By far the most difficult enclaves to deal with were the three Anhalt duchies of Bernburg, Dessau and Köthen.[1] They made a joint protest against the Prussian tariff in January 1819 and subsequently rejected Prussia's proposal that they should join her customs system on the same terms as Schwarzburg-Sondershausen. Duke Ferdinand of Anhalt-Köthen bitterly resented Prussia's action and determined to oppose her at all costs. He regarded himself as the champion of the sovereign rights of the small German States. He took advantage of the discussions on economic questions at Vienna at the end of 1819 and in the early part of 1820 to air his grievances and to attempt to secure a modification of the Prussian tariff.

When this failed he tried to evade the payment of Prussian duties by shipping goods direct to his own port of Rosslau on the Elbe. Free navigation of this river had been agreed upon in principle in the Final Act of the Congress of Vienna (1815) and he thought that Prussia would not levy duties on goods passing through her territory by this route. In June, 1820, Baruch Friedheim, an Anhalt-Köthen merchant—apparently acting on official instructions—refused to pay the Prussian con-

---

[1] The Anhalt point of view is stated by Max Dressler, *Der Kampf Anhalt-Köthens gegen die preussische Handelspolitik* (1908), the Prussian by H. von Treitschke, III, pp. 32–3, 477–81. A selection of documents on the dispute is printed by Eisenhart Rothe and Ritthaler, II, pp. 119–92.

sumption duty on 30 hundredweight of sugar and coffee which he was sending on the Elbe from Strehla (in the Kingdom of Saxony) through Prussian territory to Rosslau. Prussian customs officials detained the ship at Mühlberg. There followed an acrimonious correspondence between Anhalt-Köthen and Prussia in which Prussia stated that the extent of freedom of navigation on the Elbe depended upon the discussions which were taking place at Dresden on the carrying out of this provision of the Final Act.

As the Duke of Anhalt-Köthen was unable to obtain satisfaction from Prussia he complained to the Federal Diet in January, 1821. The matter aroused great interest throughout Germany. Metternich tried to reconcile the disputants but at the same time Adam Müller—the Austrian Consul-General in Leipzig between 1816 and 1827—apparently on his own initiative encouraged the Duke to remain firm. The Diet postponed discussion on the question in July so as to give both sides a fresh opportunity of coming to an agreement.

Meantime the Elbe Navigation Act had been signed in July, 1821.[1] It was ratified in the following December. Prussia agreed to levy import duties only on goods landed in Prussian territory and not on those in transit. So Friedheim's ship was allowed to leave Prussia without import duty being paid on the cargo. The Duke of Anhalt-Köthen, delighted at the turn events had taken, attempted to revive the dispute before the Diet by demanding compensation for duties levied by Prussia

---

[1] See *Denkschrift in Betreff des Elbeverkehrs und der Elbzölle* (Magdeburg, 1847); M. Kriele, *Die Regulierung der Elbschiffahrt*, 1819–21 (1895); and "Zur Beurteilung der Elbschiffahrtsakte von 1821", in *Zeitschrift des Vereins für Hamburgische Geschichte*, x, 1899. By the Elbe Navigation Act of 1821 dues on goods amounting to 1 thaler, 3 groschens and 6 pfennigs (*Conventionsmünze*) per Hamburg hundredweight were levied at fourteen customs houses on the 368 miles of river between Hamburg and Mělnik (Bohemia). Further charges (*Recognitionsgebühr*) on ships varied between 3 thalers, 13 groschen and 14 thalers, 16 groschen. The staple privileges and shipping monopolies of various towns and gilds were abolished.

on the Elbe since 1819. He obtained no satisfaction and eventually withdrew his complaint.

The Duke of Anhalt-Köthen now hoped to use the Elbe route to import foreign goods through Prussian territory without paying Prussian import duties. Prussia could not prevent this but she could draw a customs cordon round the Anhalt duchies and stop the *re-export* of goods which had entered duty-free. This was done in February 1822 and it broke the united front of the Anhalt duchies. Anhalt-Bernburg opened separate negotiations with Prussia and in December, 1822, she agreed that her lower Duchy should adhere to the Prussian customs system if the other two Anhalt duchies also joined. The Duke of Anhalt-Köthen refused to co-operate, so the agreement could not be carried out. Then in October, 1823, agreement was reached on the inclusion of the upper Duchy of Anhalt-Bernburg and the district of Mühlingen in the Prussian customs system.

Anhalt had meantime become a centre for smuggling foreign goods into Prussia and the Prussian exchequer consequently lost about 500,000 thalers a year. Early in 1825, therefore, Prussia tightened her customs cordon round the three Anhalt duchies. In June, 1825, Friedrich von Motz, formerly President of the Province of Saxony and one of the ablest Prussian officials of his day, was appointed Minister of Finance in place of Klewiz. He advocated that strong measures should be taken to bring the Anhalt duchies to heel.[1] His threats led to renewed discussion and in June, 1826, the lower Duchy of Anhalt-Bernburg accepted the Prussian tariff so that the whole of Anhalt-Bernburg was now within the Prussian customs system.

In February, 1827, Prussia again levied import duties on goods entering Anhalt-Köthen by the Elbe. Importers could subsequently recover the amount paid if they could show that the goods had been consumed in Anhalt-Köthen but they were seldom able to produce the necessary proof. Prussia claimed

[1] For Motz's policy with regard to the enclaves, see H. von Petersdorff, *Friedrich von Motz*, II (1913), pp. 88–107.

that this breach of the Elbe Navigation Act was justified since she had signed that agreement on the understanding that the Anhalt duchies would join her customs system. This had not taken place, so Prussia had resumed her freedom of action. Further, Prussia complained to Austria about the activities of her Consul-General at Leipzig. Adam Müller had, largely on his own responsibility, been encouraging the Duke of Anhalt-Köthen to hold out against Prussia. He had been reproved by Metternich as early as 1824 and now he was recalled. Anhalt-Köthen and Anhalt-Dessau protested to the Federal Diet in the spring of 1827 against the levying of Prussian import duties on the Elbe. A committee was set up which reported substantially in favour of the petitioners. Prussia refused to accept the Diet's decision.

Metternich at last recognised the seriousness of the dispute and tried to induce the parties to compose their differences. It was becoming clear even to Duke Ferdinand that his subjects were suffering from the quarrel and that Anhalt-Köthen must enter the Prussian customs system. The main questions at issue were the claims of Anhalt-Köthen and Anhalt-Dessau to administer the customs by their own officials and to receive compensation for the duties levied by Prussia on the Elbe. Eventually, in the summer of 1828, the two duchies agreed to enter the Prussian customs system on much the same terms as other enclaves. Those parts of Anhalt-Köthen and Anhalt-Dessau completely surrounded by Prussian territory were to have their duties collected by Prussian officials. In other parts of the duchies native officials were to be employed. Prussia agreed to pay compensation for duties she had collected on the Elbe between January 1, 1819, and February 11, 1822, and between February 16, 1827, and the coming into force of the new treaty. Thus ended Duke Ferdinand's attempt to abuse his sovereign rights by turning his duchy into a smugglers' paradise.

The tariff of 1818 affected Prussia's commercial relations not merely with enclaves but with her German neighbours. Nassau offered to open negotiations for a commercial treaty in 1819 but nothing came of this suggestion and in 1822 Nassau adopted a new tariff and collected her duties at the frontier. Hesse-Cassel's reply to the Prussian tariff was to raise her import duties on Prussian leather and iron. The South German States discussed their plans for the formation of a customs union. Hesse-Darmstadt[1] was placed in an awkward position by the Prussian tariff. Nine-tenths of her population were engaged in agriculture and they now had difficulty in obtaining cheap foreign manufactured articles. Her own manufactures were the finishing of rough cloths and carpets by domestic workers in Biedenkopf and Gladenbach, and the linen industry of Alsfeld and Lauterbach: they were injured by lack of free access to Prussian markets. The commerce of Mainz was checked.

Hesse-Darmstadt took a part in the early negotiations for the founding of a South German customs union. When they failed she determined to reform her own customs system. Financial considerations contributed to this decision, for the income from her main sources of revenue—the domain lands and land-tax—was inadequate. In April, 1824, a new tariff was introduced and duties were collected at the frontiers. It was difficult to stop smuggling owing to the length of frontier to be guarded. Hesse-Darmstadt fostered the development of Offenbach-am-Main as a rival to Frankfurt-am-Main. A fair was started at

[1] The establishment of the customs union between Prussia and Hesse-Darmstadt is described by Wilhelm Oncken, *Der preussisch-hessische Zollverein vom 14. Februar 1828* (1878); Christian Eckert, "Zur Vorge-schichte des deutschen Zollvereins. Die preussisch-hessische Zollunion, vom 14. Februar 1828", in *Schmollers Jahrbuch...*, xxvi (New Series, 1902), pp. 505–56; H. Schmidt, *Die Begründung des Preussisch-Hessischen Zollvereins vom 14. Februar 1828* (1926). A selection of documents on the negotiations is printed by Eisenhart Rothe and Ritthaler, ii, pp. 19–294, and by H. Schmidt, pp. i–xxix (Appendix). For Motz's share in the negotiations, see H. von Petersdorff, ii, pp. 108–28. The Prussian point of view is given by H. von Treitschke, iii, pp. 629–38; the Hesse-Darmstadt view in *Denkwürdigkeiten aus dem Dienstleben des Hessen-Darmstädtischen Staatsministers Freiherrn Du Thil*, 1802–48 (edited by H. Ulmann, 1921). Du Thil wrote his memoirs when he was an old man and they are inaccurate in some respects (see Eisenhart Rothe, iii, p. 12 n. ii).

Offenbach and roads were built to link up the town with the main routes to the North Sea ports and to Leipzig.[1] Hesse-Darmstadt, however, was far too small a State to be able to pursue for long an independent commercial policy, let alone to aim at any sort of economic self-sufficiency. The financial position of Hesse-Darmstadt remained unsatisfactory. Du Thil (the Hesse-Darmstadt Minister of Finance and Minister of Foreign Affairs) decided to turn to Prussia. In June, 1825, the first cautious overtures were made. Prussia suggested that joint negotiations with Hesse-Darmstadt and Hesse-Cassel were desirable rather than with Hesse-Darmstadt alone. Hesse-Cassel did not wish to negotiate and nothing came of these discussions. Bavaria and Württemberg made preliminary arrangements for forming a customs union in April, 1827, and suggestions were made that Hesse-Darmstadt should join them. But owing to her geographical position she felt unable to do so while Baden, Nassau and Hesse-Cassel stood aloof.

In August, 1827, Hesse-Darmstadt again approached Prussia, and in December Freiherr von Hofmann arrived in Berlin for the negotiations. Motz was anxious to come to terms. He favoured not a commercial treaty but a customs union between the two countries. He recognised that Prussia would gain few economic advantages from such a union. It would extend the customs frontier to be guarded and would probably involve financial sacrifices. But political advantages would be secured. Prussia's influence in North Germany would be increased and the efforts to form customs unions in South and Central Germany might be checked. Prussia would also link up her western provinces with the important Federal fortress of Mainz.

Agreement was reached on February 14, 1828. Hesse-Darmstadt adopted the Prussian tariff. Future modifications of the tariff needed the consent of both parties. Hesse-Darmstadt's share of the customs revenue was to be in the ratio of her

---

[1] See H. Görlich, *Die Entwicklung der Industriestadt Offenbach und die hessische Wirtschaftspolitik in der Gründungszeit des Zollvereins* (1922): MS. Dissertation in the Prussian State Library.

population to that of the western provinces of Prussia. This was regarded as a convenient, though rough and ready, method of comparing the amount of dutiable commodities consumed by the two regions and hence of assessing the share of the customs revenue contributed by each to the joint exchequer. Hesse-Darmstadt's customs administration was to be modelled on that of Prussia but was to remain in the hands of her own officials. Owing to the differences of internal taxation in the two countries, duties continued to be levied on certain goods—such as beer and wine—crossing the frontier between Hesse-Darmstadt and Prussia.

A secret supplementary agreement, also signed on February 14, 1828, placed Prussia in a somewhat stronger position than the public treaty. Thus, Hesse-Darmstadt gave her consent in advance to future alterations of the tariff in the eastern provinces of Prussia, to commercial treaties signed by Prussia with States whose frontiers did not touch Hesse-Darmstadt, and to measures taken by Prussia as reprisals against the economic policy of other States. The Prussian official in the customs administration at Darmstadt was given wider powers than those laid down in the principal treaty.[1]

Both Governments acted in advance of public opinion. In Hesse-Darmstadt the treaty was vigorously criticised by Count Lehrbach who complained of the "betrayal" of his country to Prussia. Du Thil subsequently wrote that it was fortunate that the Chambers were not in session when the treaty was signed. The wine-growers of Hesse-Darmstadt welcomed an agreement which would restore to them the Prussian market but the manufacturers complained bitterly that they would be ruined by Prussian competition. In Prussia, on the other hand, critics of the treaty said that Hesse-Darmstadt had got the best of the bargain and that Prussia would suffer heavy financial losses. The wine-growers in the Mosel valley feared competition from the

---

[1] The secret articles are printed by Eisenhart Rothe and Ritthaler, II, pp. 207–11; H. Schmidt, pp. xxv–xxix (Appendix), and C. Eckert, pp. 541–545.

neighbouring Hesse-Darmstadt vineyards[1] but manufacturers were glad of a new—though small—market for their products.

Many of the German States were alarmed at the treaty of February 14, 1828. It is true that Baden welcomed the agreement but "at all the other courts the first vague intelligence from Berlin was received with indescribable alarm, the news falling into the diplomatic world like a bombshell".[2] Milbanke wrote to the Earl of Dudley from Frankfurt-am-Main: "The news of this negotiation has created some clamour against Prussia and no little alarm among the merchants and others connected with the trade in this part of Germany who will undoubtly suffer considerably by it, as the Prussian custom house establishment is conducted with the utmost severity and the adoption of that system in the Duchy of Hesse-Darmstadt will have the effect of raising the duties upon a great number of articles of commerce...."[3] The Bavaria-Württemberg customs union, within three weeks of its foundation, was faced with a formidable rival. Bavaria did not disguise her displeasure at an arrangement which would mean the levying of Prussian dues on one route between Bavaria and her isolated province of the Palatinate. Württemberg was alarmed but the King admitted that "sooner or later we shall be forced to follow this example".[4] Hesse-Cassel indignantly turned down the proposal that she should join the Prussia-Hesse-Darmstadt union. Austria, too, was hostile and was soon fostering the formation of a customs union in Central Germany. Abroad, considerable interest was shown in the treaty. In England, for example, it was feared that the extension of the Prussian customs system might lead to a reduction in English commerce—both legitimate and smuggling—with German States.

---

[1] Fear of Hesse-Darmstadt competition has been given as a cause for the decline in vineyards in Prussia from 37,700 acres in 1828 to 35,643 acres in 1829 (H. von Petersdorff, II, p. 133).

[2] H. von Treitschke, III, p. 639.

[3] Milbanke to Earl Dudley, March 14, 1828 (F.O. 30/28).

[4] W. Oncken, p. 10.

Just as the treaty of 1819 between Prussia and Schwarzburg-Sondershausen served as a model for subsequent agreements by which enclaves entered the Prussian customs system, so were the terms which Hesse-Darmstadt accepted in 1828 substantially the same as those on which other German States joined Prussia to form the Zollverein a few years later. The chief difference between the treaties of 1819 and 1828 was that while Schwarzburg-Sondershausen's customs administration was run by Prussian officials, that of Hesse-Darmstadt remained in the hands of her own officials.

The years which saw the first extensions of the Prussian customs system were also a period of progress in the reconstruction of Prussia's finances and in the extension of her network of roads. Attempts were made to develop her mercantile marine.

In his five years of office as Minister of Finance (1825–30) Motz thoroughly overhauled the financial system and balanced the budget. In 1825 the agriculture of the eastern provinces was suffering from an economic crisis and from the continued difficulty of exporting corn, wool and timber. Motz assisted the tenants on the royal domains by lowering rents but he insisted that these new rents should be punctually paid. About 3000 acres of domain land were sold between 1826 and 1830. The collection of taxes was tightened up and economies were made. Prussia's credit improved and in 1830 she was able to secure a reduction of interest—from 5 to 4 per cent—on the loan she had raised in London in 1818. In 1826 the Prussian budget showed a surplus of over 1,000,000 thalers and in 1828 one of 4,400,000 thalers.[1]

Equally satisfactory was the progress made in road-building.[2]

---

[1] H. von Treitschke, III, pp. 457–63 and H. von Petersdorff, II, ch. iii.

[2] For Prussian road-building at this time, see Horstmann, "Über die Fortschritte im preussischen Staat während der Jahre 1816 bis 1829 einschliesslich", in *Verhandlungen des Vereins zur Beförderung des Gewerbefleisses in Preussen*, IX (1830), pp. 242–50; Rudolf Grabo, *Die ostpreussischen Strassen im achtzehnten und neunzehnten Jahrhundert* (Königs-

In 1815 Prussia had only about 2400 miles of main roads mostly near Berlin and in the western provinces. Between 1815 and 1829 over 2800 miles of new main roads were constructed, 11 million thalers being spent on the work in 1817–28. The chief roads completed or in course of construction in this period were two from Leipzig to Frankfurt-am-Main, one from Bremen to Wesel-am-Rhein, one from Berlin to the Rhine through Arnsberg and several in lower Silesia. Some were entirely in Prussian territory while others were partly in other States. But much remained to be done, particularly in East Prussia and upper Silesia. Road-building had both political and economic significance. It was desirable to place Berlin in as close contact as possible with the provincial capitals. It was necessary to link up natural economic resources which were on the frontiers (such as the Saar coalfield) with markets in the interior of the country. Further, Motz used the new roads to try to capture through-traffic from neighbouring States, particularly in Thuringia, that were attempting to attract foreign trade by routes on which lower transit dues were charged than in Prussia.

The development of the Prussian mercantile marine was hampered by the navigation laws of other countries and by the high Sound dues levied by the Danes. Holland charged higher harbour dues on foreign than on native ships and granted a 10 per cent. drawback on duties on all goods imported in Dutch ships. England restricted the movement of Prussian vessels in two ways. First, under her Navigation Acts the only goods which a Prussian ship might bring to England for consumption in England were those produced in Prussia or exported from a Prussian port. Prussian ships were excluded from English

berg, 1910; Dissertation); Fritz Sälter, *Entwicklung und Bedeutung des Chaussee- und Wegebaues in der Provinz Westfalen unter ihrem ersten Oberpräsidenten von Vincke*, 1815–1844 (Marburg, 1917: Dissertation); Arnold Schellenberg, *Die Entwicklung des Landstrassenwesens im Gebiet des jetzigen Regierungsbezirks Merseburg* (Halle-an-der-Saale, 1929: Dissertation); and Paul Thimme, *Strassenbau und Strassenpolitik in Deutschland zur Zeit der Gründung des Zollvereins*, 1825–35 (1931).

colonies and from the English coasting trade. Secondly, even in trades in which Prussian ships might legally take part, higher harbour dues were levied on Prussian than on English ships. In 1822, as a measure of retaliation, Prussia reserved her own coastal trade to Prussian ships and introduced a system of differential harbour dues.[1] In 1824 England signed a Reciprocity Treaty with Prussia. It did not modify the English Navigation Acts but it did equalise harbour dues on English and Prussian ships in those trades not otherwise restricted.[2] In 1826 Prussia was allowed to trade with English colonies in return for giving English commerce and navigation most favoured nation treatment.

Prussia also negotiated commercial treaties with other countries. In March, 1825, a treaty was signed with Russia and the Prusso-Russian frontier was "reopened for the importation of produce arriving from Prussia, in so far as it is not prohibited by the general tariff". Transit dues were "considerably reduced on the whole extent of the frontiers from Memel to the Oder".[3] But Russia made little attempt to carry out her obligations and trade across this frontier remained largely in the hands of smugglers. In 1828 an agreement was made with the United States on the basis of reciprocity with regard to shipping dues. The treaty contained a most favoured nation treatment clause.[4]

Despite attempts to foster the growth of the Prussian mercantile marine, it declined from about 700 ships to 640 between 1820 and 1830. But outworn vessels were being replaced by new and there was a slight rise in total tonnage.

[1] Carl Brinkmann, p. 144.
[2] J. H. Clapham, *An Economic History of Modern Britain,* 1 (1926), pp. 330–4. The Anglo-Prussian Convention of 1824 is printed in P.P. 1824, XXIV. Cf. P.P. 1839, LXVII, p. 263.
[3] Von Maltzan to Canning, December 25, 1825 (P.P. 1839, XLVII, p. 268).
[4] G. M. Fisk, *Die handelspolitischen...Beziehungen zwischen Deutschland und den Vereinigten Staaten von Amerika* (1897), pp. 60–6.

(3) THE NEGOTIATIONS FOR A SOUTH GERMAN CUSTOMS UNION, 1819–1828[1]

The three South German States—Bavaria, Württemberg and Baden—retained in 1815 most of the territories they had acquired as a result of Napoleon's reconstruction of Germany. Unlike Prussia and the Hapsburg Empire they had no non-German subjects and no territory outside the Confederation. Some of their statesmen hoped that the Southern States, in co-operation with smaller States on the Rhine and in Central Germany, would be able to form a "third Germany"[2] and to pursue a policy of their own, independent alike of Prussia and Austria. This view was clearly set forth in a pamphlet, *Manuskript aus Süddeutschland*, which was published anonymously in London in 1820. The author was Friedrich Ludwig Lindner and he appears to have been in close touch with the King of Württemberg.

Lindner considered that German unity could not be attained as the cleavage between North and South Germany was too

[1] The founding of the South German customs union is described by W. Weber, chs. ii–v; L. K. Aegidi, pp. 65–74, 93–102, 118–21; H. von Treitschke, III, ch. viii. Bavaria's policy is discussed by M. Doeberl, *Bayern und die wirtschaftliche Einigung Deutschlands* (1915); Württemberg's by Karl V. Riecke, "Zur Vorgeschichte des deutschen Zollvereins. Auszüge aus Briefen des Freiherrn K. A. von Wangenheim", in *Württembergische Vierteljahrschrift* (1879), pp. 101–11; H. von Treitschke, "Karl August von Wangenheim", in *Historische und Politische Aufsätze* (5th edition, I, 1886), pp. 196–268; and C. Albrecht, *Die Triaspolitik des Freiherrn Karl August von Wangenheim* (1914), ch. v, Nassau's by W. Menn, *Zur Vorgeschichte des deutschen Zollvereins: Nassau's Handels- und Schiffahrtspolitik...,* 1815–27 (1930); and Hesse-Darmstadt's in Du Thil's memoirs. Documents on the negotiations are printed by Eisenhart Rothe and Ritthaler, I, pp. 371–549, and by M. Doeberl, pp. 60–117. See also documents printed in *Friedrich List: Werke*, I (part ii), pp. 647–75 and in Anton Chroust, *Die Berichte der französischen Gesandten, 1816–1848* (Part I of *Gesandtschaftsberichte aus München, 1814–48*) (5 vols and index, Munich, 1935–7).

[2] Sometimes called "the pure Germany" (*das reine Deutschland*).

great. The North was a coastal region with growing mercantile and industrial interests: the South was cut off from the sea and was predominantly agricultural. In the North lack of natural frontiers necessitated the upkeep of large armies: in the South the mountains offered some defence against the invader. The North was largely Protestant, the South predominantly Catholic. There were differences in the character of the people: the German of the North were more vigorous and progressive and fonder of travelling than those of the South. Lindner tended to exaggerate these differences and he failed to give proper weight to factors favouring German unity. But his views were widely held in South Germany in the 'twenties.

The desire to give South Germany greater political influence had its economic counterpart in attempts to form a South German customs union. The failure to carry out Article 19 of the Federal Constitution, the introduction of the Prussian tariff of 1818 and the continuance of the Austrian prohibitive system forced the South German States to try to improve their economic position without reference to either Austria or Prussia.

Discussions on the possibility of forming a South German customs union began late in 1819 at Vienna where representatives of the States concerned had met for the Ministers' Conferences. On the one hand, there were discussions between small States on the Rhine—Baden, Hesse-Darmstadt and Nassau. They favoured an agreement to keep their countries open to commerce and so to secure through traffic on the trade routes they commanded. On the other hand, Bavaria and Württemberg, encouraged by the appeals of the Union of Merchants,[1] had little sympathy for these free-trade suggestions but pro-

---

[1] As early as June 23, 1819, J. J. Schnell, chairman of the Union of Merchants, suggested to the King of Bavaria that if Bavaria would make the necessary move, the setting up of "a *separate* customs union of the greater part of Germany, namely of Württemberg, Saxony, Hesse and the other smaller States, may be regarded as certain, and once these States unite the adhesion of Prussia and Austria must follow" (quoted by M. Doeberl, pp. 13–14).

posed to set up a customs union in South Germany with new duties to be collected on the frontiers. They were thus proposing to accomplish in South Germany what they were criticising Prussia for doing in the North. The difference between the plans of the Rhine States and of Bavaria and Württemberg are significant, for they show the cleavage in the economic interests of the South German States which prevented the formation of a customs union. Baden, for example, had a considerable transit trade owing to her geographical position between France, Switzerland and Germany. Her frontiers were very long in proportion to her area and it was consequently difficult to prevent smuggling. So she favoured low import duties. Bavaria, on the other hand, was a larger State with more varied agricultural resources and a few growing industries. She desired to protect her manufactures and favoured rather higher import duties.

On May 19, 1820, Bavaria, Württemberg, Baden, Hesse-Darmstadt, Nassau, Sachse-Weimar, the Saxon duchies and the Reuss principalities agreed to enter into negotiations at Darmstadt for the formation of a customs union. The basis for these negotiations was seven heads of proposals (*Punktation*). The tariffs of separate States were to be replaced by a single tariff for the whole union to be jointly administered by all members. Uniformity was to be secured in tolls on roads and inland waterways. Where special consumption duties were levied by a State, native products were not to pay more than those of other members of the union. The customs revenue was to be divided according to population.[1]

The negotiations at Darmstadt lasted from the autumn of 1820 to the summer of 1823.[2] Nebenius made strenuous efforts to secure some agreement. Representatives of the Union of

[1] The treaty and heads of proposals are printed by L. K. Aegidi, pp. 99–101, and by Hans-Peter Olshausen, pp. 297–99: Eisenhart Rothe and Ritthaler print the punctation (1, pp. 383–4), but not the treaty. Cf. F. von Weech, pp. 100–7.

[2] See A. Suchel, *Hessen-Darmstadt und der Darmstadter Handels-kongress von* 1820–23 (Darmstadt, 1922).

Merchants pressed the plenipotentiaries to bring their deliberations to a successful conclusion.[1] On the other hand, Rechberg
(the Bavarian Foreign Minister) opposed the scheme for a
South German customs union as he feared that it might endanger Bavaria's political independence, and he worked against
von Lerchenfeld (Minister of Finance)[2] who favoured the plan.
So nothing was accomplished at Darmstadt. It was not even
possible to agree to a treaty for free-trade in provisions. On
this question the discussion degenerated into a lively debate
whether snails were a "necessary of life" or not! The division
between the small States on the Rhine on the one hand and
Bavaria and Württemberg on the other was too great to be
bridged. Particularist sentiment prevented the sacrifices necessary for the achievement of unity.

There were several questions upon which no agreement
could be reached. First, there were disputes as to the height of
the proposed import duties and to the method of collecting
them. Baden favoured low duties to be collected only at the
frontier while Bavaria wanted higher duties to be levied either
on the frontier or at recognised markets in the interior. Secondly,
the method of altering the tariff caused difficulties. It was
agreed that this should be by a majority decision but while the
small States wanted each member to have one vote, Bavaria and
Württemberg favoured a scheme by which the number of votes
cast by each State should vary according to its population.
Thirdly, there were differences of opinion regarding the division of the joint customs revenue. Baden, having long frontiers, proposed that the length of frontier in common with States
outside the customs union should be considered in dividing the
revenues. Most of the other States thought that this should be

---

[1] See, for example, F. Miller, *Über die Verhandlungen zu Darmstadt...*
(1821), and *Über ein Maximum der Zölle zwischen den süddeutschen
Staaten* (1822); and Hans-Peter Olshausen, pp. 154–89.

[2] See Max von Lerchenfeld (the Younger), *Aus den Papieren des
königlich bayerischen Staatsministers Maximilian Freiherrn von Lerchenfeld*
(1887).

done according to population. Again, some States wanted the size of the population to be determined by a census but others claimed that the provisional figures used for deciding how many men a State was liable to send to the Federal army (the *Bundes-matrikel*) should be used. When the *Bundesmatrikel* had been fixed a few years before, States had been anxious to prove that they had a small population so that they should contribute only a few soldiers, but when it came to claiming a share of a customs revenue they wanted to show that they had a large population.

In July, 1823, Du Thil announced that Hesse-Darmstadt was leaving the conference as she could delay no longer in setting her customs system in order and in the following year a new Hesse-Darmstadt tariff was introduced. Nassau had already reformed her tariff (1822) and she too left the conference. The united front of the South German States against Prussia and Austria had been broken and there followed a series of tariff wars between them. But Bavaria and Württemberg on the one hand and the small Rhine States on the other still recognised that they had interests in common. Thus Baden signed a treaty with Hesse-Darmstadt for mutual reduction of duties though she also did her best to improve commercial relations with Switzerland.

Bavaria and Württemberg, alarmed at this desertion of the small Rhine States, decided to try to compose their own differences first and then to approach their neighbours again. They came to a preliminary agreement in October, 1824: the tariff of the new union was to be modelled upon that of Bavaria. Representatives of Hesse-Darmstadt and Baden met at Heidelberg in the following month and replied to the Bavaria-Württemberg agreement by drawing up a Protocol to which Nassau subsequently agreed. "Here particularism played its trump card."[1] The Heidelberg allies promised to negotiate for a South German customs union only on the basis of each State retaining control over its own customs administration.

[1] H. von Treitschke, III, p. 625.

Nevertheless, Bavaria and Württemberg invited Baden, Nassau and Hesse-Darmstadt to discuss once more the question of union. Negotiations began at Stuttgart in February, 1825, but "proved a lamentable repetition of the Darmstadt conferences, being vitiated throughout by ill-temper and mistrust".[1] The old differences barred the way to agreement and no one showed signs of making serious concessions. Once again, disputes between Bavaria and Baden on the height of the tariff and between the larger and smaller States on control of customs administration and on the division of the revenue proved fatal to the success of the conference.

Plans for the formation of a South German customs union were revived in 1826 when King Ludwig I ascended the throne of Bavaria. He was a gifted and energetic though somewhat eccentric despot, who hoped to make Bavaria a leading State in Germany, both in cultural and material affairs. Large sums were spent on new buildings and art collections. He moved the Bavarian University from Landshut to Munich and did something to reform secondary education. One of his chief political ambitions was to link the two parts of his kingdom by securing the Baden Palatinate on the right bank of the Rhine to which he had claims. Baden firmly resisted Ludwig's pretensions. This dispute was not without result upon commercial negotiations.[2]

Shortly after Ludwig I's accession the Bavarian tariff was raised. The King of Württemberg feared that this would injure the economic interests of his country. He wrote to Ludwig I to suggest that negotiations for a customs union between the two States should be resumed. Discussions began in January, 1827, and were completed a year later. The smaller Rhine States did not join in the negotiations but Hohenzollern-Hechingen and Hohenzollern-Sigmaringen had entered the Württemberg customs system in July, 1824, and so became part of the new

[1] H. von Treitschke, III, p. 626.

[2] The influence of this territorial dispute upon Ludwig I's foreign policy is discussed by Otto Westphal, "System und Wandlungen der auswärtigen Politik Bayerns in den ersten Jahren Ludwigs I, 1825–1830", in *Staat und Volkstum* (Festgabe für K. A. von Müller, 1933).

union.[1] The Bavarian Palatinate did not form part of the union.[2] The treaty for setting up the first German customs union was signed on January 18, 1828. It was to come into force on July 1. Each State retained its own customs administration but mutual inspection secured uniformity. Duties were levied at the frontier. According to the main treaty the proceeds were to be divided in proportion to population, but by a supplementary convention it was agreed that Bavaria should receive 72 per cent and Württemberg 28 per cent of the customs revenue. The duties on manufactured articles were somewhat lower than those of Prussia; the duties on the produce of tropical countries were rather higher. A customs congress was to be held annually at Munich.

The attempts to set up a South German customs union had achieved only partial success. Bavaria and Württemberg were too small to form a powerful customs union of their own. The customs revenue per head of population was only $9\frac{1}{2}$ silver groschens as compared with 24 in Prussia. Administrative costs were high and absorbed 44 per cent of the receipts. The Bavarian Palatinate was isolated economically by the customs barriers of neighbouring States and Ludwig I's claims to Baden territory made the adhesion of Baden to the Bavaria-Württemberg customs union out of the question. Hopes of securing the adhesion of Hesse-Darmstadt ended when that State joined the Prussian customs system in February, 1828.

[1] The Hohenzollern Principalities received a share of the Württemberg customs revenue calculated on the basis of population. Württemberg, however, guaranteed Sigmaringen 20,000 florins a year and Hechingen 12,300 florins a year (Wurm and Müller, p. 102).

[2] The Bavarian Palatinate (*bayrischer Rheinkreis*) was excluded from "the common customs frontier" of the South German customs union since it was separated by Baden territory from the main Bavarian lands. But its products and manufactures were to enjoy the same tariff concessions (*Zollbegünstigungen*) as had hitherto been granted to them in the main Bavarian territories or which might in future be granted by the Governments of Bavaria and Württemberg. See the protocol on the negotiations between Bavaria and Württemberg (April 4, 1827) printed by Eisenhart Rothe and Ritthaler, I, pp. 534–5.

(4) THE ESTABLISHMENT OF THE MIDDLE
GERMAN COMMERCIAL UNION, 1828[1]

"The most dramatic but also the most confused events in the history of the achievement of German unity are those leading to the establishment of the Middle German Commercial Union. Nowhere are there so many players in action, nowhere are the factors more involved, nowhere are details so significant."[2]

The establishment in January and February, 1828, of customs unions in North and South Germany raised serious problems for the States of North and Central Germany that remained outside. Hanover, Oldenburg and Brunswick were agricultural countries which wanted to continue to import foreign manufactured goods as cheaply as possible. It was in their interest to keep open the roads from the North Sea ports to the great markets of Frankfurt-am-Main and Leipzig. The Thuringian States controlled important passes in the Thuringian forest and were determined to make the most of their geographical opportunities. Saxony, on the other hand, had growing industries and feared that her markets would be seriously restricted by the customs barriers that were closing in upon her on every side. These States had few economic interests in common except a desire to keep as many of the German trade routes as possible free from the duties imposed by either of the existing customs unions.

Both Prussia and Bavaria lost little time in attempting to

---

[1] The negotiations leading to the establishment of the Middle German Commercial Union in 1828 are described by W. Weber, ch. vii; H. von Treitschke, III, pp. 649–61; H. von Petersdorff, II, pp. 129–74. The position of the Thuringian States is discussed by E. Engel, *Wirtschaftliche und soziale Kämpfe in Thüringen...vor dem Jahre* 1848 (1927). For Brunswick, see R. Wittenberg, *Braunschweigs Zollpolitik von* 1828 *bis zum Anschluss an den deutschen Zollverein* (19. *Oktober* 1841) (1930). For Frankfurt-am-Main, see R. Schwemer, *Geschichte der Freien Stadt Frankfurt-am-Main*, II (3 vols. 1910–18), ch. vi, pp. 286–350.

[2] Ritthaler in introduction to part iv of Eisenhart Rothe and Ritthaler, III, p. 297.

extend their influence over Central Germany. Prussia aimed particularly at linking up her eastern and western provinces. She tried to secure the adhesion of Hesse-Cassel, Nassau and Sachse-Weimar but they refused to join. Hanover, too, rejected Motz's overtures for a commercial treaty which might pave the way for future union. Bavaria turned to the two Hesses. Hesse-Darmstadt, however, had joined Prussia. Hesse-Cassel was attracted by Bavaria's proposal to guarantee her existing customs revenue but eventually Austria's opposition prevented her from joining Bavaria.

Meantime Saxony was approaching Sachse-Weimar and the Saxon duchies in Thuringia. Economic and political motives both played a part. The King of Saxony was anxious to secure some economic control over the only loophole in the customs barriers of Austria, Prussia and Bavaria by which his dominions were surrounded and he also desired to extend his political influence over small States governed by members of his own house. An attempt in 1822 to establish a Thuringian customs union had led to the Treaty of Arnstadt but this had never been ratified.[1] At the end of March, 1828, an agreement was made at Oberschöna on heads of proposals on which should be based future negotiations for a customs union between the Kingdom of Saxony, the Grand Duchy of Sachse-Weimar and the Saxon duchies of Thuringia. The most significant of the proposed terms of union were the obligation to refrain from joining another customs union and the promise to keep in good order the main roads for through traffic.

Proposals now began to be made for the formation of a wider customs union in Central Germany on the lines indicated by the Oberschöna agreement. The Frankfurt Senator Dr Thomas actively promoted the setting up of such a union.[2]

[1] The abortive Treaty of Arnstadt is discussed by W. Engel, p. 4, and by F. Hartung, *Das Grossherzogtum Sachsen unter der Regierung Karl Augusts* (1923), p. 453.

[2] See Dr Thomas's letters to Burgomaster Smidt of Bremen (February 28, 1828) and to Rumpf—who represented the German free cities in Paris—(March 6, 1828) in R. Schwemer, II, Appendix, pp. 750-57.

There were many difficulties to be overcome. Small States in Central Germany were flattered by the attentions of powerful neighbours. They were pressed both by Prussia and Bavaria to join their unions and by Saxony to enter a new confederation. Austria was favourably disposed towards the proposed union in Central Germany. The economic interests of the States concerned were by no means identical. Personal quarrels—such as that between the Duke of Brunswick and the King of Hanover (George IV of England)—complicated matters. By the end of April, 1828, however, a draft treaty for a middle German commercial union had been drawn up at Frankfurt-am-Main. No member of the union was to join another customs union. No increase in transit dues was to be made. Main roads for through traffic were to be kept in good order. Thus the principles of the Oberschöna agreement were to be extended over a far larger area. But Hesse-Cassel and Hanover accepted this draft treaty as a basis for negotiations only with reservations.

Foreign States favoured the formation of a low tariff commercial union in Central Germany. Thus Henry Unwin Addington, the English Minister Plenipotentiary to the Germanic Confederation, wrote from Frankfurt-am-Main on May 27, 1828: "A mere inspection of the map will...show that, in case the union be persevered in, and its principles really and practically adopted and applied, a road will, during their operation, be kept open for the free transit of British wares from Hamburg and Bremen through Hanover and Hesse-Cassel, the Rhine and Switzerland, to the frontiers of Italy, on one side, and through Saxony and the minor central German States to those of Bohemia on the other. Besides these *lawful* commercial advantages, such a state of things will afford immense facilities for carrying on the contraband trade in the dominions of Prussia, Bavaria, Württemberg and [Hesse-] Darmstadt, and may not improbably have the effect of ultimately detaching more than one of these states from the restrictive system in force amongst them."[1]

[1] F.O. 30/28, May 27, 1828: Eisenhart Rothe and Ritthaler, II, pp. 429–30.

The Netherlands, too, were anxious to keep open the great German trade routes. The sugar refiners of Amsterdam and Rotterdam feared that their exports to South Germany and to Switzerland would be reduced owing to the formation of customs unions both in North and in South Germany.[1] France favoured the formation of a middle German union which would, it was hoped, prevent the complete economic unification of Germany. The extent to which foreign countries were able to influence German States at this time should not, however, be exaggerated. It is impossible, for example, to accept the view of Treitschke that Hanover's commercial policy was habitually under English control.

Negotiations were begun at Cassel on August 22, 1828, and were completed by September 24. Last-minute attempts were made by some States to secure concessions by refusing to ratify, but at last the difficulties were overcome and ratifications were exchanged on December 8. By this treaty a Middle German Commercial Union (der mitteldeutsche Handelsverein) was set up. The members were Hanover, Saxony, Hesse-Cassel, Nassau, Brunswick, Oldenburg, Frankfurt-am-Main, Bremen, the Saxon duchies, the Reuss principalities, Hesse-Homburg, Schwarzburg-Rudolstadt and the Upper Lordship (Oberherrschaft) of Schwarzburg-Sondershausen. They agreed not to enter another customs union before the end of 1834 when the treaty between Prussia and Hesse-Darmstadt expired. Existing main roads for through traffic were to be kept in good order and new ones were to be built. Transit dues on foreign goods coming to a State within the Union were not to be raised but those on foreign goods passing through the Union might be

[1] E. Baasch, Holländische Wirtschaftsgeschichte (1927), pp. 437 ff.; J. Kortmann, Die Niederlande in den handelspolitischen Verhandlungen mit Preussen, 1815–37 (1929), pp. 63–9. A selection of documents on the question is printed by N. W. Posthumus, Documenten betreffende de Buitenlandsche handelspolitiek van Nederland in de negentiende eeuw, III (1923), pp. 246–91. For a suggestion that the Netherlands should join the Middle German Commercial Union, see a dispatch from von Lindenau to von Scherff, April 19, 1828 (N. W. Posthumus, III, pp. 277–8).

raised. It would thus be possible to hamper commerce between the eastern and western provinces of Prussia. The Middle Union was not a customs union of the type already existing in North and South Germany, and all attempts to turn it into such a union failed. Each State continued to pursue its own economic policy. Agreement had really been reached on only two points—the determination to prevent the other two unions from expanding and the desire to keep open for English goods the north-south main trade routes from Hamburg and Bremen to Frankfurt-am-Main and Leipzig but to restrict if necessary the traffic on the west-east routes in so far as they ran through Prussian lands.

Such a union was not likely to survive for long. It could not even decide through which States the new roads were to run, let alone raise the funds necessary for their construction. It soon collapsed owing to the determined opposition of Prussia. Treitschke has exhausted his extensive vocabulary of vituperation in his criticism of the Middle Union. It was "a malicious and unnatural conspiracy against the Fatherland, bearing witness, like the Confederation of the Rhine, to the inherent possibilities of the German system of petty princedoms". "Never before had particularism brought forth so monstrous, so unnatural an abortion."[1]

At the end of 1828 three customs unions had been formed in Germany. The Prussia-Hesse-Darmstadt union, though nominally an arrangement between two independent sovereign States, was, in fact, the absorption of the smaller country into the customs system of the larger. The Bavaria-Württemberg union fell far short of the great South German customs union which it had been hoped to construct. The Middle Union had no common tariff and its objects were to a great extent negative—to prevent either of the other unions from expanding.

The significance of the events of this momentous year as steps towards the economic unification of the country was fully recognised in Germany. In October, 1828, Goethe told Ecker-

[1] H. von Treitschke, III, pp. 649, 656.

mann that he looked forward to the day when Germany would be united so that "Thalers and Groschens may have the same value throughout the country and my luggage may pass unopened through all the thirty-six States (of the Confederation)".[1] Goethe died before the establishment of the Zollverein but he foresaw the influence that a customs union might one day exert in German affairs.

[1] J. P. Eckermann, *Gespräche mit Goethe*, III (edition of 1884), p. 191. It is an interesting coincidence that in this year (1828) Liebig set up a chemical laboratory at the University of Giessen. "A great part of the subsequent advance in the chemical technique of production is due to his pupils..." (Alfred Marshall, *Industry and Trade* (edition of 1932), p. 129).

Chapter III

THE FOUNDING OF THE ZOLLVEREIN,
1828–1833

(1) THE STRUGGLE BETWEEN PRUSSIA AND THE MIDDLE GERMAN COMMERCIAL UNION, 1828–1833[1]

The Middle German Commercial Union tried to develop its organisation into that of a genuine customs union and to divert through traffic from Prussia by building new roads on which only low transit dues were levied. It failed owing to the divergent interests of its own members and to the active hostility of Prussia. Motz succeeded in opening up two trade routes between North and South Germany outside the control of the Middle Union. One was by roads through the small Thuringian States of Sachse-Coburg-Gotha; the other was along the Rhine where navigation was facilitated by a treaty with Holland.

By securing the adhesion of Hesse-Cassel to her customs system Prussia at last forged a link between her two groups of provinces. Hanover and her allies protested that Hesse-Cassel, by joining Prussia, had broken the treaty by which she had become a member of the Middle Union and the matter was brought before the Diet of the Germanic Confederation. Hanover also tried to induce the Diet to take up once more the question of carrying out Article 19 of the Federal Constitution. But the Diet again failed to play a decisive part in the promotion of German economic unity.

[1] For Prussia's struggle against the Middle Union, see J. Muck, *Zur Vorgeschichte des deutschen Zollvereins insbesondere die Bestrebungen des mitteldeutschen Vereins gegen den preussischen Zollverein* (1869); W. Weber, ch. ix; H. von Treitschke, iii, pp. 661–81; H. von Petersdorff, ii, chs. vii–xi; R. Schwemer, ii, ch. vii; and the monographs by W. Engel and R. Wittenberg cited above (p. 64 note 1).

The Middle Union had been set up on December 8, 1828. A few months later—in May, 1829—a commercial treaty was made between the Prussia-Hesse-Darmstadt customs union and the Bavaria-Württemberg customs union. This *rapprochement* rendered the position of the Middle Union insecure. Its members met at Cassel in June. Hanover was satisfied with the existing arrangement of a "neutral" union having as its main object the keeping open of trade routes between North and South Germany. Saxony, on the other hand, desired to expand the Union into a proper customs union with a common tariff and a joint customs administration. In July, 1829, the news came that Meiningen and Coburg had broken the spirit—though not the letter—of their engagements to the Union by allowing Prussia to construct roads through their lands by which goods could be moved from North to South Germany without paying transit dues. Some members of the Union thereupon showed little interest in the arguments of either Hanover or Saxony but were anxious to get the best terms they could from Prussia at the earliest opportunity.

In the circumstances it is surprising that any agreement was reached at Cassel at all. But von Grote, the Hanoverian representative, worked hard to secure an extension of the Union's activities—although this was not the policy originally advocated by his own Government. A treaty was signed in October, 1829, by which the life of the Middle Union was extended to the end of 1840 (when the commercial treaty between the Prussia-Hesse-Darmstadt and the Bavaria-Württemberg customs union expired). Further, a number of supplementary treaties were subsequently made between various members of the Middle Union which were intended to pave the way for future uniformity in the tariff and in customs administration. The most important of these agreements was that made at Eimbeck (or Einbeck) in March, 1830, between Hanover, Hesse-Cassel, Oldenburg and Brunswick. These States decided to form a customs union with internal free-trade (except in salt and playing-cards) and a common customs frontier. But no agreement was reached on the common tariff and the union contemplated at Eimbeck never came into force. A few years later, however, three of the Eimbeck allies joined to form a Tax Union (*Steuerverein*).

There were many difficulties in securing the ratification of the Treaty of Cassel. Meiningen and Gotha refused to ratify it. Nassau made reservations. Saxony and Sachse-Weimar reserved to themselves the right to leave the Union after 1834. Should the existing customs unions in North and South Germany unite, then Saxony and Sachse-Weimar would consider themse'ves at liberty to join this new union.

Meanwhile, the leading members of the Middle Union were embarking upon a programme of road-building which had been discussed for some years.[1] A road had been planned to start from Frankfurt-am-Main. It was to run north-east between Hesse-Darmstadt and Bavaria. From Fulda it was to go north to Cassel, north-east to Göttingen, north again to Hanover where one branch should go to Bremen and another to Hamburg. Attempts were made by Thuringian States to link Leipzig to Frankfurt-am-Main by a new road. The old road crossed Prussian territory twice between Gotha and Leipzig, namely at Erfurt and Naumburg. To avoid Prussian territory it was necessary to go from Leipzig south to Altenburg and then west to Gera and Gotha. Between Gera and Gotha there was a choice of several routes. For example, there was a northern route through Jena and Meiningen and a southern route through Neustadt, Saalfeld, Rudolstadt, Stadt Ilm and Ilmenau. To build such a road necessitated co-operation between a number of small Thuringian States and their mutual jealousies made this impossible. Each State wanted the new road to run through its own territories as much as possible so as to develop its own internal communications even if this involved unnecessary detours for through traffic. Each State feared that as soon as its

[1] See Paul Thimme, *Strassenbau und Strassenpolitik in Deutschland...* 1825–35 (1931), and S. Wollheim, *Staatsstrassen und Verkehrspolitik in Kurhessen von 1815 bis 1840* (1931).

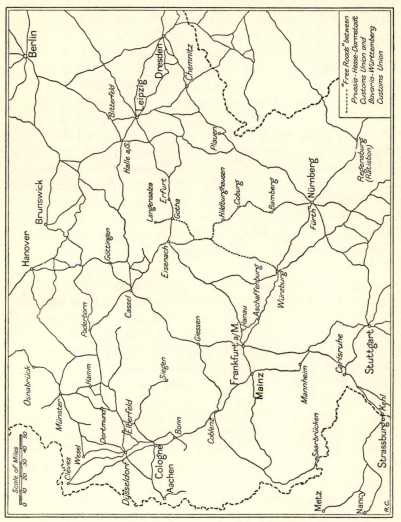

3. Main Roads in Central Germany, 1834.

own stretch of the new road had been built, a neighbour would try to secure the transit trade by constructing another road and charging lower tolls on it. These difficulties and the lack of money prevented the completion of the roads.

Motz was not intimidated by this show of activity on the part of his opponents. He was determined to frustrate their plans and to secure the construction of two great roads between North and South Germany which should be under Prussian control and which should compete successfully with the Middle Union for through traffic. In this way full advantage could be taken of the Commercial Treaty of 1829 between the Prussia-Hesse-Darmstadt and the Bavaria-Württemberg unions to promote trade between Prussia and the South German States. The first road was to be in the eastern provinces and was to run up the valleys of the Elbe and the Saale, across the Thuringian Forest and reach Northern Bavaria on the upper Main. The second road was to be in the western provinces and was to go from Bremen up the Weser valley to Minden and then south to Frankfurt-am-Main. Both roads would pass through territory in the hands of the Middle Union and careful negotiation would therefore be necessary.

Most of the western road was built. The Prussian section started at Minden—where traffic coming up the Weser valley from Bremen could be secured. It ran through Westphalia, entered Hesse-Darmstadt at Biedenkopf and then went on to Giessen and Frankfurt-am-Main. From Frankfurt there were roads to the South German States[1] and to France.[2] The disadvantage of this road was that the northern end (Bremen-Minden) lay in Hanover, which was hostile to Prussia's plans, and the southern end had to cross a small strip of Hesse-Cassel territory.

There were difficulties in securing the construction of the

[1] For example: Frankfurt-am-Main to Hirschhorn and then up the Neckar valley to Stuttgart.

[2] Frankfurt-am-Main to Mainz where the *Kaiserstrasse* to Metz was joined.

northern part of the eastern road—the section from Hamburg to Magdeburg. The direct route was through Hanoverian territory: a longer way was by the right bank of the Elbe through Lauenburg (whose Duke was King of Denmark) and Mecklenburg-Schwerin. With none of the States concerned could Prussia come to an agreement for the time being. But with regard to the vital middle section of the eastern road Motz was successful. Treaties with Sachse-Meiningen-Gotha and Sachse-Coburg-Gotha enabled Prussia to complete the road from Magdeburg to Bamberg through the hills of the Thuringian Forest. The route lay through Langensalza, Gotha, Hildburghausen and Coburg. South of Gotha this main road was joined by roads from the north-east (Erfurt) and from the south-west (Frankfurt-am-Main and Würzburg).

In negotiating with the small Saxon duchies of Meiningen and Coburg—their joint population numbered only 257,000— Motz was in a strong position. Both had territories which could be linked only by roads passing through Prussian lands. The Duke of Meiningen wanted to complete a road from Saalfeld to Pösneck but a small part of it would cross the Prussian district (*Kreis*) of Ziegenrück. The Duke of Coburg desired to unite his two residences of Coburg and Gotha by a road which would pass not only through Meiningen territory but also through the Prussian district of Schleusingen. Moreover, both dukes needed money. The Duke of Coburg had already applied unsuccessfully to the King of Saxony for funds for road-building.

Motz took advantage of the financial needs of the duchies to induce them to modify their schemes for road-building so as to make them part of his own plans for an eastern road from North to South Germany. Both Meiningen and Coburg came to terms in July, 1829. The Reuss principalities followed their example in December. They all agreed to build new roads by means of loans and subsidies supplied by Prussia. Coburg was lent 80,000 thalers and received a subsidy of 25,000 thalers. Meiningen, by a later agreement (June, 1830), speeded up road construction in return for a loan of 25,000 thalers. Through traffic on the new roads was not to pay transit dues. Various provisions were made facilitating trade between Prussia and the duchies. By secret articles the duchies agreed to enter the customs system of either Prussia or Bavaria and Württemberg as soon as their obligations to the Middle Union enabled them to do so—that is to say by January 1, 1835, at the latest.

Motz observed that "the treaties with Coburg and Meiningen for transit-free roads between Prussia, Bavaria, Württemberg and to Frankfurt-am-Main give us the great advantage of assured lines of communication with the south of Germany. The concessions made to Coburg and Meiningen are not commensurable with these great advantages, particularly as in this way a breach is made in the Middle German Commercial Union and we can confidently expect its members to take the initiative in asking for union with us."[1]

Traffic between North and South Germany was also facilitated by the treaty which Motz was able to negotiate with Holland on the question of the navigation of the Rhine.[2] In 1815 it had been agreed at Vienna that, for the subjects of States having territory on the river, traffic on the Rhine should be free *jusqu'à la mer*—not from ordinary customs dues—but (with certain exceptions) from special transit dues. The staple privileges of Cologne, Mainz and Mannheim were retained for the

---

[1] Quoted by H. von Petersdorff, II, p. 275.

[2] See C. Eckert, *Rheinschiffahrt im 19en Jahrhundert* (1900), part ii; G. Gothein, *Geschichtliche Entwicklung der Rheinschiffahrt im 19en Jahrhundert* (1903), chs. iv–vi; J. Kortmann, *Die Niederlande in den handelspolitischen Verhandlungen mit Preussen vom Wiener Kongress bis zum Schiffahrtsvertrag von 1837* (1929); P. J. Bouman, "Der Untergang des holländischen Handels- und Schiffahrtsmonopols auf dem Niederrhein, 1831–51", in *V.S.W.* XXVI (1933), p. 244: see the first section; H. von Treitschke, III, pp. 470–3; H. von Petersdorff, II, pp. 303–11; A. Zimmermann, pp. 102–4. A selection of documents on the question is printed by N. W. Posthumus, *Documenten betreffende de Buitenlandsche handelspolitiek van Nederland in de negentiende eeuw* (6 vols. 1919–31): see, for example, I, pp. 71, 78–85; III, pp. 226–46, 292–309; and v, pp. 214–18.

4. The Low Countries.

Note how the Netherlands commanded the mouths of the Rhine and Scheldt. Even after Belgium became independent, Holland's possession of territory on both banks of the Lower Scheldt enabled her to levy dues on ships going to or coming from Antwerp. The Antwerp-Cologne railway was completed in 1843.

time being so that it was still necessary for cargoes to be transferred from one ship to another at these river ports.

It was not found possible to carry out even this modest measure of freedom of navigation on the Rhine. Holland was determined to keep as much as possible of the trade on the Rhine in her own hands and she made every effort to evade the provisions of the Vienna settlement regarding freedom of navigation. "Never was a treaty more shamelessly broken", as Treitschke wrote. The Dutch not only imposed extra dues but even prohibited through traffic in several commodities including spices, tea, herrings and salt. In consequence of the Dutch imposts the cost of transporting goods along the Dutch section of the Rhine was about thirteen times as high as along a Prussian stretch of equal length.[1] Holland claimed that freedom of navigation *jusqu'à la mer* meant "*as far as* the sea" and that she was consequently entitled to levy what dues she pleased "at whatever point the *operation* of the tides commenced".[2] Other States interested in the navigation of the Rhine claimed that the obvious interpretation of *jusqu'à la mer* was "*into* the sea". Further, the Dutch held that the Rivers Waal and Leck—the most important branches of the Rhine from the point of view of navigation to and from the sea— were separate rivers and were therefore not covered by the provisions of the Vienna settlement. Holland skilfully played off England and the various German States against each other and for a time succeeded in restricting commerce on the Rhine in her own interest.

In 1820 the Dutch Government attempted to tighten Holland's hold upon the navigation of the Rhine by ordering that all goods going up the river from Amsterdam, Rotterdam or Dordrecht should be sent in vessels belonging to the shipping gilds of the ports concerned. No notice was taken of protests from German commercial interests and the attempts of German shipping companies to compete with the Dutch were unsuc-

[1] H. von Treitschke, III, p. 470.
[2] See N. W. Posthumus, V, p. 215.

cessful. The introduction of steamships on the Rhine did little to hinder Holland's virtual monopoly. In 1825 three rival shipping companies—one Dutch and two German—agreed to share the traffic and the Dutch company secured the all-important stretch of the river from Rotterdam to Cologne.

The Dutch, however, gradually began to realise that it would not be possible for them to retain permanently their monopoly of navigation on the Rhine. The strong protest of the Powers assembled at the Congress of Verona in 1822 reminded Holland of her isolation in this matter.[1] Only from France did the Dutch receive some support, for she thought that Le Havre would benefit from the dispute. It was, indeed, becoming clear that if navigation on the Rhine continued to be restricted, commerce to Central Europe would be driven to ports on other rivers.[2]

Prussia took the lead in Germany in demanding satisfaction from Holland. With much difficulty she succeeded in composing the differences of the smaller German States on the Rhine so that a united front could be presented to the Dutch. Only Nassau—whose ruling house was related to that of Holland—stood aloof. After prolonged negotiations, in which Motz took a prominent part, Holland at last gave way in the spring of 1829. In August of that year Prussia and Holland laid joint proposals before all the Rhine States assembled at Mainz.[3] The matter was delayed owing to the July Revolutions and the new Rhine Navigation Act was not signed until March, 1831. On the one hand the Dutch made important concessions. Navigation was to be free "*into* the sea" for ships belonging to

[1] For the English point of view on this question, see Wellington to Canning, November 29, 1822 in N. W. Posthumus, 1, pp. 84–5.

[2] It was, for example, often cheaper to send goods to the Rhine from Antwerp—by land or water—rather than from Amsterdam or Rotterdam (E. Baasch, *Holländische Wirtschaftsgeschichte* (1927), p. 428).

[3] See *Projet de Convention entre les Gouvernemens des États riverains du Rhin et de Règlement relatif à la navigation du dit fleuve* (August 19, 1829): a copy was sent by Addington to Lord Aberdeen (F.O. 30/29, Frankfurt-am-Main, September 10, 1829).

subjects of States on the Rhine and which were registered as vessels navigating that river.[1] The Rivers Waal and Leck were recognised as mouths of the Rhine. The monopoly of the Dutch shipping gilds came to an end. On the other hand, the obligation to change ships at Cologne,[2] Mainz and Mannheim was removed. Various dues remained—the *droit fixe* (consolidated transit dues) and "recognition duty" (*Rekognitionsgebühr*) on ships and the *octroi* on goods. The Rhine Navigation Act of March, 1831, did little more than carry out the intentions of the Vienna settlement of sixteen years before.

Motz's work in 1829 sealed the fate of the Middle German Commercial Union. The commercial treaty with Bavaria and Württemberg, the agreements on road-building with Meiningen and Gotha and the acceptance by Holland of most of Prussia's claims concerning freedom of navigation on the Rhine for subjects of the *états riverains* prepared the way for the dissolution of the Union and for the founding of the Zollverein. Motz died at the end of June, 1830, and so did not live to see the completion of his work. Motz stands out as one of the ablest Prussian statesmen of his day. His reform of the finances, his successful struggle with the Anhalt duchies, his share in the negotiations for bringing Hesse-Darmstadt into the Prussian customs system and the crushing blows which he directed against the Middle Union in 1829 helped to lay the foundations of Prussia's economic predominance in Germany in years to come. Motz's work was carried on by Maassen—the "father" of the tariff of 1818 who succeeded Motz as Minister of Finance —and by his colleague Eichhorn. More fortunate than his predecessor, Maassen lived until November, 1834, and so saw the accomplishment of the founding of the Zollverein.

It was clear that the Middle Union could not survive for long.

---

[1] This provision prevented Prussia, for example, from sending ships direct from her eastern provinces or from the Hanse towns by sea and river to her western provinces.

[2] For the last years of the Cologne staple, see M. Schwann, *Geschichte der Kölner Handelskammer*, 1 (1906), ch. xix.

The signal for its dissolution was given by the revolutions of 1830. The governments of most of the States concerned were overturned and their successors made the best terms they could with Prussia. The first to desert the Middle Union was Sachse-Weimar, which took advantage of the reservation she had made when ratifying the Treaty of Cassel. In February, 1831, Sachse-Weimar promised to join the Prussia-Hesse-Darmstadt customs union on January 1, 1835.

Hesse-Cassel was in a different position. She had agreed not to join another customs union until 1841 and she was also bound by the treaty of Eimbeck. Nevertheless, she negotiated for immediate union with Prussia. Her economic position was a deplorable one. She had an area of only 3250 square miles, yet had a customs frontier of over 700 miles to guard. Her import duties were high but smuggling was rampant, so the income from this source barely covered the cost of collection. Her transit duties were low but revenue from them was declining since merchants had begun to use the new road through Thuringia. Economic distress was partly responsible for the popular rising in the autumn of 1830. In the south of the Electorate between Fulda and Hanau customs houses were attacked,[1] the officials left their posts and considerable quantities of foreign goods entered the country without paying duty at all. Some members of the Hesse-Cassel estates began to press for a customs union with Prussia as the only solution for the country's economic troubles.

After some hesitation the Elector of Hesse-Cassel approached both Prussia and Bavaria. Prussia declined to discuss the question of union so long as the Elector negotiated with Bavaria as well and Hesse-Cassel gave way on this point. Negotiations were completed by the end of August, 1831, and Hesse-Cassel —with the exception of the isolated county (*Grafschaft*) of Schaumburg—joined the Prussian customs system on substantially the same terms as Hesse-Darmstadt. There were, however, some differences that deserve notice. On the one hand,

---

[1] See Milbanke to Aberdeen, September 29, 1830 (F.O. 30/32).

Hesse-Cassel secured privileges for the Cassel fair—a concession which led to unsuccessful demands from Hesse-Darmstadt for similar rights for her own fair at Offenbach-am-Main. Further, by secret articles, Prussia agreed not to attempt to penalise traffic passing from North to South Germany through States outside the Prussian customs system since Hesse-Cassel transit trade might suffer from such action. On the other hand, Hesse-Cassel agreed to introduce the same excise as that imposed in Prussia on the production of wine, new wine (*Most*) and tobacco. No similar provision was contained in Prussia's treaty with Hesse-Darmstadt.

For Hesse-Cassel the customs union with Prussia and Hesse-Darmstadt was an escape from an intolerable economic situation. Prussia, too, regarded the union with considerable satisfaction. She had at last linked her eastern and western provinces and she had divided the Middle Union into two parts. Hanover was now separated from the Thuringian States and from Saxony and the position of the Middle Union was more hopeless than ever.

Hanover was determined that the Middle Union should not be dissolved without a final attack upon Prussia. Hesse-Cassel's flagrant breach of her engagements to the Union gave Hanover her opportunity. Hanover demanded that Hesse-Cassel should fulfil her pledges and should refrain from raising duties on foreign goods destined for a country belonging to the Union. The raising of transit dues on goods passing through Hesse-Cassel to Frankfurt-am-Main from 3 groschens to 24 groschens was regarded as an intolerable hardship. In reply to protests, Hesse-Cassel defended her action by claiming that the Middle Union had in fact collapsed when Meiningen and Gotha allowed Prussia to build roads through their territory. The Union had failed in its main object of keeping trade routes open. Hesse-Cassel's deplorable economic conditions had forced her to enter the Prussian customs system. Nor could Hanover obtain any satisfaction at Berlin. Prussia naturally regarded the equalisation of the Prussian and Hesse-Cassel transit dues as one of the chief advantages of the new customs union. Negotiations on the subject had no result.

The matter now came before the Federal Diet of the Germanic Confederation. On May 24, 1832, Hanover, Oldenburg, Brunswick, Nassau, Bremen and Frankfurt-am-Main made a formal protest to the Diet and charged Hesse-Cassel with breaking her treaty obligations to the Middle Union. Prussia had no wish to see the Confederation intervene in economic affairs again and she sharply criticised Hanover's action both before the Diet and in representations which she made to German courts. Hesse-Cassel attempted to delay proceedings before the Diet as much as possible. She was confident that Prussia would not allow her customs union to be broken up and she recognised that the days of the Middle Union were numbered. The Diet never passed judgment upon Hesse-Cassel's breach of her treaty obligations. On the establishment of the Zollverein, trade between Hesse-Cassel and the south of Germany became internal commerce instead of foreign commerce so that the disputed transit dues were reduced to a level acceptable to Hanover.

When Hanover saw what slow progress was being made with her charges against Hesse-Cassel, she brought the question of German economic unity before the Federal Diet in another way. She laid two proposals before the Diet in August, 1832, which had as their object the carrying out of Article 19 of the Federal Act. The first proposed to facilitate transit trade through Federal States and aimed at securing a reduction in the Prussian transit dues. The second proposed to facilitate commerce between Federal States. England and Austria approved of this step. Palmerston sent a memorandum to the English representatives at the chief German courts on September 18, 1832, instructing them to give what support they could to the Hanoverian proposals. In a covering circular he told each of them "to take such steps as may appear to you best calculated to induce the Representatives of the various Courts in the Diet to support any propositions tending to facilitate the internal commerce of the German States between each other and their external commerce with other countries".[1] Metternich wrote to the Austrian Emperor that it would be desirable for Austria to modify her prohibitive tariff so as to remove an obstacle to the carrying out of Article 19. But it was too late for the Diet to do much. A committee of the Diet reported favourably on the first Hanoverian proposal but before serious progress had been made in the matter Prussia had succeeded in forming the Zollverein. The various Zollverein treaties contained a clause which provided for the dissolution of the new union should Article 19 of the Federal Act ever come into force. The contingency was not likely to arise but this clause robbed the Diet of a possible excuse for intervening in Zollverein affairs.

While Hanover was fighting for the maintenance of open trade routes for foreign goods into Germany, her former allies, Saxony and the Thuringian States, were busy discussing with Prussia the terms upon which they might enter her customs system.[2] The collapse of the Middle Union made it essential for the Kingdom of Saxony to join the Prussian customs system. Her manufacturers imported much of their raw material—particularly cotton—through Prussian territory and they were looking for wider markets than could be secured at home or by smuggling across the Bohemian frontier. Her growing industrial population needed uninterrupted access to the corn-growing province that had been ceded to Prussia in 1815. The King of Saxony was anxious to secure an increased revenue which would make him less dependent upon his parliament. But the merchants of Leipzig feared that they would suffer heavy losses if Saxony accepted the Prussian tariff which was higher than her own. Prussia entered into negotiations with Saxony with some misgivings. Her weavers and calico-printers

[1] F.O. 30/39 and 30/46; Eisenhart Rothe and Ritthaler, III, pp. 689–90.
[2] For an Austrian view of the early negotiations see Count Franz C. Colleredo's reports to Metternich from Dresden, January 17, February 7, May 11 and December 5, 1831 (Vienna Archives, *Zollvereinshandlungen*, 1830–47, fasc. 79 c).

in Silesia and in the province of Saxony were alarmed at the prospect of facing the competition of the poorly paid labour of the Erzgebirge. The fair-towns of Frankfurt-an-der-Oder and Naumburg feared the competition of the old-established fair at Leipzig. So the chief difficulty to be overcome in securing a settlement between the two countries was Saxony's desire that the Prussian tariff—particularly the transit dues—should be reduced and that the Leipzig fair should receive privileges similar to those enjoyed by the Prussian fairs.

In March, 1831, von Zeschau, the Saxon Finance Minister, arrived at Berlin and the negotiations between Prussia and Saxony began. Little progress was made and it was not until a year later that discussions were resumed. In the autumn of 1832 there was another breach, for Saxony was the first State to support Hanover's proposals to the Federal Diet for the carrying out of Article 19 of the Federal Constitution. Negotiations were opened for the third time on March 24, 1833. The fact that Bavaria and Württemberg had just come to terms with Prussia made it more necessary than ever for Saxony to enter the Prussian customs system. Agreement was reached within a week (March 30). Saxony entered the Prussian customs system on the same terms as the Hesses, Bavaria and Württemberg. She accepted the Prussian tariff and obtained a share of the customs revenue in proportion to her population. It was agreed that the rebate of duties on goods sold at the Frankfurt-an-der-Oder fair should be reduced and that the Leipzig fair should receive the same privileges as those enjoyed by the Frankfurt-an-der-Oder fair.[1] Certain Prussian import duties—

[1] The following account by Herr Zoller of the method of levying customs duties at the Leipzig fair forms part of an enclosure to F.O. 30/51, Cartwright to Palmerston (Frankfurt-am-Main, May 21, 1834):

"A merchant receives a quantity of foreign . . . goods; they are deposited at the custom house; the merchant delivers in a manifest with an account of the goods, the number of the packages with their marks, numbers and contents, and they are weighed at the custom house. The merchant then opens an account with the custom house, and his goods are sent home to him. He is debited in his account with the custom house with the whole

the most important being those on cotton and woollen yarns—
were reduced.[1]

Prussia was negotiating with the Thuringian States at the
same time as with Saxony, Bavaria and Württemberg. When
Hesse-Cassel joined the Prussian customs system, the Saxon
duchies declared that the Middle Union had been dissolved and
that they considered themselves at liberty to approach Prussia.
Meiningen, Gotha and Weimar were already pledged to join
Prussia in 1835. But many difficulties had to be overcome before terms of union could be arranged. Bavaria and Württemberg wanted their negotiations with Prussia to be completed
before the claims of the Thuringian States were considered.
Saxony demanded the right to participate in discussions concerning the Saxon duchies. Prussia was determined to keep the
Thuringian negotiations as much as possible apart from discussions with other States. Moreover, Prussia did not wish to

weight of his goods, and during the fair, as he goes on selling for exportation...he sends an account to the custom house, which sees them
weighed, packed up and sent off, and delivers to the purchaser the
necessary certificate which enables him to send the goods to their destina-
tion without being subject to any visitation or vexation.

"At the end of the fair the goods remaining in the merchant's warehouse are weighed, and their weight is added to the weight of those
already exported, and these two sums are deducted from the whole weight
of the goods he is debited with in the custom house books, and he pays
the duty according to the tariff upon the balance; for those goods must
have been sold for home consumption."

For the development of the Leipzig fair in the nineteenth century see
P. Heubner, "Hundert Jahre Wandel und Wachstum der Leipziger
Messen", in *Schmollers Jahrbuch* (October 1937), LXI, v, pp. 77–94.

[1] For Saxony's adhesion to the Prussian customs system, see F. von
Raumer, *Über den Anschluss Sachsens an die deutschen Zoll- und Handels-
vereine* (1833); F. L. Runde, *Auch ein Wort über Sachsens Anschluss an den
preussischen Zollverband...* (1833); Cunow, *Sachsens Anschluss an den
preussischen Zollverband* (1833); J. H. Thierot, *Welchen Einfluss auf dem
Felde des sächsischen Gewerbefleisses und Handels hat der Anschluss des
Königreichs Sachsen an den preussisch-deutschen Zollverein bis jetzt gehabt?*
(1838: French translation, 1840); W. Thieme, *Eintritt Sachsens in den
Zollverein und seine wirtschaftlichen Folgen* (1914).

negotiate with each Thuringian State separately. She wanted the Thuringian States to form a customs union among themselves and then to approach Prussia together. The mutual petty jealousies of the Thuringian States held up negotiations and at one time Prussia threatened to enforce her enclave system against Meiningen.

At last all difficulties were overcome. The Customs and Commercial Union of the Thuringian States (*Zoll- und Handelsverein der Thüringischen Staaten*) was established on May 10, 1833, between Sachse-Weimar, the smaller Saxon duchies, the Reuss principalities, the Prussian districts of Erfurt, Schleusingen and Ziegenrück and the Hesse-Cassel district of Schmalkalden. On the following day this union entered the Prussian customs system on the usual terms and also adopted the Prussian system of indirect taxation. A General Inspector, appointed by Sachse-Weimar, was to reside at Erfurt and supervise the affairs of the Thuringian customs union. The Thuringian States were to be jointly represented at the Zollverein congress and they had only one joint vote. "This federation within a federation, which Prussian statesmen had favoured since 1819, proved to be so simple and so natural that the dissolution of the Thuringian customs union was never contemplated—not even during the most serious crisis of the Zollverein."[1]

Hanover and Brunswick had no intention of following the example of Hesse-Cassel, Saxony and the Thuringian States. The two Guelph States did not join the Zollverein but on May 1, 1834, they formed a Tax Union (*Steuerverein*) which came into operation on June 1, 1835. Oldenburg joined in 1836, Lippe-Schaumburg in 1838. The Tax Union was to last, in the first instance, for seven years. Actually it survived for twenty years though Brunswick's scattered territories were incorporated in the Zollverein in the 'forties. Unlike the Middle Union, the

---

[1] H. von Treitschke, IV, p. 379. Cf. G. F. Kraus, *Der grosse preussisch-deutsche Zollverein in besonderer Beziehung auf den thüringischen Zollverband...* (1834), and K. Wildenhayn, *Der thüringische Zoll- und Steuerverein...* (1927).

Tax Union was a genuine customs union with a common tariff and a joint customs administration. Common excises were levied on spirits (*Branntwein*) and—to 1839—on beer. Administrative expenses accounted for over 20 per cent. of the gross customs revenue. Duties on manufactured articles and on the products of tropical countries were lower than those levied by the Zollverein and consumption in relation to population was greater. The Tax Union obtained a revenue of a thaler per head of population from these duties—about a third more than was raised by the Zollverein. By 1840, however, the revenue per head of population was much the same in the Zollverein and the Tax Union. In return for the manufactured goods and colonial products imported through Hamburg and Bremen, Hanover exported agricultural produce. At first it seemed as if the Tax Union intended to carry on the hostile anti-Prussian policy of the Middle Union but, after early difficulties had been overcome, Hanover recognised the wisdom of adopting a more conciliatory attitude towards her powerful neighbour. In 1837 it was agreed to co-operate to reduce smuggling and to transfer enclaves to the customs union in which they were situated.

(2) THE NEGOTIATIONS BETWEEN PRUSSIA AND THE BAVARIA-WÜRTTEMBERG CUSTOMS UNION, 1828—1833[1]

It has been seen that the attempts of the South German States to set up a customs union failed largely owing to differences of interests between, on the one hand, the two large States—Bavaria and Württemberg—and, on the other, the smaller States on the Rhine. When negotiations on this question were

---

[1] The negotiations between Prussia, Bavaria and Württemberg are described by W. Weber, chs. viii, x, xi; H. von Treitschke, III, pp. 665–8; IV, pp. 364–71; H. von Petersdorff, II, ch. ix; and M. Doeberl, pp. 30–60. A selection of documents on the negotiations is printed by Eisenhart Rothe and Ritthaler, III, pp. 421–730, and by M. Doeberl, pp. 60–115.

revived shortly after the accession of King Ludwig I of Bavaria, it was found possible to secure a customs union between Bavaria and Württemberg. Any hopes that Ludwig I may have had that this union would form the nucleus of a wider union were disappointed by the formation of customs unions in North and Central Germany in the same year (1828). Territorial disputes barred the way to an understanding with Baden. Their common distrust of the Middle German Commercial Union helped to bring Prussia, Bavaria and Württemberg together.

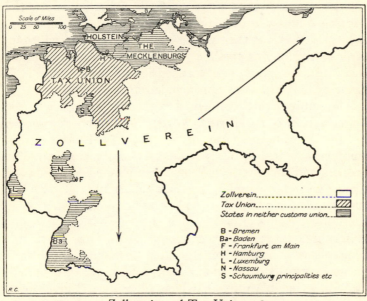

5. Zollverein and Tax Union, 1834.

The first overtures were made by Bavaria and Württemberg through Baron Johann Friedrich von Cotta, the well-known publisher and founder of the influential Augsburg *Allegemeine Zeitung*.[1] He paid three visits to Berlin in the winter of 1828–29

[1] Seymour, the English ambassador at Berlin, wrote to Aberdeen on September 29, 1829, that this newspaper had "the most extensive circulation and influence of any published within the Confederacy" (Eisenhart Rothe and Ritthaler, III, p. 578).

and his discussions with Motz laid the foundations of union between Prussia and the South German States.[1]

It was thought that the best method of paving the way to a
customs union was by means of a commercial treaty. Official
negotiations began on March 26, 1829, and a commercial treaty
was signed on May 27, 1829, between the Prussia-Hesse-Darmstadt and the Bavaria-Württemberg customs unions. It provided that after January 1, 1830, certain articles produced at
home might be sent duty free from one union to another, and
on other articles—such as textile goods and articles made from
leather—duties were to be reduced by 25 per cent. Efforts were
to be made to bring the customs system of the two unions into
as close harmony as possible. Annual conferences were to be
held "for the support and expansion of this treaty". The
Bavarian Palatinate was not included in the treaty.[2]

The nature of this commercial treaty was clearly described in
a circular note of the Prussian Foreign Minister which was sent
to Prussian embassies (August 18, 1829): "It is not a customs
union such as that formerly made between Bavaria and Württemberg and later between Prussia and Hesse-Darmstadt. It is
characterised not so much by the establishment of a common
tariff legislation as by close co-operation in administering and
collecting customs duties, which depends—it is true—upon
uniformity of tariffs. It is a commercial treaty but of a far more
comprehensive nature than any other of its kind. Such agreements are usually confined to certain definite products of native
growth or manufacture, to which preference is given in the
mutual trade between the contracting States. But this treaty

[1] A selection of von Cotta's correspondence on these discussions is
printed by Eisenhart Rothe and Ritthaler, III, pp. 421–38, 448–56, 460–1,
and by M. Doeberl, pp. 73–84. For von Cotta, see A. E. F. Schäffle, *Zum
hundertjährigen Andenken an Friedrich Freiherrn von Cotta* (1888).

[2] The treaty is printed by Eisenhart Rothe and Ritthaler, III, pp. 501–7;
cf. M. Doeberl, p. 105. Treitschke points out that "in all respects the treaty
had a provisional character; it established the narrowest form of commercial
union, all that was possible so long as the lands of the allies were not
geographically contiguous" (III, p. 668).

establishes complete freedom of trade in all products of native growth and manufacture between the contracting States: there are only a few exceptions and even of these, some are only temporary. The States which have signed the treaty have agreed, first, to secure uniformity in customs administration, secondly, to treat in the same way as their own produce that imported from the territory of another party to the agreement, and thirdly, to place each other's subjects on the same footing as their own as regards the carrying on of business and also to make all communications and other facilities for trade and commerce reciprocally available and to make the use of them as cheap as possible. An attempt has been made to remove, as far as trade and commerce are concerned, the frontiers dividing the various States from each other. In so far as this object has not been completely attained by the present treaty, efforts will be made to approach ever more closely to it at the annual conferences which it has been agreed to hold."[1]

Two months after this treaty had been signed Motz concluded his agreements with Gotha and Meiningen for the construction of roads on which goods could pass between North and South Germany without paying transit dues. His negotiations with Holland for facilitating commerce on the Rhine were practically completed when he died in June, 1830.

A year before his death Motz submitted to the King of Prussia a memorandum which may be regarded as his political testament (June, 1829).[2] It discussed the importance of the commercial treaty with Bavaria and Württemberg and advocated its ratification. Motz began by observing that the Germanic Confederation had made no serious attempt to facilitate commerce in Germany. He blamed Austria for refusing to modify

[1] Quoted by Eisenhart Rothe and Ritthaler, II, p. 555, and by M. Doeberl, p. 49.

[2] Reprinted by Eisenhart Rothe and Ritthaler, III, pp. 525–41. Cf. H. von Treitschke, III, p. 670; H. von Petersdorff, II, pp. 261–5; F. Schnabel, *Deutsche Geschichte im 19en Jahrhundert*, II, pp. 301, 402. The first draft of the memorandum was by Geheimrat Menz but Motz was responsible both for the leading ideas and for the detailed corrections.

her prohibitive commercial system and criticised other German States, which had non-German territories, for favouring the economic development of the latter at the expense of their possessions within the Confederation. He deplored the tariff wars which had checked German commerce in the 'twenties. The hope that the founding of customs unions in North and South Germany early in 1829 would lead to the economic unification of Germany had been frustrated by the establishment of the Middle Union. Motz considered that the only way to secure economic prosperity in Germany was to extend the Prussian customs system to Bavaria and Württemberg and to any other States that might be willing to negotiate. This would foster internal commerce and increase the customs revenue. Equally important would be the political and military advantages of a customs union between North and South Germany. Austria would be isolated. The support of the South German armies might turn the scale in a war against France for the defence of the Rhine.

Negotiations between the customs unions of North and South Germany were opened in December, 1831, but came to an end in May, 1832, without any result being achieved. In January, 1833, von Mieg, the Bavarian Minister of Finance, arrived in Berlin and negotiations were reopened. The treaty between Prussia, the Hesses, Bavaria and Württemberg was signed on March 22, 1833.[1] The chief provisions were similar to those contained in the treaties which Prussia had made previously with the two Hesses. There were, however, some differences. Although the customs revenues were to be divided according to population, Prussia received a lump sum of 100,000 thalers a year in return for handing over to the Zollverein exchequer the shipping dues she levied on the Oder and Vistula. Some States adopted (partly or entirely) the Prussian

---

[1] The treaty is printed in German and in English translation in P.P. 1838, XLV. Translations also appear in J. MacGregor, *Commercial Statistics* (1843), I, pp. 491–505 and (abridged) in J. R. McCulloch, *Dictionary of Commerce* (1847), II, pp. 1022–4.

system of internal taxation when they entered the Prussian customs system but Bavaria and Württemberg did not do so. Consequently, where an excise was levied—on tobacco or wine for example—by one member of the Zollverein a countervailing duty (*Ausgleichungsabgabe*) might be charged on such a product imported from another State in the Zollverein. Some local monopolies were maintained.

Further, Bavaria and Württemberg secured the right to negotiate commercial treaties but Prussia alone could negotiate with Russia with regard to commerce with Russian Poland. "The competence to conclude commercial treaties, a treasure grasped by Bavaria with such passionate zeal, proved in practice a harmless toy...."[1] The southern States seldom made use of this concession and Prussia undertook all important negotiations with foreign countries on behalf of the Union. Zollverein affairs were to be regulated by annual General Congresses at which unanimity was necessary before anything could be done. Actually only fifteen were held between 1834 and 1863.

There was some delay before Bavaria and Württemberg ratified the treaty. Ludwig I criticised his plenipotentiary for agreeing to the immediate provisional introduction of the Prussian customs system into Bavaria. Von Mieg resigned. In July, 1833, Eichhorn went to Munich and agreed to the withdrawal of the clause to which Bavaria had taken exception. The King thereupon ratified the treaty. There was a bitter struggle in the Württemberg Landtag before that body passed a resolution agreeing to the treaty. It may be observed that on October 9, 1834, Bavaria and Württemberg signed a secret "reinsurance treaty" by which they agreed to revive their own customs union in the event of the dissolution of the Zollverein.[2] Meantime, Saxony and the Thuringian States had joined Prussia and the Zollverein treaties came into force on January 1, 1834.

---

[1] H. von Treitschke, IV, p. 368. For the negotiations of the South German States with Switzerland see F. Ruckert, *Die Handelsbeziehungen zwischen Deutschland und der Schweiz* (1926), pp. 87–90.

[2] M. Doeberl, pp. 58, 112–15.

There was thus established in Germany a customs union of eighteen States with an area of 162,870 square miles,[1] and a population of nearly 23½ millions. Thirty years after its foundation Gustav Fischer declared that "the elder generation can still remember how joyfully the opening hour of the year 1834 was welcomed by the trading world. Long trains of waggons stood on the high roads, which till then had been cut up by tax barriers. At the stroke of midnight every turnpike was thrown open, and amid cheers the waggons hastened over the boundaries, which they could thenceforward cross in perfect freedom. Everyone felt that a great object had been attained."[2]

Germans had every reason to rejoice at the successful completion of the arduous negotiations for the construction of a customs union. The Zollverein of 1834, however, was incomplete in several respects. In the north the Tax Union, the three Hanse Towns, the two Mecklenburgs, Schleswig, Holstein and Lauenburg were outside the new union and the Zollverein therefore did not touch the North Sea coast and was cut off from the mouths of some of the chief German rivers and from the principal German seaports. In South-west Germany, Nassau, Baden and Frankfurt-am-Main retained their economic independence for a brief period. In the south, the Hapsburg Empire remained aloof. The prohibitive tariff system of this Empire and the customs frontier between Austria and Hungary prevented the Hapsburgs from co-operating effectively in economic matters with German States. Moreover, within the Zollverein itself complete freedom of trade had not yet been attained owing to differences of internal excise. Monopolies—such as those on salt and playing-cards in Prussia—and countervailing duties continued to hamper commerce in Germany.[3]

[1] W. H. Dawson, *Protection in Germany* (1904), gives the area of the Zollverein as "7,719 square miles" (p. 19). These are *German* square miles.

[2] G. Fischer, "Über das Wesen und Bedingungen eines Zollvereins", in *Hildebrand's Jahrbücher für Nationalökonomie und Statistik*, II (1865), p. 375.

[3] The following brief surveys of the founding of the Zollverein

(3) RECEPTION OF THE ZOLLVEREIN ABROAD[1]

The Zollverein was founded after fifteen years of bitter economic strife that followed the issue of Prussia's tariff of May 1818. The notion that it was set up as the result of the rise of a German national consciousness and was a touching example of brotherly co-operation on the part of the various States will not bear examination for a moment. Benaerts points out that "the formation of the German customs union was characterised by the very opposite of this 'national movement' which legendary history and inaccurate writings subsequently ascribed to it".[2] The States concerned fought for their own narrow interests and many of them joined the Zollverein only when economic depression and empty exchequers made further resistance to Prussia impossible.

The opposition of Germany's neighbours to the formation of the Zollverein was undoubtedly a factor which delayed union but its importance should not be exaggerated. Some German historians—such as Treitschke—have shown a tendency to stress this factor unduly and to accuse foreigners of conspiring to check the attainment of German unity. Actually the "intervention" of other States was only one element in a very complicated situation.

Austria was alarmed at the establishment of the Zollverein. Metternich's attitude was indicated in a private memorandum to the Austrian Emperor on June 24, 1833. It may be regarded as his reply to Motz's striking memorandum of June, 1829.

deserve notice: H. Richelot, *L'Association Douanière Allemande* (1845), part i, ch. ii; É. Worms, *L'Allemagne Économique ou Histoire du Zollverein Allemand* (1874), ch. i; E. Franz, "Ein Weg zum Reich. Die Entstehung des deutschen Zollvereins", in *V.S.W.* XXVII (1934); O. von Zwiedeneck-Südenhorst, "Zur Entstehungsgeschichte des deutschen Zollvereins", in *Jahrbücher für Nationalökonomie und Statistik*, CXLII (1935), pp. 25–34; and E. Hölzle, "Der deutsche Zollverein. Nationalpolitisches aus seiner Vorgeschichte", in *Württembergische Jahrbücher für Statistik und Landeskunde* (Jahrgang 1932–33; published 1935).

[1] See P. Benaerts, ch. ii. [2] P. Benaerts, p. 67.

Treitschke considered that a comparison of the two shows "why the Vienna court was bound to lose its leadership of Germany".[1]

Metternich complained that "the appearance of the Prussian Zollverein is most disadvantageous and threatening to the Germanic Confederation as such and to Austria in particular". "In the great Confederation there is arising a smaller subsidiary union, a *status in statu* in the full sense of the term, which will only too soon accustom itself to achieve its ends by its own machinery in the first place and will only pay attention to the objects and the machinery of the Confederation in so far as they are compatible with the former."[2] The Hapsburg Empire would be injured from the economic point of view by the expansion of industries in the new customs union and by the fact that the Zollverein would control communications between Austria and Northern Europe. Austria would be injured politically by the new pressure that Prussia would be able to exercise upon those members of the Confederation who were also members of the Zollverein. Metternich feared the possible development of a Zollverein *bloc* at the Federal Diet which would vote solidly for Prussia. The only remedy that Metternich could suggest was that the Government departments concerned should be asked to report on what modifications of the Austrian customs system would be necessary to enable Austria to secure the carrying out of Article 19 of the Federal Act!

Although Metternich recognised the danger of the Zollverein to Austria's position in the Confederation, he did not face boldly the alternatives before Austria in this matter. He should have recognised that the time was past for using the machinery of the Confederation. The only effective policy for Austria was either to try to break up the Zollverein (by using to the full her influence over some of its members) or else to undertake a

---

[1] H. von Treitschke, IV, p. 384. On the other hand, Heinrich Ritter von Srbik thinks highly of the memorandum and feels that Treitschke's opinion is "open to serious criticism" (*Metternich*, II (1925), p. 770); cf. Srbik, I, pp. 524–39.

[2] *Aus Metternich's nachgelassenen Papieren*, V (1882), pp. 507, 509.

radical reform of her own customs system so as to be able to make a serious attempt to force her way into the Zollverein. By either of these means she could have disputed Prussia's leadership in German economic affairs. Metternich did neither. He thought that it would be unwise to work openly against the Zollverein since he needed Prussia's political support at this time. He felt that it was equally out of the question to modify the tariff of the Hapsburg Empire sufficiently to make it possible to open negotiations for adhesion to the Zollverein. He saw that to do this he would have to overcome serious opposition both from the Austrian industrialists (who favoured high protective duties) and the Magyars (who had their own customs system). So Metternich maintained, on the whole, an attitude of neutrality regarding the Zollverein. On the other hand, Austria's representatives at German courts—often acting on their own initiative—tended to act in a hostile manner towards Prussia in economic matters.[1]

Britain, too, was hostile to the construction of the Zollverein —but for different reasons.[2] While Austria feared that Prussia's political prestige would increase now that she was head of the Zollverein, Britain feared that her own exports of manufactured articles and colonial goods to Central Europe would decline. British interests had unquestionably been injured by commercial developments in Germany since 1815. A striking example of this was given by Cartwright in a dispatch to the Duke of Wellington on December 1, 1834. He wrote: "Before 1819 British cotton manufactured goods were only subjected to a very trifling duty on their introduction into Bavaria. By the tariff of 1819 that duty was fixed at twenty florins (Gulden) the

[1] See A. Branchart, *Österreich und die Anfänge des preussisch-deutschen Zollvereins* (1930).

[2] For an English point of view of Prussian commercial policy on the eve of the founding of the Zollverein, see articles in *The Times* on January 7, 10 (leading article) and 19, 1833: German translations of these articles and comments upon them appear in "Ein Preusse", "Reden und Gegenreden in Sachen Preussischer und Englischer Handelspolitik" (1833).

Bavarian hundredweight. In 1825 it was increased to fifty florins. In 1828, when Bavaria united with Württemberg, the duty was still further increased to sixty florins, which was considered very high; and now, under the regulations of the Prussian Union, it stands at nearly ninety-five florins. Therefore that which in 1819 only paid a duty of twenty florins is now subjected to a duty of ninety-five florins, a most rapid and immense augmentation, to the detriment of British trade; and if these high duties are persisted in, it is feared that the demand for British goods must decrease every year." [1]

The attitude of the Committee of the Privy Council for Trade to the construction of the Zollverein may be seen from the alarm that was felt in the spring of 1833 when the English Consul-General at Hamburg reported a rumour that Hanover intended to enter the Prussian customs system. In a letter of May 25 Thomas Lack wrote to Sir George Shee that "their Lordships observe with regret the perseverance of the Prussian Government and the success which has attended its endeavours to establish and to extend a system, the manifest object of which is that of combining commercial monopoly with political aggrandisement". He referred to the Zollverein as "an alliance conceived in a spirit of hostility to British industry and British commerce". He observed that "the Lords of this Committee entertain the hope that a combination founded upon false principles, and under which the natural advantages of every other party must be sacrificed to the selfish views of Prussia cannot long be effectively sustained. Their Lordships will further bear in mind, in any reduction of duties which they may possibly have to propose, in regard to imports from the shores of the Baltic, the war which they conceive to have been declared by Prussia upon British commerce and will be strongly inclined to favour the productions of countries actuated by a more liberal and friendly spirit." [2] Lord Palmerston wrote to Baron Ompteda, the Hanoverian minister in London, on the subject on

[1] F.O. 30/53, no. 135.
[2] F.O. 34/23 (May 25, 1833); Eisenhart Rothe and Ritthaler, III, p. 719.

June 7, 1833,[1] and was informed that Hanover had no intention of joining the Zollverein.

It has been seen that Lord Palmerston had in September, 1832, instructed British ministers at the chief German courts to support Hanover's attempt to secure the carrying out of Article 19 of the Federal Act. He had signed a commercial treaty with Frankfurt-am-Main in May, 1832, by which the contracting parties agreed not to give any preference to a third State. Further, he viewed with undisguised satisfaction the founding of a Tax Union between Hanover, Oldenburg and Brunswick with low duties. A few years later he admitted that while the British Government had "never looked with a favourable eye upon the Prussian commercial league...there seems some reason to hope that the effect of this commercial union may not prove so injurious to the trade of this country as had been imagined; and at all events, the political consequences which may possibly result from the League, are by no means such as to give rise to uneasiness and apprehension".[2] But the development of manufactures in the Zollverein in the 'thirties alarmed English exporters. In 1841, for example, Richard Tottie wrote to Lord Aberdeen: "It may be unnecessary to inform your Lordship of the extent and perfection that has for some years been progressing in the manufactures of Germany, and that the competition with ours, both in quality and price, has become so formidable, as to have greatly reduced the demand and estimation for British fabrics in the great markets of Europe. Several descriptions of them are almost wholly supplanted, and the sale of all is fearfully reduced. For many years after the Peace, our exports were almost entirely composed of finished goods—now the great bulk consists of cotton twist and worsted yarn."[3]

---

[1] F.O. 34/23 (June 7, 1833).

[2] Palmerston to Sir Edward Cromwell Disbrowe, September 24, 1841, F.O. 37/227 (printed by N. W. Posthumus, v, pp. 75–6).

[3] Richard Tottie to Lord Aberdeen (Hull, October 14, 1841) in F.O. 33/91.

The attitude of the Netherlands to the growing Zollverein resembled that of England. Both countries supplied Germany with manufactured articles and colonial goods in return for agricultural produce such as corn from the Baltic ports. Both countries felt that the Zollverein would foster the expansion of German industry, commerce and shipping at their expense. Both countries had a certain political influence in Germany— Britain through the personal union with Hanover, the Netherlands through the personal union with Luxemburg and their family connections with the ruling house of Nassau. When it was in their power to do so the Dutch did not hesitate to hamper Prussia's commercial policy. Their obstinate attitude on the question of free navigation on the Rhine has already been discussed. In the early 'thirties the Belgian revolt kept the Dutch fully occupied and they were unable to offer serious opposition to the establishment of the Zollverein.

France disliked the Zollverein both for political and economic reasons.[1] She had no wish to see a powerful Prussia rising on her eastern frontier and she viewed with concern the prospect of a decline of German consumption of her wines and silks. France had retained some political influence in certain courts of South and Central Germany from the days of the Confederation of the Rhine and she tried to use it to prevent some of the German States from adhering to the Prussian customs system. But her own high tariff of July, 1822, alienated possible allies in Germany. When the South German States saw that their exports—for example of cattle—to France were about to be re-

[1] When Count de Rumigny, the French chargé d'affaires at Munich, heard in the spring of 1829 that a treaty was about to be signed between the Prussia-Hesse-Darmstadt and the Bavaria-Württemberg customs unions he wrote in alarm that this convention was "one of the most important events after the religious Reformation" for "Prussia is about to include in a vast system, formed by this alliance of North and South, all the States lying between them and this Power will exercise over its associates a preponderance which will surpass anything of this kind that hitherto existed and anything that it is possible to imagine" (quoted by P. Benaerts, p. 15).

stricted they promptly retaliated by raising their duties on French imports. France had skilful agents in Germany—such as Engelhardt, the French Consul at Mainz—but she failed to keep the South German States out of the Zollverein. She signed a commercial treaty with Nassau (1833) by which she hoped to prevent that State from joining Prussia. Nassau, however, broke her agreement in 1835 and adhered to the Zollverein. In July, 1836, France signed a commercial treaty with Mecklenburg with the object of increasing the sale of her wines there. Doubtless she expected that some would be smuggled from Mecklenburg into Prussia.[1]

The founding of the Zollverein was an example to States such as the Hapsburg Empire and Switzerland where commerce was still hampered by internal customs frontiers. Italy lacked both national and economic unity. Duties were levied not merely at the frontiers of separate States but at town gates. There were, for example, eight customs houses on the road between Milan and Florence. Italians envied the progress that was being made in Germany in the direction of abolishing internal tariffs. It has been observed that the *Annali universali di statistica* "hailed as an event of good omen for Italy the treaty providing for the completion of the Zollverein in 1834; and the journalists of Lombardy, and of the whole peninsula, proceeded to exploit it to the limit as an instrument of propaganda ideally suited to their purposes. It was a working model of what they wanted, consecrated by immediate success...."[2]

Friends and foes both watched with interest the consolidation and expansion of the Zollverein in the years that followed its foundation.[3] When it became clear that little less than a revolu-

[1] P. Benaerts, pp. 78–88.
[2] K. R. Greenwood, *Economics and Liberalism in the Risorgimento* (1934), p. 233.
[3] The attempts of foreigners to interfere in the affairs of Zollverein Congresses should not be exaggerated. In this connection the following letter from the British Foreign Office to H. F. Howard (chargé d'affaires at Berlin), June 9, 1846, is of interest:
"I have to inform you that Mr Ward, Her Majesty's Consul-General in

tion in Germany would be necessary to shake the new customs union the attitude of those who had once opposed its formation changed. They showed both a certain readiness to conclude commercial treaties with the Zollverein and tried to influence decisions at its Congresses by lobbying the delegates.

Saxony, will visit Berlin during the meeting of the deputies of the States of the Zollverein for the purpose of watching their proceedings in so far as they may have reference to the interests of British commerce. Mr Ward is directed to take especial care not to assume any official position himself or to countenance any supposition on the part of others that Her Majesty's Government, in sending an agent to the place of meeting, are desirous to obtain any influence over discussions with which they may be supposed to have no direct concern; the sole object of his journey to Berlin being to report on questions affecting British interests which have been his peculiar study..." (F.O. 64/262). Even so, von Canitz was "both astonished and annoyed" when Mr Ward appeared in Berlin (Sir George Hamilton to Lord Aberdeen, June 8, 1846, F.O. 64/264).

Chapter IV

THE ZOLLVEREIN ON TRIAL, 1834–1841[1]

(1) THE EXPANSION OF THE ZOLLVEREIN, 1834–1841[2]

However gratified Prussian statesmen might have been at the successful conclusion of the wearisome negotiations which

[1] For general developments between 1834 and 1841, see C. F. Nebenius, *Der deutsche Zollverein, sein System und seine Zukunft* (1835); "Über die Entstehung und Erweiterung des grossen deutschen Zollvereins", in *Deutsche Vierteljahrschrift* (1838), Heft ii, pp. 315–59; H. Richelot, *L'Association Douanière Allemande* (1845), part i, chs. v–vii; C. F. Wurm and F. T. Müller, pp. 156–82, 196–236; W. Weber, chs. xii–xviii; H. von Festenberg-Packisch, ch. viii; H. von Treitschke, IV, pp. 393–406, 569–98; S. von Walterhausen, pp. 77–86; and P. Benaerts, pp. 166–71.

[2] Negotiations with Baden are discussed by C. F. Nebenius, *Denkschrift für den Beitritt Badens zu dem...Zollverein* (1833), K. Mathy, *Betrachtungen über den Beitritt Badens zu dem deutschen Zollverein* (1834), H. von Treitschke's essay on Mathy in *Historische und politische Aufsätze*, I (5th edition, 1886), pp. 484–99, and F. Wallschmitt, *Der Eintritt Badens in den deutschen Zollverein* (1904); with Nassau by Karl Braun, "Nassau mit Frankreich gegen Preussen...", in *Vierteljahrschrift für Volkswirtschaft und Kulturkunde*, IV (1866), pp. 55–85; with Frankfurt-am-Main by R. Schwemer, II, chs. x–xii and by the *Geschichte der Handelskammer zu Frankfurt-am-Main* (issued by the Frankfurt Chamber of Commerce, 1908), part ii, ch. ii; with the Tax Union by H. Arning, *Hannovers Stellung zum Zollverein* (1930), G. von Berg, *Oldenburgs Anschluss an den deutschen Zollverein* (1842), R. Wittenberg, *Braunschweigs Zollpolitik von 1828 bis zum Anschluss an den deutschen Zollverein...* (1930), and the first ten documents in *Der grosse Zollverein deutscher Staaten und der Hannover-Oldenburgsche Steuerverein am 1. Januar 1844* (eine Staatsschrift mit Belegen, Hannover, 1844). For the Hanse towns, see E. Baasch, "Hamburg und Bremen und die deutschen wirtschaftlichen Einheitsbestrebungen von der Begründung des Zollvereins bis zum Anschluss Hannovers 1854", in *Hansische Geschichtsblätter*, XXVII (1922), p. 115, and A. Wohlwill, "Beiträge zu einer Geschichte C. F. Wurms", in *Zeitschrift des Vereins für Hamburgische Geschichte*, XXII (1918), ch. vi, pp. 60–70.

culminated in the establishment of the Zollverein they had every reason to regard the future with some misgivings. The treaties ran for eight years only. The new customs had hostile critics both at home and abroad.[1] A number of States had joined it mainly because that appeared to be the only way to avoid economic and financial collapse. They had grave doubts whether they would derive substantial advantages from the step they had taken. Thus, in Bavaria there was difficulty in securing a smooth working of the new system as the easy-going local officials disliked the rigour of Prussian methods of administration. J. MacGregor, for example, reported from Munich on July 9, 1836: "It appears that the other States complain of Bavaria not being sufficiently strict in guarding the frontiers towards Switzerland and not paying the douaniers as agreed to, which has led to their being very generally bribed."[2] In Prussia itself there was some discontent, particularly in Berlin where industries suffered temporarily from the competition of cheap Saxon goods. "Many manufacturers of this capital moved their factories to small provincial towns so as to reduce their costs."[3] Before the Zollverein treaties expired on January 1, 1842, Prussia had to convince not only her allies but many of her own people that the system was worth retaining. Alvensleben, who was Prussian Finance Minister at this time (1835–42), was not a man of the same calibre as his predecessors Motz and Maassen. Kühne, a Civil Servant upon whose advice great reliance had been placed in commercial affairs, was now pushed into the background somewhat. Nevertheless, Prussia's commercial policy achieved a sufficient measure of success to prevent any defections. She succeeded in completing the Zollverein in South-west Germany by securing the adhesion of Baden, Nassau and Frankfurt-am-Main.

Baden had an area of 5740 square miles and her population in 1835 was 1,240,000. It has been seen that her position between France, Germany and Switzerland made it difficult for her to

---

[1] See S. Bab, *Die öffentliche Meinung über den deutschen Zollverein zur Zeit seiner Entstehung* (1930), and P. Benaerts, ch. ii.   [2] B.T. 1/324.
[3] H. Richelot, *L'Association Douanière Allemande* (1845), p. 140.

adopt a tariff which would involve a strict supervision of her 780 miles of frontier. Her import duties were low—the highest rate was 3 thalers, 28 groschens per (Prussian) hundredweight —while her transit dues were comparatively high. The customs revenue, though much smaller than that of Prussia per head of population, was not inconsiderable. Over a million florins were collected annually between 1829 and 1833 and only 14 per cent. of this was spent upon customs administration. This compared favourably with the administrative costs of the Bavaria-Württemberg customs union which amounted to 44 per cent. of the gross revenue.

At the end of the Napoleonic Wars Baden's neighbours— with the exception of France—had low import duties. Baden was predominantly an agricultural country and she was able to send her produce—wine, tobacco, hemp, hops and cattle—to neighbouring German States. She had only a few small domestic industries. After the failure of the attempts to form a South German customs union in the early 'twenties Bavaria and Württemberg raised their import duties and Hesse-Darmstadt removed the collection of duties to her frontiers. This had two effects upon Baden's export trade. First, a considerable smuggling trade developed, particularly on the 370 mile frontier with Württemberg (part of which ran through the Black Forest). The Baden Government made no serious attempt to stop it. Secondly, there was an increase in trade between Baden and neighbouring Swiss cantons which were also suffering from the recent raising of tariffs in South and Central Germany. Switzerland imported agricultural produce from Baden and exported cattle, hides, cotton cloth and cotton goods. Baden also increased her trade with Holland. The Dutch sent colonial goods and received in exchange hemp, timber and cattle.

Baden had taken part in the abortive Darmstadt and Stuttgart conferences of 1820–25 but had remained aloof from the subsequent negotiations which led to the establishment of three customs unions in Germany in 1828. Disinclination to give up her policy of free trade, fear of a restriction of her political independence, and the territorial dispute with Bavaria were factors which help to explain her attitude. In May, 1828, the two Baden Chambers, in private session, drew up an address to the Grand Duke in which they declared that, if the establishment of a general German customs union were impossible, the question of adhesion to one of the three existing unions should be considered. If it were decided not to enter into negotiations with one of these unions, Bavaria and Württemberg should be approached with regard to the conclusion of a commercial treaty and, should this proposal be rejected by the South German union, then Baden should reply by raising her duties on imports from Bavaria and Württemberg.[1] In 1830 Prussia, whose court was on good terms with that of Baden, co-operated with Württemberg in an attempt to mediate on the vexed problem of Bavaria's territorial claims on Baden. Commercial questions were discussed at the same time and by a preliminary convention of July 10, 1830, Baden agreed to enter into negotiations with Bavaria and Württemberg with a view to adhering to their customs union. These negotiations were unsuccessful. The mutual suspicions of the South German States were as strong as they had been ten years before. Bavaria would not give up her territorial demands. Württemberg was alienated by the persistent smuggling across her Black Forest frontier and Baden attempted to secure reductions in the Bavaria-Württemberg tariff which neither of these States was prepared to accept.[2]

On May 17, 1831, the Baden second Chamber was informed, in a private session, of the negotiations on commercial affairs and on the territorial dispute with Bavaria. A unanimous decision was reached on October 5 not to join the Bavaria-Württemberg union, but by thirty-five votes to twenty-three

---

[1] For Prussia's views on Baden's position towards the end of 1829 see a note from the Prussian Foreign Ministry to Otterstedt, the Prussian minister in Carlsruhe, August 21, 1829 (Eisenhart Rothe and Ritthaler, III, pp. 560–5). The Baden Foreign Ministry replied on September 4, 1829 (*ibid*. III, pp. 568–76).

[2] Eisenhart Rothe and Ritthaler, III, pp. 598–9 (agreement of July 10, 1830), and III, pp. 601–2 (instructions to the Baden plenipotentiaries, September 1, 1830).

the Government was authorised to negotiate with Prussia and other German States for the construction of a general German customs union.[1] The terms the Chamber wanted to obtain were, however, so unreasonable that it was nearly eight months later before the Government ventured to ask Prussia to open negotiations. Prussia recognised that such negotiations would prejudice her chances of coming to an agreement with Bavaria and Württemberg and she saw that Baden was not yet prepared to make serious concessions. No discussions were undertaken at this time and Baden took no part in the final negotiations for the construction of the Zollverein.

With the establishment of the Zollverein it became clear that Baden's agriculture and commerce would suffer from her isolated situation. Trade with Switzerland and Holland was no adequate compensation for the loss of German markets. The more smuggling was reduced by the strict supervision of the Zollverein frontiers the more difficult would Baden's position become. Nebenius, who had long been working to secure the formation of a German customs union, saw that his dream was coming true though not in the form he had hoped when he wrote his famous memorandum in 1819. He recognised that Baden had now no choice but to join the Zollverein and he put forward this point of view in November, 1833, in a memorandum—*Denkschrift für den Beitritt Badens zu dem...Zollverein.* He received some support in Baden but there were still many who opposed the adhesion of the country to the Zollverein. This became clear when Böckh, the Minister of Finance, discussed the question with representatives of agriculture, commerce and industry. Economic objections were advanced by merchants—particularly those interested in smuggling—who thought that they would lose trade if Baden adopted the Zollverein tariff. Political objections came from enthusiastic Liberals who wanted no alliance, even of a purely economic nature, with absolutist Prussia.

Preliminary negotiations took place in the autumn of 1834.

[1] The address of the second Chamber to the Grand Duke is printed by Eisenhart Rothe and Ritthaler, III, pp. 638–40.

Prussia insisted that they should not be complicated by discussions on Bavaria's territorial claims. It soon became clear
that five main difficulties had to be overcome. First, Baden desired a substantial reduction of the import duties levied by the
Zollverein. To this Prussia would not agree. It was indeed unreasonable to expect a customs union which included a population of over 23 millions to remodel its tariff to oblige a small
country with a little over 1¼ million inhabitants. Secondly,
Baden desired a free hand in future commercial negotiations
with Switzerland. Prussia and Hesse-Cassel were not prepared
to grant Baden a privilege which might lead to the introduction
into the Zollverein of cheap Swiss silk and cotton goods.
Thirdly, Baden was charging higher shipping dues on the Main
and Neckar than were acceptable to other States on those rivers.
Bavaria and Württemberg had, on joining the Zollverein, declared that they would agree to the adhesion of Baden only if
a satisfactory agreement on this question could be reached.
Fourthly, there was the problem of introducing into Baden the
Zollverein system of a frontier district (*Grenzbezirk*). This was
normally the region between the frontier and a line drawn some
nine miles inland and in it customs officials kept strict watch to
prevent smuggling. So broad a frontier district would cause
considerable hardship in Baden which had a long frontier with
France. Fifthly, as in previous negotiations with Bavaria, a
difficulty arose as to the method of introducing the new tariff.
It was desired to avoid a repetition of what had occurred in
Saxony and the Thuringian States where large quantities of
foreign goods had been imported between the signing of the
treaties and actual entry into the new customs union. There had
been difficulty in levying retrospective duties (*Nachversteuerung*) upon these goods.[1]

[1] The retrospective levying of duties can be done in different ways.
"The mildest form is to make a rough estimate (of liability). A stricter
method is to demand a declaration (of dutiable goods held). The most
efficient but also the most burdensome method is for the customs officials
to make an inventory (of goods liable to duty)" (R. Schwemer, II,
p. 694 n.).

Little progress was made in the preliminary negotiations which had begun in August, 1834. The Württemberg Government, in particular, showed extreme reluctance to make any concession whatever to Baden. But a declaration by Bavaria on August 20 that she was prepared to leave for future discussion the chief questions regarding navigation on the River Main, raised hopes that this difficulty need not stand in the way of Baden's adhesion to the Zollverein. In October representatives of the three southern States met at Munich and agreed upon the privileges that they should demand jointly regarding future commercial negotiations with Switzerland.

Negotiations at Berlin were resumed on November 18, 1834, but it was not until May 12, 1835, that a treaty was signed. Even then Württemberg stated that she would ratify only if she obtained satisfaction regarding her demands for a reduction of the dues on the River Neckar and for compensation for those of her customs officials who could no longer be employed owing to the abolition of one of her customs frontiers. Baden accepted the Zollverein tariff with only minor modifications and introduced it provisionally on the night of May 17–18. Repayment of excess duties levied was promised in the event of the treaty not being ratified. This prompt action took the Baden merchants by surprise and prevented vast importations of foreign goods at the old low rates of duty. Baden was granted a narrower frontier district than was usual. She shared with Bavaria and Württemberg a limited right to make commercial agreements with Switzerland. By a secret article Baden secured a few concessions regarding her trade with Switzerland. Thus home-grown corn and native timber might be imported from or exported to Switzerland without payment of duty. A few Swiss products (such as wine from the Lake of Constance, cheese and parts of watches) were to pay less than the normal Zollverein import duties.[1]

There was considerable criticism of the treaty both on

[1] See E. Dietschi, "Die Schweiz und der entstehende deutsche Zollverein, 1828–35", in *Zeitschrift für die Geschichte des Oberrheins*, XLIV (New Series, 1931), pp. 287–344.

economic and political grounds in Baden. Many petitions were presented against it. A committee appointed by the second Chamber to examine the treaty produced an unfavourable majority report. Eventually, on July 2, 1835, the Chamber agreed by forty votes to twenty-two to join the Zollverein on the terms laid down by the treaty. Ratifications were exchanged in Berlin at the end of July. Only Hesse-Cassel stood aloof and continued to raise objections. A sharp note from Prussia was necessary before she agreed to ratify the treaty on September 1. The adhesion of Baden gave the Zollverein an easily guarded river frontier in the south-west in place of a difficult frontier in the hills of the Black Forest. Baden regained the German markets that she had partially lost. Her agriculture and commerce revived. Sugar refining was introduced under the protection of the Zollverein tariff. Baden's trade with Switzerland, however, declined.

The next State to join the Zollverein was Nassau. This small duchy had an area of 3940 square miles and a population of only 300,000. Its geographical location was advantageous, for it lay on the right bank of the middle Rhine and there was easy access to many of the main roads of Central Germany. The ruling family—a branch of the house of Orange—succeeded in maintaining its independence after the Napoleonic Wars. It feared both Prussia and Bavaria and endeavoured to retain the goodwill of the Hapsburgs so as to maintain Nassau's position as a sovereign member of the Germanic Confederation.

Nassau was mainly an agricultural region. Exports to neighbouring German States included wheat and oats from the fertile valleys of the Lahn and Aar and fat oxen from the Westerwald. The wines of the Rhine, Main and Lahn and the State-owned mineral waters of Selters and Fachingen were sent further afield. They had a European reputation. Industry was comparatively undeveloped. It was closely connected with agricultural pursuits and was carried on almost entirely in the home. The most important was the working up of linen, wool and cotton. Progress was slow owing to competition from England,

Hanover and Prussia. There was a small but active iron industry in the valleys of the Dill and Lahn. Such large-scale commerce as did exist was controlled not by local traders but by the merchants of Mainz and Frankfurt-am-Main. The economic position of Nassau after the Napoleonic Wars was unsatisfactory. The high tariffs of France and Holland checked exports and the appearance of cheap English goods endangered the home market. Agriculture suffered from the bad harvest of 1819.[1]

So long as Nassau had reasonably free access to the main commercial routes of Germany and to the chief markets of her neighbours she might hope to retain her economic independence without suffering serious inconvenience. But the failure of the Confederation to establish a customs union, the persistence of the high Dutch shipping dues on the Rhine, and finally the introduction of the Prussian tariff of 1818, forced Nassau to reconsider her position. Marschall, her leading statesman at this time, was above all anxious to maintain unimpaired the sovereignty of the duchy. Consequently, he rejected all suggestions for closer economic co-operation with Prussia. He took part in the Darmstadt conferences where he opposed the proposal to set up a South German customs union with a single customs administration to collect duties at the frontiers. All he wanted was an agreement to drop internal duties and to keep commerce as free as possible. When the conferences failed, however, Nassau herself removed to the frontiers the collection of her import duties. Marschall wished on the one hand to retaliate against the new tariffs of Prussia and other neighbouring States and on the other to increase the revenues of the duchy. Manufactured articles were to pay high duties, colonial goods moderate duties, while agricultural produce might be imported free. Nassau attended the Stuttgart conferences where fresh but unavailing efforts were made to set up a South German customs union.

The establishment of a customs union between Prussia and Hesse-Darmstadt in 1828 seriously threatened the economic

[1] W. Menn, pp. 5–16.

independence of Nassau. The Hanoverian minister in Berlin wrote to his sovereign that Prussia now "controls the navigation of the Rhine from Mannhein to Emmerich" and "the Duke of Nassau, completely enclosed by Prussia and Hesse-Darmstadt, is thus placed in a very difficult position and will probably be forced to make a similar agreement" with Prussia.[1] But the duchy was not *completely* isolated. The road to Frankfurt-am-Main was still open. Nassau was thus able to join the Middle German Commercial Union and her people could trade with South and Central Germany without crossing Prussian territory. The old hostility to Prussia was as powerful as ever. Marschall wrote to the Oldenburg representative at the Diet that it was not in the interest of States lying between the eastern and western provinces of Prussia to join her customs system since the division of that country into two parts was the surest guarantee against an undue increase of Prussia's power in Germany.[2]

The collapse of the Middle German Commercial Union and the final negotiations of 1833 for the completion of the Zollverein appeared to seal the doom of Marschall's policy. Nevertheless, he made a last effort to stave off economic union with Prussia. He turned to France. The signing of the Rhine Navigation Act of 1831 facilitated communication on that river between the *états riverains,* and it was possible for Nassau to trade with France by water without hindrance from the Zollverein tariff. France had recently raised her duties on foreign mineral waters but was prepared to reduce them if Nassau remained outside the Prussian customs system. Since the Nassau mineral waters were State property, the duke was strongly tempted to increase his revenue in this way. On September 19, 1833, a commercial treaty was signed between France and Nassau. Its terms were not made public until 1866.[3] France

---

[1] Eisenhart Rothe and Ritthaler, III, p. 24 (Reden to George IV, March 6, 1828).   [2] R. Schwemer, II, p. 303.
[3] The Franco-Nassau treaty of 1833 was first published by Karl Braun in the *Vierteljahrschrift für Volkswirtschaft und Kulturkunde,* IV (1866), pp. 65–6. The date of publication is significant.

promised to lower her duties on mineral waters while Nassau agreed not to raise her duties on French wines and silks for five years. Since the Zollverein duties on wines and silks were higher than those of Nassau, this provision bound the duchy to abstain from entering the Prussian customs system for five years.

The export of mineral waters to France was, however, no adequate compensation for loss of markets elsewhere. It became daily more obvious that Nassau's only hope of economic revival lay in union with Prussia. Baden's adhesion to the Zollverein in May, 1834, was the last straw. Marschall's death in January, 1834, made it easier for Nassau to change her policy. She evaded her obligations to France in a singularly dishonourable manner. In July, 1834, the French Government was informed that Nassau no longer considered herself bound by the treaty of 1833 because the French Chambers had failed to ratify it in their session of 1833–34. France had reduced her duties on mineral waters by royal decree and it was merely pressure of business that had delayed consideration of the treaty by the Chambers. Although Nassau appears to have been technically within her rights[1] the French Government had every reason to feel aggrieved. For some months the Duke of Nassau waited for Prussia to take the first step towards opening negotiations for Nassau's entry into the Zollverein. But Prussia did not do so and in October, 1834, Nassau swallowed her pride and approached Prussia herself. The negotiations for the ratification of the treaty with Baden kept Prussian officials busy at this time and Nassau had to wait until July, 1835, before her proposals were considered. Meantime, Nassau raised many of her duties and was thus able to tax the large quantities of colonial goods which speculators were importing in view of the impending adhesion of the duchy to the Zollverein.

Despite her long record of hostility to Prussia, Nassau hoped for generous treatment when she joined the Zollverein. Treitschke considered that she showed "amazing effrontery" in the

[1] See Article 3 of the Franco-Nassau treaty of 1833.

negotiations. She asked for the maintenance of local shipping dues on the Rhine and Main, the privileges of fairs for the Nassau spas and the grant of a larger share of the Zollverein revenues than that to which she was entitled on a basis of population. Nassau argued that the presence of many visitors in spas like Wiesbaden and Ems raised the consumption of foreign goods above the normal. Eichhorn—who was in charge of the negotiations on the Prussian side—far from being prepared to grant privileges to Nassau wanted to place her in an inferior position by not giving her a full vote at the Zollverein conferences. Eventually a compromise was reached. Nassau secured her full vote and retained her shipping dues but gave up her special claims and entered the Zollverein on the usual terms in December, 1835. Ratifications were exchanged on February 24, 1836. The treaty benefited both parties. Prussia had completed the construction of her customs union in South-west Germany—for Frankfurt-am-Main was on the point of joining the Zollverein too. Nassau had an opportunity of recovering her old markets and her customs revenue increased.

The last State in South-west Germany to join the Zollverein was Frankfurt-am-Main.[1] This free city of some 60,000 inhabitants was a sovereign State of the Confederation and the seat of the Diet. Its favourable location on the Main gave its inhabitants easy access to the Rhine. Its position on the chief trade routes of Western and Central Germany favoured the development of commerce. It was a great centre for the distribution of foreign—particularly British—goods to Central Europe. Its fairs attracted buyers from almost all parts of the world. As the home of the house of Rothschild it became one of the most important European banking centres.

A city whose prosperity was based largely on the profits of transit trade and banking naturally favoured the greatest possible freedom of commerce in Germany. It has been seen that

[1] Documents on the commercial policy of Frankfurt-am-Main are printed by Eisenhart Rothe and Ritthaler (see, for example, III, pp. 486, 499–500, 548–54, 588–96, 629–30, 653–4), and R. Schwemer, II, Appendix.

the introduction of the Prussian tariff of 1818 adversely affected Frankfurt and turned some of its legitimate trade into smuggling. The establishment of the customs union between Prussia and Hesse-Darmstadt ten years later was another blow to

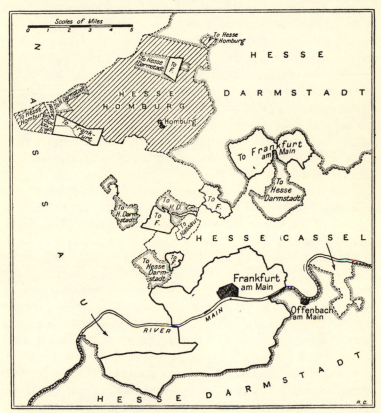

6. The Free City of Frankfurt-am-Main and neighbouring territory in 1833. This map illustrates the territorial confusion in Germany at this time. (After August Ravenstein.)

Frankfurt's fortunes, for the fair of Offenbach-am-Main—a neighbouring Hesse-Darmstadt town—developed at Frankfurt's expense. The free city took a leading part in the formation of the Middle German Commercial Union.

When it became clear that Prussia was succeeding in her policy of breaking up the Middle Union, Frankfurt turned to Britain as Nassau turned to France. But whereas Nassau was anxious to find new markets for her exports to replace those she was losing owing to the extension of the Prussian customs system, Frankfurt hoped to obtain political support from Britain for her policy of keeping open some of the main German trade routes. She wanted Britain to help Hanover in her attempts to prop up the crumbling Middle Union and to secure a solution of Germany's economic problems through the Confederation. Unfortunately, Frankfurt had little to offer in return. She had already lowered her import duties so that there was hardly room for further reduction and she would obviously keep out of Prussia's commercial system as long as possible without any bribe from Britain to do so.

Britain was approached three times. Nothing came of two proposals in 1830 and a third attempt was made after the conclusion of the Rhine Navigation Act of March, 1831. Cartwright wondered "how a treaty which is based upon the reciprocal admission of flags into the ports of the contracting parties can be made applicable to a town situated upon a river the depth of which in the summer months is almost insufficient to float large barges, and which does not possess a single vessel by any means capable of putting to sea".[1] He might have added that since Britain was not an *état riverain* her ships might not come direct from a home port to one on the Rhine.[2]

The adhesion of Hesse-Cassel to the Prussian customs system at the end of August, 1831, drew the Prussian net closer round Frankfurt and early in January, 1833, Dr Harnier (a Frankfurt Senator) and Koch (the British Consul at Frankfurt) arrived in London. It still seemed somewhat pointless to begin

[1] Cartwright to Lord Palmerston, June 18, 1831 (Eisenhart Rothe and Ritthaler, III, pp. 629–30).

[2] A Dutch official wrote in October, 1845: "Neither English, Belgian, Hanoverian or other flag has the privilege of *direct transit*, nor can such ships have a *patent*" (N. W. Posthumus, v, p. 216).

discussions since Frankfurt had little to offer. "Nevertheless, Palmerston did enter into negotiations because he was able to fit them into his general policy—namely, an energetic foreign policy, protection of England's economic interests, support for all small States seeking assistance against Great Powers, opposition to members of the Holy Alliance."[1] A treaty between Britain and Frankfurt was signed on May 13, 1832. It was to last for ten years. Ships were to be treated on the basis of reciprocity, goods on that of the most favoured nation. The significance of the treaty was political, not economic. Britain openly supported Frankfurt in her struggle to maintain her economic independence and the free city, by implication, pledged itself not to join the Zollverein for ten years.

Frankfurt's hopes that Prussia's plans for the extension of her customs system would be thwarted were disappointed. The establishment of the Zollverein left the free city and its neighbour Nassau in isolation. Many Frankfurt merchants regarded the future with alarm. A petition of December 2, 1833, to the Senate pointed out that by the founding of the Zollverein "a direct line of communication will be formed over Offenbach; all the Saxon manufacturers who have hitherto visited our fairs will in future proceed to Offenbach; the remaining portion of our transit and active trade will follow in the same channel; our retail trade with the immediate neighbourhood, already so considerably impaired, will be almost entirely ruined, and the majority of our fellow-citizens will in vain seek their livelihood, whilst our neighbours will reap the fruits of this new formation of the trade of our German Fatherland from the enjoyment of which we shall wilfully have excluded ourselves." The petitioners suggested that the only way out of the difficulty was for Frankfurt to join the Zollverein.[2]

The fears of the petitioners were not without justification. In 1834 legitimate trade with the rest of Germany declined

---

[1] R. Schwemer, II, p. 467.
[2] This petition appears in English translation in F.O. 30/53, no. 135, Cartwright to Wellington (December 1, 1834), Enclosure C.

though smuggling increased. In June, 1835, a Prussian commissioner reported to the Prussian Minister of Finance that it was notorious that both open and secret "smuggling on a very large scale takes place from Frankfurt to all the neighbouring parts of the Zollverein...". "Open smuggling is done partly by carriers...and partly by vehicles, particularly coaches, which travel in large numbers every day between Frankfurt and Offenbach: large quantities of goods are smuggled in the vehicles and in the clothes and on the persons of the passengers. Secret smuggling is generally done by means of forged customs-seals with the co-operation of those who issue certificates of origin. It is generally considered—and it has recently been proved—that customs officials are not averse from acting in collusion with smugglers. The frontier is weakly and inadequately guarded. Those in charge of the customs administration do not perform their duties satisfactorily."[1] The carriers who openly defied the Zollverein customs officials usually left Sachsenhausen—the southern suburb of Frankfurt—by the *Affentor* in the evening, went to the village of Oberrad and then avoided the Hesse-Darmstadt customs houses by going through the woods to the village of Giesheim. From Giesheim,* which was beyond the Zollverein frontier district (*Grenzbezirk*), smuggled goods were taken to Darmstadt, Hanau, Offenbach and Aschaffenburg.[2]

Trade depression forced the Frankfurt authorities to consider the question of joining the Zollverein. There were serious differences of opinion to be overcome. Those who favoured adhesion to Prussia argued that Frankfurt's commerce would be ruined if she remained isolated much longer. They agreed that economic independence was an honourable state but they held that the free city had virtually no choice in the matter. Their

---

[1] Yet a year before, Cartwright had written to Palmerston: "The customs officers at the different stations on the Hesse-Cassel and Hesse-Darmstadt frontiers exercised their duties with great and unusual rigour..." (F.O. 30/50, no. 51, April 12, 1834).

[2] The report is printed by R. Schwemer, II, pp. 770–2.

* For Giesheim *read* Griesheim.

opponents feared that adhesion to the Zollverein would mean a loss of prestige and might lead to a diminution of political independence. In the last twenty years Frankfurt had played by no means an insignificant part in economic affairs in Germany. The formation of the Middle Union, the treaty with Britain, the complaint against Hesse-Cassel at the Diet, the attempts to secure the fulfilment of Article 19 of the Federal Act—in all these matters Frankfurt had shown her influence. As a Zollverein member she might become a mere satellite of Prussia.

In April, 1834, the Frankfurt Senate resolved to open negotiations with Prussia. Early in the following year a Frankfurt mission went to Berlin. It was composed of opponents to Prussia who regarded adhesion to the Zollverein as a necessary evil. They demanded a full vote at the Zollverein Congress, the same rights for the Frankfurt fair as Leipzig possessed, the maintenance of local gild privileges, and the introduction of only a mild form of retrospective duties. Further, since Frankfurt was a wealthy town consuming large quantities of foreign goods she demanded a "preferential payment" (*Präzipuum*)—a larger proportion of the Zollverein revenues than that to which she would be entitled on a basis of population. Prussia, on the other hand, wanted Frankfurt to share a vote at the Zollverein Congress with another State and to pledge herself to agree to future changes in the Zollverein tariff and to commercial treaties with foreign States. A severe form of levying retrospective duties was proposed. Prussia agreed, however, to the principle of a "preferential payment". The divergence of opinion between the two parties was considerable and by the beginning of April, 1835, no agreement had been reached. Frankfurt now asked Britain if she would be prepared to release her from the obligations undertaken by the treaty of May, 1832, and early in July Britain agreed to this. But Frankfurt held on to the treaty with Britain to the last as a bargaining weapon against Prussia. By December, 1835, it was clear that further delay would be dangerous since Nassau's adhesion to the Zollverein completed Frankfurt's isolation. On January 2, 1836, a treaty was signed by which Frankfurt joined the Zollverein.[1]

The terms on which Frankfurt-am-Main entered the Zollverein were, on the whole, generous.[2] On many points her representatives succeeded in getting their point of view accepted. Frankfurt's share of the joint revenue was fixed at 4⅔ florins (or 2 thalers, 15 silver groschens and 5⅕ pfennigs) per head of her urban population, and 1 florin (or 17 silver groschens, 1⅐ pfennigs) per head of her rural population.[3] (In 1836 and in 1837 she was to receive 230,000 florins.) This worked out at about four and a half times as much as she would have obtained if her share of the revenue had been calculated in the ordinary way. Frankfurt obtained the same rights for her fair as those possessed by Leipzig. She retained many of her gild privileges.[4] On the other hand, although she was nominally a full member of the customs union, Frankfurt agreed that normally her interests at Zollverein Congresses should be in the hands of the Nassau delegate. She promised to accept commercial treaties between the Zollverein and foreign Powers. She reluctantly agreed that the Offenbach fair should be held at the same time as her own. Further, she accepted the levying of retrospective duties on goods already imported, on condition that she received 10 per cent. of the proceeds. The levying of these duties

[1] This was technically a breach of the commercial treaty with Britain which was still in force. A few days later, however, Dr Harnier reported from London that Lord Palmerston had agreed not merely to cancel the treaty of 1832 but to date this cancellation *before* January 2, 1836. For a report of Karl Sieveking (of Hamburg) to Dr Thomas, July 7, 1835, giving the results of a discussion with Palmerston on the question of Britain's attitude to the proposed adhesion of Frankfurt to the Zollverein, see H. Sieveking, *Karl Sieveking, 1787–1847*, III (1928), pp. 242–4.

[2] An English translation of the treaty of January 2, 1836, was enclosed in a report from Cartwright to Palmerston, June 8, 1836 (B.T. 1/326).

[3] For calculating this payment the urban population was estimated at 50,000 and the rural population at 10,000.

[4] See *Aktenstücke der hiesigen Gewerbeverhältnisse insbesondere die Aufhebung der Zunftbeschränkungen betreffend* (Frankfurt, 1861) for documents on gild regulations in Frankfurt-am-Main.

caused considerable inconvenience. It had been estimated that they would bring in three million florins but actually less than half that sum was collected.[1]

Prussia had now completed the construction of the Zollverein in South-west Germany. So long as Baden, Nassau and Frankfurt-am-Main retained their economic independence South-west Germany could not obtain the full benefit of the establishment of the Zollverein. The smuggling of large quantities of foreign goods into this part of Germany was a continual source of anxiety to Prussia. But now—with the exception, of course, of Alsace—the whole of the Rhine valley from the Dutch to the Swiss frontiers formed part of a single customs area. It has been seen that Baden and Nassau benefited from the new régime. So did Frankfurt. Good business was done at the first fair after her adhesion to the Zollverein and Frankfurt observed with satisfaction the decline of her rival Offenbach.[2]

In England the expansion of the Zollverein between 1834 and 1836 caused some alarm. The Manchester Chamber of Commerce, for example, told Palmerston that it "viewed with concern the formation of this great league without any successful effort being made to stem its progress towards completion" and expressed the hope "that something may yet be done, if not to lessen, at least to provide against a further extension of the meditated injury to the commerce of this country". Palmerston replied that "the Chamber of Commerce must be aware, that the English Government has neither the power nor the right to prevent independent States from entering into such arrange-

[1] Between 1836 and 1839 the amount raised in retrospective duties was 1,217,229 florins. For the development of Frankfurt's trade under the Zollverein, see O. von Aufsess, "Der Warenhandel und Verkehr der Freien Stadt Frankfurt seit deren Anschluss an den Deutschen Zollverein (1836–1860)", in *Beiträge zur Statistik der Freien Stadt Frankfurt* (1862), Band 1, Heft iv.

[2] See Heber's account of the Offenbach-am-Main Easter fair, 1836, in H. Görlich, *Die Entwicklung der Industriestadt Offenbach und die hessische Wirtschaftspolitik in der Gründungszeit des Zollvereins* (unpublished Dissertation, Frankfurt-am-Main, 1922), pp. 324–5.

ments with respect to their mutual commerce as may appear to them best calculated to promote their respective interests".[1]

The completion of the Zollverein in the south-west of Germany left only Austria and a part of North Germany in economic isolation. This included the predominantly agricultural States of Hanover, Brunswick, Oldenburg, the Schaumburg principalities, the two Mecklenburgs and the (Danish) provinces of Schleswig, Holstein and Lauenburg as well as the commercial seaports of Hamburg, Bremen and Lübeck. Prussia desired their adhesion to the Zollverein to link together more firmly her eastern and western provinces—then united only by Hesse-Cassel—and to secure access to the North Sea. The interests of the North German States, however, were apparently so divergent from those of the Zollverein that no union seemed possible for the time being.

In Hanover, the largest of the States concerned (14,600 square miles), nine-tenths of the population of 1,730,000 were interested in agriculture. The linen industry, once so important, had declined and there was little to take its place. Some road-building was undertaken in the 'twenties and 'thirties to improve communications with the North Sea ports. Shipping was confined to local coasting trade. Hanover pursued a policy of free-trade since she wished to import manufactured articles, colonial goods and wines as cheaply as possible.[2] Oldenburg, which had an area of 2100 square miles and a population (1816) of only 182,000, was almost entirely an agricultural region.[3] Hamburg and Bremen, on the other hand, were great centres of transit trade. They supplied Central Europe with large quantities of manufactured articles and colonial goods. They had a share of the growing emigrant traffic to North America. Hamburg and Bremen favoured a policy of free-trade. They feared that adhesion to the Zollverein would lead to a loss of some of their transit trade. Certainly so long as neighbouring North

[1] M.Ch.C., January 20 and 27, 1836.
[2] See F. W. O. L. Reden, *Das Königreich Hannover...* (1839).
[3] See P. Kollmann, *Das Herzogtum Oldenburg...* (1893).

German States stood aloof it was hardly in their interest to join the Zollverein. "It was undeniable that the enormous mass of the population of the North Sea littoral had no desire to surrender its separate existence. Klefeker in Hamburg, Berg in Oldenburg, von der Horst in Hanover and a few other far-seeing publicists who advised adhesion to the Zollverein, could effect nothing in face of the universal prejudice."[1]

Shortly after the Zollverein had been formed, Hanover, Brunswick and Oldenburg formed a customs union known as the Tax Union. Import duties, on the whole, were low. The revenue was divided, as in the Zollverein, in proportion to population. To some extent this union might be regarded as a successor to the ill-fated Middle German Commercial Union. Both favoured the introduction of cheap foreign manufactured articles and colonial goods. Both turned a blind eye to smuggling into neighbouring territories which had adopted the Prussian customs system. Cartwright referred at the end of 1834 to the smuggling of British goods to Leipzig "across the Hanoverian frontier in the Harz Mountains". He stated that he was assured "that a contraband trade is now carrying on to a great extent along that frontier, and that the Prussian Government are aware of the circumstance but are totally unable to put a stop to it".[2] The interests of the Zollverein were also injured in another way. The Tax Union levied its full import duties on goods passing from Prussian enclaves through its territory to the main Prussian dominions.

Negotiations were undertaken in the hope of improving relations between the two customs unions. They were held up for a time owing to Hanover's desire to extend the Tax Union by securing the adhesion of the Schaumburg principalities (Schaumburg-Lippe[3] and Lippe-Detmold) as well as the Hesse-Cassel county (*Grafschaft*) of Schaumburg. The negotiations with Schaumburg-Lippe were successful and (by a treaty

[1] H. von Treitschke, v, p. 445.
[2] Cartwright to Wellington, Frankfurt-am-Main, December 1, 1834 (F.O. 30/53, no. 135).　　　[3] Also known as Lippe-Bückeburg.

signed in November, 1837) she joined the Tax Union on January 1, 1838. Lippe-Detmold, however, remained aloof and Hesse-Cassel refused to agree to the adhesion of the county of Schaumburg. On November 1, 1837, a number of agreements were made between the Zollverein and the Tax Union. Measures were to be taken to put down smuggling between the two unions. The Prussian town and district of Minden were to join the Tax Union. There was to be an exchange of enclaves and other small districts so as to simplify the frontier between the two unions. The chief districts to enter the Zollverein by this arrangement were the Brunswick territories of Blakenberg, Walkenried and Calvörde and the Hanoverian districts of Hohnstein and Elbingerode. Provision was also made for the lowering of transit dues on local frontier traffic. Although these arrangements at first improved somewhat the relations between the Zollverein and the Tax Union, there were many complaints on both sides that traffic between the two unions was being unnecessarily hampered and in December, 1840, the Tax Union denounced the agreements of 1837.

It was not to be expected that the negotiations for a new agreement would be begun at once, since the treaties establishing the Zollverein and the Tax Union expired on January 1, 1842, and both Prussia and Hanover were engaged in discussions with their allies for prolonging these unions. But the position was complicated by a quarrel between the two Guelph houses and by the sudden decision of Brunswick to leave the Tax Union. This small agricultural State, with a population of rather more than a quarter of a million, had for the last twenty-five years taken advantage of the central location of its scattered territories to play off its powerful neighbours, Prussia and Hanover, against each other. The breach with Hanover in 1840–41 was caused largely by Brunswick's fear that Hanover was neglecting her interests in agreements that were being made with Prussia on the construction of railways and roads in North Germany. She desired the rapid completion of the lines from Magdeburg to Brunswick, Hanover and Minden and from

Celle to Hanover, Hildesheim and Brunswick. Further, Brunswick was dissatisfied at the construction through Prussian and Hanoverian territory of a new road from Magdeburg to Hamburg which would probably take traffic from the old route running through her own territory. The Hanoverian section of this road from Ülzen to Salzwedel was nearly finished at the end of 1840 and would obviously soon be open to through traffic. Brunswick's protest against its construction was therefore somewhat belated. But Brunswick was free to leave the Tax Union if she wished to do so, for although the treaty of renewal had been signed both parties had ratified only with reservations on road-building and railway construction. In March, 1841, Brunswick announced that she was leaving the Tax Union.

Amsberg,[1] the leading Brunswick economist of his day, who had had considerable experience in commercial negotiations, went to Berlin to try to secure the adhesion of Brunswick to the Zollverein. Prussia agreed to negotiate. If Brunswick were left isolated in North Germany, she might become a great smuggling centre, while if she joined the Zollverein, another step would have been taken to link Prussia's eastern and western provinces. There was little difficulty in drawing up a treaty. Brunswick entered the Zollverein on the usual terms and accepted the Prussian excises on beer, wine, brandy and tobacco. She did not receive a full vote at the Zollverein Congress. Hanover was alarmed at the turn events had taken, since Brunswick's adhesion to the Zollverein meant that her provinces of Göttingen and Grubenhagen would be completely cut off from the main part of the State. Eventually it was agreed to preserve the economic unity of Hanover *for one year* by allowing the Brunswick territories on the Weser and in the Harz Mountains to remain temporarily in the Tax Union. Their inhabitants, however, were to be allowed to export *native* products freely to the Zollverein and to import freely the native products of that part

---

[1] Ten years before this, P. A. von Amsberg had put forward his views on the problem of German economic unity in a pamphlet entitled *Ueber die Einigung der Handels-Interessen Deutschlands* (Brunswick, 1831).

of Brunswick which was in the Zollverein. It was hoped that this would give Prussia and Hanover sufficient time to negotiate for the admission of the Tax Union to the Zollverein. The treaty between Prussia and Brunswick was signed on October 19, 1841, and was ratified before the end of the year. In December the treaties of 1837 between the Zollverein and the Tax Union were renewed with modifications for one year. The southern part of the Hanoverian district of Fallersleben joined the Zollverein.

Lippe-Detmold and the Waldeck county of Lippe-Pyrmont also agreed in October, 1841, to join the Zollverein. This meant that the Hesse-Cassel county of Schaumburg was no longer isolated from Zollverein territory and this district, too, entered the Prussian customs system.

No negotiations were undertaken by Prussia with the North German States that were not members of the Tax Union. It was necessary to tighten up the customs administration on the Mecklenburg-Strelitz frontier to prevent the smuggling of French wines which were being imported cheaply under a commercial treaty with France which had been signed in July, 1836, and was to run for ten years. The question of joining the Prussian customs system was considered in Mecklenburg-Schwerin. When Colonel G. H. Hodges, the recently appointed British Consul-General at Hamburg, visited the court of Mecklenburg-Schwerin in the autumn of 1841 he was told by von Lützow, the Grand Duke's chief minister, that "our Grand Duchy is peculiarly situated: sooner or later we shall be forced to join the Prussian League...".[1] But public opinion in Mecklenburg-Schwerin was, on the whole, against adhesion to the Zollverein. Hamburg, Bremen and Lübeck showed little inclination to join the Prussian customs system, though there was some discussion on the subject in local newspapers and in pamphlets.[2]

---

[1] Colonel Hodges to Lord Aberdeen (Hamburg, September 24, 1841) in F.O. 33/91.

[2] See, for example, the pamphlet, *Ueber das Verhältniss der freien Hansestadt Bremen zum Zollvereine*, Von einem Bremer Kaufmann (Bremen, 1837).

In 1842, when the new Zollverein treaties came into force, Prussia could regard with satisfaction her work in the past eight years in expanding the Zollverein. The gaps in the south-west —Baden, Nassau and Frankfurt-am-Main—had been filled. In the north the Tax Union had suffered a serious loss by the defection of Brunswick and was pledged to negotiate immediately for union with the Zollverein.

(2) COMMERCIAL RELATIONS WITH FOREIGN COUNTRIES, 1834–1841[1]

So long as Germany possessed no economic unity it was not easy for individual States to secure favourable terms in commercial negotiations with foreign Powers. This is illustrated by the great difficulty that was experienced by Prussia in coming to an agreement with the Dutch on the vexed question of freedom of navigation on the Rhine. It was hoped that this state of affairs would change after the establishment of the Zollverein. It was felt that Prussia, at the head of a customs union which by 1836 included most of Germany would be in a position to secure better terms than before for the export of German commodities. But traditions die hard and neighbouring States had been accustomed for so long to take advantage of Germany's internal

[1] For the Zollverein's commercial policy in 1834–41 see A. Zimmermann, book iv, and treaties printed by C. A. C. H. von Kamptz, *Die Handels- und Schiffahrtsverträge des Zollvereins...* (1845). Negotiations with Holland may be studied in the documents printed by N. W. Posthumus, iv, pp. 1–490, and v, pp. 3–56, in Rudolf Häpke, "Die Wirtschaftspolitik der Niederlände, 1815 bis 1830" (in *V.S.W.*, xvii, pp. 152–5), E. Gothein, *Geschichtliche Entwicklung der Rheinschiffahrt im 19en Jahrhundert* (1903), chs. vii–ix, J. Kortmann, *Die Niederlande in den handelspolitischen Verhandlungen mit Preussen vom Wiener Kongress bis zum Schiffahrtsvertrag von 1837* (1929), P. J. Bouman, *Rotterdam en het Duitsche achterland, 1831–51* (1931), and an article in *V.S.W.* xxvi (1933), pp. 244–66, and Franz Haumer, *Die Handelspolitik der Niederlande, 1830–1930* (1936), pp. 26–32; with Britain in J. H. Clapham, "The Last Years of the Navigation Acts", in *E.H.R.* xxv (1910), see pp. 495–7, and *Cambridge History of British Foreign Policy*, ii, ch. xi, sect. i; and with the Hapsburg Empire in A. Beer, pp. 74–6.

divisions that some time elapsed before they adjusted their commercial policies to new conditions. In these circumstances Prussia's first negotiations on behalf of the Zollverein were not uniformly successful.

Commercial relations with the Dutch soon demanded the attention of Prussian statesmen. Holland was in a difficult position at this time. The recently signed Rhine Navigation Act had weakened the Dutch hold on shipping on that river. The establishment of an independent Belgium had caused a decline in Holland's political prestige and the Dutch were alarmed at the prospect of the development of the commerce of Antwerp[1] and the industries of Liége and other towns. The founding of the Zollverein, it was feared, would also lead to the expansion of new industrial regions. Particularly alarming was the progress that was being made in the Rhineland. Energetic leaders like Krupp, Harkort, Stinnes, Hansemann, Camphausen and Mevissen thoroughly appreciated the vast industrial and commercial potentialities of the district. They fully recognised the need for constructing railways and for developing steam navigation. They urged the Prussian Government to adopt a forward commercial policy so that the natural resources of the Rhineland could be exploited. The rise of two comparatively new industrial regions so near her borders was a danger to Holland in various respects. It was likely that Belgium and the Zollverein would gradually use more of their own manufactured articles instead of foreign goods and would import the products of tropical countries direct and not through Holland. The Dutch anticipations of a fall in their transit trade and a decline in their not inconsiderable profits as financiers and middle-men were well founded. In the 'thirties and 'forties, with the exception of trade in coffee from Java and Brazil, the Dutch middlemen were faced with ever-increasing competition in the Zollverein from German rivals.

[1] Holland was able to hamper 'Antwerp's trade to some extent by levying tolls at the mouth of the River Scheldt. Both sides of the river below Antwerp were in Dutch hands. See Map 4 above (p. 77).

In the circumstances it is not surprising to find von Maltzan reporting from The Hague in August, 1834, that the Dutch Finance Minister had spoken to him of the advantages which both Holland and Prussia would derive from a commercial treaty. He even mentioned the possibility of Holland joining the Zollverein.[1] Nothing came of this suggestion. Holland proceeded to injure the interests of the Zollverein in various ways. First, she continued to levy high duties on the importation of grain. The prohibitive duties of 1825 were, it is true, abolished but in 1835 new duties on corn were introduced on a sliding scale. The East Prussian farmers and exporters of grain were hard hit by this measure. Secondly, Dutch sugar refiners adopted the practice of sending partially refined sugar (*Lumpenzucker* and *Melis*) to Germany, declaring that it was unrefined. Thus they paid a low duty instead of a high one. This reduced the revenue of the Zollverein and injured the growing German sugar refining industry. Thirdly, under a law of 1821, Holland granted a 10 per cent drawback on goods entering Dutch ports in Dutch ships although Dutch vessels were allowed to enter Prussian ports on the same terms as national shipping. Fourthly, despite the Rhine Navigation Act of 1831, the Dutch still harassed German river shipping in various ways. Germans complained of the failure to dredge the Leck and the Waal, the lack of adequate warehouses in Dutch ports, and the unnecessary formalities and delays at Dutch customs houses. Finally, in July 1833, the Dutch levied a new import duty (two florins per 1000 lb.) upon coal that came to Holland in foreign ships. Prussia retaliated to these unfriendly acts by levying extra dues on Dutch ships entering Prussian ports in the Baltic and also—except for colliers—on the Rhine and by taxing partially refined sugar as if it were completely refined.

Negotiations were undertaken to remedy this unsatisfactory state of affairs. A navigation treaty between Prussia and Holland was signed on June 3, 1837. It was to last for three years

[1] Von Maltzan to von Ancillon, August 22, 1834 (in N. W. Posthumus, IV, pp. 17–19).

in the first instance. As far as *direct* voyages from one country
to the other were concerned, it was agreed to abolish discriminating harbour and import dues and to observe the principle of reciprocity in dealing with each other's vessels. This did
not apply to the Dutch colonial trade or to *indirect* voyages
from Prussian ports to Holland. Since Prussia did not penalise
the indirect voyages of Dutch ships in the same way, she received, as compensation, the right to participate in the Dutch
coasting trade. Concessions were also made regarding Rhine
shipping. Prussia agreed to treat Dutch ships using her ports
on the river in the same way as those belonging to a member of
the Zollverein. The Dutch abolished the *octroi* on goods coming
down the Rhine to be consumed or warehoused in Holland and
halved it on goods going up the river. Holland extended this
concession to other Zollverein States on the Rhine in 1839.
Purely transit traffic on the Rhine through Holland, however,
paid the *droit fixe* as usual. It was agreed to regulate steam
navigation so as to avoid undue competition.

Although Prussia had obtained some not unimportant concessions from the Dutch in 1837, to conclude a navigation treaty
without at the same time securing a commercial agreement was
probably a mistake from the Prussian point of view. By admit-
ting Dutch ships to her Rhine harbours without obtaining a
reduction of duties on the chief German exports to Holland,
Prussia weakened her position in subsequent negotiations. Yet
it was particularly desirable to secure favourable terms on this
occasion because, while the navigation treaty concerned only
Prussia and Holland, the commercial treaty was negotiated by
Prussia for the Zollverein as a whole. After long discussions
between Prussia and Holland and among the Zollverein States
themselves, a commercial treaty was signed on January 21, 1839.
Like the navigation treaty it was to last in the first instance for
only three years. The Zollverein halved its import duties on
Dutch partially refined sugar [1] on cattle and on dairy produce.

---

[1] Hamburg (December 12, 1839) and Bremen (July 4, 1840) secured a
similar reduction of duty on their exports of semi-refined sugar to the
Zollverein.

It reduced its duty on Dutch refined sugar to 10 thalers per hundredweight and on rice to 2 thalers per hundredweight. Holland reduced her duties on Zollverein wine, corn, timber and certain textiles. The Zollverein might trade with the Dutch colonies on most favoured nation terms.[1]

The Dutch had secured the best of the bargain. The export of Dutch refined sugar to Germany declined but the amount of unrefined sugar going up the Rhine from Amsterdam rose from under 30,000 kg. in 1838 to 12,790,000 kg. in 1841.[2] On the other hand, the tariff concessions made by Holland brought little benefit to Zollverein exporters. The Cologne Chamber had protested against a reduction in the duty on Dutch semi-refined sugar.[3] The disadvantageous results of the commercial treaty of 1839 aroused a storm of protest in the Zollverein. Refiners of cane sugar combined both with those who grew and those who refined beet sugar to denounce the benefit conferred upon their Dutch competitors. It was clear, writes Treitschke, "that the first diplomatic achievement of the new national commercial policy was both a bad blunder and a departure from the fundamental principles of the Zollverein, which normally rejected all differential duties but on this occasion granted dangerous privileges to an unfriendly neighbour".[4] The approaching expiry of the original Zollverein treaties caused Prussia to pay particular attention to the complaints of her allies. A commission of enquiry was set up and, as a result of its investigations, it was decided to denounce the

[1] This last concession was of very little value since by its discriminating duties the Dutch tariff discouraged trade between foreign countries and the Dutch colonies. See, for example, an article in the Augsburg *Allgemeine Zeitung*, August 18, 1842 (printed by N. W. Posthumus, v, pp. 91–105).

[2] P. J. Bouman (*V.S.W.*, xxvi, 1933), p. 254 n.

[3] Memorandum of the Cologne Chamber of Commerce, September 5, 1838 (N. W. Posthumus, IV, pp. 400–2). A. Zimmermann (p. 159) is wrong in supposing that no one in Germany had foreseen the negligible benefit that Zollverein exporters would obtain from the treaty.

[4] H. von Treitschke, IV, pp. 573–4.

treaty.[1] When the commercial treaty expired at the end of 1841, the duty on semi-refined sugar was raised to 10 thalers per hundredweight.

Treitschke considers that by securing the denunciation of this commercial treaty German "public opinion won its first well deserved victory" in influencing commercial policy.[2] It would be truer to say that a new German industry, artificially fostered by protective duties, had become powerful enough to impose its will upon the Zollverein as a whole. The interests of the consumers of sugar were sacrificed to those of the home producers.

Britain, like Holland, had good reason to be alarmed at the founding of the Zollverein. British manufacturers could not view with equanimity the prospect of the development of German industries under the protection of the Zollverein tariff. Britain had tried to prevent the expansion of the new customs union. Now that it had been established she studied the Zollverein with some interest. J. MacGregor, who was collecting commercial statistics in Europe in the 'thirties, visited Germany on several occasions and reported to the Board of Trade and to the Foreign Office on the economic position of the Zollverein.[3] Richard Cobden made "the tour of Germany" in 1838 and gave "some attention to the progress of manufactures in the countries through which he had passed".[4] In July, 1839, Dr John Bowring was instructed by the Foreign Office "to report on the progress, present state and future prospects of the Prussian

[1] The Prusso-Dutch navigation treaty of 1837, however, remained in force and the Dutch continued to grant the concessions regarding the *octroi* to *all* Zollverein States on the Rhine.

[2] H. von Treitschke, IV, p. 574.

[3] See, for example, MacGregor's letters from Leipzig (April 29, 1836), Chemnitz (May 2, 1836) and Mainz (May 8, 1836) in B.T. 1/322, and from Munich (July 9 and 14, 1836) in B.T. 1/324. Cf. his *Commercial Statistics* (1843), I, sect. vi, pp. 483–799.

[4] See Cobden's speech to Manchester Chamber of Commerce, December 13, 1838 (W. H. Dawson, *The Evolution of Modern Germany* (1911), pp. 76–7). Cf. Cobden to W. Neild, September 30, 1838, printed by E. Hughes in the *Bulletin* of Rylands Library (October, 1938), pp. 409–14.

Commercial League". The result of these investigations was his *Report on the Prussian Commercial Union* (1840) which is still a valuable source of information on the Zollverein at that time.[1]

English policy was directed on the one hand to keeping the North German coastal States out of the Prussian customs system and, on the other, to trying to induce the Zollverein to lower some of its import duties on manufactured articles and colonial produce. Prussia, for her part, wanted England to reduce her duties on corn and timber and to modify her Navigation Laws. In January and in March, 1836, England proposed that the Zollverein should lower its duties on her woollen and cotton goods in return for a reduction of English import duties on German timber. Nothing came of this suggestion. In July of the same year MacGregor was at Munich—at the time of the first Zollverein congress—but he was unable to secure any reduction in Zollverein duties. Kühne told him that "if any arrangement be entered into, you must begin at Berlin, and a reduction of your corn duties to a fixed rate must be preliminary to any understanding as to a reduction on our part of duties on your commodities".[2]

MacGregor went to Vienna and discussed with Metternich the question of renewing the Anglo-Austrian reciprocity treaty of 1829 which would soon expire.[3] Metternich was not unwilling to extend the scope of the treaty somewhat, for he was beginning to feel that new commercial agreements to foster trade might strengthen the Hapsburg Empire in relation to the Zollverein.

[1] Dr Bowring's letters to the Foreign Office are in F.O. 97/326. His report is printed in P.P. 1840, XXI. Bowring subsequently went to some of the chief English cities to lecture on the Zollverein. For his visit to Manchester, see M.Ch.C., November 14, 1839 (Special General Meeting relative to the Prussian Commercial Union); to Hull, see the third Annual Report of the Hull Chamber of Commerce (1840), p. 11.

[2] J. MacGregor to C. P. Thomson, President of the Board of Trade, July 14, 1836 (B.T. 1/324).

[3] MacGregor's letters to the Foreign Office from Vienna are in F.O. 7/262–7/277.

A commercial and navigation treaty was signed by Austria and England on July 3, 1838. Austria promised to replace some prohibitions on English manufactured articles by import duties. England—with an eye to possible future developments in river steamship traffic in Central Europe[1]—agreed to give most favoured nation treatment to Austrian exports by certain non-Austrian routes ("through the northern outlet of the Elbe and the eastern outlet of the Danube"). Further, Austrian ships were allowed to bring "enumerated articles", such as timber and corn, from Turkish ports on the Danube to England to be consumed there.[2] This infringed the English navigation code and a special Act of Parliament was passed in 1840 to put the matter right.

Prussia at once demanded similar concessions regarding "natural outlets" to those granted to Austria. England wanted to secure the same reductions of duties on the importation of rice and sugar into Zollverein territory as had been given to Holland in 1839. Prolonged negotiations eventually led to the conclusion of the Anglo-Zollverein convention of March 2, 1841.[3] It was to last in the first instance until January 1, 1842 (when the commercial treaty between the Zollverein and Holland expired) but, unless denounced six months before that

[1] It has been observed that "the formation of the Austrian Danube Steam Navigation Company in 1830 captured the imagination of many enthusiasts who hoped that the Danube, so little known and so rarely used as a long-distance route, would justify in the future Napoleon's designation of it as the 'King of Rivers'" (G. East, *An Historical Geography of Europe* (1935), p. 386). For a description of a voyage by steamship from Budapest to Rustchuk in 1834, see M. J. Quin, *A Steam Voyage down the Danube* (2 vols. 1835), I, chs. i–xi.

[2] By Article 4 "all Austrian vessels arriving from the ports of the Danube, as far as Galacz inclusive, shall, together with their cargoes, be admitted into British ports exactly in the same manner as if such vessels came direct from Austrian ports". The Anglo-Austrian treaty of 1838 is printed in P.P. 1839, L.

[3] The Anglo-Zollverein commercial and navigation convention of 1841 is printed in P.P. 1841, XXXI, p. 197, von Kamptz, pp. 124–32, and F. A. de Mensch, *Manuel pratique du Consulat...* (1846), pp. 218–21.

date, it would remain in force for another six years. British vessels and their cargoes, wherever they came from, might enter Zollverein ports on the same terms as Zollverein ships. British subjects might send sugar and rice to the Zollverein on most favoured nation terms. England accepted the principle that the Zollverein had "natural outlets" beyond her own frontiers. Zollverein ships coming to England from ports between the Elbe and the Meuse were to be treated as if they came from a Zollverein port. This was a reasonably generous interpretation of the Zollverein's "natural outlets". It did not, however, include either, the Russian ports on the Baltic (from which Prussian ships wished to carry timber direct to England) or Antwerp.[1]

The Anglo-Zollverein convention of 1841, like the Dutch commercial treaty of 1839, was severely criticised in Germany. But while the attacks on the Dutch treaty came mainly from the North German sugar "interest", those against the English convention came mostly from the South German protectionists and were made on more general grounds. It was held that the small Prussian mercantile marine would derive little immediate benefit from the "natural outlets" clause and that this was no adequate compensation for concessions regarding the importation of English rice and sugar. It was pointed out that no reduction in the English corn and timber duties had been obtained. List complained that Prussia had "deprived herself for eight years of the possibility of making those concessions to the Hanse Towns which alone could secure their adhesion to the Zollverein".[2] The agitation against the English convention did not

---

[1] Other German States claimed similar privileges. In 1844–5 Hanover, Oldenburg, the Hanse towns and the Mecklenburgs were granted as "natural outlets" all ports between the Elbe and the Meuse and between the Trave and the Niemen. At first the Mecklenburgs secured (in the Baltic) only the ports from the Trave to the Oder but this was later extended. Mecklenburg-Strelitz, it may be noted, had no sea-coast. See, for example, F.O. 33/101, nos. 2 and 3, Lord Aberdeen to Colonel Hodges, October 23, 1845.

[2] F. List, *Über den Wert und die Bedingungen einer Allianz zwischen Grossbritannien und Deutschland*, 1846 (edition of 1920), p. 40. The

have the same immediate success as that against the Dutch treaty. But Prussian statesmen watched closely the rising free-trade agitation in England in the 'forties and were quick to take advantage of any change in British commercial policy.

Discussions between Prussia and Austria in the early years of the Zollverein did not lead to any commercial agreement. In June, 1833, Metternich had still hoped that Article 19 of the Federal Act might be carried out. He soon recognised, however, that the Zollverein had come to stay. Metternich saw the desirability of reducing smuggling on the Zollverein frontier and it was suggested to Prussia that a convention might be signed for this purpose. Prussia, on the whole, favoured such an agreement if she could obtain a relaxation of Austria's restrictions on local frontier traffic and some reduction in Austria's duties on imports from Silesia. The linen industry of this province was particularly hard hit by the prohibitive tariffs of Austria and Russia. Kühne went to Vienna in 1836 to sound Austrian statesmen on these suggestions. In 1837 and 1838 the questions were discussed but no agreement was reached.[1] An effort was also made to facilitate trade between the Polish districts of Prussia and Austria and in 1839 Prussia agreed to reduce her transit dues on Galician corn. Meantime, as has been noticed, Metternich was trying to encourage trade with England by the Anglo-Austrian treaty of 1838. But the concessions that were made in the new Austrian tariff of March 1, 1839, were a disappointment to optimists who had hoped that it would herald a more liberal era of Austria's commercial policy. "The changes were unimportant", is Beer's terse comment.[2]

Prussian Government replied to criticisms of the Anglo-Zollverein Convention in articles in the *Allgemeine Preussische Staatszeitung*, June 16 and 18, 1841, which were subsequently reprinted as *Die Handels- und Schiffahrts-Convention zwischen dem Zollverein und England vom 2. März 1841.*

[1] The Prussian point of view may be seen in a note from von Jordan to von Trauttmannsdorff, the Austrian Ambassador in Berlin (May 2, 1837), printed by A. Zimmermann, pp. 471–9.

[2] A. Beer, p. 15.

When the Zollverein treaties were renewed at the end of 1841 Metternich gave expression once more to his old anxiety at the growing power of Prussia in German economic affairs. He wrote to Kübeck on October 20, 1841, that the import duties of the Zollverein bore heavily on growing Austrian industries. Bohemia was particularly hard hit. Despite the failure of negotiations in the 'thirties, Metternich hoped that it would be possible to conclude an Austro-Zollverein commercial treaty which would enable Austria to exercise more influence in German economic affairs. He considered that the development of railways in Germany had given the Hapsburg Empire a new opportunity. She could co-operate with South German States in building new lines from the upper Danube to the plain of Lombardy and to the Adriatic. This would be the first step towards identifying Austrian economic interests to some extent with those of the Zollverein.[1] In December, 1841, it was decided to pursue this policy and to construct, at the expense of the State, lines from Vienna to Munich, Dresden, Triest and Milan.[2]

Few results of importance came from other negotiations undertaken by Prussia at this time. It was found impossible to secure concessions of any value from Russia or France which adhered firmly to their prohibitions and high duties or from Denmark whose Sound dues hampered Baltic commerce. Discussions with the United States of America, too, were unsuccessful. Henry Wheaton, who arrived in Berlin in 1835, wanted the Zollverein to reduce its import duties on American rice and tobacco but was unable to offer adequate concessions in return.[3] Prussia, however, was able to sign a navigation and com-

---

[1] Metternich's note is printed in *Aus Metternich's nachgelassenen Papieren*, VI (1883), pp. 531–9.

[2] Heinrich Ritter von Srbik, *Metternich*, II (1925), p. 106.

[3] See *Verhandlungen der General-Konferenzen in Zollvereinsangelegenheiten*, II (1838), Beilage xvii; V (1842), sect. xiv, and G. M. Fisk, *Die handelspolitischen...Beziehungen zwischen Deutschland und den Vereinigten Staaten von Amerika* (1897), pp. 81–91.

mercial treaty with Greece in 1839 to which other members of
the Zollverein could adhere if they wished. In October, 1840,
a commercial convention was signed with the Porte which gave
subjects of States belonging to the Zollverein substantially the
same rights as those enjoyed by Englishmen and Frenchmen.[1]

(3) INTERNAL DEVELOPMENTS, 1834–1841[2]

The benefits derived from establishing the Zollverein were felt
sooner in South Germany than in the North. Prussia obtained
only a comparatively small extension of markets and this was
offset by a decline in customs receipts. Bavaria and Württemberg, however, could now send their products to the populous
districts of North Germany. So there was an expansion of
Southern industries. Cotton imports, for example, rose from
121,000 cwt. in 1834 to nearly 243,000 cwt. in 1842. As early as
1836 the Manchester Chamber of Commerce expressed its
serious concern at the progress of the German cotton industry.[3]
Some protection against foreign competition was afforded by
the Zollverein tariff. Certain duties had been raised a little
since 1818 and as they were *specific* the recent fall in prices led
to a rise in duties when compared with the *value* of goods.
Further, in 1840 the Zollverein hundredweight (50 kg.) was
used instead of the slightly heavier Prussian hundredweight in
weighing dutiable goods and this raised the tariff somewhat.[4]
Nevertheless Bavaria and Württemberg, which only a few years

[1] The conventions with Greece and Turkey are printed by von
Kamptz, pp. 26–99, 138–61: the convention with Turkey is also printed
by F. A. de Mensch, pp. 212–18.

[2] See W. Weber, chs. xv–xviii, and H. von. Treitschke, IV, pp. 569–98.
For the Zollverein General Congresses, see the *Verhandlungen der
General-Konferenzen in Zollvereinsangelegenheiten* (15 vols. 1836–63)—
cited as *Verhandlungen*. These proceedings are a valuable source of
information on the history of the Zollverein.

[3] Manchester Chamber of Commerce to the Board of Trade, June 15,
1836 (B.T. 1/323), and M.Ch.C., June 1, 1836, and February 13, 1837.

[4] Bowring to Palmerston, August 28, 1839 (F.O. 97/326).

before had criticised the Prussian tariff as being too high, now complained that it was too low.[1]

The first General Congress of the Zollverein met early in June, 1836, and lasted until the middle of September. It secured agreement on various reforms to ensure greater uniformity in customs administration throughout the Zollverein.

Two meetings were held in Dresden in 1838—a monetary convention[2] and the second Zollverein General Congress. At this time each German State issued its own money and there were in circulation many different kinds of coins and notes. Silver was the standard money (except in Bremen where there was a gold thaler) and there was a bewildering variety of silver coins. To compare their value it was necessary to know the so-called "foot measure"—that is to say, the number of pieces coined from a Cologne mark of fine silver which weighed 233·856 grammes. In North Germany (Prussia, Hanover and other States) the "foot measure" was 14 (thalers), in the Hapsburg dominions 20 (florins),[3] in the South German States 24 (florins) and in Hamburg and Lübeck 34 (marks). Even where the same "foot measure" was used, the silver coin was divided in different ways. Thus the Prussian thaler was divided into 30 groschens and 300 pfennigs, but the Hanoverian thaler was

[1] Palmerston wrote in 1846: "When first the Zollverein was established those two Kingdoms had few manufactures and they were advocates for low duties being interested therein as consumers....Now Bavaria and Württemberg are advocates for higher protecting duties; by means of which a few manufacturers in those Kingdoms are enabled to make the consumers of Germany pay more than they ought to pay for articles which they want" (from a memorandum printed by A. Zimmermann, p. 552).

[2] For German monetary conditions, see A. Lips, *Der deutsche Zollverein und das deutsche Mass- Gewicht- und Münz-Chaos...* (1837), and J. F. Hauschild, *Geschichte des deutschen Mass-᾽ und Münzwesens in den letzten sechzig Jahren* (1861). For early negotiations on monetary unification see *Verhandlungen*, I (1836), Besonderes Protokoll v vom 6. September das Münzwesen betreffend, nebst Beilagen A und B.

[3] This was the "Convention Foot Measure" as established by a convention of 1753.

divided into 24 groschens and 288 pfennigs. There were also many gold coins in circulation—friedrichs d'ors, louis d'ors, pistoles, ducats and so forth—which varied in value with the price of silver. Prussia, however, fixed the silver-gold ratio at $15\frac{9}{13}$ to 1 in 1832.

When the Zollverein was founded it was agreed to negotiate for the unification of monetary systems. Duties might be paid either in Prussian thalers or in florins at the rate of 7 florins to 4 thalers. There were, however, no florins in existence of exactly that value, so the South German 24 "foot measure" was adopted in practice although there was a difference of 2 per cent between the nominal and actual values of the florins. To get out of this difficulty a new South German valuation (*Süddeutsche Währung*) was established in August, 1837, at the rate of $24\frac{1}{2}$ florins to the Cologne mark of fine silver. In 1838 the ratio of 4 to 7 was established between the Prussian thaler and the new South German florin. Fourteen thalers or $24\frac{1}{2}$ florins were to be coined from a Cologne mark. Thus, a ratio which had been originally introduced to facilitate the calculation of customs duties was now used to secure a fixed relationship between the more important coins actually in circulation in Germany. It was also agreed that, in addition to their own coins, the Zollverein States should issue a double thaler worth 2 Prussian thalers or $3\frac{1}{2}$ South German florins. This was popularly known as the "champagne thaler". These arrangements lasted until 1857. Particularist prejudice stood in the way of the acceptance of Saxony's sensible proposal that the Zollverein should adopt a uniform monetary system based on a unit worth one-third of a Prussian thaler. Not until thirty-three years later was such a coin (the mark) introduced throughout Germany.

At the second Zollverein Congress (1838) the difficult question of settling the accounts of the customs union for the year 1834 was discussed. On entering the Zollverein Saxony and the Thuringian States had levied retrospective duties on goods already imported but Bavaria and Württemberg had not. It was decided that the two southern States should together contribute

175,000 thalers to the Zollverein exchequer in lieu of such duties. Saxony paid the Zollverein 100,000 thalers and the Thuringian States 78,800 thalers out of the receipts of retrospective duties.[1] Prussia suggested the imposition of an excise on beet-sugar. She pointed out that the considerable revenue which was derived from import duties on raw colonial cane-sugar would be endangered if great progress were made in the production of beet-sugar at home. No decision was reached on this question either in 1838 or in 1839.[2]

The third Zollverein Congress met between July and September, 1839, and was shortly followed by the fourth between October, 1839, and May, 1840. Both were held in Berlin. At the third congress a new tariff was drawn up, while at the fourth various administrative problems were settled. The main discussions, however, were behind the scenes, since the question of renewing the Zollverein treaties would soon have to be considered. The presence of Bowring[3] and Engelhardt in Berlin at this time showed that England and France fully appreciated the significance of the meetings there.

On the eve of the renewal of the Zollverein treaties it was to be expected that the financial results of the last few years should be carefully studied. Most of the middle and small States had every reason to be satisfied. Bavaria, for example, had drawn a little over 2,100,000 florins from the revenues of the Bavaria-Württemberg customs union in the financial year 1831–32, but obtained nearly 3,860,000 florins as her share of the receipts of the Zollverein in the first year of its existence (1834). Prussia's receipts, on the other hand, declined at first. In 1833 they had

---

[1] *Verhändlungen*, II (1838), Besonderes Protokoll, xiii. Bavaria paid 126,437 thalers, 15 silver groschens; Württemberg 48,562 thalers, 15 silver groschens.

[2] *Verhändlungen*, II (1838), Hauptprotokoll, sects. xxv, xxvi, xxvii, and Beilagen iii, iv and xxi; III (1839), Hauptprotokoll, sect. xv, and Besonderes Protokoll in Betreff der Besteuerung der Runkelrübenzucker-Fabrikation.

[3] See Bowring's letters to Palmerston from Berlin, August 7, 13, 28, and September 17, 1839, in F.O. 97/326.

amounted to 20 silver groschens per head of population. In the following year they sank to 15½ silver groschens and only in 1838 was the old level reached again. At each distribution of the Zollverein revenues Prussia made substantial payments to nearly all her fellow-members. Saxony was the most important exception. There was considerable criticism in Prussia at these financial losses for which, it was held, no adequate compensation had been obtained. Complaints were made of the low consumption of colonial goods in the southern States, of the privileges of the Leipzig fair and of the continuance of smuggling across the Erzgebirge. Prussia's hopes of securing a new influence in the Federal Diet as a result of her predominance in the Zollverein had been disappointed.

Prussia hoped to secure some financial concessions by the new Zollverein treaties which would come into force in 1842. In a memorandum of December 22, 1839, her Government observed that "it had received no declaration from any members of the Zollverein which left any doubts as to their genuine desire to preserve the customs union....Although Prussia fully recognises that its subjects have shared in the general advantageous results of the customs union, yet the position is quite different when viewed from the financial standpoint.... Prussia, in considering her position at the beginning of a new period of the Zollverein, has good reasons for having considerable misgivings if it is to hold no other prospect save that of new financial sacrifices in the future while all other members of the union can look forward to a permanent increase of customs revenue."[1]

In this memorandum and in a memorandum of August 16, 1840, Prussia explained what reforms of the Zollverein she considered desirable. The most important concerned the difficult question of dealing with those products which paid a consumption tax in certain States but not in others. In 1834 it had been agreed that goods passing from a State where they were not subject to such a tax to a State where they were, should pay "compensatory duties" (*Ausgleichsabgaben*). Thus, Prussia and

[1] Quoted by W. Weber, p. 185.

States which adopted her system of internal taxation levied taxes on wine, beer, brandy and tobacco produced at home (whether consumed at home or not) and compensatory duties on these products imported from other Zollverein States. The system was a complicated one, since the amount of duty levied varied according to the rate of taxation in the States from which they came. After much discussion the compensatory duties were replaced by fixed "transition duties" (*Übergangsabgaben*). Another change proposed by Prussia and eventually accepted by other members of the Zollverein was the levying of an excise on beet-sugar—originally on a temporary basis. The new treaties were signed on May 8, 1841, and the Zollverein was renewed for twelve years.

The customs union had thus survived the period of trial. However dissatisfied some Germans might be at the small measure of success achieved by Prussia in commercial negotiations with foreign countries, the financial results of the years 1834–41 alone were sufficiently satisfactory for there to be no question of any of the middle or smaller States leaving the union. Indeed, they were prepared to make a few concessions to Prussia to ensure the renewal of the Zollverein treaties, and it is significant that it was Bavaria who insisted that the new treaties should run for twelve years while Prussia favoured six years.

When the second period of the Zollverein began, Germany was still predominantly an agricultural country exporting raw materials and grain in return for manufactured and colonial goods. It has been seen that twenty years of peace followed by the achievement of a considerable measure of economic unity had not been without results on the industrial development of the South and of the Rhineland. There were, however, still many factors which hindered progress. Germany lacked capital. The rate of interest was $4\frac{1}{2}$ or 5 per cent at a time when $2\frac{1}{2}$ or 3 per cent was being charged in England. Further, despite the road-building of the 'twenties and 'thirties, communications were still inadequate. "It was the railways which first shook the nation out of its economic stagnation, completing what the Zollverein had surely begun. So vigorously did they influence all habits of life that by the 'forties Germany had already assumed a completely different aspect."[1]

The success of the railways between Stockton and Darlington (1825) and between Manchester and Liverpool (1830) had led to the building of new lines in England and in North America.

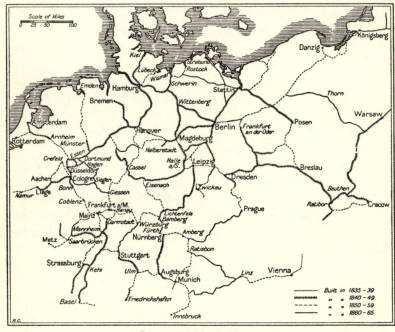

7. German Railways, 1835–65.

Based on the map in P. Benaerts, *Les Origines de l'Industrie Allemande*, p. 318.

On the Continent Belgium led the way. As soon as she secured her independence she determined to make full use of her geographical position which attracted trade to Central Europe. Undeterred by the criticism that "to construct a great railway

---

[1] H. von Treitschke, IV, p. 581. For German railways, see D. Lardner, *Railway Economy* (1850), ch. xix, A. von Mayer, *Geschichte und Geographie der deutschen Eisenbahnen* (2 vols. 1891), and P. Benaerts, ch. viii.

at the expense of the taxpayer would be as useless and ruinous an enterprise as to build a pyramid",[1] the Belgian State decided in 1834 to construct a national railway system and in 1836 the Brussels-Antwerp line was opened. Holland, which had also an advantageous geographical position and competed with Belgium for transit trade, lagged behind.

In Germany the more far-seeing officials and industrialists soon grasped the possibilities of railway development in that country. Motz, for example, discussed with Ompteda in June, 1828, the project of a railway from Wesel on the Rhine to Rheine on the Ems which would take some of the traffic that then paid heavy tolls to go through Holland by river to the Rhineland. The same desire to avoid the Rhine tolls lay behind the suggestion of the Westphalian *Landtag* in 1831 that a line should be built from Lippstadt to Minden. Harkort, a leading Westphalian industrialist, agitated in favour of a railway from Cologne to Minden. Commercial considerations were uppermost in his mind but he referred to the strategic advantages of such a line. "A hundred and fifty [railway] carriages could take a brigade from Minden to the Rhine in a day. A telegraph line from Mainz to Wesel would make it impossible for the French to cross the Rhine."[2] In Bavaria King Ludwig watched railway developments abroad with great interest. He considered various plans for building railways to link Bavaria with North Germany and with Austria. Fieldmarshal Wrede suggested to him the construction of a Bavarian network of strategic lines radiating from the fortress of Ingolstadt. But Ludwig's enthusiasm was a passing phase. He was more interested in his project for a canal from the Rhine to the Danube.

List, too, was putting forward in pamphlets and articles suggestions for a German railway system. His best known publica-

---

[1] This remark by T. Cordier, a French engineer, is quoted by E. Mahaim, "La politique commerciale de la Belgique", in *Schriften des Vereins für Sozialpolitik*, XLIX (1892), p. 199 n.

[2] Harkort's memorandum to the Westphalian *Landtag*, November 1833, quoted by P. Benaerts, p. 299 n.

tion on this subject was a pamphlet of 1833 on a proposed Saxon railway system which was to form a nucleus for a network of lines for the whole of Germany.[1] List foresaw the decisive part that railways would play "in the development of national productive forces".[2] He showed remarkable prescience in his views on the routes that should be followed by the German trunk lines.

These pioneers had to face much criticism. The Bavarian. College of Physicians is said to have prophesied all sorts of unpleasant effects both for passengers on trains and for spectators.[3] In Prussia the Director-General of Posts complained that the construction of railways would ruin his service of post coaches. Others said that railways would never pay in Germany and that the chief result of their construction would be a loss of revenue from road tolls.

The first German railway was opened in Bavaria in December, 1835—less than a year after the Zollverein treaties came into force. It was a line from Nürnberg to Fürth and was only about four miles long.[4] In 1838 the Berlin-Potsdam railway was completed and was soon so busy that a night service was introduced. Both were built and run by private companies. The line between Brunswick and Wolfenbüttel (1838) was the first State railway in Germany. These three railways were short suburban lines. In 1839 a longer and more important railway was completed. This was the 70-mile line from Dresden to Leipzig. The advantages of rapid communication between the capital and the

---

[1] F. List, *Über ein sächsisches Eisenbahn-System als Grundlage eines allgemeinen deutschen Eisenbahn-Systems*... (1833). List edited a short-lived periodical, *Das Eisenbahnjournal*, which was founded in 1835.

[2] G. Bousquet, "List et les Chemins de Fer", in *Revue d'Histoire Économique et Sociale*, XXI (1933), p. 270.

[3] But F. Schnabel states that no memorandum to this effect has been found in the archives of the Bavarian College of Physicians (*Deutsche Geschichte im neunzehnten Jahrhundert*, III (1934), p. 435), So this oft-repeated story may not be true.

[4] Earlier "railways", such as that from Steele to Kupferdreh and Langenberg in the Ruhr, used horse-traction.

chief commercial city of the Kingdom of Saxony were obvious. In 1840 four lines were completed—Leipzig to Magdeburg, Munich to Augsburg, Frankfurt-am-Main to Mainz, and Mannheim to Heidelberg. This was followed in the next year by the opening of railways from Berlin to Anhalt, from Düsseldorf to Elberfeld, and from Cologne to Aachen. The last line was part of a new route through Belgium to Antwerp which would enable Rhineland industrialists to avoid Dutch tolls on the Rhine. It was completed in October, 1843.[1] By the end of 1846 there were over 2000 miles of line open in Germany and 725 in Austria. "The German railway system", wrote Bourgoing to Guizot in September, 1847, "is being daily extended and completed with an ever increasing activity which enables one to forecast that this country will be far ahead of other continental States in this respect."[2]

The building of railways in Germany had many important results. "The German Empire", declared Wilhelm Raabe enthusiastically, "was founded with the construction of the first railway between Nürnberg and Fürth."[3] Railway shares were indeed "bills drawn upon Germany's future unity".[4] The new lines undoubtedly helped to weaken local prejudices by bringing Germans into closer contact with one another. Goethe's prophecy in October, 1828, that Germany's "good roads and future railways" would do their share in promoting unity was justified by events.[5]

Economic progress, too, was fostered by the railways. Industrial regions like upper Silesia, which had remained undeveloped owing to lack of adequate communications with distant markets, benefited from the reduction in transport costs

---

[1] See, for example, L. Camphausen, *Zur Eisenbahn von Köln nach Antwerpen* (1835), and A. Bergengrün, *David Hansemann* (1901), ch. iv.

[2] Quoted by P. Benaerts, p. 305.

[3] Quoted by L. Pohle, *Das deutsche Wirtschaftsleben seit Beginn des neunzehnten Jahrhunderts* (6th edition, 1930), p. 11.

[4] Karl Beck, quoted by H. von Treitschke, IV, p. 597.

[5] J. P. Eckermann, *Gespräche mit Goethe*, III (edition of 1884), p. 191.

for heavy materials. The construction of rails and sleepers, the building of engines and carriages, the provision of coal, gave some industrialists new markets for their products—though here, as elsewhere, keen foreign competition had to be faced.

At the same time as railways were being built the traffic of steamships on the great German rivers was increasing. As early as 1816 a steamship had made its way from Rotterdam to Cologne.[1] By 1830 twelve steamers were plying on the Rhine. Towards the end of the 'thirties steamers appeared on the Danube. At first the main work of river steamers was to carry passengers but later the transportation of goods became more and more important. In 1841 a company provided a service of tugs to draw barges on the Rhine.[2]

The advantages derived from the establishment of the Zollverein and from the improvement of communications were considerable but there was another side of the picture. As early as 1828 Lieutenant-General von Horn commented upon the poor physique of army recruits from the industrial districts of the Rhineland. In the 'forties the poverty-stricken linen-weavers of Silesia and the struggling peasants of parts of South-west Germany were faced with hard times. Riots broke out in 1844 among the upper Silesian weavers, who attempted to destroy textile machinery. Factory conditions in Germany were worse than those in Britain. Macaulay, in a speech on the Ten Hours

[1] E. Baasch, *Holländische Wirtschaftsgeschichte* (1927), p. 429 n.

[2] The increase of goods traffic on the Rhine in the early years of the Zollverein may be seen from the following table (A. Sartorius von Waltershausen, p. 109):

Goods passing the customs houses on the Rhine (tons, omitting 000)

		1836		1840	
		Up	Down	Up	Down
Emmerich	(Dutch frontier)	87·8	241·5	128·0	253·8
Coblenz	(Prussia)	81·4	72·9	163·2	128·3
Kaub	(Hesse-Cassel)	76·3	69·0	160·8	113·9
Mainz	(Hesse-Darmstadt)	70·4	54·0	135·5	79·9
Mannheim	(Baden)	42·4	61·8	43·0	48·7

Bill in 1846, scoffed at the notion that Britain was in any danger of serious competition from "a race of degenerate dwarfs".[1] In the 'forties, writes Treitschke, "complaints were already rife concerning starvation wages, child labour, the maltreatment and exploitation of workpeople".[2] Emigration was increasing. It was estimated that about 100,000 emigrants left Germany in 1847—a year of exceptional depression of trade.[3] This suggested that, despite all economic progress, Germany was unable to maintain her growing population at the standard of living to which it was accustomed.[4]

[1] J. Kuczynski, *Labour Conditions in Western Europe* (1937), p. 84.

[2] H. von Treitschke, v, p. 510.

[3] W. Mönckmeier, *Die deutsche überseeische Auswanderung* (1912), pp. 16–17. This estimate is quoted from Hübner's *Jahrbuch für Volkswirtschaft und Statistik* (Jahrgang 1852–61). Mönckmeier's own estimate for German emigration in 1847 is 78,800.

[4] Kuczynski's cost of living index for Germany (base year 1900, 100) is as follows: 1820, 49; 1825, 35; 1830, 50; 1835, 46; 1840, 53. His index for gross real wages in industry, transport and agriculture (base year 1900, 100) is: 1830–39, 78; 1840–49, 71 (pp. 94–5).

Chapter V

THE ZOLLVEREIN IN THE 'FORTIES, 1842–1847[1]

(1) NEGOTIATIONS WITH LUXEMBURG AND THE TAX UNION, 1842–1847[2]

Shortly after the new Zollverein treaties came into force Luxemburg joined the Prussian customs system. Luxemburg, whose Grand Duke was King of the Netherlands, was a member of the Germanic Confederation and had a Federal fortress in its capital. Treitschke considered the Luxemburgers to be "a

---

[1] See G. Höfken, *Der deutsche Zollverein in seiner Fortbildung* (1842); T. C. Banfield, *Industry of the Rhine* (2 vols. I, 1846, II, 1848); C. F. Wurm and F. T. Müller, pp. 182–298; W. Weber, chs. xix–xxii; A. Zimmermann, book iv; R. von Delbrück, *Lebenserinnerungen* (2 vols. in I, 1905); H. von Festenberg-Packisch, ch. viii; H. von Treitschke, v, pp. 433–93; and A. Sartorius von Waltershausen, pp. 77–94.

[2] The Prussian view of the negotiations with Luxemburg is given by H. von Treitschke, v, pp. 436–41, the Luxemburg view by A. Calmes, *Der Zollanschluss des Grossherzogtums Luxemburg an Deutschland* (2 vols. 1919). Cf. A. Widung, *Anschluss des Grossherzogtums Luxemburg an das Zollsystem Preussens und der übrigen Staaten des Zollvereins* (1912). The points at issue in the Zollverein-Tax Union negotiations are stated in publications (which include documents) issued by the Governments concerned: *Der grosse Zollverein deutscher Staaten und der Hannover-Oldenburgsche Steuerverein am 1. Januar 1844* (Hanover, 1844), *Bemerkungen auf Veranlassung der Königlich Hannoverischen Staatsschrift...* (Berlin, 1844), *Der Anschluss Braunschweigs an den Zollverein...* (Brunswick, 1844). For Hanover's point of view, see also G. Zimmermann, *Bruchstücke aus dem Thema vom Anschluss Hannovers an den Zollverein* (1843), and *Politische Predigten, gehalten im Jahre 1843 auf verschiedenen Dächern der Hauptstadt* (1843) (written under pen name "Dr Faber"). For Brunswick's attitude, see *Die Verhandlungen zwischen Hannover, Braunschweig und dem Zollverein über Hannovers Anschluss* (1844: reprinted from the *Kölnische Zeitung*).

mongrel people without a Fatherland and consequently without honour".[1] They were of German stock and spoke a German dialect. But French and Walloon influences were strong. The upper classes were generally educated in France. The laws, administration, monetary system and official language were French.

A few years after Belgium became independent, Luxemburg was partitioned. The larger portion became a Belgian province, the smaller (which included the capital) retained its independence, its membership of the Germanic Confederation, its Federal fortress and its personal union with Holland. It had an area of 1000 square miles and a population of 175,000. It was mainly an agricultural region. The chief industry was the production of iron. Eleven furnaces were at work in 1842.

Luxemburg was now cut off from Holland. If she were to retain her economic independence, she would have to pursue a policy of free-trade since she was too small to adopt protection and aim at self-sufficiency. But Luxemburg needed a revenue from import duties to strengthen her finances. She had therefore to decide which of her three neighbours she should try to join—Belgium, France or Prussia. On economic grounds many of her farmers favoured union with Belgium, for this would prevent the setting up of a customs frontier between the Grand Duchy and the part ceded to Belgium. The industrialists, on the other hand, thought that adhesion to the Zollverein would bring them a large protected market for their products. The Grand Duke had no love for the Belgians who had just succeeded in breaking up his Kingdom of the Netherlands as established in 1815. Union with France appeared to be impossible since other Powers would object to the extension of French influence in a country containing a fortress of the Germanic Confederation. It was on military grounds that some Prussian statesmen favoured the adhesion of Luxemburg to the Zollverein. From the economic and financial point of view Prussia would gain little if Luxemburg joined her customs

[1] H. von Treitschke, v, p. 441.

system. The tanners of the Prussian frontier towns of Malmedy and St Veit complained that they would be ruined by their Luxemburg rivals. The Prussian Finance Ministry opposed union at first since it would probably involve fresh financial sacrifices and the guarding of a new and difficult customs frontier. It was seen, however, that it was better to secure the adhesion of Luxemburg than to allow her to become a nest of smugglers on the Prussian frontier.

Negotiations between Prussia and Luxemburg took place between October, 1839 and July, 1840. Partly owing to the accession of William II of Holland there was a break in the discussions for about a year. A treaty was signed on August 8, 1841. Luxemburg accepted the Prussian tariff and system of internal taxation. She was to receive a share of the Zollverein revenues in proportion to her population and was to be represented at Zollverein Congresses by Prussia. Prussian officials were to supervise her customs administration. But William II would not ratify the treaty. He also declined to ratify an agreement for the inclusion of Luxemburg in the Prussian postal system. Perhaps he feared that the customs treaty would lead to a reduction of the concessions made in the Belgian Law of July 6, 1839, to facilitate trade between the two parts of Luxemburg. Possibly he still hoped to recover all Luxemburg and felt that his hands would be tied by the treaty with Prussia. But he made no satisfactory defence publicly of his action. Palmerston observed that the treaty had been "concluded by the Dutch plenipotentiary in strict conformity with the instructions of his sovereign; nor is there any valid reason assigned by the King himself for his reluctance to ratify the agreement".[1] Discussions were resumed. Prussia refused to make new concessions of any importance and at last the Dutch negotiators gave way and on February 8, 1842, signed a treaty which was shortly afterwards ratified by both parties. The terms were substantially the same as those of the earlier treaty but Prussia agreed that the number

[1] Palmerston to Sir Edward Cromwell Disbrowe, December 24, 1841 (F.O. 37/227; printed by N. W. Posthumus, v, p. 76).

of Prussian customs officials in Luxemburg should be reduced somewhat.

The treaty benefited both parties. Prussia gained a certain influence over a State containing an important Federal fortress and her iron manufactures obtained a useful supply of ore. Luxemburg gained financially and found new markets for her iron ore, hides and agricultural produce. She was so satisfied with her position that although she did not become a member of either the North German Confederation (1867) or the German Empire (1871) she remained within the German customs system until 1919.

Prussia's negotiations with Hanover between 1842 and 1845 were, to a large extent, unsuccessful. They did not lead to the adhesion of the Tax Union to the Zollverein but merely to the incorporation of the Harz and Weser districts of Brunswick and to a new agreement to stop smuggling. At the beginning of 1842 the position was this: Brunswick had joined the Zollverein but her Harz and Weser provinces were to remain in the Tax Union for a year so as to give Prussia and Hanover time to discuss the adhesion of the whole of the Tax Union to the Zollverein. The agreements of 1837 for the suppression of smuggling between the two unions and for the rectification of the customs frontier by the exchange of enclaves were also extended (with slight modifications) for a year. Prussia hoped that the threat of including Brunswick's Harz and Weser districts in the Zollverein and so isolating Göttingen and Grubenhagen from the rest of the Tax Union would force Hanover to come to terms. She was to be disappointed.

The opposition of King, Government and people in Hanover to joining the Zollverein was so great that the negotiations were virtually doomed from the outset.[1] Hanover feared that adhesion to the Prussian customs system would involve loss of sovereign rights and would lead to a rise in the cost of living.

[1] For the King of Hanover's attitude to "this cursed affair of the Zollverein", see *Letters of the King of Hanover to Viscount Strangford* (1925), pp. 51–4 (August 21, 1844), and p. 64 (November 3, 1844).

Her duties were generally low and she exchanged her agricultural produce for manufactured articles and colonial goods. Hanover was determined not to pay more for her textiles, rails, sugar, tea, coffee and tobacco. The popular sentiment was well expressed in a ballad which appeared in 1843 and was sung to the tune of the new anti-French patriotic song: "Sie sollen ihn nicht haben den freien deutschen Rhein" ("They shall not have the free German Rhine").

Wir wollen ihn nicht haben	We will not have it, ever,
Den preussischen Zollverein;	Their Prussian Zollverein;
Ob sie wie gier'ge Raben	For all their screeching, never
Sich heisser danach schreien.	With them will we combine.

.   .   .   .

Wir lassen ihn nicht sinken	Our coffee we'll not let it
Den indischen Kaffee;	Be kept beyond the sea;
Wir wollen ferner trinken	And, further, we'll still get it,
Den echten China Tee.	The best of China tea.

.   .   .   .

Wir wollen ferner brauchen	Whenever punch we're making,
Zum Punsch den echten Rak;	Real rum is what we need;
Wir woll'n auch ferner schmauchen	And when a smoke we're taking
Ein gutes Blatt Tabak.[1]	We want no home grown weed.

.   .   .   .

Hanover was in no hurry to begin negotiating with Prussia in 1842 for she had no serious intention of joining the Zollverein. England was naturally anxious that Hanover should remain outside the Prussian customs system and should retain her low import duties. The King of Hanover informed his minister in London that he opposed adhesion to the Zollverein and that whatever happened he would avoid injuring England's interests. "No one could take this amiss in an English Prince",

---

[1] A copy of this ballad was sent by von Kress to Metternich from Hanover on September 15, 1843 (Vienna Archives, fasc. 79c, *Zollvereinsverhandlungen*): H. von Treitschke (v, p. 442) quotes a few lines.

he added.[1] Negotiations were kept alive, however, in the hope of securing the permanent adhesion to the Tax Union of that part of Brunswick which divided the southern provinces of Hanover from the main part of the Kingdom. For seven months Hanover discussed the matter with her ally Oldenburg. At last, in August, 1842, a note was sent to Berlin suggesting a possible basis for negotiation on the question of adhesion to the Zollverein. Hanover refused to introduce the Zollverein salt monopoly, to levy retrospective duties, or to give up the revenues derived from her tolls on roads and on the Weser and Elbe. She wanted a relaxation of the restrictions in the Zollverein frontier districts and a reduction of Zollverein import duties on colonial products and wine. Hanover demanded a preferential payment—a larger share of the Zollverein revenue than that calculated on the basis of population—since she consumed more colonial products and wine per head of population than the Zollverein and she also wanted compensation for the loss of revenue from transit dues.[2]

There were precedents for some of these demands. Thus, Prussia was compensated for relinquishing to the Zollverein the proceeds of shipping dues levied on the Oder and Vistula. Frankfurt-am-Main received a greater revenue than that to which she would have been entitled on a basis of population. Bavaria and Württemberg had avoided the levying of retrospective duties on joining the Zollverein by paying a lump sum instead. Baden had secured a smaller customs frontier region (*Grenzbezirk*) than was usual. But Hanover was so exigent that it seemed hopeless to expect agreement. Preliminary negotiations, however, were begun in Berlin in October, 1842. In the same month Bunsen, the Prussian minister in London, was instructed to seek English co-operation in bringing pressure to bear upon Hanover to adopt a more accommodating attitude towards the Zollverein on the question of union and on that of

[1] H. von Treitschke, v, p. 443.
[2] Hanover's note is printed in *Der grosse Zollverein deutscher Staaten . . .* (Hanover, 1844), pp. 37–47, and in A. Zimmermann, pp. 538–46.

lowering the Stade tolls. He was to represent that it was in England's interest for Hanover to join the Zollverein since her adhesion would strengthen the free-traders in Germany against the rising protectionist feeling of the southern States. England, however, declined to put any pressure on Hanover of the kind desired by Prussia.

8. Adhesion of Brunswick to the Zollverein, 1837–44. Dates indicate when various Brunswick lands entered the Zollverein.

Little progress was made in the discussions between Prussia and Hanover and in December, 1842, it was decided to gain time by allowing Brunswick's Harz and Weser districts to remain in the Tax Union for yet another year. But Prussia declared that no further extension of temporary arrangement would be permitted after the end of 1843. The negotiations of 1843 were no more successful than those of 1842. Agreement might have been possible on some of the Hanoverian demands but on the question of a preferential payment Prussia remained adamant. She firmly refused to negotiate on the basis of granting a financial privilege of this sort to Hanover. Negotiations for the adhesion of Hanover to the Zollverein were therefore dropped.

Since the two customs unions were to continue side by side, a new agreement to facilitate commerce between them was desirable. The treaties of 1837 for the prevention of smuggling and for the exchange of enclaves—already modified in 1841—would have to be remodelled in view of Brunswick's adhesion to the Zollverein. As Brunswick refused to allow her Harz and Weser districts to remain in the Tax Union and Hanover refused to permit her provinces of Göttingen and Grubenhagen to join the Zollverein, the position was a difficult one. Prussia wanted to prevent the Harz and Weser districts from becoming a smuggling centre while Hanover wanted to secure her communications with her now isolated southern regions. Despite long negotiations no treaty was signed before the end of 1843. It was not even found possible to secure a provisional agreement at the last moment.

The treaties of 1837 and 1841 expired at the end of 1843 and were not renewed for the time being. Hanover, however, announced her intention of continuing to take measures to stop smuggling into Zollverein territory. On January 1, 1844, Brunswick's Harz and Weser districts were incorporated in the Zollverein. The ordinary Zollverein duties were levied in that part of the newly acquired region lying *west* of the River Leine. But, owing to the difficulty of controlling commerce in the wooded Harz Mountains, it was arranged that goods entering the district *east* of the Leine should pay lower duties. Since Brunswick received a share of the Zollverein revenue on the basis of her total population—that is to say including the inhabitants of the region east of the Leine—she derived a slight financial advantage from this arrangement.

Hanover was exasperated at Brunswick's desertion of the Tax Union. That customs union now included only Hanover,

Oldenburg and Schaumburg-Lippe. Its influence in Central Germany was irreparably weakened by the inclusion of the whole of Brunswick in the Zollverein at a time when new railways and roads were being planned in this part of the country. The Hanoverian Government vented its wrath on Brunswick by publishing in January, 1844, a justification of its conduct in the recent negotiations supported by the evidence of a number of official documents. Brunswick issued a reply shortly afterwards. "This gives a full and exact account of how Brunswick left the Tax Union with several remarkable details, the revelation of which at that time was rightly regarded with astonishment."[1] "The way in which the two embittered Guelph courts washed their dirty linen in public was not edifying."[2] In April there appeared an official Prussian answer to the Hanoverian charges. This controversy and the revealing of official documents to support the arguments of the courts concerned showed how anxious the Governments were to secure public support in economic matters and was a tribute to the rising influence of the commercial and manufacturing middle classes. The dispute aroused great interest in Germany and abroad. Prussia was, on the whole, supported by the Press of members of the Zollverein. Sympathy for Hanover was generally confined to the Hanse towns and to foreign countries such as England, which had an interest in preventing the extension of the Zollverein to the North Sea coast.

The controversy lasted throughout 1844 and "almost assumed the character of a public scandal".[3] England and Austria made unsuccessful attempts to mediate between Hanover and Prussia. Hanover turned to England for support. By the Anglo-Hanoverian Navigation Treaty of July, 1844, England agreed to recognise as Hanover's "natural outlets" not merely the North Sea ports between the Elbe and the Meuse but also the Baltic ports between the Trave and the Niemen. Hanover reduced the Stade tolls on English ships and granted England

[1] W. Weber, p. 268.
[2] H. von Treitschke, v, p. 447.   [3] W. Weber, p. 288.

most favoured nation treatment with regard to import duties. Hanover's obligations under this treaty would make it difficult for her to join the Zollverein before 1848. "The Guelph kingdom, even after its detachment from the English Crown, thus remained for British commercial policy a bridgehead upon the continent."[1]

Early in 1845 negotiations between Prussia and Hanover were reopened and a treaty and six supplementary agreements between the Zollverein and the Tax Union were signed on October 16 of that year.[2] There was an exchange of enclaves: steps were to be taken to stop smuggling and to facilitate frontier traffic. Ratification was delayed by the unexpected opposition of Bavaria, Württemberg and Baden to the permission given to the Tax Union to export *handwoven* linen-yarn cloth to the Zollverein free of duty. The controversy between free-traders and protectionists had come to a head at the Zollverein Congress of 1845 and the South German protectionists took this opportunity to oppose Prussia on a comparatively minor point. Prussia stood firm and the South German States gave way. In September, 1846, ratifications were exchanged and the relations between the Zollverein and the Tax Union were at last placed upon a more satisfactory basis. Yet, in the same year, Hanover placed a new obstacle in the way of future negotiations for her entry into the Zollverein by making important tariff concessions to the United States of America. Oldenburg followed suit in 1847.

Prussia's failure to include Hanover and Oldenburg in her customs system seemed to render hopeless any approach to other North German States in the early 'forties. Hamburg and Bremen were determined to maintain their economic independence and low import duties.[3]

---

[1] H. von Treitschke, v, p. 448.

[2] *Gesetz-Sammlung für den Königlichen Preussischen Staat*, no. 37 (December 1, 1845).

[3] See, for example, T. Hansen, *Hamburg und die zollpolitische Entwicklung Deutschlands im neunzehnten Jahrhundert* (1913); A. Wohlwill,

It was said that in Hamburg after the destructive fire of May, 1842, certain citizens favoured "a junction with the Zollverein and some are even bold enough to declare that such a step can alone restore Hamburg to the position she held before the fire". Three years later Colonel Hodges wrote that supporters of the Zollverein in Hamburg were "haranguing many of the influential community at select meetings set up for this purpose". "Formerly there could scarcely be found an individual on the Exchange of Hamburg bold enough to venture a surmise of a junction between this great commercial mart and the German League but now many sober-minded men, and some even among the members of the Chamber of Commerce declare that ere long Hamburg will be compelled to make some sort of arrangement with the League, though none give utterance to the idea of an absolute junction with it." But, on the whole, supporters of adhesion to the Zollverein were in a small minority.[1]

In Lübeck, trade depression led some citizens to advocate economic union with Prussia. On the one hand, the free city had to face severe competition from the port of Stettin which Prussia favoured in every possible manner. On the other hand,

"Beiträge zu einer Geschichte C. F. Wurms", in *Zeitschrift des Vereins für Hamburgische Geschichte*, XXII (1918), ch. vi, Hamburg und der Zollverein (pp. 60–70); E. Baasch, "Hamburg und Bremen und die deutschen wirtschaftlichen Einheitsbestrebungen von der Begründung des Zollvereins bis zum Anschluss Hannovers 1854", in *Hansische Geschichtsblätter*, XXVII (1922), p. 115; and Carl J. H. Blume, *Hamburg und die deutschen wirtschaftlichen Einheitsbestrebungen* (Hamburg, 1934; Dissertation).

[1] Colonel G. L. Hodges to Lord Aberdeen, May 31, 1842 (F.O. 33/93); February 4, 1845 (F.O. 33/101), and February 28, 1845 (F.O. 33/102). Hodges was British Consul-General at Hamburg from 1841 to 1860. His successor declared that "the men of business at Hamburg soon discovered that he possessed but a slender knowledge either of trade or of German politics, nor did he even acquire the German language during the nineteen years in which he represented British interests at that great commercial port" (J. Ward, *Experiences of a Diplomatist...*, 1840–70 (1872), pp. 177–8).

Lübeck suffered from the commercial jealousy of Denmark. Lübeck, for example, desired the construction of a railway to Hamburg or—if this were not possible—of a branch line to the Berlin-Hamburg railway. But the former would pass through Holstein and the latter through Lauenburg and the King of Denmark (the ruler of these German duchies) refused his assent. The Danes wanted no competition with the Altona-Kiel railway which ran entirely through Holstein territory.[1] Colonel Hodges was told in 1844 that Denmark's hostility "would probably do irretrievable mischief to that city and (would) ultimately compel it to join the German Commercial League, although such a step would not take place until the junction of Mecklenburg thereto".[2]

Mecklenburg-Schwerin, however, still favoured economic isolation.[3] She signed a commercial and navigation treaty with Britain in May, 1844, to which Mecklenburg-Strelitz adhered. The two States were granted generous "natural outlets" and Colonel Hodges thought that this concession would keep them out of the Zollverein. In 1847 Mecklenburg-Schwerin made a commercial agreement with the United States which the American negotiator considered "a terrible blow" to the Zollverein.[4]

(2) COMMERCIAL NEGOTIATIONS WITH FOREIGN COUNTRIES, 1842–1847 [5]

The first commercial treaty to be made after the new Zollverein treaties came into force was that with Belgium in 1844. It was

---

[1] See, for example, F.O. 33/100 (memorandum on Lübeck and Hamburg Railroad), F.O. 33/104 (Colonel Hodges to Lord Aberdeen, July 24, 1846) and F.O. 33/106 (Colquhoun to Lord Palmerston, August 22, 1846 —enclosing map).

[2] Colonel Hodges to Lord Aberdeen, August 23, 1844 (F.O. 33/98).

[3] See, for example, J. L. Schumacher, "Der preussische Zollverein und Mecklenburg", in *Rau und Hanssens Archiv der politischen Ökonomie*, VIII (New Series, 1849), p. 33.   [4] R. von Delbrück, I, p. 170.

[5] See A. Zimmermann, book iv and documents on pp. 555–624. For commercial relations with Belgium, see W. Weber, ch. xx; H. von Festenberg-Packisch, pp. 224–31; M. Sering, *Geschichte der preussisch-*

in Prussia's interest to maintain amicable commercial relations with Belgium after she had secured her independence. It might be advantageous to her merchants to use the port of Antwerp rather than that of Amsterdam or Rotterdam. Once Cologne was linked by rail with Antwerp there was a short route to the North Sea on which the payment of Dutch tolls could be avoided. Heinrich von Arnim, the Prussian Minister at Brussels, and David Hansemann, an influential Rhineland industrialist, were among those who had great hopes of the development of German transit trade through Belgium.

On the other hand, some German manufacturers were uneasy at the rapid development of Belgian industries. Belgium was "the one country in Europe which kept pace industrially with England in the first half of the nineteenth century. She had an ancient urban civilisation and brilliant economic traditions".[1] In the 'thirties she produced over six million tons of coal a year. Her production of pig-iron rose from 221,000 tons to 591,000 tons between 1821 and 1847. Her engineering industry—particularly John Cockerill's great factory at Seraing (near Liége)—was the most advanced on the Continent and supplied large quantities of machines to Holland, Germany and Russia. Belgium's prosperity, however, was temporarily checked in the late 'thirties owing to the separation from Holland and the consequent loss of free access to markets in Holland and in the Dutch colonies. In 1838 there was a commercial crisis.[2]

---

deutschen Eisenzölle... (1882), ch. ii, sect. iii and R. von Delbrück, 1, pp. 155–62; with Holland, see E. Gothein, ch. ix–xi; P. J. Bouman's article in V.S.W. XXVI (1933), pp. 244–66 and documents in N. W. Posthumus, v, pp. 57–338; with England, see J. H. Clapham's articles in E.H.R. XXV (1910); with France, see H. Richelot, L'Association Douanière Allemande (1845), part iii, ch. ii; with the U.S.A. see G. M. Fisk, pp. 81–91; and with Austria, see A. Beer, pp. 16–34, 76–82, and Heinrich Ritter von Srbik, Metternich, II (1925), pp. 104–10.

[1] J. H. Clapham, The Economic Development of France and Germany (3rd edition, 1928), p. 57.

[2] For Belgium's early industrial expansion, see for example V. Briavionne, De l'Industrie de la Belgique (1839), M. Dunn, View of the Coal

Belgium took over the Dutch customs system and navigation laws, and discussions with the Zollverein on their modification made little progress in the 'thirties. It was suggested that Belgium might enter the Zollverein but there were two objections to negotiating on this subject. First, Prussia thought it undesirable for a non-German State to be included in the Zollverein. Secondly, if the discussions broke down, Prussia could hardly object if negotiations for a Franco-Belgian customs union were opened. Though the inclusion of Belgium in the Prussian customs system was impracticable, the conclusion of a commercial treaty was desirable. But so long as the Prusso-Belgian frontier was not fixed, it was not easy to try to regulate trade. The partition of Luxemburg in April, 1839, partially removed this difficulty by settling the political—though not the economic—future of the Grand Duchy. In August, 1839, Belgium submitted drafts of commercial and navigation treaties to Prussia but the ensuing conference led to no result.[1] Belgium turned to France and the question of establishing a Franco-Belgian customs union was discussed in 1841. The negotiations failed largely owing to opposition from Austria and England. Palmerston observed in August, 1841, that the five Great Powers had guaranteed Belgium's integrity and independence. "It is manifest that when two countries of very unequal extent and power enter together into exclusive commercial engagements, by which they grant to each other privileges and advantages of commerce, which they are not prepared to concede to all other nations, the political independence of the lesser power must be impaired by such a compact."[2]

Negotiations with France having failed Belgium turned to Prussia again but the discussions held in the autumn of 1841

Trade (1844), J. Thomson, *Notes on the Present State of Calico Printing in Belgium* (1841), and E. Mahaim, "Les débuts de l'établissement John Cockerill à Seraing", in *V.S.W.* III (1905), pp. 627–48.

[1] A. Zimmermann prints the Belgian projects and Prussia's reply (pp. 588–97).

[2] Quoted by A. Zimmermann, p. 271.

were unsuccessful. Two difficulties arose in 1842. First, when Luxemburg joined the Zollverein, Belgium threatened to withdraw her concessions regarding trade between the two portions of the partitioned Grand Duchy unless the Zollverein reduced its import duties on wool. Belgium offered to reduce her import duties on silk goods and wines. Secondly, in June, 1842, France made a fresh effort to gain commercial influence over Belgium. She doubled her duties on linen yarn and cloth. Belgium was hard hit by this measure and in July secured a reduction of the French duties to the old level by agreeing to raise her own duties on German and English linen yarn and cloth to the same high rate which France charged on all such wares except those coming from Belgium. Consequently English and German exporters of linen yarn and cloth were now faced with almost prohibitive duties in France and Belgium. The Zollverein threatened to retaliate by raising her duties on Belgian iron. So Belgium reduced (until August 1, 1843) some of her duties on German silks and wines—but not on linens.

At the Stuttgart Zollverein Congress of 1842 agreement was reached on the concessions to be offered to Belgium regarding goods coming from Belgium and passing through Zollverein territory on their way to Austria, Switzerland and other countries. In November, 1842, Prussia offered to resume negotiations. It was feared that undue delay might give France another opportunity of putting economic pressure upon Belgium and of concluding an advantageous commercial treaty with her. This would not be so dangerous to Prussian interests as a Franco-Belgian customs union[1] but it might well lead to an undue extension of French political influence in Belgium. Prussia recognised that she must make economic sacrifices to prevent the conclusion of such a treaty. The Belgians fully appreciated the strength of their position and hoped to play Prussia and France

[1] For proposals for a Franco-Belgian customs union in the early 'forties, see F. De Lannoy, "Les Projets d'Union Douanière Franco-Belge en 1841–42", in *Revue Catholique des Idées et des Faits* (Brussels, December, 1922).

off against each other. They declined to negotiate with Prussia unless the proposed transit concessions were made at once. Prussia agreed to lower her transit dues on Belgian goods arriving by the Antwerp-Cologne railway to half a silver groschen per hundredweight after the beginning of January, 1843. Belgium thereupon declared that she would enter into negotiations for a navigation and commercial treaty (May, 1843).

The plenipotentiaries met in Berlin in the autumn of 1843 and their deliberations lasted for a year. At first little progress was made in the negotiations; commercial relations between the two countries became worse and a tariff war began to develop. Belgium, for example, refused to renew the concessions of 1842 regarding the importation of German wines and silks and even abolished the repayment of Scheldt dues on Prussian ships. Prussia retaliated by announcing a special increase in her import duties on Belgian iron. Eventually cooler counsels prevailed. The chief difficulty was to meet the Belgian demand for a substantial reduction of the Zollverein duty on iron which was one of Belgium's chief exports. The Zollverein States had only recently agreed, after long discussions, on a revision of the tariff on iron. A low duty was paid on the importation of pig-iron (formerly admitted free) and the tariff was raised somewhat on wrought-iron, iron rails and so forth. Prussia consulted the Governments of the Zollverein States on the subject and they agreed that Belgium should be offered a reduction by half of the new iron duties. Belgium accepted this proposal and a navigation and commercial treaty was signed on September 1, 1844. It was to come into force on January 1, 1845, and was to last for six years.

The clauses on shipping established the principle of reciprocity with regard to the treatment of vessels of one country entering the ports of the other. The Zollverein halved its transit dues on Belgian goods, its import duties on Belgian iron and cheese, and its duty on the export of certain wools to Belgium. Fifteen thousand sheep might be sent annually duty free from

Belgium to the Zollverein. Belgium, on the other hand, made comparatively few concessions. She reduced a few import duties on Zollverein goods and admitted mineral waters duty free. She agreed to maintain the following existing arrangements which she had more than once threatened to abolish permanently—the freedom of transit on the Cologne-Antwerp railway, the concessions regarding the import of linen yarn from Westphalia and Brunswick and of German silks and wines, and the special arrangements on the Luxemburg frontier.[1]

Belgium had played her cards well. She did little more than promise not to treat the Zollverein worse than she had done in the past. In return she secured preferential treatment in an important market for one of her chief exports. Prussia, fearing the extension of French commercial and political influence in Belgium, had made substantial concessions and had little to show for them. The trouble that had occurred over the granting of a preference to Dutch semi-refined sugar in 1839 might have warned Prussia of the danger of giving a preference to Belgian iron. During the six years that the treaty was in force the importation of Belgian iron increased very considerably. In 1850 it amounted to over 75,000 tons—nearly 70 per cent. of Germany's total iron imports. German ironmasters had every reason to complain of the severity of Belgian competition. On the other hand, the Zollverein secured virtually no compensating advantages from the treaty. Transit traffic through Belgium did not develop as rapidly as had been hoped. The financial results of the treaty were also unsatisfactory. It was estimated that the Zollverein revenue was reduced by 842,000 florins in 1847 owing to the concessions that had been made whereas Belgium gave up only 76,500. Belgium also succeeded in concluding advantageous commercial agreements with France in December, 1845, and with Holland in July, 1846. Prussia denounced the commercial treaty with Belgium in 1850.

[1] The commercial and navigation treaty between the Zollverein and Belgium, 1844, is printed by von Kamptz, pp. 198–233, and by F. A. de Mensch, pp. 221–33.

The commercial treaty of 1844 between the Zollverein and Belgium influenced the economic relations of Holland and the Zollverein. Although transit traffic on the Antwerp-Cologne railway did not increase so rapidly as optimists had expected, the competition on the railway with shipping on the Rhine was severe enough to alarm the Dutch. It is true that the carriage of most goods was cheaper by ship than by rail.[1] Prices were kept down both by the keen competition between Dutch, German and English river steamship companies[2] and by Camphausen's introduction of an improved type of tug on the Rhine. On the other hand, the Antwerp-Cologne railway had the advantage of speed. The Dutch wanted a further reduction in the cost of transporting goods on the Rhine. Their commerce by this route was of two kinds. On the one hand, the export of coffee from Java and Brazil to Germany was still largely under the control of Dutch middlemen who secured profits both from financing the trade and from shipping the goods—a lucrative trade both to merchants and to the State. It was said that "without the large export of coffee to Germany the Dutch could not find the interest for their huge national debt: one cent more or less per pound makes a difference of a million Gulden. In relation to the Zollverein coffee is as important to Holland as iron is to Belgium."[3] On the other hand, the export of other colonial products and of manufactured and semi-manufactured articles was coming under the control of German importers who either used Dutch intermediaries merely as commission agents or got into direct touch with the producers. The Dutch were thus losing their middlemen's gains and were anxious to retain their profits as carriers. The nature of some of this carrying

[1] See table of comparative costs in van Hall to Delasarraz, November 24, 1843 (N. W. Posthumus, v, pp. 119–29).

[2] The chief companies were the Nederlandsche Stoomboot Maatschappij, the Kölner Schiffahrtsverein (1833), the Dampfschiffgesellschaft für den Mittel- und Niederrhein (Düsseldorf, 1836), and the Steam Navigation Company.

[3] Von Koenigsmarck to von Bülow, September 9, 1844 (N. W. Posthumus, v, p. 155).

trade was changing in another way. In the 'forties the export of semi-manufactured articles was replacing that of completely manufactured products. Thus finished textile goods were giving place to yarn and refined sugar to semi-refined sugar. German factories were manufacturing the yarn into garments and were refining the sugar.

In the 'forties trading relations between the Zollverein and Holland were only partially regulated by treaty, for although the navigation convention of 1837 remained in force the commercial treaty of 1839 expired in 1841 and was not renewed. Both countries raised some of their duties but there was no tariff war. Prussian statesmen made no attempt to follow the advice of some of the more violent German protectionists who wanted to force Holland into the Zollverein by boycotting the importation both of her native and colonial products.[1] Holland's anxiety to retain her carrying trade in the changing economic conditions of the 'forties made her try to secure a general reduction of the Rhine tolls. In 1843 she proposed that these dues should be abolished but nothing came of the suggestion. The Dutch tariff of 1845 reduced the Rhine dues in Holland. General abolition needed the co-operation of all the *états riverains* and this was not forthcoming owing to the opposition of some of the smaller States such as Hesse-Darmstadt and Nassau.

On several occasions between 1844 and 1846 Holland indicated to Prussia her willingness to negotiate for a commercial treaty which should include a general diminution of Rhine dues.[2] Little progress was made in the discussions. Howard observed to Lord Aberdeen that "the difficulties which Holland

---

[1] See the violent article in the Augsburg *Allgemeine Zeitung*, August 24, 1842 (N. W. Posthumus, v, pp. 105–7).

[2] See, for example, von Koenigsmarck to von Bülow, September 9, 1844 (reporting statement of the Dutch Finance Minister: "The time has come when we must reach an understanding with Prussia..."), von Bülow to Schimmelpenninck van der Oye, December 19, 1844, von Canitz to Schimmelpenninck van der Oye, February 5, 1846 (N. W. Posthumus, v, pp. 153–6, 210–13, 231).

interposed from the year 1815 until the conclusion of the Convention of Mayence (Mainz) in 1831, in the way of the navigation of the Rhine and the former exclusive policy it pursued, are still borne in mind in Germany, and have left behind them, as Baron Bülow assured me in a late conversation I had with him in Berlin, a certain degree of disinclination towards Holland, whilst a much greater disposition exists in the States of the Zollverein towards a closer commercial connection with Belgium".[1] Holland now signed a commercial treaty with Belgium (July, 1846) and reduced her duties on certain imports from that country.

In March, 1847, she sent a note to Prussia stating more precisely the terms which might form a basis for negotiations. The Dutch offered the Zollverein most favoured nation treatment both in Holland and in her colonies and was even prepared to admit certain German goods to the Dutch East Indies on the same terms as Dutch goods. Holland's duties on various German imports were to be lowered and the Rhine *octroi* would be abolished. In return Holland asked for the reduction of certain Zollverein import duties (including that on semi-refined sugar) and the removal of the Rhine dues. Prussia was not prepared to negotiate on these terms. She could hardly reduce the duties on semi-refined sugar in view of the violent protests that had been made in Germany against such a concession in 1839. She did not want to discuss the question of the Rhine dues at the moment. In 1849 Prussia denounced the navigation treaty of 1837 but agreed to continue to observe its provisions so long as negotiations for a new treaty of commerce continued.[2]

[1] Henry Francis Howard to Lord Aberdeen, April 17, 1845 (F.O. 37/251, N. W. Posthumus, v, pp. 213–14).

[2] Schimmelpenninck van der Oye to von Canitz, March 27, 1846 (Dutch terms for commercial treaty) (P. J. Bouman, *V.S.W.* xxvi (1933), p. 264 gives the date "March 1847" instead of March, 1846), and April 27, 1846, von Canitz to Schimmelpenninck van der Oye, October 26, 1846 (Prussia's reply), von Koenigsmarck to Lightenvelt, July 20, 1849 (denunciation of navigation treaty of 1837) N. W. Posthumus, v, pp. 240–2, 246, 315–16, and A. Zimmermann, pp. 586–8.

Meantime, the influence of the Dutch free-traders was increasing. They argued that Holland should adopt a policy of free-trade whether her neighbours followed suit or not. As in Britain the chief struggle was over the Corn Laws. In 1847 the sliding scale of duties, which had been in force since 1835, was replaced by a low import duty. In 1850 three navigation laws were passed abolishing transit dues, differential duties in favour of Dutch shipping and the prohibition of the registration of foreign-built vessels as Dutch ships. The Meuse dues were removed in 1851. These concessions were favourably received in Germany. Prussia was able to secure the consent of the *états riverains* to the inclusion of the question of reducing the Rhine tolls in the discussions with Holland. Negotiations were undertaken in the autumn of 1851 and a commercial and navigation treaty was signed on December 31. Holland gave up the *droit fixe* and the "recognition duty" on the Rhine and Prussia made generous concessions to Dutch shipping. The treaty was to run until January 1, 1854, after which it might be terminated by either party by giving a year's notice. Actually it lasted until 1923. Thus Holland lost her monopolistic position at the mouth of the Rhine.[1]

As in Holland so in England the increasing influence of the free-traders had its effect upon relations with the Zollverein. Prussia hoped that the Zollverein would soon benefit from the removal of the more serious obstacles that British commercial policy placed in the way of German trade and shipping. Sir Robert Peel's reduction of many import duties in his budget of 1842 was a serious breach in the traditional protective system. This did not, however, improve our relations with the Zollverein as much as might have been expected. In Germany there were complaints that England's concessions were inadequate and it was pointed out that the English navigation laws, corn laws and high timber and sugar duties remained. At the same time pressure from the German protectionists was forcing Prussia to agree to certain increases in the Zollverein tariff

[1] See P. J. Bouman, *V.S.W.* XXVI (1933), p. 266.

which were severely criticised in England. Banfield, an obser-
vant traveller in the industrial regions of the Rhineland, lamented
that "from the period of its foundation the history of the Zollverein is unhappily that of a gradual departure from the sound
principles on which it was originally based".[1]

At the Zollverein Congress of 1842 the import duties on
mixed cotton and woollen printed goods were raised from 30 to
50 thalers per hundredweight.[2] In 1843 England protested in
vain against the new Zollverein duty on pig-iron and the raising
of duties on iron bars and rails. In the following year relations
between the Zollverein and England were embittered by the
conclusion of the Anglo-Hanoverian navigation treaty which
granted Hanover more "natural outlets" than had been conceded to the Zollverein in 1841. The English navigation code
was re-enacted in 1845. Few changes were made and it remained more restrictive than that of any German State. It was
hardly surprising that there should be discussions in Germany
at this time on the possibility of concerted action on the part of
German maritime States to force England to adopt a more
liberal navigation policy. Peel's budget of 1845 provided for
further removals and reductions of import duties. The abolition
of the English duty on the importation of raw cotton alarmed
the German protectionists. They feared that this would enable
English cotton manufacturers to lower their prices of finished
goods. So a fresh increase in the Zollverein duties on textiles
was proposed. The Manchester Chamber of Commerce protested against "this further inroad upon British commerce".[3]
The Zollverein Congress at Carlsruhe (1845), however, could
come to no agreement on these duties and they were left at the
old level.

In May, 1846, when the English cabinet was fully occupied
with the debates on the abolition of the Corn Laws, Bunsen

---

[1] T. C. Banfield, *Industry of the Rhine*, II (2 vols. in 1, 1846–48), p. 12.
[2] Westmorland to Aberdeen, November 8, 1842 (P.P. 1843, LXI,
pp. 281–8).
[3] Memorial to the Board of Trade (M.Ch.C. June 4, 1845).

(the Prussian Minister in London) presented a memorandum to Lord Aberdeen on the question of renewing the Anglo-Zollverein convention of 1841 which would expire on January 1, 1848. The note criticised the British navigation code. It suggested that the navigation laws had done their work and that the British mercantile marine had secured a position of undisputed supremacy in the world. "Certainly Prussia and the German Union of Customs never can think of disputing this preponderant power." Bunsen criticised the concessions regarding "natural outlets" which had recently been made to North German maritime States outside the Zollverein. He expressed the hope that the convention of 1841 would be renewed "on the principle of true reciprocity". Aberdeen passed the memorandum on to his colleagues Dalhousie and Gladstone who both criticised it vigorously. Dalhousie admitted that the navigation code could not be permanently maintained but he did not think that Prussia had "any fair right to demand such concessions". He observed that the Zollverein was raising its duties against Britain at the very time that Peel's reform of the British tariff was benefiting the Zollverein. Gladstone declared that Prussia's commercial policy was as protectionist as that of any other country "and only differed from them in that this course of proceeding had been accompanied by constant vapourings about the principles of freedom of trade."[1]

Nothing came of Bunsen's demands in 1846. Equally unsuccessful were the efforts of List (who was in London at this time) to secure closer economic and political co-operation between Britain and Germany. In a memorandum submitted to leading statesmen of both countries he argued that the rise of

---

[1] For Bunsen's memorandum (received by the Foreign Office on May 12, 1846, and endorsed "answered verbally by the Earl of Aberdeen") and comments by Dalhousie and Gladstone, see F.O. 64/268, and J. H. Clapham in *E.H.R.* xxv (1910), pp. 693–4. For correspondence in the spring of 1846 between Bunsen and Karl Sieveking (of Hamburg) on Anglo-German commercial relations, see H. Sieveking, *Karl Sieveking*, 1787–1847..., iii (1928), pp. 737–8.

a strong and friendly Germany would be in Britain's interest in view of a possible hostile Franco-Italian alliance and he suggested that Germany could gain economic power only by adopting a policy of protection. Palmerston considered that List's political views were "just and well founded: his commercial doctrines do not appear to be exactly correct". He agreed that Britain would gain by having a powerful ally in Central Europe but did not think that Germany would benefit by adopting a high tariff. Palmerston observed that the Zollverein had fostered commerce and industry by establishing a large free-trade area in Germany. It should follow a free-trade policy in its relations with foreign countries. Peel informed List that the sentiments expressed in his memorandum "in favour of the policy and reciprocal advantage of an intimate union between this country and Germany have my cordial concurrence as complete and unqualified as is my dissent from your view as to the mode by which that intimate union can be most effectually promoted".[1]

The failure of attempts to secure Anglo-Zollverein agreement in 1846 led to fresh attacks upon Britain's commercial policy in the German protectionist Press and, early in 1847, English agents in Germany received an official statement (drawn up by MacGregor) of the English point of view to enable them to reply to these criticisms. Colonel Hodges wrote an article "based upon the reasoning contained in Mr MacGregor's

[1] See F. List, *Über den Wert und die Bedingungen einer Allianz zwischen Grossbritannien und Deutschland*, 1846 (edition of 1920). The comments of Palmerston and Peel are printed by A. Zimmermann, pp. 550–5. A letter from List to the King of Prussia (July 31, 1846) is printed by H. von Treitschke, v, pp. 766–7. For a discussion of List's project for an Anglo-German alliance, see Ludwig Sevin, "Die Entwicklung von Friedrich Lists kolonialen und weltpolitischen Ideen bis zum Plane einer englischen Allianz 1846", in *Jahrbuch für Gesetzgebung, Verwaltung und Volkswirtschaft*, herausgegeben von Gustav Schmoller, XXXIII (1909), Heft iv, pp. 299–341, and "Die Listsche Idee einer deutsch-englischen Allianz in ihrem Ergebnis für Deutschland", *ibid.* XXXIV (1910), Heft i, pp. 173–222.

letter" and arranged for its publication in the *Börsen-Halle* (*Hamburgische Abendzeitung*) on April 3, 1847.[1]

The Navigation Laws were suspended by the new Whig ministry in January, 1847, to facilitate the importation of food. In May Prussia denounced the Anglo-Zollverein Convention of 1841. Bunsen offered to renew it temporarily if England would recognise *all* Baltic ports as "natural outlets" of the Zollverein. Palmerston agreed to make the same concessions to the Zollverein as had been made to the two Mecklenburgs so as to secure a provisional extension of the agreement of 1841. He also held out hopes of recognising the Baltic ports as "natural outlets" of the Zollverein if Prussia would agree to a permanent convention. In February, 1848, Bunsen accepted the Mecklenburg list under protest. The English navigation code was repealed in July, 1849.[2] Thus a long-standing cause of dispute between England and Prussia was removed.[3] The terms of the Anglo-Prussian Convention of 1841, as modified in 1847, were maintained provisionally subject to six months' notice from either side. This arrangement lasted until 1865.

The establishment of greater freedom of trade, which did so much to improve the relations of the Zollverein with Holland and England, had little influence upon the commercial policy of France in the 'forties. High import duties, strict navigation laws and restrictions regarding colonial trade were the order of the day. The Zollverein desired the facilitation of local frontier traffic, reciprocity regarding shipping and reductions of duties on the chief German exports to France (such as wool, timber,

[1] Colonel Hodges to Lord Palmerston, April 6, 1847 (F.O. 33/108). Shortly afterwards Hodges was authorised to pay for the insertion of articles of this sort (F.O. 33/107). Foreign Office draft to Colonel Hodges, September 24, 1847.

[2] The coasting trade, however, was still reserved to national ships. Three-quarters of the crew of every vessel on the British register had to be of British nationality.

[3] For the Prussian point of view in 1847, see von Canitz to Bunsen, July 13, 1847 (printed by A. Zimmermann, pp. 555–61); in 1849, see von Bülow to Lord Westmorland, February 21, 1849 (P.P. LI, pp. 229–30).

cattle and certain manufactured articles). In return she was prepared to reduce her own import duties on wines and spirits.
The Stuttgart Zollverein Congress of 1842 decided to double
the import duties on various French imports (such as gloves
and cognac) if France failed to come to terms. France thereupon reduced some of the high duties on imports from the
Zollverein but—in order to bring Belgium to terms—she raised
her duties on linens, a course of action which injured Germany
as much as Belgium.

In December, 1842, Count Bresson sent Bülow a long note
on Franco-German commercial relations. He represented that
Zollverein exports to France were increasing while Zollverein
imports from France were decreasing and that France had been
anxious for some time to negotiate for a trade agreement but
was only waiting for Prussia to make the first move. Bülow replied in March, 1843, that France only imported such German
raw materials as were indispensable to her industries. She levied
high duties on German manufactured articles but she was able
to send her chief exports to the Zollverein on payment of
moderate duties. Moreover, France sent goods to the Zollverein not merely across the land frontier but also by sea
through various North Sea ports.[1] In September, 1843, and in
December, 1844, France offered to lower various duties if the
Zollverein would come to terms but Prussia considered that the
proposed concessions were inadequate and in December, 1845,
she announced that she would not enter into negotiations with
France.

Unsatisfactory as were the Zollverein's relations with France
in the 'forties, those with Russia were worse. Since 1836 Russo-
Zollverein commerce had not been regulated by treaty. The
high and prohibitive Russian duties hindered German commerce and conditions on the frontier were thoroughly unsatisfactory. Both economic and political motives lay behind
Russia's determination to reduce German imports as much as

---

[1] See memorandum to the Prussian note to Bresson, March 7, 1843
(printed by A. Zimmermann, pp. 561–85).

possible. Kankrin, the Russian Finance Minister, was pursuing a ruthless mercantilist policy which aimed at making the country self-sufficient. The Czar favoured a reduction of all traffic on the Prussian frontier so as to prevent Poles with revolutionary ideas from entering his own Polish Kingdom. Prussia was able to turn the Czar's fear of revolution to her own advantage. In 1831, after the Polish revolt, Prussia had agreed to an exchange of political fugitives and, since very few Prussians fled to Russia, the main result of the convention was that Prussian frontier officials were kept busy sending Polish refugees back to Russia. This agreement was due to expire in 1842 and Prussia indicated that she would renew it only in return for commercial concessions.

In June, 1842, the Czar announced his intention of lowering the Russian duties on certain Prussian exports including silk, wool and iron. Prussia explained that these reductions would be valueless if they were confined to Prussian products: they must be extended to the goods of all members of the Zollverein. Eventually an agreement was reached in 1844. Russia stated that she would give the benefit of the reduced duties to the Prussian goods in question if they were certified as originating from free internal commerce. Thus, although the Zollverein was not specifically mentioned, its silk, wool and iron exports might enter Russia at the new rates of duty. Prussia reduced her transit dues on Russian cereals coming by river and she renewed the agreement for the exchange of fugitives for twelve years. Trade between Germany and Russia improved a little. In 1850 a new Russian tariff was issued which reduced some duties and in the same year the customs frontier between Russia and Russian Poland was abolished.

Austria, like Russia, remained faithful to her prohibitive system. It has been seen that in October, 1841, Metternich had recognised the desirability of improving commercial relations with the Zollverein. On November 17 a ministerial conference at Vienna decided upon a radical reform of the Austrian tariff. Prohibitions were to be replaced by adequate protective duties and the customs frontier between Austria and Hungary was to be removed. A committee was set up to enquire into the state of Austria's industries. Shortly afterwards it was decided to construct several important railways. By February, 1843, the proposed new tariff had been completed. As soon as the Austrian industrialists heard of the possibility of duties being lowered, they protested vigorously and the plan fell to the ground. Both in Germany and in the Hapsburg Empire the proposed reform of the Austrian tariff and the question of Austria's entry into the Zollverein aroused lively discussion. List, for example, wrote in 1841 that "nothing is so desirable as that the Zollverein and Austria at a later period, after the industry of the Zollverein States has been better developed and has been placed in a position of greater equality to that of Austria, should make, by means of a treaty, reciprocal concessions in respect of their manufactured products".[1] Louis Kossuth, on the other hand, in a series of articles in the Budapest newspaper *Pesti Hirlap*, declared that both from the national and economic standpoint it was not desirable for Hungary to join the Zollverein.[2]

Austria's failure to reform her tariff in the early 'forties made it useless to negotiate with Prussia for a commercial treaty, let alone for an Austro-Zollverein union. There were, however, discussions between the two countries on a minor matter—the future of the free city of Cracow. This remnant of an independent Poland pursued a free-trade policy and had become a centre for smuggling English and German manufactured goods to Russia and Austria-Hungary. From both economic and political motives the Hapsburgs desired to annex Cracow and to include it in their customs system. In April, 1846, Austria, Prussia and Russia agreed to the Austrian occupation of Cracow. Prussia demanded commercial concessions from Austria before consenting to the absorption of the city in the Austrian customs system. Agreement was reached in October, 1847. The Austrian customs regulations regarding the im-

[1] F. List, *The National System of Political Economy*, 1841 (English edition of 1928), p. 348.

[2] L. Kossuth, *Ungarns Anschluss an den deutschen Zollverband* (1842: translated from the Magyar).

portation of Silesian linen yarn and cloth into Bohemia and Moravia were made less restrictive. Local frontier traffic, particularly in agricultural produce, was also facilitated. Prussia thereupon accepted the inclusion of Cracow in the Austrian customs system. Delbrück considered that Austria secured the best of the bargain.[1]

The commercial relations of the Zollverein with other countries were of less importance. Reciprocity treaties were signed with Portugal in 1844 and Sardinia in the following year.[2] (In 1850 Sardinia gave up her differential dues.) Mutual tariff concessions were arranged with Denmark in 1846 and the Sound dues were lowered somewhat.[3] A commercial treaty with the Porte led to a reduction of some Turkish duties.

Prussia signed a commercial treaty with the United States in March, 1844.[4] The United States undertook to reduce her duties on various imports from the Zollverein and, in return, was to secure a reduction of duties on her tobacco and lard. The United States Senate Committee of Foreign Relations, however, received the treaty unfavourably and adjourned further discussion on it by twenty-six votes to eighteen. This was equivalent to rejecting the treaty since the time limit for ratification was running out. Negotiations with Brazil did not lead to the signing of a commercial treaty. But in October, 1847, Brazil decided to levy differential dues against nations which treated her ships less favourably than their own. At the same time she offered to conclude reciprocity treaties with various countries. Prussia accepted the proposal and reciprocal treatment of shipping (excluding coastal trade) was arranged by exchange of notes.[5]

[1] For economic conditions in the Hapsburg Empire see J. Marx in *V.S.W.* XXXI, iii, 1938, pp. 242–82.

[2] The Zollverein-Sardinia commercial and navigation treaty of 1845 is printed by F. A. de Mensch, pp. 233–40.

[3] For the Prussian point of view on the Sound dues, see H. Scherer, *Der Sundzoll...* (1845).

[4] The unratified United States-Zollverein commercial treaty of 1844 is printed by A. Zimmermann, pp. 599–606.

[5] See Declaration by de Moraes in A. Zimmermann, p. 624.

(3) THE STRUGGLE BETWEEN PROTECTIONISTS AND FREE-TRADERS, 1842–1847[1]

It has been seen that after the Napoleonic Wars most of the German States (except Austria) favoured low tariffs since their industries were undeveloped and they exchanged their food-stuffs and raw materials for foreign manufactured articles and colonial products. Even Prussia, which might have set up a high tariff in 1818, levied import duties which were much more moderate than those of any other European Great Power though they were higher than those of her smaller German neighbours. It has been observed, too, that there was some increase in the Prussian tariff in the 'twenties and 'thirties. Certain duties were raised directly. Moreover, since duties were specific, their *ad valorem* rate increased with the fall in prices in this period and after they were levied on the Zollverein hundredweight instead of the heavier Prussian hundredweight some of them were automatically raised a little.

[1] See W. Weber, ch. xxi; H. von Treitschke, v, pp. 448–86; A. Zimmermann, book iv, ch. i; G. Schmoller, "Wandlungen in der europäischen Handelspolitik des 19en Jahrhunderts", in *Schmollers Jahrbuch*, XXIV (1900), pp. 373–82; Max Schippel, *Grundzüge der Handelspolitik* (1902), chs. ii and iii; Percy Ashley, *Modern Tariff History* (1904), part i; R. von Delbrück, chs. vi–viii; K. Rathgen, "Freihandel und Schutzzoll", in *Die Entwicklung der deutschen Volkswirtschaftslehre im neunzehnten Jahrhundert*, essays presented to G. Schmoller on his seventieth birthday (2 vols. 1908; II, ch. xxvii); and documents in A. Schneer, *Aktenstücke betreffend die Differenzial-Zoll-Frage* (1848). For the German protectionists, see F. List, *Werke (Schriften, Reden, Briefe)* (8 vols. 1927–33) and *National System of Political Economy*, 1841 (English translation of 1928); A. Duckwitz, *Denkwürdigkeiten aus meinem öffentlichen Leben von 1841–66* (1877); O. Paulus, *Die Stellung des Rheinlands zur Schutzidee...bis um die Mitte des neunzehnten Jahrhunderts* (1926). The development of free-trade ideas may be studied in John Prince Smith, *Gesammelte Schriften* (3 vols. 1871–80, edited by Michaelis and Braun); L. Grambow, *Die deutsche Freihandelspartei zur Zeit seiner Blüte* (1903); L. Katzenstein, *Die Zeit der preussischen Freihandelspolitik* (1913); and E. Baasch, "Der Verein für Handelsfreiheit in Hamburg, 1848–68", in *Zeitschrift des Vereins für Hamburgische Geschichte*, XXIV (1920), pp. 32–60.

The founding of the Zollverein extended the home market of many German manufacturers and the improvement of communications by roads, inland waterways and railways brought isolated industrial regions like Silesia into closer touch with their customers. Existing manufactures expanded: new industries developed. Industrialists—particularly ironmasters and cotton manufacturers—complained that they had great difficulty in meeting English competition and demanded high protective duties. Bavaria, Württemberg, Silesia and the Rhineland had strong protectionist sympathies. In the Prussian industrial regions there had been requests for protective tariffs in the difficult years that followed the Napoleonic Wars. Bavaria and Württemberg, on the other hand, had changed their views, for in the 'twenties they had objected to joining Prussia's customs system since the tariff was too high.

The leading exponent of protectionist ideas in Germany at this time was List who had already played an important part in agitating for the establishment of economic unity and for the building of railways. In 1841 his *National System of Political Economy* appeared. In this famous work, in his newspaper the *Zollvereinsblatt* and in the Augsburg *Allgemeine Zeitung* List pleaded for the establishment of high protective tariffs in Germany. He made use of two main arguments. First, he put forward the old mercantilist view that the State is the natural unit of economic production. The State should regulate agriculture and industry so as to increase its own power. Individuals might suffer but their interests must give way to those of the whole community. Secondly, he used the "infant industries" argument. He admitted that world free-trade was a worthy ideal but held that it could not be attained so long as England's industries were so powerful in comparison with those of Germany. He observed that Spain in the sixteenth century, Holland in the seventeenth century, England in the late eighteenth and early nineteenth centuries had all attained commercial greatness under the shelter of tariff barriers and navigation laws. Germany's weak struggling industries needed the protection afforded by high import duties so that they could compete on equal terms with English rivals. List was wrong in supposing that Germany could not develop her industries without high protective duties. Without them her manufacturers had made astonishing progress before the revival of protection in 1878. In 1841 List had opposed the imposition of import duties on agricultural produce but in the different circumstances of 1878 the German farmers were as loud as anyone in their demand for protection.

While the rising industrialists were clamouring for protection in the 'forties, substantial merchants and shippers interested in foreign commerce, big agriculturists engaged in the export trade rather than in supplying the home market, and the professional middle classes who regarded the matter from the consumer's point of view, were generally free-traders. While Bavaria and Württemberg were complaining that the Zollverein import duties were too low, the Tax Union, the Mecklenburgs and the Hanse towns declared that they would remain outside the Zollverein so long as its tariff was so high. Prussia continued to favour moderate duties. She had to consider the interests of her agricultural eastern provinces as well as those of her manufacturing districts. She thought, too, that so long as her duties remained fairly low it would be impossible for Austria (with her high tariff) to attempt to enter the Zollverein and to gain a new influence in German economic affairs. One of the leading free-traders in Germany was Prince Smith, an Englishman who had settled in Prussia. Organisations such as the Free-Trade Leagues of Frankfurt-am-Main, Hamburg and Berlin helped to spread free-trade views. The distinctions that have been suggested between regions and classes supporting free-trade and protection are, of course, only rough and ready. The Prussian bureaucracy, for example, was regarded as a firm supporter of moderate as opposed to high duties. Yet there was a sharp division of opinion between the Prussian Ministry of Finance and the Board of Trade (*Handelsamt*) which was established in 1844 under the presidency of von Rönne. The former had much less sympathy with the protectionists than the latter.

It may be observed that there were significant differences between the fiscal controversies in Germany and Britain. In Germany the agricultural districts generally supported free-trade, while the growing industrial centres wanted protection. In Britain the bulk of the landlords and farmers desired to retain protection (particularly the Corn Laws) while important manufacturing regions, such as Lancashire, agitated in favour of free-trade. In both countries, however, manufacturers who did not feel strong enough to face foreign competition tended to favour protective duties. In Germany it was free-traders who were alarmed at the rise of factories and desired to preserve domestic workers—such as handloom weavers—from destruction. In Britain the free-traders regarded the decline of domestic industry as inevitable and it was left to protectionists to plead for its preservation. Again, in Britain the free-traders were on the offensive and the protectionists were defending an old established commercial system. In Germany both parties were on the offensive. The free-traders wanted a lower Zollverein tariff, the protectionists a higher tariff. In Britain the struggle was over fairly quickly. In Germany it was more prolonged. For years Prussia tried to satisfy both parties by lowering a duty here only to raise another elsewhere. Not until the early 'sixties did the German free-traders achieve most of their aims. There were differences, too, in the political outlook of free-traders and protectionists in the two countries. The British free-trader was generally a Radical or a Whig, the protectionist a Tory. In Germany, at any rate in the south, "it was regarded as a truism that every liberal must be a protectionist, and that every free-trader was necessarily a reactionary".[1]

In the 'thirties the opposition between German free-traders and protectionists was not serious and seldom disturbed the deliberations of the Zollverein Congresses. But the uproar over

---

[1] H. von Treitschke, v, p. 451. In the Rhineland the Liberals were divided on the fiscal question. Among the great industrialists, for example, Mevissen and Hansemann were protectionists, while L. Camphausen was a free-trader. Cf. K. Buchheim, *Die Stellung der Kölnischen Zeitung im vormärzlichen rheinischen Liberalismus* (1914), ch. ii, sect. ii, pp. 292–305.

Prussia's concessions to Holland regarding the importation of semi-refined sugar showed that new German industries were becoming strong enough to put pressure on the Zollverein. In the 'forties the matter was brought to a head by the demands of the textile and iron industries for higher import duties.

At this time "the textile industries were the strongest industrial interest which opposed the great landlords".[1] There was a considerable export of German woollen goods in the 'forties. The cotton industry had not attained so important a position in the world market owing to strong English competition. The linen industry was in a very different position. It was "the one manufacture in the Zollverein in which there was a decline in exports between 1836 and 1864".[2] In the 'twenties and 'thirties the German textile weavers used mainly English yarn. Consequently the weaving industry was far more advanced than the spinning industry. The Saxon cotton weavers, for example, secured English yarn on payment of a duty of only 2 thalers per hundredweight but the goods they produced were protected by a tariff of 30 or 40 thalers a hundredweight.[3] The South German spinners complained that they could not compete with their more advanced English rivals and demanded sufficient protection to enable them to capture the home market. Free-traders, on the other hand, criticised a proposal which would raise the price of yarn to the struggling handloom weavers and stocking makers.

At the Stuttgart General Congress of 1842 Bavaria and Württemberg demanded increased import duties on both cotton and linen yarn. Prussia objected and in a memorandum, which was sent to members of the Zollverein, she complained of the

[1] Gertrud Hermes, "Statistische Studien zur wirtschaftlichen und gesellschaftlichen Struktur des zollvereinten Deutschlands", in *Archiv für Sozialwissenschaft und Sozialpolitik*, LXIII (1930), i, p. 136.

[2] *Ibid.* p. 139.

[3] By 1845 "Saxon hosiery had almost driven English out of American and many Continental markets (partly...because of cheapness attained by a very large use of cotton as a material)". Saxon operatives were paid only from 3s. 6d. to 4s. 6d. a week (Alfred Marshall, *Industry and Trade* (edition of 1932), p. 767 n. 2).

attitude of the South German protectionists. The note criticised the South German cotton spinners for their persistent selfish clamour for assistance and their disregard for the interests of other industries and of consumers.[1] The question was discussed at the Zollverein Congresses of 1842 and 1843 but no agreement was reached.

The German iron industry was not so important as the manufacture of textiles in the 'twenties and 'thirties. There was no import duty on pig-iron and only moderate duties on wrought-iron. While German weavers depended to a great extent upon English yarn, German ironworkers preferred native charcoal-smelted iron to English pig-iron smelted with coke or to English bar-iron which had been passed through a reverberatory furnace and had then been puddled and rolled. But in the 'forties came the demand for iron rails in Germany. The German industry was unable to meet the demand and the importation of English pig-iron, wrought-iron and iron rails increased rapidly. While between 1834 and 1839 the amount of foreign iron used in Germany fluctuated between 12 and 24 per cent. of the total consumption, in 1843 no less than 55 per cent. of the iron used in Germany came from abroad.

In the circumstances German ironmasters felt justified in demanding the imposition of an import duty on pig-iron and the raising of existing duties on wrought-iron and iron rails. Prussia opposed their demands. She feared that such duties would lead to a rise in the price of iron goods and consequently to complaints from consumers. Nor did she wish to offend England at a time when a reduction of English import duties seemed possible. At the fifth Zollverein General Congress, which was opened at Stuttgart on July 4, 1842, Nassau proposed that the duties on iron should be raised. Prussia, on the other hand, suggested a reduction of the import duties imposed on certain iron manufactures. Nothing was accomplished. The

[1] The Prussian note of August 25, 1842, was written by Michaelis: extracts are printed by A. Zimmermann, pp. 189–93, and by M. Schippel, pp. 119–21.

question was again discussed at the sixth Congress, which was held in Berlin in 1843.[1] Negotiations were continued after the Congress broke up and agreement was at last reached on duties on iron which came into force on September 1, 1844. Pig-iron paid 10 silver groschens (a shilling) a hundredweight and existing duties on wrought-iron, iron rails and so forth were raised. But on the same day that the new duties came into force, Prussia signed a commercial treaty with Belgium which reduced the import duties on Belgian iron to half the normal rate. The importation of Belgian iron increased and German ironmasters complained of the concession made to a serious foreign competitor.

In March, 1845, von Rönne, President of the Prussian Board of Trade, set up a committee to enquire into the tariff question —apparently without consulting the Ministry of Finance. The manufacturers who were invited to attend were protectionists and the committee's report favoured an increase in textile duties. The seventh Zollverein Congress, which was opened in Carlsruhe in July, had as its chief task the triennial revision of the tariff. It was the stormiest congress in the history of the customs union but the heated debates ended in a deadlock and no far-reaching reform of the tariff was undertaken.[2] It is said that Sir Alexander Malet, the English representative at Carlsruhe, was so delighted that he invited the delegates to a dinner: Radowitz's intervention, however, frustrated his hospitable intentions.[3]

The Prussian point of view on the agitation of the South German protectionists was forcibly repeated in January, 1846, in a circular note to members of the Zollverein.[4] In May there

---

[1] *Verhandlungen*, VI (1843), Hauptprotokoll, sect. xxi.

[2] Lord Westmorland to Lord Aberdeen, Berlin, October 15, 1845 (F.O. 64/258). Cf. H. F. Osiander, "Über den Karlsruher Zollkongress...", in *Konstitutionelle Jahrbücher*, I (1846), pp. 1–77.

[3] W. Weber, p. 229; H. von Treitschke, V, p. 472.

[4] The Prussian note of January 27, 1846, and an accompanying explanatory memorandum are printed by A. Zimmermann, pp. 500–8.

appeared a pamphlet by Kühne entitled *Der deutsche Zollverein während der Jahre* 1834 *bis* 1845 which analysed the financial results of the Zollverein since its establishment. The Zollverein's revenue had increased by 89 per cent. although the population had risen by only 21 per cent. Expenses had declined from a sixth to a twelfth of the revenue.[1] Bavaria's net profit in the years 1834–45 had been 22 million thalers, Württemberg's 10 million, the Thuringian States' nearly 4 million and Baden's over 3 million. This was a timely reproof both to grumblers in the south and to critics nearer home such as von Rönne.[2] Shortly afterwards, at the Berlin Congress, something was done to meet the wishes of the protectionists by raising slightly various duties on textiles (1846).[3]

Meanwhile, Prussia was promoting a scheme which, it was hoped, would receive some support from both protectionists and free-traders. This was a plan to foster German shipping by means of an agreement between the Zollverein and the North German maritime States to levy differential duties against nations—such as Britain—which maintained restrictive navigation laws. A proposal of this sort had been discussed in Hamburg and Bremen a few years before.[4] Burgomaster Smidt of

---

[1] Cf. A. Bienengräber, *Statistik des Verkehrs und Verbrauchs im Zollverein für die Jahre* 1842–64 (1868), p. 14.

[2] This was the view expressed by Trauttmansdorff in a report to Metternich from Berlin, May 5, 1846 (Vienna Archives, Zollvereinsverhandlungen, 1830–47, fasc. 79c). Cf. Lord Westmorland to Lord Aberdeen, May 6, 1846 (F.O. 64/264: English précis of Kühne's book enclosed).

[3] See *Verhandlungen*, VI (1843), Hauptprotokoll, sects. xix, xxii, xxiii, and Beilage ii; VII (1845), Besonderes Protokoll den Vereinszolltarif betreffend, sects. iv, xiii, xv, xviii; VIII (1846), Hauptprotokoll, sects. v, ix, xi, xiii.

[4] For Hamburg see *Die Hansestädte in ihrem Verhältnis zu den Staaten des deutschen Zollvereins* (1839), and C. W. Asher, *Der deutsche Zollverein, die "Augsburger Zeitung" und die neueste englische Zollgesetzgebung* (1841); for Bremen see *Bremische Denkschrift vom* 1. *Juli* 1842, in C. F. Wurm and F. T. Müller, pp. 351–62, and A. Duckwitz, *Der deutsche Handels- und Schiffahrtsbund* (1848).

Bremen had asked both Prussia and Austria to consider such a scheme in 1841–43 and the activities of "this crafty politician"[1] caused some concern to Colonel Hodges, the English Consul-General at Hamburg.

The idea was taken up by German protectionists and also received some support in the North German Press. In Prussia the Board of Trade supported the plan and issued a memorandum on the subject in April, 1845.[2] The Ministry of Finance, however, opposed the scheme.[3]

In March, 1847, a Prussian project of a treaty was produced for establishing a Shipping and Commercial Union between the Zollverein and other States of the Germanic Confederation.[4] Prussia hardly expected that Austria would join but she hoped

[1] The phrase was used by Colonel Hodges in a letter to Lord Aberdeen, May 31, 1842 (F.O. 33/93). Later, Hodges referred to Smidt in less uncomplimentary terms. He wrote to Lord Aberdeen on November 29, 1844, that "Burgomaster Smidt...is deservedly looked up to by the three Hanse Towns as an experienced politician" (F.O. 33/98). See also Colonel Hodges to Lord Aberdeen, April 28, 1846 (F.O. 33/104). Smidt was the far-sighted founder of the Bremen outport of Bremerhaven which was built 35 miles below Bremen on the right bank of the River Weser upon land bought from Hanover (1827).

[2] *Denkschrift des preussischen Handelsamts*, April, 1845, in C. F. Wurm and F. T. Müller, pp. 362–84.

[3] See L. Kühne's criticism of the scheme in *Über Differenzialzölle: nur ein Beitrag zur Beleuchtung dieser Frage für den Zollverein* (1846) and reply by R. von Patow, *Denkschrift betreffend die Begünstigung des direkten Verkehrs zwischen den Staaten des Zollvereins und aussereuropäischen Ländern* (1846: printed by A. Zimmermann, pp. 508–35). These two pamphlets are discussed, from the protectionist point of view, by Heinrich von Arnim, *Ein handelspolitisches Testament* (2nd edition, 1846): English précis enclosed in Lord Westmorland to Lord Aberdeen, March 18, 1846 (F.O. 64/263). The case for differential duties may also be studied in C. H. Carl, *Deutschlands Zolleinigung und Differenzialzölle* (1848) and in the anonymous pamphlets *Zollvereinsfragen Anfang 1846* (Berlin, 1846), and *Verteidigung des für den Zollverein in Vorschlag gebrachtes Differenzialzollgesetzes* (Berlin, 1848); the case against in W. Beer, *Die Gefahren der Differenzialzölle und der Revision des Zoll-Tarifs* (1848).

[4] The Prussian draft treaty is printed by A. Zimmermann, pp. 212–15. Cf. English translation in P.P. 1847–8, LIX.

that it might be possible to secure the adhesion of the North German maritime States. She was especially anxious to secure the co-operation of Hamburg and Bremen. Von Patow visited both towns in 1847 to explain the Prussian point of view to the leading citizens. The influence of Smidt and Duckwitz secured the support of Bremen for the plan.[1] But Hamburg rejected it. A committee of the Hamburg Senate declared that German shipping interests were "not likely to be benefited by this system, in a measure at all comparable to the great development which they have already attained through the unaided exertions of our shipowners". "The increase occasioned in the direct imports of non-European produce would be of very little importance. The import trade in general, on the other hand, would be injured. Transit trade would be greatly endangered. The great German markets (*Weltmärkte*), instead of growing to importance, would on the contrary decline...."[2]

Colonel Hodges suggested that the opposition between Hamburg and Bremen in this matter was due to differences in their commercial relationships with foreign countries. He wrote: "There is, no doubt, a great distinction to be made in the relative interests of Bremen and Hamburg, the trade of the former being principally connected with that of the United States of America, while Hamburg in a far greater degree is dependent on her trade with Great Britain. Bremen is thus enabled without risk to her commercial interests to unite in the popular and national views assumed by Prussia, which distinction between the two towns draws down much odium upon Hamburg for her want of nationality."[3]

In the circumstances Prussia decided to postpone further consideration of the question until it was known whether England was about to repeal her Navigation Laws or not.

[1] A. Duckwitz, *Denkwürdigkeiten*... (1877), pp. 44–57, prints comments by Bremen and Hanover on the Prussian proposal.

[2] *Das Differenzialzollsystem*... (Hamburg, 1847): English translation in P.P. 1847–48, LIX. Cf. F.O. 33/108, Colonel Hodges to Lord Palmerston, July 30 and August 16, 1847.

[3] Colonel Hodges to Lord Palmerston, April 9, 1847 (F.O. 33/108).

At the end of 1847 the South German protectionists had little cause for satisfaction. Several years of intensive propaganda had led to only a slight raising of duties on iron, textiles and a few other imports. The scheme for a shipping union of the Zollverein and the German North Sea States to levy differential dues had fallen through. In Prussia the moderate protectionist views of the Board of Trade had made little headway against the more liberal policy of the Ministry of Finance. List, the inspiring leader of the protectionists, had died by his own hand in November, 1846.

The German free-traders, on the other hand, were more hopeful. They had lost little ground to their rivals. They were heartened by the triumph of free-trade in England. The free-traders of Elbing offered their congratulations to Peel on the repeal of the English Corn Laws.[1] Richard Cobden received an enthusiastic reception from free-traders when he visited Germany in the autumn of 1847.[2] Trauttmansdorff gave Metternich an account of Cobden's reception in Berlin and expressed the opinion that free-trade ideas were gaining ground in Prussia. He added, however, that "the resistance of the protectionists, who have strong support in the South and West of Germany, must be considered and it is consequently impossible to prophesy the course of events".[3]

Trauttmansdorff was right. Even towards the end of 1847 there were few who could have foretold the events of the following year! The revolutions of 1848 led to a reconsideration of the whole question of German economic unity.

[1] The Elbing address of July 14, 1846, and Peel's reply of August 5, 1846, are printed in J. Prince Smith, III, pp. 260 ff.

[2] For Cobden's visit to Germany in 1847, see the extracts from his diary printed by John Morley, *Life of Richard Cobden*, I (2 vols. 1881), pp. 446–50. Cobden wrote on July 31, 1846: "...In the evening attended a public dinner given to me by about 180 free-traders of Berlin, the mayor of the city in the chair; he commenced speaking at the second course and it was kept up throughout the dinner, which was prolonged for nearly three hours...."

[3] Trauttmansdorff to Metternich (Berlin, August 12, 1847) in the Vienna Archives, Zollvereinsverhandlungen, 1830–47, fasc. 79c, no. 129E.

Chapter VI

THE FIRST ZOLLVEREIN CRISIS, 1848–1853

(I) THE FRANKFURT NATIONAL ASSEMBLY AND ECONOMIC PROBLEMS, 1848–1849[1]

At the beginning of 1848 there was serious political and economic unrest in Germany. There was a strong desire not only to secure political rights in various German States but also to obtain a thorough revision of the constitution of the Germanic

[1] For a survey of the literature on the Frankfurt National Assembly, see J. A. Hawgood, "The Frankfurt Parliament of 1848–49", in *History* XVII (July, 1932), pp. 147–51. A standard work on the German revolutions of 1848–49 is Veit Valentein (the younger), *Geschichte der deutschen Revolution, 1848–49* (2 vols. 1930–31). Cf. A. W. Ward, *Germany, 1815–1890*, I (1916), ch. vi. Collections of speeches made at the Assembly have been edited by E. Mollat (1895) and by Paul Wentzcke (1922). For the economic activities of the Assembly, see, for example, H. von Festenburg-Packisch, ch. ix; L. Oelsner, "Die wirtschafts- und sozialpolitischen Verhandlungen des Frankfurter Parlaments", in *Preussische Jahrbücher*, LXXXVII (1897), pp. 81–100; E. Baasch, "Adolph Soetbeer in Frankfurt-am-Main, 1848", in *Hamburgischer Correspondent* (1904), nos. 557, 559, 561; H. Pahl, *Hamburg und das Problem einer deutschen Wirtschaftseinheit im Frankfurter Parlament, 1848–49* (1930); P. Albrecht, *Die volkswirtschaftlichen und sozialen Fragen in der Frankfurter National Versammlung* (1914); W. Schneider, *Wirtschafts- und Sozialpolitik im Frankfurter Parlament* (1923); and the documents printed in *Die Resultate der Beratungen der Regierungs-Kommissaire in Frankfurt-am-Main, 1848–49, zur Herstellung der Zolleinheit im Deutschen Reiche* (Halle-an-der-Saale, 1851). See also Karl Marx, *Revolution and Counter Revolution; or Germany in 1848* (edited by Eleanor Max Aveling: edition of 1937). For an examination of the introduction and meaning of the terms *Grossdeutsch* and *Kleindeutsch* in 1848–49, see Heidrun von Möller, *Grossdeutsch und Kleindeutsch. Die Entstehung der Worte in den Jahren 1848–49* (1937). For Britain's attitude to German unity at this time, see Hans Pecht, *Englands Stellung zur deutschen Einheit, 1848–50* (1925), part ii, ch. iv.

Confederation. Reactionary rulers, such as the King of Hanover, were faced with demands for the establishment of a constitution, the freedom of the Press, the right of free assembly,
and the introduction of trial by jury. Many reformers looked
beyond the frontiers of their own States and advocated the re-
placement of the existing weak Confederation by a strong
central German executive authority.

The existence of social—as distinct from political—unrest
was hardly surprising. It has been seen that, despite the economic benefits secured by the establishment and extension of
the Zollverein, there was still much economic distress in
Germany. The economic crisis of 1847 showed that Germany
could not escape from the periodic slumps of the kind that had
afflicted British industry at fairly regular intervals in the last
seventy years or so.[1] Some factory workers were beginning to
demand a share in the profits of industry. German emigration
in 1848–54 was due less to political causes than to unsatisfactory
conditions in certain agricultural districts. Political revolution
and reaction occurred all over Germany, yet emigration was
mainly from the south-west. Here agricultural arrangements
were still largely feudal. But the medieval agrarian system was
being undermined by the division of common lands and the
decrease of the forests. The small peasant proprietors were thus
losing rights of pasture and the sources of their supply of fuel.
But, on the whole, their standard of living was rising and they
chafed against the game laws and other feudal disabilities. The
position in 1848 was aggravated by the failure of the potato
crop. Peasants were not merely short of food but had no money
to pay interest on loans contracted a year or two before—when
failures of commercial houses had led lenders to invest in agriculture. To add to this distress came the cholera epidemic of
1849.[2]

[1] For an account of economic and social distress in Prussia between
1845 and 1849, see Hugo C. M. Wendel, *The Evolution of Industrial
Freedom in Prussia*, 1845–49 (New York University Press, 1921), ch. ii.

[2] See M. L. Hansen, "German Emigration in the 'Fifties (1848–54)",

The revolution in Paris in February, 1848, which led to the fall of Louis Philippe and the establishment of the second French Republic, was the signal for risings in many of the German middle and small States. In Bavaria, King Ludwig abdicated and Lola Montez (his unpopular mistress) left the country. In Hesse-Darmstadt the reactionary Grand Duke had to allow Heinrich von Gagern to form a ministry and in Hesse-Cassel the Elector was forced to grant a Liberal constitution. The Duke of Nassau tried to placate his exasperated subjects by declaring his extensive domains to be State property. In Württemberg a rising was suppressed but a reformer (Friedrich Römer) was admitted to the cabinet. The obstinate King of Hanover had to grant a constitution. In Saxony reforms were promised. There were risings, too, in many of the smaller States and various concessions were granted.

A rising in Vienna led to the resignation of Metternich, who went into exile in London. Before the end of 1848 Austria was engaged in putting down risings in North Italy and in Hungary. In Prussia there were riots in Berlin and a Liberal Ministry was appointed. The King exasperated his followers by his inability to make up his mind what to do and he eventually retired to Potsdam. The unpopular Crown Prince went to England.

Having secured a considerable measure of success in various States, German reformers turned to the problem of establishing a greater measure of national unity than had been secured under the Confederation of 1815. A preliminary parliament (*Vorparlament*), which met at Frankfurt-am-Main on March 31, 1848, arranged for elections throughout Germany to choose representatives for a single-chamber national assembly.

On May 13, the National Assembly met in the Pauluskirche at Frankfurt-am-Main. It appointed an Imperial Vicar (*Reichs-*

in *Journal of Economic and Business History* (August, 1930), pp. 630 ff. J. Kuczynski's cost of living index for Germany (base year 1900, 100) in the 'forties is as follows: 1840, 53; 1845, 57; 1847, 79; 1850, 49 (*Labour Conditions in Western Europe* (1937), p. 94.)

verweser) to whom the old Federal Diet handed its powers. Much time was spent in debates on the fundamental rights of the German people and then the labours of the Assembly were interrupted by the Schleswig-Holstein crisis[1] and by riots in Frankfurt.[2] In October, 1848, the Assembly resumed its discussions of the proposed constitution for the whole of Germany. It is not necessary to deal with these proceedings, for the constitution never came into force. The blunders of the Assembly itself, the hostility of Austria and the lack of adequate support from Prussia all contributed to the failure of the labours of those assembled at Frankfurt.

The economic activities of the Assembly deserve notice. Although 564 members belonged to the professional classes (Civil Servants, lawyers, university teachers, doctors) and only 77 were engaged in agricultural, commercial or industrial pursuits, economic affairs were not neglected. An economic committee (*volkswirtschaftlicher Ausschuss*) of 30 members was set up. Its first chairman was von Rönne, who had been in charge of the Prussian Board of Trade. He was succeeded by Eisenstück, a prominent Saxon industrialist. The vice-chairman was Bruck, who was to play an important part in Austrian and German economic affairs in the next few years. These three men were protectionists. So were two other leading members of the committee—von Mevissen, the Rhineland industrialist, and Karl Mathy, the Baden Minister of Finance and Commerce. The discussions of the committee show how strong was the influence of List's ideas upon its members. The debates also indicate that there was a strong feeling in the committee in favour of the economic unification of Germany. It was held

---

[1] The Danish blockade of the Elbe during the Schleswig-Holstein War of 1848 injured German commerce and also hampered the export of English textiles to Central Europe. See *Memorial of the Manchester Chamber of Commerce to Lord Aberdeen on the Interruption of British Commerce owing to the Danish War of 1848* (M.Ch.C. May 4, 1848).

[2] R. Schwemer, *Geschichte der Freien Stadt Frankfurt-am-Main, 1814–66*, III (1915), part i, pp. 210–43.

not merely that the whole of Germany should be included in a single customs union but that sea and river shipping, postal arrangements, coinage and so forth should all come under a unified central control.[1]

Prussia followed with close attention the discussions of the Frankfurt Assembly's proposals for absorbing the Zollverein in a larger customs union. That Prussia recognised the importance of setting her own house in order as far as economic affairs were concerned may be seen from the fact that a Ministry of Commerce was set up in April, 1848. The recently established Board of Trade and two departments of the Ministry of Finance were absorbed by the new Ministry. Four Ministers of Commerce—von Patow, Milde, von Bonin and Pommer-Esche—were appointed between April and November, 1848, but in December the post was given to von der Heydt, the head of an old-established Elberfeld banking house which was interested in industrial enterprises. He held the post for nearly fourteen years.[2]

The Zollverein General Congress, which should have met in 1848 to settle the tariff for the years 1849 to 1851, was postponed. In August, 1848, however, expert commissioners (*Regierungs-Kommissaire*) from the German States arrived in Frankfurt-am-Main to assist the Assembly in its economic deliberations,[3] and the opportunity was taken to hold an extraordinary meeting of representatives of Zollverein States. Prussia proposed various reductions in the tariff. Bavaria was prepared to accept them but Württemberg was not. So in

[1] P. Albrecht, pp. 8–17.

[2] Lord Bloomfield stated in 1851 that von der Heydt "is not considered a person of talent and has no influence in the Cabinet, where he occupies a place solely as the representative of the manufacturing interests" (Lord Bloomfield to Lord Palmerston, September 18, 1851: F.O. 64/332). For von der Heydt's work as Minister of Commerce, see A. Bergengrün, *Staatsminister August Freiherr von der Heydt* (1908).

[3] See *Die Resultate der Beratungen der Regierungs-Kommissaire in Frankfurt-am-Main, 1848–49, zur Herstellung der Zolleinheit im Deutschen Reiche* (Halle-an-der-Saale, 1851).

October, 1848, it was agreed to prolong the existing tariff indefinitely.[1]

The deliberations of the National Assembly continued in 1849 and in March a draft German constitution was issued. It provided that the Reich "shall be united for purposes of commerce and tariffs and shall be surrounded by a common customs frontier. All internal dues shall be abolished." But "the Federal authority may exclude certain places and districts from the customs union".[2] The Federal authority alone was to legislate on the customs administration and on common taxes and excises. It could regulate and supervise the collection of these dues. "A fixed portion of the customs revenue shall be used to defray the normal expenses of the Federal Budget. The remainder shall be divided among the separate States. A special Federal Law will regulate this." Navigation on German rivers was to be freed from transit dues. Charges made at harbours and locks were not to exceed the cost of the services rendered to shippers.[3]

These proposals were not carried into effect. The German Constitution of March, 1849, remained a dead letter. In April the King of Prussia virtually rejected the Federal Assembly's

[1] The transactions of this extraordinary meeting of Zollverein States were not published in the regular series of proceedings of General Congresses but were issued separately—*Verhandlungen der in den Jahren 1848 und 1849 zu Frankfurt-am-Main abgehaltenen Konferenz in Zollvereinsangelegenheiten* (Frankfurt-am-Main, 1849).

[2] For a discussion of the desirability of making Hamburg a free port, see, for example, the anonymous pamphlets—*Die deutsche Handels- und Zollverfassung und das Freihafensystem. Mit besonderer Rücksicht auf Hamburg* (Frankfurt-am-Main, 1848) (supported free port) and *Kann bei einer einheitlichen Handels- und Zollverfassung Hamburg aus der deutschen Zollinie ausgeschlossen bleiben?* (Frankfurt-am-Main, 1848) (criticised free port proposal).

[3] Draft Federal Constitution, 1849, part ii, sects. xxiv–xxvii (rivers), and xxxiii–xxxvii (customs and excise), printed in *Die Resultate der Beratungen der Regierungs-Kommissaire in Frankfurt-am-Main, 1848–1849, zur Herstellung der Zolleinheit im Deutschen Reiche* (Halle-an-der-Saale, 1851), pp. 1, 368.

offer of the German Crown, for he stated that his decision must depend upon the views of other German sovereigns. By the end of 1849 the Imperial Vicar had handed over his powers to Austria and Prussia. The attempt of the National Assembly to establish a unified Germany with a parliamentary government had failed.

(2) ECONOMIC REORGANISATION OF THE HAPSBURG EMPIRE, 1849–1852[1]

In October, 1849, a fresh and important proposal for the economic unification of Germany was made. This was Karl Ludwig Freiherr von Bruck's scheme for a customs union which should include the whole of the Germanic Confederation and the Hapsburg Empire.

Bruck was born in Elberfeld. But, unlike his fellow-townsman von der Heydt, who had made his reputation in the Rhineland, Bruck had left Germany as a young man and had settled in Triest. There he took a leading part in founding the Austrian Lloyd shipping company.

Bruck recognised that the Mediterranean was at last beginning to recover some of the importance that it had had before the opening of the great trade routes round the Cape of Good Hope to India and across the Atlantic to America. He hoped to see the Hapsburg Empire dominating the commerce of the Eastern Mediterranean[2] and helping to develop Egypt and the Levant.

---

[1] See *Ungarn und seine Zoll-Zwischenlinie* (anonymous pamphlet, Prague, 1844); G. von Höfken, *Die Reform des österreichischen Zollwesens und die österreichisch-deutsche Zolleinigung* (1850); Karl Czörnig, *Österreichs Neugestaltung, 1848–58* (1858); Alexander (Sándor) Matlekovits, *Die Zollpolitik der österreichungarischen Monarchie von 1850 bis zur Gegenwart* (1877), pp. 1–17; K. Mamroth, *Die Entwicklung der österreichisch-deutschen Handelsbeziehungen . . .* (1887), pp. 2–65; L. Láng, *Hundert Jahre Zollpolitik* (1906), pp. 182–204; R. Sieghart, *Zolltrennung und Zolleinheit. Die Geschichte der österreichisch-ungarischen Zwischenzoll-Linie* (1915), and A. Beer, ch. v.

[2] J. R. McCulloch observed in 1847 that "since the loss of Flanders the mercantile navy of Austria has been confined wholly to the ports of

He saw the possibility of turning Triest into a great port on the route from Britain to India. Triest did benefit from the activity of the Austrian Lloyd but it failed to secure the English passenger and mail traffic to India. After 1854 this traffic went through France to Marseilles and then by sea to Alexandria.[1]

Bruck had won the reputation of being one of the ablest leaders in the growing Austrian world of commerce. He considered that the vast economic potentialities of Central Europe could be adequately developed only by the formation of an Austro-German customs union which would encourage industry by adopting a policy of protection.[2] His interest in

the Adriatic. But it is, notwithstanding, very considerable and engrosses at this moment a very large share of the trade of the Mediterranean and Black Sea..." (*Dictionary of Commerce*, edition of 1847, II, p. 1297). Cf. "Triest and the Participation of Austria in the Commerce of the World during the last ten Years, 1832–41", in *The Merchants' Magazine and Commercial Review*, New York, x, pp. 495–521; translation of article in the *Journal des Österreichischen Lloyds*.

[1] This was fifteen years before the opening of the Suez Canal. As Dr Fay points out, "the canal was thus the culmination of change, rather than the starting point of it" (*Imperial Economy* (1934), p. 116).

[2] In the 'forties there had been numerous suggestions in books, pamphlets and in the Press that the Zollverein should be expanded into a Central European customs union by securing the adhesion of the Hapsburg dominions, the Tax Union and other North German maritime States and even small neighbouring countries such as Holland, Belgium, Denmark and Switzerland. List advocated an Austro-Zollverein union in his paper the *Zollvereinsblatt* (1843, no. 15, pp. 225–37, and no. 16, pp. 241–8, reprinted in *Schriften, Reden, Briefe*, VII (1931), pp. 186–92) and elsewhere. Gustav Höfken, who later served under Bruck in the Austrian Ministry of Commerce, expressed somewhat similar views in *Der deutsche Zollverein in seiner Fortbildung* (1842). Several articles in the Augsburg *Allgemeine Zeitung*, the *Deutsche Vierteljahrschrift* (both published by Cotta) and the *Kölnische Zeitung* (then edited by Karl Andree) supported the idea of Austro-Zollverein union. Moritz Mohl (the Württemberg particularist) in twenty-three articles in the Augsburg *Allgemeine Zeitung* in 1842 regarded the question mainly from the point of view of the South German manufacturers. Gustav von Mevissen (a leading Rhineland industrialist) mentioned the desirability of certain Hapsburg provinces—

List's views on protection may be seen from the fact that the *Journal des Österreichischen Lloyds* published in 1843 a series of articles favouring protection on the lines suggested by List. The influence of List's ideas may be seen on almost every page of the memoranda which Bruck wrote a few years later in favour of an Austro-German customs union.

It has been seen that Bruck was a member of the economic committee of the Frankfurt National Assembly. In November, 1848, he was appointed Austrian Minister of Commerce and he soon brought into the field of practical politics his plans for the economic unification of Austria and Germany.

Bruck recognised that it would be necessary to abolish the Austro-Hungarian customs frontier and to reform the prohibitive Hapsburg tariff before there could be any hope of negotiating for union with the Zollverein. The maintenance of the internal customs frontier had been inevitable so long as the systems of taxation of Austria and Hungary were so different. In Austria direct taxation took the form of a land-tax. Indirect taxation was levied by monopolies on salt and tobacco, by taxes on imports and exports and by excises on wines, spirits, meat and other articles. Hungary, on the other hand, had virtually no land-tax and had no tobacco monopoly, while her excises were levied upon different articles from those in Austria. The prices charged for salt were different in various parts of Austria and Hungary. The internal customs frontier had therefore been maintained.

The existence of this frontier explains to some extent the failure of early attempts to modify the strictness of the Austrian prohibitive system and to improve commercial relations with German States. It has been seen that Metternich's attempts in

---

particularly Bohemia—adhering to the Zollverein (in a letter written early in 1848 to Anton Freiherr von Doblhoff and printed by J. Hansen, *Gustav von Mevissen*, II (1906), pp. 319–23). These and many other writings in the 'forties on the establishment of an economic "Mitteleuropa" are discussed by Otto Wagner, *Mitteleuropäische Gedanken und Bestrebungen in den vierziger Jahren*, 1840–48 (Marburg, 1935: Dissertation).

the 'thirties and 'forties to secure the carrying out of Article 19 of the Federal Act and to improve economic relations with the Zollverein had met with little success. Even in the summer of 1848 when the expert commissioners from German States were discussing at Frankfurt the setting up of a customs union for the whole of Germany, the Austrian delegate (Freiherr von Geringef) stated that Austria could not join such a union and took no further part in the conference.

But the Austro-Hungarian customs frontier was abolished in 1850, the prohibitive Hapsburg tariff in 1852. For many years the Magyars had protested that their economic interests were being sacrificed to those of Austria: time and time again they demanded the removal of the frontier. In September, 1844, the Hungarian Protection League (*Schutzverein*) was founded to encourage the development of native manufactures and its hundred thousand members pledged themselves to use as far as possible only the products of Hungarian industry.[1] A month later the Hungarian Estates petitioned the Emperor in favour of a reform of the tariff and the abolition of the customs frontier.[2]

It was abolished, however, in circumstances very different from those of 1844. In 1848 Hungary rose in revolt only to be defeated by the Austrians with the help of a Russian army. The Magyars capitulated at Világos on August 13, 1849, and their political liberties were drastically curtailed. Hungary's financial independence was swept aside. Her customs administration was dissolved and her landed aristocracy lost its freedom from taxation. She had to accept the detested tobacco monopoly. All the Hapsburg dominions were organised as a single customs area (June, 1850). Although this arrangement was far from being acceptable to Magyar patriots, Hungary made considerable economic progress in the 'fifties and 'sixties. When her political

---

[1] See *Aktenstücke zur Geschichte des ungarischen Schutzvereins* (Leipzig, 1847).

[2] The petition of the Hungarian Estates is reprinted by R. Sieghart, pp. 146–52.

liberties were restored in 1867, she retained the customs union with Austria although she was then strong enough to repudiate it had she wished.

The ground had been prepared for a change from prohibitions to protection by the writings of List and other economists. A number of manufacturers, too, recognised that Austrian industry was no longer so helpless that it had to avoid foreign competition at all costs. They expected adequate protective duties but they were prepared to dispense with the prohibition of many imports. A commission was set up early in 1849 to reform the Austrian customs system, and on February 1, 1852, the new tariff came into force. It was considerably simplified and duties replaced prohibitions both with regard to exports and imports. Import duties were somewhat reduced but were still high. Export and transit dues were often so low as to be merely nominal. Differential duties, bounties and drawbacks were not normal features of the new tariff.[1]

The revision of the Austrian tariff and customs administration was only a part of the administrative reforms undertaken in the Hapsburg dominions at this time. Bruck was closely associated both with the setting up of the Austrian Ministry of Commerce and the improvement of communications. The new Ministry was organised in four departments—foreign trade, internal commerce, the carrying out of commercial legislation,

---

[1] The following examples of reductions made in the Austrian tariff of 1852—in florins (2s. 1d.) per hundredweight—are taken from A. Matlekovits, pp. 16–17.

	Before Reduction	After Reduction
Tea	90	15
Sugar	16	14
Cotton yarn (unbleached)	10	7
Cotton goods (average)	116	75
Woollen goods (average)	183	75
Silk goods	1000	600

The province of Dalmatia, however, retained the highly protective tariff of 1830 (A. Matlekovits, p. 41).

and the drawing up of new laws.[1] Bruck encouraged railway construction. Austrian shipping—both on the sea and on inland waterways—was fostered. The Austrian postal system was reformed and postage was reduced. A postal convention was signed between Austria and Prussia, and other German States adhered to it. The network of telegraphs in Austria was extended.

Bruck regarded all these reforms as necessary preliminaries to economic union with Germany.[2] But he did not wait until they were completed before pressing forward with his plans for "Mitteleuropa". This was doubtless advisable in view of the leisurely pace at which Austrian officialdom proceeded, but the fact that reforms often existed only on paper placed Bruck at a disadvantage during discussions with German States. In the critical years of negotiations Bruck could draw rosy pictures of the reformed economic organisation of the Hapsburg dominions in the near future but he could point to few reforms that were actually working. The new Austrian tariff was not brought into operation until some months after his resignation.

These reforms had largely been made possible by the revolution of 1848 and by the subsequent reaction which had crushed political opposition and led to the temporary impotence of Hungary. Similarly, revolution and reaction in Germany appeared to pave the way for economic change. Schwarzenberg, no unworthy successor to Metternich, became Austrian Chancellor in November, 1848, and was determined to recover for the Hapsburg Empire her dominant political position in Germany. This he did by the Convention of Olmütz (November 29, 1850) when Prussia gave up her attempt to secure political

---

[1] The Austrian Ministry of Commerce was abolished in 1859 and its functions were shared among other Government departments. The Ministry of Finance, for example, took charge of the railways, the post office and telegraphs.

[2] H. Friedjung, "Mitteleuropäische Zollunionspläne, 1849–53", in *Historische Aufsätze* (1919), p. 65. With pardonable exaggeration he refers to Bruck's reforms as an achievement "almost equal to the founding of the German Zollverein".

leadership in a reorganised Germany and agreed to Austria's proposal that the Germanic Confederation should be re-established in its old form. Schwarzenberg followed up this success by attempting to deprive Prussia of her leadership in German economic affairs. The Zollverein treaties were due to expire at the end of 1853 and Schwarzenberg planned to absorb the Zollverein into a wider customs union in which Prussia could play only a subordinate role. It was with this end in view that he sponsored Bruck's schemes. Schwarzenberg and Bruck both favoured an Austro-German customs union but their objects were very different. Schwarzenberg was preparing for a new political triumph over Prussia but Bruck was thinking of the economic future of the seventy million inhabitants of a great Central European customs union. Schwarzenberg died in April, 1852—too early to achieve his purpose—and Bruck (already out of office) was able to secure only a very modest instalment of his far-reaching plans.

(3) BRUCK'S PLANS FOR MITTELEUROPA, 1849–1851[1]

The first sketch in broad outline of Bruck's scheme for an Austro-German customs union appeared in an article in

[1] A list of books and articles on various proposals for the economic unification of Central Europe has been compiled by Imre Barcza, *Bibliographie der Mitteleuropäischen Zollunionsfrage* (Budapest, 1917). For plans in the 'forties to secure greater political and economic unity in central Europe, see Otto Wagner, *Mitteleuropäische Gedanken und Bestrebungen in den vierziger Jahren*, 1840–48 (Marburg, 1935: Dissertation). Bruck's career and projects are described by Richard Charmatz, *Minister Freiherr von Bruck. Der Vorkämpfer Mitteleuropas* (Leipzig, 1916). Careful studies of Austro-Zollverein relations between 1849 and 1853 are those of Alfred Gaertner, *Zollverhandlungen zwischen Österreich und Preussen von 1849 bis Olmütz* (1908), and *Der Kampf um den Zollverein zwischen Österreich und Preussen von 1849 bis 1853* (*Strassburger Beiträge zur neueren Geschichte*, 1911). Contemporary accounts include K. D. H. Rau, "Über die Krisis des Zollvereins im Sommer 1852" and "Die Krisis der Zollunion", in *Rau und Hanssens Archiv der politischen Ökonomie* (1853); Bamberg, "Le Zollverein et l'Union Douanière Austro-Allemande", in *Revue des Deux Mondes*, XVI (October, 1852), pp. 356–88. See also

the official newspaper, the *Wiener Zeitung*, on October 26, 1849.[1]

Bruck pointed out that Austria, the Zollverein and the North German States which were not members of the Zollverein all needed commercial reforms and he advocated union in order to attain them. He suggested that union should be brought about in four stages. In the first period there should be "mutual internal tariff reform". The Austrian prohibitive system was being replaced by protective duties and it was hoped that the Zollverein would raise its duties so that there would be closer approximation between the two tariffs. "Native raw materials, food and unworked metals" should be exchanged without payment of duty. In the second period "the duties on manufactured articles exchanged between Austria and Germany will be mutually reduced to three-quarters of the normal rate levied on foreign goods". The third stage would see those duties reduced to "a half of the normal rates on foreign goods". In the fourth period there would be a further reduction of these duties to a quarter of the normal rates. Finally, there would be a new treaty for assimilating German tariffs.

W. Weber, chs. xxi–xxviii; H. von Festenberg-Packisch, ch. x; Alfred Zimmermann, book v; Adolf Beer, ch. vi, and A. Sartorius von Waltershausen, pp. 152–6. For the Prussian point of view, see Rudolph von Delbrück, I, chs. ix–xiv and Alexander Bergengrün, ch. vi. For Austria's point of view see Otto Hübner, *Die Zolleinigung und die Industrie des Zollvereins und Österreichs* (1850); Karl Hock, "Die Verhandlungen über ein österreichisch-deutsches Zollbündnis, 1849–64", in *Österreichische Revue*, III (1864), pp. 39–75; J. Frühauf, "Das Projekt einer Zollunion Österreichs mit Deutschland...", in *Unsere Zeit* (1866), and K. T. Helfferich, *Mitteleuropas Vorkämpfer. Fürst Felix zu Schwarzenberg* (1933); D. C. Long, "Efforts to secure an Austro-German Customs Union in the Nineteenth Century" in *University of Michigan Historical Essays* (University of Michigan Press, 1937: edited by A. E. R. Boak), pp. 45–74. For a brief survey of central European problems in the nineteenth century, see W. O. Henderson, "Germany and Mitteleuropa", in *German Life and Letters*, II, iii (April, 1938), pp. 161–74.

[1] Reprinted by Richard Charmatz, pp. 157–63. The original draft of this article is in Gustav von Höfken's handwriting and is preserved in the Vienna Archives (*Nachlass Höfken*, Schriften i).

Miles
0 50 100 150

Unattached

TAX
UNION

ZOLLVEREIN

HAPSBURG
EMPIRE

Austro-Hungarian
customs frontier
abolished 1850

R.C.

9. Bruck's proposed Austro-German Customs Union, 1849.

Bruck considered that there would be three advantages in forming an Austro-German customs union. First, there would be an increase in customs revenue owing to the reduction of smuggling and the saving of certain administrative costs. Secondly, industries would benefit by securing new markets. Thirdly, the new customs union would be stronger politically than the existing separate German commercial groups.

This article aroused discussion in the Austrian and German Press but in official circles there were doubts whether the proposals were seriously meant. It seemed curious that the first indication of the Austrian intentions on so important a matter should appear in a newspaper article. But there were two Prussian officials who did take Bruck seriously. They were Count Bernstorff[1], the Prussian Ambassador in Vienna, and Rudolf von Delbrück who, though only thirty-one years of age, held an important position in the Prussian Ministry of Commerce.

In Delbrück, Bruck met an opponent of his own intellectual calibre, an astute negotiator and a hard bargainer. Delbrück had a thorough knowledge of economic conditions in Germany and Austria. He saw at once both the strength and the weakness of Bruck's programme and from the first he was determined to defeat any scheme which might injure Prussia's political and economic interests. Delbrück replied to Bruck's *Wiener Zeitung* article in the official *Preussischer Staatsanzeiger* on November 7, 1849.[2] He welcomed attempts to reduce smuggling and proposals for co-operation on coinage, railways, postal arrangements and so forth but he rejected as impracticable the proposal to set up an Austro-German customs union. He pointed out how different were the tariffs of the various German customs areas and observed that it would be difficult for Austria to join a wider customs union so long as her tobacco monopoly remained in force. Nevertheless, at Delbrück's suggestion, the

---

[1] For Bernstorff see Karl Ringhoffer, *The Bernstorff Papers* (2 vols. 1908).

[2] Delbrück states in his memoirs (1, p. 251) that he wrote the article himself. A. Zimmermann (p. 350) ascribes it to von der Heydt.

Prussian Government approached Austria and offered to negotiate on the questions raised in Bruck's article.

This prompt action forced the Austrian Government to show
its hand more clearly and Bruck produced an official memorandum on the proposed Austro-German customs union (December 30, 1849).[1] He now suggested that the transitional
period before the establishment of the union should be as short
as possible and that its four intermediate stages might be reduced to two. He claimed that Austria's contribution to the
reforms of the first period of transition—the revision of her
tariff—removed "every doubt as to her determination to
achieve German economic unity".

Bruck attempted to convince his opponents that they would
receive ample compensation for any disadvantages that might
result from adhering to the union. Austria would benefit
financially and her industries "will be encouraged and have their
deficiencies made good by German industries to which they in
their turn will prove a stimulus; and—strengthened by a protective commercial system in the extended area at their disposal
—they will soon be able to face all foreign competition of the
world market". The Zollverein manufacturers would secure
the advantages of greater protection against foreign competition
and a wider market for their goods. Bruck observed that "the
draft German tariff...drawn up by the General German Union
for the Protection of Home Industries (*Allgemeiner deutscher
Verein zum Schutze der vaterländischen Arbeit*)[2]...is based upon

[1] Reprinted by R. Charmatz, pp. 163–77.

[2] The constitution of this protectionist association (November 9,
1848) is reprinted by Friedrich Lenz, *Friedrich List. Der Mann und das
Werk* (1936), pp. 422–6. See also *Zoll-Tariff für Deutschland vorgeschlagen
vom Allgemeinen deutschen Vereine zum Schutze der vaterländischen Arbeit*
(Frankfurt-am-Main, 1849). In the introduction to this proposed tariff
it was stated that "a tariff which failed to satisfy Austria's interests would
divide Germany more sharply than any other event of recent times for
it would also alienate the interests and sympathy of the South-East and
would perhaps destroy the last means of linking together the two great
parts of the nation" (p. 11).

the same principles and the same system of scientific gradation as the Austrian tariff". He criticised the existing Zollverein tariff since "the protective element is completely sacrificed for the sake of simplicity". The North German States were told frankly that they must give up their low import duties since "the need of Austrian and German manufacturers for protection...must be satisfied if the Austro-German customs union is ever to be formed". But by joining this union the North German coastal States would obtain uninterrupted access to the whole of Central Europe and would "secure the advantages of the respectful treatment of their flags on all seas, the greater facility for concluding favourable commercial and shipping treaties and the security of their trade...".

The Prussian Government, in a note of February 28, 1850, maintained the position that Delbrück had indicated in the *Preussischer Staatsanzeiger*—no Austro-German customs union but readiness to negotiate on other matters. Delbrück himself was sent to Vienna early in March, 1850, to learn the views of the leading Austrian statesmen. He was impressed by Bruck who might have been prepared to open then those direct negotiations with Prussia which were in fact undertaken nearly three years later. But after he had seen Prince Schwarzenberg, Delbrück recognised how different was the policy of the Chancellor from that of his Minister of Commerce. Schwarzenberg spoke glibly of entering into discussions with all German States for the formation of a new customs union on the basis of Article 19 of the Federal Act and he obviously regarded plans for an Austro-German customs union simply as a means of weakening Prussia.

Delbrück was therefore anxious to strengthen Prussia's position in the Zollverein by attempting to placate the protectionist malcontents and he prepared a scheme for tariff reform which included the raising of the import duties on linen, woollen and cotton yarns and the granting of drawbacks on the export of articles manufactured from such yarns. The proposals were to be submitted to the next Zollverein General Congress at Cassel early in July, 1850. Schwarzenberg, on the other hand, was anxious to induce the middle States of South and Central Germany—particularly Bavaria, Württemberg, Baden, and Saxony—to support at this congress the Austrian plan for an Austro-German customs union.

Bruck once more explained this scheme in a long memorandum (of May 30, 1850) which elaborated many of the arguments previously used in its favour.[1] The memorandum broke new ground in its detailed description of the proposed administrative organs of the new union. Hitherto Bruck seems to have envisaged a union between Austria, the Zollverein, the Tax Union and such German States as were not in any customs union. Each of these customs areas would maintain its own organisation and the necessary financial and administrative adjustments would be made by consultation between them. But now there were few references to the existing customs areas and it was apparently assumed that they would disappear and that the administrative organs of the revived Germanic Confederation and the proposed Austro-German customs union would be linked as closely as possible.

The central authority of the new economic federation was to have wide powers. It would determine the tariff; regulate the customs administration; appoint consuls abroad; conclude commercial and navigation treaties with foreign Powers; and supervise shipping, railways and postal and telegraph services[2]

---

[1] Reprinted by R. Charmatz, pp. 177–241. Bruck's *Wiener Zeitung* article of October 26, 1849, and his memoranda of December, 1849, and May, 1850, were published in book form in Vienna and Leipzig in 1850. See also G. Rigaud, *Bemerkungen über die Österreichische Denkschrift...* (1850), H. von Langermann, "Zwei Staatsdokumente zum Problem des mitteleuropäischen Wirtschaftsbündnisses", in *Deutsche Revue*, LXI (1916), pp. 205 ff. and H. von Srbik, *Mitteleuropa* (1938), p. 23.

[2] It may be observed that shortly before the issue of Bruck's memorandum, Austro-Prussian negotiations for a postal convention (initiated by von der Heydt) were successfully concluded. A postal convention was signed on April 6, 1850, and all German States (except Holstein and Luxemburg) adhered to it. Prepaid letters could now be sent between almost all parts of Germany and Austria by the shortest route. Hitherto

throughout the customs union "without itself taking a direct part in the administration of these services".

There was to be an advisory Federal Council for Commerce and Shipping composed of a large council to be summoned annually and a subcommittee in permanent session. The main Council would consist of representatives selected by Chambers of Commerce and of persons nominated by State Governments. Its function should be to report to the central authority on commercial matters. The duty of the subcommittee should be to "prepare work for the main Council and to assist it in carrying out its decisions". A Federal Minister of Commerce should be appointed and a Federal Statistical Bureau set up.

Thus, on the eve of the ninth Zollverein General Congress the aims of Austria and Prussia had been clearly stated. Austria favoured the creation of an Austro-German customs union. Prussia offered no more than an Austro-Zollverein commercial treaty. The position of the smaller German States was less plain. As far as possible they avoided coming to any decision but hoped to make satisfactory terms—especially financial terms—for themselves by playing off one German Great Power against another.

The Zollverein General Congress was opened at Cassel on July 7, 1850. Delbrück suggested various increases in the tariff in the hope of placating the southern States. The proposed raising of import duties on cotton, linen and woollen yarn brought a protest from Britain.[1] Palmerston declared that since

the sender had paid the cost of transport in the postal area in which the letter was posted: the recipient had paid the charges incurred in crossing other postal areas. An Austro-Prussian telegraph convention was signed in July, 1850.

[1] For a discussion of the tariff changes proposed at Cassel in 1850, see R. von Patow, *Beleuchtung der auf der Zollconferenz in Cassel vorgeschlagenen Zolltarifs-Veränderungen* (1850); L. Kühne, *Fliegendes Blatt als Zustimmung und Nachtrag zu der von Patow'schen Beleuchtung der vorgeschlagenen Zolltarifsveränderungen* (1850); and Lord Westmorland to Lord Palmerston, June 8, 1850, enclosing letter from Schleinitz to Lord Westmorland (F.O. 64/318).

"Great Britain had now abolished the duty on foreign corn and has placed foreign shipping, with the single exception of the coasting trade, upon a footing of complete equality with British shipping...Her Majesty's Government think they are fairly entitled to expect that the same principles of enlightened policy which have dictated these changes in the commercial system of England shall be manifested in the regulations to be established by the Zollverein with regard to the commerce of Great Britain with Germany."[1] The suggested increase in the tariff was vetoed by the single vote of Brunswick. John Ward (Consul-General at Leipzig), who was in Berlin to watch over British interests at the Congress, considered "that Prussia did not wish to push the matter further, and that the opposition of Brunswick was merely collusive...".[2]

The only important change made in the Zollverein tariff at Cassel in 1850 was the raising of the import duty on cigars. It was hoped that this would benefit the Zollverein revenue but actually the receipts from the cigar duty declined since the principal importers—the Bremen cigar manufacturers—moved their factories into Zollverein territory and so evaded the import duty.

Bruck's scheme for an Austro-German customs union was brought before the Zollverein General Congress by the Bavarian representative but little progress was made. It was decided that Prussia, Bavaria and Saxony should negotiate with Austria on this question on behalf of the Zollverein.

Thus, on the one hand, Delbrück failed to secure the changes in the Zollverein tariff that he considered necessary and, on the other hand, Bruck had little reason to be satisfied with the reception accorded to his plans.

[1] Lord Palmerston to Henry Howard, August 14, 1850 (F.O. 64/312). See also Lord Palmerston to Howard, August 30, 1850 (F.O. 64/312). Lord Westmorland wrote to Schleinitz on the matter on June 23, 1850 (F.O. 64/318) and Howard sent a note to Schleinitz on August 17, 1850 (*Memorandum drawn up from Letter of Board of Trade relative to some proposed Changes in the Tariff of the Zollverein*, F.O. 64/319). Cf. A. Zimmermann, p. 389.

[2] J. Ward, *Experiences of a Diplomatist...* 1840–70 (1872), p. 99.

The Zollverein General Congress was adjourned early in November, 1850, owing to an outbreak of cholera and to the constitutional struggle in Hesse-Cassel which led to the occupation of the capital by Prussian troops. An Austro-Bavarian force was at Hanau and war seemed imminent.[1] Then Prussia gave way at Olmütz (November 29, 1850).

Schwarzenberg hoped that Prussia would be amenable in economic matters. Even Bruck began to stress the political advantages to Austria of his plans.[2] But he recognised that it might not be possible to set up an Austro-German customs union at once. The alternative would be for Austria to negotiate with the Zollverein for further discussions on the question of union.

Early in 1851 German economic affairs were discussed at two conferences. Representatives from the German States met at Dresden towards the end of December, 1850, to consider various constitutional problems that had arisen owing to the recent re-establishment of the Germanic Confederation. A committee of experts was appointed to advise on economic affairs. Bavaria and Saxony submitted to this committee memoranda in favour of the gradual economic unification of Germany through negotiations between Austria, the Zollverein, the Tax Union and those States which were not in any customs union. Eventually

[1] Howard informed Lord Palmerston on November 17, 1850, that Manteuffel had read to him a note which he had sent to Bunsen on November 13. Howard reported Manteuffel as saying that Prussia would not have opposed Austria's intervention in Hesse-Cassel "if the Electorate did not nearly everywhere border upon the Prussian frontiers, if it did not separate the eastern from the western Provinces of Prussia, and if it were not traversed by military roads the use of which is of vital importance and has been guaranteed to Prussia by formal treaties" (F.O. 64/321).

[2] In December, 1850, Bruck submitted to Schwarzenberg a confidential memorandum in which he stated that "only by the establishment of the Austro-German customs union can Austria secure her proper position as leader in German affairs: so long as she is not a member of the Zollverein all material interests gravitate towards Prussia". Quoted by A. Gaertner, *Der Kampf um den Zollverein zwischen Österreich und Preussen von 1849–53* (1911), p. 118.

the committee produced a draft treaty which was intended to pave the way for economic unification. But it was not signed and the experts' labours had no immediate practical result. Later, however, several clauses of the draft treaty were incorporated in the Austro-Prussian commercial treaty of February, 1853.

At the same time the ninth Zollverein Congress (which had been adjourned at Cassel) was continuing its deliberations at Wiesbaden. Saxony suggested that the problems under discussion at Dresden should not be dealt with by the Zollverein Congress. Prussia objected, but since unanimity was necessary Saxony was able to get her way. So only matters of comparatively minor importance were discussed. It was agreed, for example, to reduce the Zollverein transit dues from 15 to 10 silver groschens per hundredweight.[1]

Bruck saw that for the time being there was little hope of an Austro-German customs union. He had introduced important reforms in the Hapsburg dominions but it would take time to show their value. He recognised, too, that further reforms were necessary. The depreciated Austrian paper currency, for example, was a serious barrier to close economic co-operation with the German States. In Austria itself opinions on Bruck's plans were still divided. Support came from certain Austrian industrialists, such as the clothmakers of Reichenberg and the scythe-makers of upper Austria who had little fear of German competition and from Magyar landowners who wanted wider markets for their produce. Opposition came from industrialists in Bohemia[2] and lower Austria.

In Germany, too, there were differences of opinion. That influential newspaper the Augsburg *Allgemeine Zeitung*, and the protectionist manufacturers' association (the General German Union for the Protection of Home Industries) supported Bruck.

---

[1] *Verhandlungen* (1851), IX, Besonderes Protokoll den Vereins-Zolltarif betreffend, sect. xiv, pp. 113–29 (Durchgangsabgaben).

[2] See, for example, *Denkschrift des böhmischen Gewerbevereins über den Anschluss Österreichs an den deutschen Zollverein* (Prague, 1848).

But there was implacable hostility on the part of German free-traders who were ably led by John Prince Smith and who were following the example of the English Anti-Corn Law League in developing modern methods of political propaganda. In the South German States the "Trias" tradition was as strong as ever. Von der Pfordten,[1] the Bavarian Foreign Minister, was particularly anxious that the middle States should present a united front to Prussia's pretensions to either political or economic leadership in Germany. But it was clear that the South German States would not push their dislike of Prussia to the extent of losing money by leaving the Zollverein. They made it plain that they would accept Bruck's proposal for an Austro-German customs union only if they were guaranteed a customs revenue at least equal to that which they were drawing from the Zollverein. Prussia, of course, firmly opposed Bruck's scheme.

Bruck fully appreciated these difficulties. Moreover, his position in Schwarzenberg's ministry was becoming more and more uncongenial as the political reaction in Austria gained in influence. He differed with Kübeck on financial and railway questions. On May 23, 1851, Bruck resigned office and returned to Triest to resume his work as a director of the Austrian Lloyd.

(4) HANOVER'S ADHESION TO THE ZOLLVEREIN AND THE AUSTRO-PRUSSIAN TREATY OF 1853[2]

The retirement of Bruck did not mean that Austria had given up hopes of forming a customs union with German States. But some months elapsed before Baumgartner, the new Minister of Commerce, and Hock, who had been the Austrian expert at Dresden, were able to press forward again with Bruck's plan. There were, it is true, discussions at Frankfurt-am-Main where a committee of the Federal Diet examined the report of the

---

[1] See E. Franz, *Ludwig Freiherr von der Pfordten* (1938).

[2] See works cited in section (3) of this chapter and list of references in W. Weber, p. 326 n.

Dresden experts, but once again little progress was made. Delbrück used this period of comparative Austrian inactivity to deal what proved to be a fatal blow to all hopes of an Austro-German customs union. He succeeded in securing the adhesion of Hanover to the Zollverein.

It has been seen that negotiations in the 'forties between Prussia and Hanover had failed because Prussia had not been prepared to grant the far-reaching concessions demanded by Hanover. She had asked, for example, for a greater share of the Zollverein revenue than that calculated on the basis of population, a reduction in the Zollverein import duties on colonial goods and exemption from the Zollverein salt monopoly. She still hoped to secure these and other concessions but her unsatisfactory financial position made her more ready to undertake serious negotiations than before. Prussia was prepared to grant much that she had previously refused since she was faced with the possibility of the defection of the South German States when the existing Zollverein treaties expired at the end of 1853. In these circumstances the adhesion of Hanover would, to some extent, compensate Prussia for her loss of economic influence in South Germany.

The negotiations were in the hands of Delbrück for Prussia and Klenze for Hanover and were conducted with the greatest possible secrecy since neither party wished Austria to have any suspicion of what was going on.[1] A treaty was signed on September 7, 1851, and ratifications were exchanged a few days later. Although it was an agreement for the amalgamation of

---

[1] It is interesting to find Bismarck writing from Frankfurt-am-Main to General Leopold von Gerlach on June 22, 1851: "I should very much like to know if the negotiations between the Zollverein and Hanover are still in being and are making progress. The consolidation of the healthy North German elements by means of the bond of material interests—even if it involved the Zollverein in the loss of its South German members— would not fail to advance the conservative cause in our own internal politics and would justify us in regarding Federal political developments with greater composure" (*Bismarckbriefe*, 1836–72, edited by Horst Kohl, 6th edition (1897), p. 81).

the Zollverein and the Tax Union on January 1, 1854, the treaty was signed only by Prussia and Hanover. Prussia had not consulted any member of the Zollverein and Hanover had not consulted Oldenburg or Schaumburg-Lippe. But both the Zollverein and Tax Union treaties were due to expire in 1853 and Prussia and Hanover were prepared to make acceptance of the agreement of September 7, 1851, a condition for renewing them.

Hanover had little difficulty in obtaining the consent of Schaumburg-Lippe (September 25, 1851) and Oldenburg (March 1, 1852)[1] to these arrangements but Prussia had serious difficulty in securing the acceptance of the September Treaty by other members of the Zollverein.

Hanover obtained very favourable terms. Her share of the Zollverein customs revenue was fixed at 75 per cent more than she would have secured on a basis of population. (But so far as Hanover's share of the revenue from import duties and from the excise on beet-sugar was concerned this extra payment was not to exceed 20 silver groschens for each inhabitant of the country.) On the renewal of the Zollverein in 1854 the import duties on coffee, tea, tobacco, syrup, cognac and wines were to be reduced and the import duty on beet-sugar was to be raised. Rails needed for the completion of Hanover's railway system were to be admitted duty free. Hanover was not to introduce a salt monopoly and arrangements were to be made by neighbouring States to prevent the smuggling of cheap salt from Hanover into their own territories. Hanover retained

[1] Schaumburg-Lippe's adhesion to the September treaty was in the form of an agreement between Schaumburg-Lippe and Hanover alone but Oldenburg's adhesion was by a treaty between Hanover and Prussia on the one hand and Oldenburg on the other. On the same day that Oldenburg adhered to the September treaty she signed an agreement with Hanover by which the two States adopted the same system of internal indirect taxes. These treaties are printed by F. Houth-Weber, *Der Zollverein seit seiner Erweiterung durch den Steuerverein* (1861), pp. 23–43. It may be added that in 1854 Oldenburg ceded to Prussia a strip of territory on Jahde Bay. Here the naval port of Wilhelmshaven was built.

her existing tolls on roads and on the Rivers Elbe and Weser. To avoid the necessity of levying retrospective duties Hanover agreed to introduce the most important parts of the new Zollverein tariff before March 1, 1853.[1]

Hanover could not long have maintained an isolated position in North Germany and she had made an excellent financial bargain. Prussia had made considerable financial sacrifices but in return had secured a link between her eastern and western provinces in the event of the collapse of the Zollverein at the end of 1853. She had succeeded in extending her customs area to the North Sea where Hanover was making every effort to foster the development of her port of Harburg on the Elbe.[2] Moreover, the free-trade party in Prussia was strengthened by the adhesion of Hanover and it was now very improbable that Austria would ever be able to force her way into the Zollverein. Her duties were high and the Zollverein was not likely to raise its tariff to a level acceptable to Austria. In the circumstances Prussia was satisfied with the treaty. It was reported from Berlin that the treaty "had rendered Baron Manteuffel very popular and (has) added considerably to the strength of his government".[3]

Prussia followed up this success by sending a circular note in November, 1851, to all members of the Zollverein denouncing the Zollverein treaties.[4] She stated that she would renew the treaties only with the modifications rendered necessary by the

[1] The treaty between Prussia and Hanover of September 7, 1851, was printed in the *Preussische Zeitung* on September 12, 1851. See also the documents printed in F. Houth-Weber, *Der Zollverein seit seiner Erweiterung durch den Steuerverein* (1861) and in an official Prussian publication, *Beiträge zur Beurteilung der Zollvereinsfrage* (1852: cited as *Beiträge*... in future). Cf. W. Seeling, *Der preussisch-hannoverische Vertrag vom 7. September 1851 in seiner Bedeutung für Hannover* (1852).

[2] See, for example, Bligh to Lord Palmerston, June 27, 1851 (F.O. 34/64).

[3] Lord Bloomfield to Lord Palmerston, September 11, 1851 (F.O. 64/332). Manteuffel was Prussian Minister President, 1850–8.

[4] See extract printed by W. Weber, pp. 301–2.

Prusso-Hanoverian treaty of September, 1851, and she invited members of the Zollverein to a conference to be held in Berlin early in 1852 to discuss the matter. The German middle States were thus left with the alternative of accepting the Prussian arrangements with Hanover or of making the best bargain they could with Austria.

Schwarzenberg's retort to the September treaty was to publish the revised Austrian tariff on November 25, 1851, and to announce that it would come into force on February 1, 1852. On the same day Austria invited all the German States to a conference to be held in Vienna to discuss, first, a commercial treaty and, secondly, an Austro-German customs union.[1] At about the same time Thun suggested to Bismarck in Frankfurt that the competence of the Germanic Confederation should be extended to customs affairs. Bismarck firmly rejected this proposal.[2] Prussia declined to take part in the Vienna conference. She merely offered to negotiate with Austria for a commercial treaty *after* the Zollverein treaties had been renewed.[3]

The Vienna conference was opened by Schwarzenberg on January 4, 1852. It was not a meeting of all German States. Prussia was absent. No representatives were sent either from the Thuringian and Anhalt States, which were economically

[1] See circular note of the Austrian Government, November 25, 1851, printed in the official Austrian collection of documents, *Die Wiener Zoll-Conferenzen* (1852), pp. 3–5, and in *Beiträge...* (1852), pp. 76–9.

[2] See A. O. Meyer, *Bismarcks Kampf mit Österreich am Bundestag zu Frankfurt* (1927), pp. 69–72. Bismarck criticised the Austrian intrigues among South German States on the eve of the Vienna conference. He wrote from Frankfurt-am-Main to General Leopold von Gerlach on November 26, 1851: "An honest Brandenburger can have no conception of the way in which Hock lies and intrigues here, up and down the Rhine: the South Germans—these children of nature—are very corrupt" (*Bismarckbriefe*, 1836–72, edited by Horst Kohl, 6th edition (1897), p. 81). Cf. F. W. Lange, *Bismarck und die öffentliche Meinung Süddeutschlands während der Zollvereinskrise*, 1850–53 (Giessen, 1922: Dissertation).

[3] Manteuffel to von Arnim and Circular Note from Manteuffel to Prussian representatives abroad, December 5, 1851: printed in *Beiträge...* (1852), pp. 81–9.

dependent upon Prussia, or from the Mecklenburgs and Holstein. But the conclusion of the treaty of September, 1851, did not prevent Hanover from taking part in the conference.

Three schemes were discussed at Vienna. The first (proposal A) was the draft of a commercial treaty to prepare the way for a general customs union. The second (proposal B) provided for the union itself and was to come into force in 1859.[1] The third (proposal C) was the result of secret negotiations between Austria on the one hand and Bavaria, Württemberg, Baden, Saxony, Nassau[2] and the two Hesses on the other. It provided for a customs union between these States in the event of the first two proposals failing owing to Prussian opposition. Schwarzenberg hoped that the middle States would desert the Zollverein as they had deserted Prussia's political "Union" in 1850. But none of the treaties discussed at Vienna were signed at this time, for there were several points upon which no agreement could be reached.

A meeting of the middle States was held at Darmstadt in April, 1852. It was decided to sign the A and B Vienna proposals[3] and to propose at the forthcoming Berlin conference of Zollverein States that they should form the basis of negotiation between the Zollverein and Austria. The middle States (except Baden) further agreed that if Prussia declined to negotiate with Austria they would refuse to renew the Zollverein treaties. They would themselves form a customs union and would negotiate for eventual union with the Hapsburg dominions on the basis of the Vienna proposal C. It was intended to keep these agreements secret but they appeared in full in the Berlin newspaper, the *Vossische Zeitung*, on April 24.[4] Prussia sharply

[1] Proposals A and B were printed in *Die Wiener Zoll-Conferenzen* (1852), pp. 11–41.

[2] For Nassau's policy during the first Zollverein crisis, see Hermann Toelle, *Das Herzogtum Nassau und die deutsche Frage*, 1852–57 (Marburg, 1914: Dissertation), ch. iii, pp. 59–81.

[3] This was done at Vienna on April 20, 1852.

[4] The Darmstadt agreements were printed in *Beiträge...* (1852), pp. 119–23. The Vienna proposal C was signed on February 22, 1853

criticised this new attempt of the middle States to play an independent part in German economic affairs.

On the second day of the Darmstadt negotiations the news of Schwarzenberg's death was made known and it was clear that the possibility of Austria's plans for the future economic organisation of Germany were more remote than ever. Schwarzenberg was succeeded by Buol and it was announced that Austria's economic schemes remained unaltered. Austrian representatives at South German courts were officially informed at the end of May, 1852, that "according to information we have received, the opinion is gaining ground that the Imperial Government will not in future pursue its commercial policy with the same vigour and zeal as hitherto. This opinion is mistaken...".[1] But, as Delbrück observed in his memoirs, "those who knew the two men had no doubt that the creative power and the ruthless energy behind these plans had been extinguished".[2]

Meantime, the members of the Zollverein had met in Berlin on April 19, 1852, to discuss the renewal of that customs union. The Darmstadt confederates promptly suggested that before the Zollverein was renewed negotiations should be opened with Austria—on the basis of the Vienna proposals A and B—for the formation of an Austro-German customs union. In a declaration of June 7, 1852, the Prussian Government explained why it would not agree to this suggestion. It observed that "the measures necessary to protect the tobacco monopoly in Austria would hamper the movement of goods from the Zollverein to Austria to such an extent as to be incompatible with the main

(though dated February 17) but the conclusion of the Austro-Prussian commercial treaty of February 19, 1853, made it virtually certain that the Zollverein treaties would be renewed and that therefore proposal C would not come into force. Cf. F. Werner, *Die Zollvereinspolitik der deutschen Mittelstaaten*, 1852. *Die Darmstädter Konferenz.*

[1] Copy of a circular note to the Imperial (Austrian) Embassies in Munich, etc. (May 31, 1852) in the Vienna Archives, Pol. Arch. II, 65 (fol. 1–336): Zoll- und Handelsvertrag vom 19. Februar, 1853.

[2] R. von Delbrück, I, p. 305.

object of the customs union". Owing to its provisional nature the Austrian plan "is unsuitable as a means of fixing one of the most important sources of income of the State. The tariff, the main part of the general customs legislation, is left in a state of uncertainty and the successful introduction of the whole plan is therefore prejudiced from the start". "The Prussian Government is of opinion that these deficiencies of the plan are no mere fortuitous blemishes which could be eliminated by thorough discussions but lie in the very nature of the project itself and cannot at present be removed." Prussia repeated her offer to enter into negotiations with Austria *after* the Zollverein treaties had been renewed.[1] No agreement was reached at Berlin and the conference was adjourned on July 9, 1852.

Then another move was made largely owing to the intervention of Russia. The Czar had already, in 1850, put strong pressure upon Prussia and Austria to compose their political differences. He was now anxious to secure, as far as possible, a united front in Europe against France, where Louis Napoleon's *coup d'état* had taken place on December 2, 1851. Russia had no wish to see the middle States of Germany break away both from Prussian and Austrian influence only to become dependent upon France. The Czar and his Chancellor, Nesselrode, visited both Vienna and Berlin in May, 1852, and impressed upon Austria and Prussia the desirability of settling their economic differences. The King of Prussia thereupon decided to send Bismarck (then Prussian representative at the recently revived Federal Diet at Frankfurt-am-Main) to Vienna to discuss these matters.

No way out of the difficulty was found, however. Many years later Bismarck declared in his memoirs that neither in 1852 nor later did he favour the setting up of an Austro-German

[1] The Prussian declaration of July 7, 1852, is printed in *Beiträge*... (1852), pp. 143–7. Several other documents on the Berlin conference of 1852 appear in this work. For a criticism of *Beiträge*..., see the anonymous pamphlet, *Zum Verständnis der Zollvereins Krisis*... (Giessen, 1852).

customs union. "The difference in the consumption of dutiable articles between Hungary and Galicia on the one hand and the Zollverein on the other is so great that it appears to be impossible to establish a customs union between them."[1] At the time, Bismarck blamed the Austrians for the failure of the negotiations. He wrote that the Austrians "either feel that there is no necessity for them to come to an agreement with us or else they think that we are in greater need of making a settlement than is in fact the case. I fear that the opportunity of coming to an agreement will be let slip. This will have an unfortunate reaction in Prussia where it is thought that my mission was a very conciliatory move. It will be a long time before we again send (to Vienna) anyone who has such a free hand as myself and who is, at the same time, so anxious to arrive at a settlement."[2]

In the autumn of 1852 the Darmstadt confederates continued their deliberations, first at Stuttgart and then at Munich, and the Berlin conference of Zollverein States held a second fruitless session.[3] So in September, 1852, Prussia declared that she would in future negotiate separately with each State on the renewal of its Zollverein treaty.[4]

[1] *Gedanken und Erinnerungen von Otto Fürst von Bismarck*, 1 (edition of 1922), p. 105.

[2] Bismarck to his wife, June 16, 1852, in *Bismarckbriefe*, 1836–72 (edited by Horst Kohl, 6th edition, 1897), p. 84.

[3] In a memorial of July 3, 1852, the Manchester Chamber of Commerce complained that "few sessions of the deputies of the Zollverein have been hitherto held without some short-sighted endeavour to disturb the commerce of this country...". Lord Stanley replied on Lord Malmesbury's behalf on July 13, 1852, "that any official interference on the part of Her Majesty's Government in the internal arrangements or the financial administration of Germany, could not fail to increase the jealousy which already exists of some of the States in question with regard to the commercial policy of this country, and might even tend to promote the adoption of that very prohibitory system which it is equally in the interest of England and the intention of Her Majesty's Government to discourage..." (M.Ch.C., vol. v, August 5, 1852).

[4] Dispatch of Manteuffel, September 27, 1852, printed in *Beiträge...* (1852), pp. 184–5.

The deadlock was complete. It was learned that Prussian officials were inspecting the Hesse-Cassel frontier to decide on suitable places for erecting new customs houses and this suggested that Prussia was fully determined to end the Zollverein if her allies refused to give way. Many German manufacturers were dismayed at the prospect of the collapse of the Zollverein[1] and several German States, which had been receiving large sums annually as their share of the Zollverein revenue, began to doubt the wisdom of supporting Austria.

In September, 1852, Bruck emerged from his political retirement, visited Vienna, and urged the Foreign Minister to approach Prussia directly. In the middle of October, Buol wrote a private letter on the subject to Manteuffel, the Prussian Minister President; and Prussia gave way to the extent of agreeing to sign a commercial treaty with Austria *before* renewing the Zollverein treaties. The Austrian representative was Bruck; the Prussian representatives were Delbrück and Pommer-Esche. So in December, 1852, the direct Austro-Prussian negotiations, which might well have begun in 1850, were at last opened. The discussions led to the Austro-Prussian commercial treaty of February 19, 1853.[2]

[1] Bismarck reported from Frankfurt-am-Main early in 1853 that the "superabundance of money is attributed by Rothschild to the fact that, partly through fear of war, and partly through the uncertainty regarding the future of the customs union, the spirit of enterprise has vanished, so that money is flowing back from business without being reinvested" (quoted by E. C. Corti, *The Reign of the House of Rothschild* (1928), p. 333).

[2] The Austro-Prussian commercial treaty was signed on February 20 but as this was a Sunday it was dated February 19, 1853. A. Zimmermann (pp. 735–69) prints the Vienna proposal A (1852) which formed the basis of the discussions and the alterations made in it during the negotiations. Cf. *Draft of Treaty between Prussia and Austria*, enclosed in Lord Bloomfield's dispatch to Lord John Russell, February 8, 1853 (F.O. 64/353). Delbrück states in his memoirs (1, p. 331 n.) that the account of the negotiations leading up to the Austro-Prussian commercial treaty of February 19, 1853, which is given by W. Weber (ch. xxvii) is "often mistaken, probably because the author made use only of the information supplied by Austria to the Darmstadt confederates".

The commercial treaty of February 19, 1853,[1] though signed by only Austria[2] and Prussia was, in fact, a treaty between Austria and the Zollverein since the obligations which Prussia undertook would—like those of the September Treaty (1851) with Hanover—have to be incorporated in the new Zollverein treaties. It owed much to the labours of the experts at Dresden in 1851 and of those who had drawn up proposal A at Vienna in 1852. The treaty was to last for twelve years—from January 1, 1854, to December 31, 1865.

It was agreed that—with a few exceptions—no goods should be prohibited from crossing the Austro-Zollverein frontier. No import duties were to be charged on certain raw materials and semi-manufactured articles. Lower import duties than those paid by goods coming from other countries were to be levied on various manufactured articles. The reduction in import duty generally amounted to about 25 per cent *ad valorem*. New tariff concessions made by one of the contracting parties to a third State were to be automatically enjoyed by the other contracting party.[3]

[1] See *Handels- und Zoll-Vertrag zwischen Seiner Majestät dem Könige von Preussen und Seiner Majestät dem Kaiser von Österreich* (copy in Lord Bloomfield to Lord John Russell, February 22, 1853: F.O. 64/353) and *Verträge und Verhandlungen über die Bildung und Ausführung des deutschen Zoll- und Handelsvereins*, IV (1858), pp. 227–69.

[2] It may be added that the Principality of Liechtenstein and the Duchies of Parma and Modena had recently formed customs unions with the Hapsburg dominions and were included in the Austro-Prussian commercial treaty of February 19, 1853. In 1857 Parma and Modena both left the Austrian customs system. Modena signed a new commercial treaty which was nominally an agreement for a customs union. Actually many duties were different in the two countries and an Austro-Modena customs frontier was set up again. Both parties agreed in 1858 to abrogate the commercial treaty signed the year before. See R. von Delbrück, II, pp. 106–7.

[3] In an article on "Free Trade in Austria" the *Economist* (October 20, 1866) summarised the statistics of Austrian trade between 1851 and 1865. The *Economist* stated that it was apparent "that interchange of commodities with the States of the Zollverein by the help of low duties increased

Thus a system of differential duties was set up which marked an important change in the tariff policy of the Zollverein. Hitherto preferences—such as those granted to Dutch semi-refined sugar (1839–41), to Belgian iron (1844–53) and (by the South German States) to certain Swiss products (1835–51)—had been exceptional concessions made only in special circumstances.

Austria and Prussia also pledged themselves to discuss various matters in the future. The first negotiations were to deal with further facilitation of transit trade and local frontier traffic and the establishment of an Austro-German monetary convention. In 1860 there were to be negotiations for the setting up of an Austro-German customs union.

Bruck could claim that he had achieved a certain measure of success and had rescued something from the wreck of his ambitious schemes. Prussia had given way on a formal point by signing the February Treaty before renewing the Zollverein treaties. She had agreed to a system of differential import and transit duties which—in conjunction with the postal and telegraph conventions of 1850[1]—bore some resemblance to the first stage towards Austro-German economic unity envisaged in Bruck's article in the *Wiener Zeitung* of October 26, 1849. Prussia was under obligation to undertake negotiations in 1860 for the establishment of a customs union between the Zollverein and the Hapsburg dominions.

But whatever satisfaction Bruck might obtain from these provisions, the February Treaty was in fact a Prussian success which to some extent balanced the "humiliation" of Olmütz. The chief obstacle in the way of renewing the Zollverein treaties

at a far greater ratio than the trade with foreign countries, stunted as it was by an almost prohibitory tariff, the imports from Germany having augmented by 220 per cent. and the exports thither by 300 per cent. In fact, the general increase of the Austrian export business is owing to its growth with Germany specially, where, from the lowering of duties in 1852, its total ruin had been predicted by the protectionists" (p. 1228).

[1] See above p. 208, n. 2.

had been removed and further negotiations for Austria's admission to the Zollverein had been postponed until 1860. This gave Prussia the opportunity of strengthening the free-trade and anti-Austrian elements in the Zollverein. Prussia had prevented Austria from entering her customs union, had frustrated the attempt to detach the South German States from the Zollverein and had secured the adhesion of the Tax Union. Hock, an influential official in the Austrian Ministry of Finance, recognised this when he referred to the February Treaty as "a not very advantageous armistice".[1]

In the years 1848–54 Prussia was fully occupied with internal troubles and with the political and economic struggle against Austria. She had little time for negotiations with other States. An additional convention to the treaty of 1845 with Sardinia was signed in 1851. Sardinia extended to the Zollverein the tariff concessions she had recently made to France, England and Belgium. In view of the increase in the Swiss tariff—particularly on iron imported from South Germany—the South German States withdrew, in 1851, the preferences granted since 1835 to the importation of certain Swiss goods. Negotiations at Carlsruhe for a new settlement were at first unsuccessful. On July 27, 1852, however, Switzerland and Baden agreed to facilitate frontier traffic and to reduce shipping tolls on the Rhine between Constance and Basel.[2] Between 1846 and 1849 Great Britain had abolished her corn laws and navigation code and had reduced her import duties on timber. German landowners, farmers and shippers derived considerable benefit from England's new commercial policy.

The commercial treaty with Belgium (1844) was denounced by Prussia but was prolonged—by a convention of February, 1852—until the end of 1853. The preference granted to Belgian

---

[1] Quoted by E. Franz, *Der Entscheidungskampf um die wirtschaftspolitische Führung Deutschlands*, 1856–67 (1933), p. 4.

[2] See W. D. Christie to Lord Palmerston, July 16, August 25, September 3 and 16, 1851 (F.O. 100/69); F. Ruckert, *Die Handelsbeziehungen zwischen Deutschland und der Schweiz . . .* (1926), p. 100.

iron imported into the Zollverein had been severely criticised in Germany and was now reduced by a half. After the expiry of this convention Belgian iron no longer entered the Zollverein on better terms than iron from other countries.[1] For ten years commercial relations between the Zollverein and Belgium were not regulated by treaty. It has been observed that the progress of free trade in Holland had important results in Germany. In December, 1851, Prussia was able to conclude a treaty with Holland which placed the economic relations of the two countries upon a satisfactory basis for over seventy years.

Several questions of comparatively minor importance had been shelved at the Berlin conference on the continuation of the Zollverein so that the discussions should not be unduly prolonged. When this conference had successfully accomplished its task it was decided that the tenth Zollverein General Congress should be held before the new treaties came into operation. The Congress met at Berlin in June, 1853, but did not complete its labours until February of the following year. The new Zollverein tariff was approved. Few duties were altered since the continued opposition of free-traders and protectionists made it impossible to secure the unanimity that was necessary before changes could be made. Prussia, for example, wanted to reduce the Zollverein import duty on pig-iron from 10 to 5 silver groschens per hundredweight, an arrangement which would have removed the awkward preference given to Belgian iron.[2] But the protectionist South German States refused to agree to this. The import duty on corn, however, was abolished.

The twelve years that had elapsed since the coming into force of the new Zollverein treaties at the beginning of 1842 had seen important changes in Germany's economic development and

---

[1] See Nothomb's memorandum of November 25, 1853; Manteuffel's reply of December 3, 1853; and Manteuffel's dispatch to von Bockelberg of December 7, 1853 (printed in A. Zimmermann, pp. 780–94).

[2] At this time Belgian pig-iron paid $7\frac{1}{2}$ instead of 10 silver groschens per hundredweight. If the normal duty were reduced to 5 silver groschens it would not be necessary to grant any preference to Belgian pig-iron.

prospects. The construction of a network of railways was fostering German economic progress. The amalgamation of the Zollverein and the Tax Union had established a customs union which included the whole of the territory of the future German Empire except a few regions in the north—Schleswig, Holstein and Lauenburg (three duchies in personal union with Denmark), the two Mecklenburgs and the three Hanse towns. Most of the political gains of the German revolutions of 1848–49 had been lost in the subsequent reaction but many of the economic gains remained. There was, for example, little danger of any attempt to re-establish feudal burdens on the peasants.

The more liberal economic policies of England and Holland had opened new prospects for the expansion of German agriculture and commerce. The abolition of the Austro-Hungarian customs frontier (1850), the adoption of the revised Austrian tariff (1852), and the conclusion of the Austro-Prussian commercial treaty (1853) had raised hopes that German manufacturers would gain new markets in the extensive Hapsburg dominions. Elsewhere in Europe, too, customs barriers had fallen. The new Swiss constitution of 1848 had provided for the abolition of internal customs dues and for the establishment of a uniform tariff for the whole federation. The frontier between the main part of Russia and the Czar's Polish dominions had been abolished on January 1, 1851.

On the other hand, relations between Prussia and the South German States had been embittered both by the rise of the fierce controversy between free-traders and protectionists and the attempt of Austria to gain economic (as well as political) leadership in Germany. Bavaria and Württemberg disliked Prussia's predominant position in the Zollverein more than ever—yet they were not prepared to leave a customs union from which they derived considerable economic and financial advantages. The economic depression of the early 'forties, the commercial crisis of 1847, the cholera epidemic of 1849 and the political uncertainties of revolution caused much distress. In the 'fifties even more than in the 'forties thousands of Germans crossed the Atlantic to a country which offered them greater opportunities.

The Great Exhibition of 1851 enabled Germans to compare their manufactured products with those of their principal competitors. Britain and France were clearly the leading industrial countries in the middle of the nineteenth century and the technical excellence of many of their exhibits was manifest. Only a few German exhibits, such as Siemens and Halske's telegraphic apparatus, attracted much attention. A correspondent of the *Allgemeine Zeitung* complained that "German industry has no peculiar character. In the Exhibition (from which alone we judge) it appears as if every national character were carefully avoided. Everywhere German industry appears to lean on some foreign industry and to imitate it.... Here one beholds the supporting hand of France, there that of England."[1] This criticism was probably not unjust. But in certain manufactures, such as metal work and chemical industries, Germans had little to learn from their foreign rivals.

In 1854 John Ward (British Consul-General at Leipzig) visited the German Industrial Exhibition at Munich and in his memoirs he commented upon the substantial advances made by German manufacturers since 1844.[2] A few years later he reported that "the manufacture of German cutlery has very greatly improved in the last fifteen years". The progress of German industry was tending "towards the exclusion of English cutlery from the German markets".[3] It was clear that German economic life was recovering from the temporary setback received in the years of revolution.

[1] Quoted by the *Economist*, June 28, 1851, and by J. H. Clapham, *An Economic History of Modern Britain*, II (1932), p. 20.

[2] John Ward, *Experiences of a Diplomatist...1840–70* (1872), p. 130. Cf. *Bericht der Beurteilungs-Commission bei der allgemeinen deutschen Industrie-Ausstellung zu München im Jahre 1854*, edited by F. B. W. von Hermann (1855).

[3] John Ward to Lord Bloomfield, July 1, 1858, in Ward's papers in the Perne Library, Peterhouse, Cambridge.

Chapter VII

THE ZOLLVEREIN IN THE 'FIFTIES, 1854–1859

(1) ECONOMIC PROGRESS AND TARIFF DEADLOCK, 1854–1859[1]

The years 1854–59 were a period of economic progress in Germany. "Tall chimneys grew like mushrooms" in her industrial regions.[2] Various factors were favourable to economic expansion at this time.

First, the revolutions of 1848–49 were followed by a period of political reaction. The commercial middle classes had little share in governing the country. They turned their energies to economic affairs and endeavoured to recover some of the financial losses they had suffered in the troubled revolutionary years.

Secondly, the recent removal of various customs barriers in Europe began to benefit German trade. Customs frontiers had been abolished between the Swiss cantons; between Austria and Hungary, Liechtenstein, Parma and Modena;[3] between Russia and her Polish provinces; between the Zollverein and the Tax Union; and between Denmark and the duchies of Schleswig,

---

[1] Accounts of various aspects of German economic affairs in 1854–59 are given by R. von Delbrück, ii, chs. xv–xxvi and by A. Bergengrün, *Staatsminister August von der Heydt* (1908), chs. vii–xi. See also W. Weber, ch. xxix; H. von Festenberg-Packisch, ch. xi; É. Worms, *L'Allemagne Économique . . .* (1874), ch. iii, and S. Maiboom, *Studien zur deutschen Politik Bayerns in den Jahren 1851–59* (1931).

[2] Max Wirth, *Geschichte der Handelskrisen* (4th edition, 1890), p. 309.

[3] The customs union between Austria and the duchies of Parma and Modena, however, came to an end in 1857–58; see above p. 223 n. 2.

Holstein and Lauenburg. The example given by England and Holland in reducing import duties was followed to some extent by Belgium, Switzerland and Sardinia and even by Austria and France. In 1852 Austria replaced her prohibitive duties by a reformed tariff and in 1856 she made further reductions in certain import duties. Between 1853 and 1856 France reduced her import duties on various raw materials and foodstuffs. In the 'fifties Russia modified somewhat the stringency of her prohibitive system of tariffs. The reduction of duties by the United States in 1846 and the opening of Japan to foreign trade in 1854 also deserve notice.[1]

Thirdly, the improvement of communications—particularly railway construction—continued in the 'fifties and this enabled industrial regions to come into closer contact with consumers. Railway construction between 1848 and 1865 was characterised by the linking up of railway systems both between German States themselves and between German States and neighbouring countries. The coalfields of the Saar, the Ruhr, Saxony and upper Silesia and the salt-mines of the Prussian province of Saxony were tapped by new lines. By 1865 three railway systems linked West and East Germany—one across the North German Plain (Aachen–Hanover–Berlin–Danzig–Königsberg), another through Central Germany (Essen–Cassel–Dresden–Breslau–Beuthen), and a third in the south (Mannheim–Stuttgart–Munich and so to Vienna). There were also three systems linking North and South Germany. In the east there was a railway from Stettin to Berlin where lines ran south to Prague and south-east to Breslau and Beuthen. In Central Germany lines from Hamburg and Bremen ran to Cassel and so to South and West Germany. In the west the railways in the

[1] See Hermann Wätjen, "Die Anfänge des deutsch-japanischen Handelsverkehrs im neunzehnten Jahrhundert", in *Zeitschrift des Vereins für Hamburgische Geschichte*, xxxv (1936), pp. 1–21, and E. Baasch, "Die Anfänge des modernen Verkehrs Hamburgs mit Vorderasien und Ostasien", in *Mitteilungen der Geographischen Gesellschaft in Hamburg*, xiii (1879), pp. 113 ff. In the late 'fifties the first German commercial house in Japan—Louis Kniffler and Co.—was founded by Louis Kniffler of Düsseldorf and Hermann Gildemeister of Bremen.

Rhine valley from the Dutch to the Swiss frontiers were completed in 1856.[1]

Transport was facilitated, too, by the removal of a number of old-established restrictions on important commercial routes. By the Treaty of Paris (1856) the Danube became a "free river" and an international commission was empowered to improve the approaches to the river. The Sound dues were abolished in the following year. Outside Europe, commerce was encouraged by the construction of two short but very important railways in the 'fifties—one across the Isthmus of Panama (1855) and another from Alexandria to Suez (1858).

Fourthly, it was on the whole a period of peace in Germany. Louis Napoleon declared to the Bordeaux merchants that "l'Empire c'est la paix" and his active promotion of the economic welfare of France had favourable reactions upon neighbouring countries. The Second Empire did not enjoy peace for long but neither the Crimean War (1854–56) nor the Italian War of 1859 had serious effects upon German economic life. During the Crimean War German vessels were liable to be searched by the British and French for contraband and enemy dispatches.[2]

---

[1] P. Benaerts, pp. 313–17. The Prussian State alone raised loans of £6,370,000 for railway construction in 1852–57 (Heinrich Stuebel, *Staat und Bank im Preussischen Anleihewesen von 1871–1913* (1935), p. 5).

[2] For the blockade of Russia during the Crimean War see the documents printed by A. Soetbeer, *Sammlung offizieller Aktenstücke in Bezug auf Schiffahrt und Handel in Kriegszeiten, Feb. 1854–April 1855* (Hamburg, 1855) and by G. B. Henderson in *The Journal of Modern History*, x, ii, June 1938, pp. 232–41. On November 6, 1855, Moustier (the French Minister in Berlin) informed Walewski (the French Foreign Minister) that Russia was obtaining considerable military supplies from the Zollverein. Some of these supplies were produced in the Zollverein: others were made elsewhere but were sent to Russia through Zollverein territory. Moustier, in effect, favoured an Allied blockade of Prussia (Eugène Guichen, *La Guerre de Crimée, 1854–56, et l'attitude des puissances européennes*, Paris (1936), p. 300). Under the International Law doctrine of "continuous voyage" an Allied blockade of Prussia could prevent most contraband goods—intended ultimately for Russia—from entering Prussia. But contraband produced in Prussia and exported to Russia by land could be stopped only by war or threat of war.

The Russian prohibition of the export of gold coins made it difficult for German firms to obtain payment for goods sent to Russia. There was some loss of direct trade with Russian Baltic ports but profits were made by transporting Russian goods by land to Prussian Baltic harbours[1] and from services rendered to the fleets of the Western Powers. The short Italian War of 1859 severely strained Austria's resources and resulted in the loss of Lombardy. The German States remained neutral and suffered few economic inconveniences though Prussia had the expense of mobilising a part of her army.

A fifth factor of importance was a general rise in prices. Between 1820 and 1845 Germany, like the rest of Europe, suffered from falling prices. Then, in the late 'forties and early 'fifties, gold was discovered in California, Victoria and New South Wales. Owing to more efficient methods of transport the new supplies were distributed more rapidly than they would have been in the earlier part of the century and their effect upon prices was soon felt. In the United States of America there was a land boom and a speeding up of railway construction. Trade improved. More raw materials and wheat were sent to Western Europe and more manufactured articles were received in return. German traders received a share of the increase of commerce both in the United States and in Europe.

The production of silver also increased. This was due less to the opening of new mines than to the discovery (in California) of new supplies of quicksilver which was used as an amalgam

---

[1] The Hull Chamber of Commerce reported in 1855: "The frontiers of Prussia being open for the transport of goods to and from Russia, it appears that the articles of flax, hemp, tallow and linseed, to some extent, have been able to bear the heavy land carriage and charges for shipment from Memel and Königsberg, so that the importation of these articles (except linseed) has been fully adequate to the consumption of this district" (quoted in *The Quarterly Review*, XCVIII (December, 1855), p. 273). Dundee, too, secured flax from Prussian instead of Russian Baltic ports. In 1853 she had imported 30,687 tons from Russia. In 1854, on the other hand, Dundee obtained only 2983 tons from Russia and no less than 20,487 tons from Prussia (P.P. 1856, XVI, p. 713).

in the production of silver. At the same time, however, Europe's consumption of colonial products—such as tea and rice—from the Far East was increasing. There was a "drain" of silver from Europe to the Far East to pay for these imports.

A sixth influence which promoted agricultural and industrial activity in the 'fifties was a general extension of credit. Here the Second Empire led the way by the founding of the *Crédit foncier* and the *Crédit mobilier*. The former made advances on the security of land; the latter promoted industrial joint-stock enterprises. In the German middle States and small States and in Austria somewhat similar institutions were founded—such as the Darmstadt Bank for Commerce and Industry and the Austrian Credit Institute for Commerce and Industry. Some of the German institutions were too liberal with their credits and so encouraged unwise speculation. In Prussia banks of a rather different character were established. Three of the most important were the *Diskontogesellschaft* (reorganised 1856), the *Berliner Handelsgesellschaft* and the *Schlesischer Bankverein* (both founded in 1856). The share-capital of banks founded in Germany in 1853–57 amounted to 200 million thalers. It was at this time, too, that Frankfurt-am-Main became an international centre for the exchange of State bonds.

Meantime the Zollverein prospered. Its gross revenue increased from $22\frac{1}{2}$ million thalers in 1854 to 28 million thalers in 1858.[1] The consumption of colonial goods increased. Between 1850 and 1860 the amount of (cane and beet) sugar consumed rose from 94,100 to 118,300 tons. The cotton industry made progress, the number of spindles increasing from $\frac{3}{4}$ million in 1846 to $2\frac{1}{4}$ millions in 1861. The production of coal increased in value from 10,200,000 thalers in 1850 to 27,600,000 thalers in 1857. In 1860 $12\frac{1}{3}$ million tons of coal and $4\frac{1}{2}$ million tons of lignite were produced. At this time coke was replacing charcoal for iron smelting. Between 1851 and 1857 twenty-four new coke blast furnaces were fired in the Ruhr district.[2] The consumption

[1] *Verhandlungen*, xiv (1859), pp. 174–5, and xv (1863), pp. 212–14.
[2] P. Benaerts, p. 456.

of pig-iron in the Zollverein rose from 393,000 to 900,000 tons in the ten years 1854–64 while the imports of pig-iron declined from 125,000 to under 100,000 tons.[1] The excess of wheat exports over imports was considerably greater in the 'fifties than in the 'forties but was declining a little.[2]

German States outside the Zollverein, particularly Hamburg and Bremen, shared in this prosperity. Hamburg recovered from the setback she had received owing to the fire of 1842 and the blockade of the Elbe during the Danish War of 1848–50.[3] Her African and Pacific commerce developed. Hamburg firms were active in both West Africa and East Africa and in 1855 a commercial agreement was made by the Hanse towns with the Sultan of Zanzibar.[4] The house of Godeffroy was gaining control of the Samoa copra trade in the late 'fifties. Bremen's commerce with the United States increased and the North German Lloyd shipping company was formed in 1857.

Austria, on the other hand, did not participate in this general prosperity. Shortly after her new tariff came into force the Crimean War broke out. Although Austria remained neutral she was, for a time, on the verge of hostilities and she occupied Moldavia and Wallachia when the Russians evacuated these principalities. Austria's Mediterranean commerce was hard hit and the Austrian Lloyd shipping company lost 949,000 florins in the financial year 1854–55. The finances of the country were disorganised and Austria's paper money sank in value. This depreciation enabled some Austrian industrialists to increase

---

[1] A. Bienengräber, *Statistik des Verkehrs und Verbrauchs im Zollverein für die Jahre 1842–64* (1868), pp. 32–3, 197, 263, 265, 286.

[2] *Ibid.* p. 135. The heading of the third column of the first table on this page should be *Mehrausfuhr* and not *Mehreinfuhr*.

[3] For Hamburg in the 'forties and 'fifties see, for example, *Bestrebungen und Wirksamkeit der Commerz-Deputation in Hamburg . . .* 1840–64 (Hamburg, 1865).

[4] For the development of German trade with Africa in the early 'fifties, see Ernst Hieke, "Das hamburgische Handelshaus Wm O'Swald & Co. und der Beginn des deutschen Afrikahandels, 1848–1853", in *V.S.W.* IV (1937), pp. 347–74 and note in *V.S.W.* IV (1937), pp. 261–5.

their exports to German States in 1854. But in the next year the florin rose somewhat and there was an increase in the importation of manufactured articles from the Zollverein. It needed only the commercial crisis of 1857 and the Italian War of 1859 to complete Austria's discomfiture. In the circumstances it was hardly surprising that many Austrian industrialists began to demand the revision of the new tariff and the imposition of higher import duties.

In the Zollverein, however, the position was different. The fact that agriculture and commerce were making progress told against German protectionists. They had made little enough headway in the 'forties when they had been able to argue that a high tariff would help to alleviate trade depression. In the more prosperous period of the 'fifties their influence declined and no great leader came forward to take List's place. Protectionist politicians like Varnbüler and Moritz Mohl were no match for the free-traders. The cotton-spinners of South Germany and the iron manufacturers of the Rhineland and Westphalia remained the most vigorous supporters of protection but they were fighting a losing battle.

The free-traders had no lack of leaders. John Prince Smith, Otto Michaelis, Victor Böhmert, Julius Faucher, Karl Braun, Karl Heinrich Brüggemann and Adolf Lette claimed that the example of Britain and Belgium should be followed and that the process of reducing import duties should be continued. The North German free-trade Press gained in influence.[1] Free trade was the economic doctrine of the day, the accession of the Tax Union had strengthened the position of free-traders in the Zollverein, and low duties were necessary to keep the Hapsbur̪g Empire out of the Zollverein. Delbrück, Pommer-Esche and

---

[1] The chief free-trade papers in North Germany at this time were the *Bremer Handelsblatt* (edited by Böhmert), the *Berliner Nationalzeitung* (commercial editor was Michaelis), the *Kölnische Zeitung* (edited by Brüggemann) and the *Stettiner Ostseezeitung*. Cf. K. H. Brüggemann, *Meine Leitung der Kölnischen Zeitung und die Krisen der preussischen Politik von 1846–55* (Leipzig, 1855).

Philipsborn—the Civil Servants who had most influence over Prussia's economic policy at this time—held free-trade views, and Manteuffel (the Prussian Minister President in the 'fifties) was in close touch with Prince Smith.

In 1858 the Union of German Economists (*Verein deutscher Volkswirte*) was founded. This powerful organisation held annual conferences at which demands were made for a thorough simplification and reform of the Zollverein tariff. The Union desired the removal of the "general import duty" (*allgemeine Eingangsabgabe*)—that is to say, the duty levied on all imports which were neither on the free list nor subject to a specific duty under the tariff. It favoured the abolition of import duties on agricultural products (particularly foods) and on raw and semi-manufactured materials which were needed by manufacturers and craftsmen. It also demanded the removal of differential duties, transit dues and tolls on river shipping.[1]

But the free-traders made only slow progress. The protectionists could hardly hope to secure an increase in the tariff but the need for unanimity at Zollverein General Congresses enabled them to hold up many proposals for new reductions of import duties.

This legacy of the bitter struggle between protectionists and free-traders in the 'forties as well as the sharp antagonisms that had been aroused in the Zollverein crisis of 1849–53 had unfortunate results in the 'fifties. At a time of comparative prosperity, when world economic conditions were clearly changing, the Zollverein failed to adapt its tariff to new conditions. Delbrück remarked that "under the influence of the stern struggle which had only recently terminated (without any genuine reconciliation) some of the Governments were more than ever determined to follow their own aims ruthlessly and

---

[1] See *Berichte über die Verhandlungen der Kongresse Deutscher Volkswirte* (Berlin, 1864); Adolf Lette, *Der volkswirtschaftliche Congress und der Zollverein* (Berlin, 1862); W. Lotz, *Die Ideen der deutschen Handelspolitik von 1860 bis 1891* (1892), pp. 10–26, and Max Schippel, *Grundzüge der Handelspolitik* (1902), pp. 194–6.

to agree to measures which would benefit everyone or would satisfy their neighbours only in return for concessions regarding their own particular interests".[1] This was seen in the deliberations of the four Zollverein General Congresses between 1854 and 1859. Deadlocks occurred with monotonous regularity. Bavaria, for example, stubbornly refused to agree to Prussian proposals for tariff reductions so long as Prussia persisted in retaining her "transition duties" (*Übergangsabgaben*) on wines at the existing level.

It was becoming clear to Prussian statesmen that when a favourable opportunity occurred an end must be made of the *liberum veto* in the Zollverein General Congress. Bismarck, for example, told Rechberg in 1857 that Prussia "was being hindered by the veto of individual German States from improving her internal financial legislation and that if the Prussian Government wished to regulate the budget (*Finanzhaushalt*) it would have to dissolve the Zollverein so as to permit its reconstruction in an improved form".[2] In the following year Bismarck declared that Prussia's "position in the Zollverein has become impossible (*verpfuscht*)". "We must denounce the whole Zollverein as soon as we are legally entitled to do so."[3]

Although the tenth Zollverein General Congress did not complete its deliberations until February, 1854, the eleventh Congress met at Darmstadt in September of the same year. Prussia was anxious to secure a number of reductions in import duties—particularly those on iron[4]—and to settle the difficulties that had arisen over the privilege given to merchants at

[1] R. von Delbrück, II, pp. 42–3.

[2] Rechberg to Buol, June 17, 1857 (A. O. Meyer, *Bismarcks Kampf mit Österreich am Bundestag zu Frankfurt* (1927), p. 551).

[3] Bismarck to von Below-Hohendorf, April 3, 1858, in *Bismarckbriefe, 1836–72* (edited by Horst Kohl, 6th edition, 1897), p. 162. See also Bismarck's memorandum on the Solution of the German Question (*Eine Denkschrift Bismarcks zur Lösung der deutschen Frage*, 1861), *ibid.* p. 220.

[4] For the German iron industry in the 'fifties, see W. Oechelhäuser, *Die Eisenindustrie des Zollvereins* (1855) and F. Harkort, *Beleuchtung der Eisenzollfrage...* (1859).

the Leipzig Fair to keep running accounts at the customs house. Prussia had complained at the previous General Congress that "it must be recognised that these facilities give opportunity for the exchange of free goods—that is to say, goods intended for export that have been made at home or have paid duty on importation—for warehoused goods which should remain in the Zollverein and are therefore liable to duty. Such exchange of goods and the consequent exportation of free goods, reduces the merchant's liability in respect of a corresponding amount of warehoused goods, and avoids payment of import duty upon it."[1] The South German States desired a reduction of "transition duties" levied by Prussia on wine from certain Zollverein States. Little was accomplished at Darmstadt. Prussia failed to secure a reduction of duties on iron and refused to give way on the question of "transition duties" on wine. Saxony declined to change the arrangements for collecting duties at the Leipzig Fair.

The twelfth General Congress was held in 1856. It met at Eisenach and was later adjourned to Weimar. Again there was a deadlock because Prussia refused to agree to the Bavarian demand for a reduction of the "transition duties" on wine and Bavarian opposition prevented the acceptance of Prussia's proposal for a reduction of import duties on iron. There were also long discussions on Prussia's suggestion that the Zollverein's revenues should be increased by raising the import duty on raw tobacco from 4 to 6 thalers per hundredweight and by levying an excise of 10 thalers on every *Morgen*[2] of land on which tobacco was grown in the Zollverein.[3] No agree-

---

[1] See Prussian memorandum in *Verhandlungen*, x (1854), Beilagen zum Hauptprotokoll, vi. Saxon replies are given in *Verhandlungen*, x (1854), Beilagen..., vii, and in *Verhandlungen*, xi (1854), Beilagen..., vii. Contrast the eighteenth-century practice in England with regard to goods warehoused for re-export described by E. H. Rideout in *Transactions of the Lancashire and Cheshire Historic Society*, vol. LXXXII (1930), pp. 1–41.

[2] The Berlin *Morgen* was equal to about two-thirds of an acre.

[3] *Verhandlungen*, xii (1856), Hauptprotokoll, sect. xvi and Beilagen zum Hauptprotokoll, vii.

ment could be reached on this question. Few results were achieved by the twelfth Congress. Import duties on wheat, meal and leguminous plants (*Hülsenfrüchte*) were, however, reduced.

At the thirteenth General Congress, which met at Hanover in 1858, the duties on iron and the "transition duties" on wines were once more discussed without any agreement being reached. Another problem was that of the abolition of the Zollverein transit dues. It was argued that they unduly hampered transit trade which had greatly increased since the construction of railways. Austria, Hamburg and Bremen were pressing for the removal of transit dues since much of their trade passed through Zollverein territory. Prussia had long resisted on financial grounds any proposal to abolish or to reduce these dues which were bringing in about 450,000 thalers a year. In 1857, during negotiations with Austria, she had refused to abolish them. In 1858, however, Prussia stated that she was prepared to accept the removal of transit dues. Baden, on the other hand, declared that she would agree to this only if the Rhine shipping dues were abolished at the same time. Von der Heydt (Prussian Minister of Commerce) was prepared to see transit and Rhine dues disappear together but his colleague von Bodelschwingh (Finance Minister) objected to both proposals. Moreover, Hesse-Darmstadt and Nassau were unwilling to lose the revenue provided by the Rhine dues and—as in the 'forties—they refused to accept their abolition. A decision on the question of these dues could not, in any case, be made at the General Congress since this was a matter on which all States with territory on the Rhine had to be consulted. So both the Zollverein transit dues and the Rhine dues remained. Once more particularist interests stood in the way of reform. The practical results of the Hanover Congress were insignificant.

The fourteenth General Congress of the Zollverein met at Harzburg in June, 1859, and was adjourned to Brunswick in September. Many proposals were put forward for changes in the tariff but the old disputes, particularly those between Prussia and Bavaria, prevented agreement except upon minor matters.

There was a reduction of import duties on a few articles such as tallow, rubber, oil in barrels, and pipes made from malleable iron. The allowance for tare on bales of over 8 cwt. (gross weight) was reduced.

Prussia had every reason for dissatisfaction at her failure to secure substantial tariff reductions at the Zollverein General Congresses held between 1854 and 1859. Many of her leading statesmen and Civil Servants were convinced that lower duties were essential from both an economic and political point of view. Every reduction of import duties would make it more difficult for Austria to join the Zollverein. On May 19, 1856, the King of Prussia informed his Ministers of Finance and Commerce that he was appointing a commission to prepare the way for a reform of the tariff and stated that it was "a political necessity to proceed with such a reduction of the Zollverein tariff so that Austria cannot follow suit too soon".[1] Yet by 1859 virtually no progress had been made and negotiations with Austria were due to begin in the following year.

In the circumstances Prussia had to be content to carry out economic reforms within her own frontiers. Monetary affairs demanded attention. It has been seen that while the value of gold was declining, that of silver was increasing slightly. Between 1852 and 1855 the average price of silver in London rose from 60 pence to $61\frac{3}{8}$ pence per ounce. The demand for silver for Far Eastern trade was rising and, since this metal was standard money in German States, fears began to be expressed that there might be a shortage of silver coins. Further, the general rise in prices encouraged business. An increase not merely of coins but of bank-notes was necessary. The Bank of Prussia—which had been founded in 1846 as a semi-private concern under public control—might issue notes only up to a total of 21 million thalers and certain private banks might together issue another three million thalers. This was not enough and many notes circulated which had been issued by banks (of

[1] Quoted by E. Franz, *Der Entscheidungskampf um die wirtschafts-politische Führung Deutschlands, 1856–67* (1933), p. 6.

somewhat doubtful standing) in small neighbouring States. So in 1856 the Prussian Bank was freed from restrictions regarding the number of notes to be issued. Permission was given to certain provincial private banks to issue up to one million thalers of notes each. In 1857 the use of foreign bank-notes was forbidden in Prussia.[1] Bavaria and Saxony took similar action. The conclusion of the Austro-Zollverein Monetary Convention of 1857 was another step towards the regulation of monetary affairs in Central Europe.

The Prussian Ministry of Commerce actively promoted the completion of a code of commercial law (*Allgemeines Deutsches Handelsgesetzbuch*) which, it was hoped, would be accepted by all German States. As early as 1836 Württemberg had proposed at the first Zollverein General Congress that a German commercial code should be drawn up.[2] Nothing came of this plan. The Frankfurt Parliament had begun the compilation of a commercial code but it was never adopted. At the tenth Zollverein General Congress of 1853–54 Württemberg again drew the attention of German States to this problem[3] and Prussia thereupon submitted a draft of her own which was, to a great extent, based upon the proposals made at Frankfurt in 1848. Still no agreement was reached.

In 1856 Bavaria took the lead but instead of bringing the question before the Zollverein General Congress she approached the Federal Diet at Frankfurt. She hoped to deprive Prussia of leadership in Germany as far as this important

[1] Prussia had previously (May, 1855) forbidden the settlement of accounts under 10 thalers in foreign bank-notes or foreign paper money.

[2] *Verhandlungen*, I (1836), Hauptprotokoll, xl, p. 95 and Beilage zum Hauptprotokoll, xi. In 1846 Württemberg suggested that the Zollverein should draw up a general German Law concerning Bills of Exchange (*Wechselrecht*). The draft of such a law was subsequently drawn up by the Frankfurt Parliament (1848) and was accepted by the Germanic Confederation. See S. Borchardt, *Die Allgemeine Deutsche Wechselordnung* (5th edition, 1869).

[3] *Verhandlungen*, x (1854), Hauptprotokoll, liv, pp. 153–7. Cf. VIII (1846), Hauptprotokoll, xxiv, pp. 63–7.

reform was concerned. Bavaria succeeded in making the discussions on the proposed commercial code a Federal and not a Zollverein matter. But she was not able to keep Prussia in the background for, contrary to her wishes, the Prussian draft formed the basis of the new German commercial code. Negotiations on the code at Nürnberg and Hamburg were prolonged and it was not until 1861 that the code was ready. It was immediately introduced into Prussia. By 1865 all German States except Holstein, Lauenburg and Schaumburg-Lippe had adopted it. Modifications were introduced in 1870 (when the code was adopted by the North German Confederation) and in 1884. The code remained in force until 1897.[1]

Various other reforms were undertaken in Prussia. The administration of the Prussian postal and telegraph system was improved and much attention was paid to railway building. A factory law of 1853 forbade the employment of children under the age of twelve and provided that young persons between the ages of twelve and fourteen, who worked in factories, should attend school for three hours a day. Inspectors were appointed to see that the law was carried out. The founding of friendly societies and savings banks under the control of local authorities was encouraged.

Contemporaries viewed from different angles the position of the German workers in the period of industrial expansion in the 'fifties. At the same time that Lassalle referred to the "eighty-nine per cent. of the population living under conditions of the greatest oppression" Wirth was writing of the "continued improvement in working class conditions which is obvious to everyone".[2] There is an element of truth in both statements. It is difficult to generalise on the social condition of a large section of the population which included persons in many occupations working under a great variety of conditions. The

---

[1] See R. Delbrück, II, pp. 161–7, and A. O. Meyer, *Bismarcks Kampf mit Österreich am Bundestag zu Frankfurt* (1927), pp. 309–20. Cf. Moritz Mohl, *Ein Beitrag zur Erörterung des deutschen Handelsgesetzbuches* (Stuttgart, 1857).   [2] Quoted by P. Benaerts, p. 593.

unskilled labourer who might be earning as little as $1\frac{1}{2}$ or 2 thalers a week and the skilled piano-maker whose wages amounted to as much as 17 thalers a week were both members of the working class but their economic positions were very different. Available statistics suggest that gross real wages in Germany in industry, transport and agriculture declined between 1850 and 1855 and then rose steadily.[1] The Ruhr coal-miners certainly secured a substantial increase in real wages in the 'fifties.

Though some factory workers and artisans shared in the general prosperity of the 'fifties, there was also much poverty and distress among the worst-paid men and among those who clung to dying trades. The labourer was still usually denied his *Gewerbefreiheit*—the freedom to enter what trade he pleased. Social discontent had been rife in the revolutionary years 1848–49 and many industrial workers and peasants had emigrated in despair. In the 'fifties the police were sufficiently vigilant to prevent disorder among the distressed. Communist writers found it more convenient to live outside Germany. But the way was being prepared for the Socialist movement which gained strength and importance during the 'sixties.

Germany's economic progress in the 'fifties was not un-interrupted. Many industries were affected by the widespread depression of 1857–59.[2] High prices and ample credit had encouraged industrial and commercial expansion in many parts of the world. There was much speculation and many doubtful

---

[1] J. Kuczynski's index of gross real wages in Germany (base year 1900, 100) is as follows: 1850, 83; 1851, 76; 1852, 64; 1853, 61; 1854, 55; 1856, 56; 1857, 71; 1858, 73; 1859, 74 (*Labour Conditions in Western Europe* (1937), p. 95).

[2] See anonymous article, "Die Handelskrisis...", in *Deutsche Viertel-jahrschrift*, XXI (1858), pp. 256–420; Otto Michaelis, *Volkswirtschaftliche Schriften*, I (1873), pp. 237–387 (eight essays on the commercial crisis of 1857); Max Wirth, *Geschichte der Handelskrisen* (4th edition, 1890), ch. xi; and Hans Rosenberg, *Die Weltwirtschaftskrisis von 1857–59* (1934). A list of books and articles on the crisis is given by Hans Rosenberg on pp. 9–12.

ventures were undertaken. In 1857 there was a good harvest. The re-establishment of normal commercial relationships between Russia and Western Europe after the Crimean War and the construction of new railways in the fertile Hungarian plain increased the amount of grain appearing on the world market. The price of wheat fell and the whole American market was affected. The failure of the Ohio Life Insurance and Trust Company in August, 1857, was the signal for a general panic.

In Britain two Scottish banks, one Liverpool bank and two leading London bill-broking houses failed within a month (October 12–November 11, 1857). Many firms went bankrupt owing either to the suspension of American remittances or to the undue extension of "open credits" to persons abroad to draw upon British houses. There was a drain of money to India owing to the expenses brought about by the Mutiny.[1]

The English failures and the rise of the London bank-rate had very serious results upon the commerce of Hamburg.[2] The outstanding acceptances of its merchants amounted to 400 million marks banco (£30,000,000).[3] On November 23, 1857, Colonel Hodges reported that "commercial confidence is entirely at an end among the merchants and moneyed capitalists of Hamburg; and that only bills on *three* or *four* of the first houses are negotiable at the highest rate of discount". On December 1 he

[1] L. H. Jenks, *The Migration of British Capital to* 1875 (1927), p. 190. Another cause of the high exports of silver to the Far East in 1856–57·was the necessity of paying for unusually high imports of raw silk owing to a bad silk harvest in Southern Europe.

[2] See Max Wirth, pp. 389–412; H. Treutler, "Die Wirtschaftskrise von 1857", in *Hamburger Übersee-Jahrbuch* (1927), pp. 301 ff., and contemporary articles cited by H. Rosenberg, p. 128 n.

[3] L. H. Jenks, p. 190. The Hamburg mark banco "consists of the sums inscribed in the books of the bank opposite to the names of those who have deposited specie or bullion in the bank, or got it transferred to them at the rate of 27½ marks banco to the Cologne mark of silver. The value of marks banco, taking silver at five shillings an ounce, is consequently 1s. 5½d. . . .". The Hamburg mark current, on the other hand, was worth about 1s. 2d. (J. R. McCulloch, *A Dictionary of Commerce*, I (edition of 1847), p. 624).

wrote that "the embarrassments of the mercantile community here still continue undiminished". One hundred and fifty firms collapsed and their total liabilities amounted to some 200 million marks banco (£15,000,000). A Discount Guarantee Association, whose funds amounted to 13 million marks banco (£1,000,000) was formed to discount bills drawn upon Hamburg but it was unable to allay the panic.[1] Efforts to raise money in Berlin failed but eventually a loan of 10 million marks banco (£750,000) was granted by the Austrian National Bank to enable Hamburg to re-establish its credit.[2]

Other parts of Germany did not suffer quite so much as Hamburg. Bremen, for example, escaped with only fourteen failures. Yet the effects of the depression were somewhat alarming. Prices fell rapidly and trade declined. The total value of Zollverein imports and exports sank from 994,000,000 thalers in 1857 to 886,000,000 thalers in 1859. There were many failures particularly among grain merchants and business men engaged mainly in export trade. Palmié Brothers of Berlin, for example, went bankrupt with liabilities of over $1\frac{1}{2}$ million thalers. The Prussian Bank raised its rate to $7\frac{1}{2}$ per cent in November, 1857. Austrian industries were more seriously hit than German industries. One of the worst failures was that of the Vienna and Budapest firm of Boskowitz, which had been speculating in grain.

When recovery came in the early 'sixties many inefficient and unsound undertakings had disappeared. The need for organising more stable and "rationalised" units of production was recognised. The early phase of the Industrial Revolution was over. Germany was shortly to enter her great era of industrial progress.

[1] Colonel Hodges to Lord Clarendon, November 23, 24 and December 1, 1857 (F.O. 33/156).
[2] See E. Baasch, "Zur Geschichte der Handelskrisis von 1857", in *Zeitschrift des Vereins für Hamburgische Geschichte*, XXX (1929), pp. 81–105.

(2) BRUCK'S SECOND ATTEMPT TO FOSTER AUSTRO-GERMAN ECONOMIC UNION, 1855–1859[1]

In the later 'fifties Bruck—who became Austrian Finance Minister in 1855—made a second attempt to foster Austro-German economic union. It met with even less success than the first. Except for the formation of the German Monetary Union of 1857 Bruck had little to show for his labours when the outbreak of the Italian War of 1859 prevented him from pressing forward with his schemes. In 1860 he was dismissed from office and he committed suicide. The discussions between Austria and the Zollverein in the years 1855–59 were not without importance since they formed an essential link between the previous negotiations which had culminated in the commercial treaty of February, 1853, and those which later led to the commercial treaty of April, 1865.

It has been seen that the Austro-Prussian commercial treaty of February 19, 1853, had provided that discussions should begin in 1854 for the further facilitation of transit trade, and in 1860 for the formation of a customs union. From the first these obligations to negotiate were regarded in a very different light in Vienna and Berlin. Austria had failed to enter the Zollverein but she had not given up her plan for an Austro-German customs union. She had merely agreed that negotiations should be postponed to a more favourable moment. She hoped that the

---

[1] For the commercial negotiations between the Zollverein and Austria in the later 'fifties, see K. Hock, "Die Verhandlungen über ein österreichisch-deutsches Zollbündnis 1849–64", in *Österreichische Revue*, parts i, ii, iii; A. Matlekovits, *Die Zollpolitik der österreichisch-ungarischen Monarchie von 1850 bis zur Gegenwart* (1877), pp. 40–65; K. Mamroth, *Die Entwicklung der Österreichisch-Deutschen Handelsbeziehungen...* 1849–65 (1887), ch. ii; R. Charmatz, *Minister Freiherr von Bruck* (1916), ch. vii; E. Franz, *Der Entscheidungskampf um die wirtschaftspolitische Führung Deutschlands 1856–67* (1933), ch. i; A. Beer, ch. vi; and R. von Delbrück, II, ch. xxi. For Bruck's economic reforms in Austria in this period, see letters from Henry Elliot to Lord Clarendon, September 5, 1855 (F.O. 7/457, no. 93); October 10 and 24, 1855 (F.O. 7/458: nos. 149, 168); October 31 (two letters) and November 21, 1855 (nos. 180, 183, 211).

discussions which were to begin in 1854 would pave the way to union. Prussia, on the other hand, continued to oppose the scheme for an Austro-German economic union. She felt that the treaty of February, 1853, had placed the commercial relations of the two parties on a reasonably satisfactory footing. She had agreed reluctantly to the provisions for future negotiations and viewed with satisfaction the delay between the signing of a protocol on February 20, 1854 (which elaborated various provisions of the commercial treaty of February, 1853) and its ratification in August, 1855. Prussia pursued a policy of procrastination and the negotiations on the further facilitation of trade which should have begun in 1854 were not undertaken until 1858. Meanwhile, however, the Austro-Zollverein monetary convention of 1857 had been signed.

In the interval both parties prepared for the negotiations. Austria's steps were directed towards ensuring their success, Prussia's towards ensuring their failure.

Bruck was appointed Austrian Finance Minister in March, 1855. His views on the future of Austro-German economic affairs had changed little from the time when, as Minister of Commerce, he had worked for the establishment of a Central European customs union. He still favoured this plan and regarded the February Treaty as the first step towards its fulfilment. But he recognised more clearly the difficulties that had to be overcome.

Bruck saw that just as it had been necessary to undertake various reforms—such as the abolition of the Austro-Hungarian customs frontier and the revision of the Hapsburg tariff—before the previous negotiations with German States could be undertaken, so now it was essential to carry out further economic reforms before discussions with Prussia could be commenced.

It has been observed that the Hapsburg dominions did not share in the general prosperity of the 'fifties. Despite the reforms of 1849–53 the economic condition of Austria was unsatisfactory when Bruck took office again. Commerce languished. At the end of 1851 the national debt had amounted to over 1500 million florins and in the next four years (1852–55) the deficit on the budgets amounted to nearly 390 million florins. Depreciated Austrian paper money had fluctuated violently between 1849 and 1854[1] and silver coins had practically been driven out of circulation. The mobilisation during the Crimean War had severely strained the national finances. Military expenditure amounted to 375 million florins in the three years 1854–56. It had been necessary to raise a large (virtually forced) loan.[2]

Bruck lost no time in getting to work. In October and November 1855, he strengthened the position of the National Bank by arranging for Crown Lands (valued at 155 million florins) to be placed at its disposal. He helped to extend credit facilities by fostering the formation of two important institutions. The first was a Mortgage Bank (*Hypothekenbank*)[3]—a branch of the National Bank—with a capital of 35 million florins. The second was the Austrian Credit Institute for Commerce and Industry (*Österreichische Kreditanstalt für Handel und Gewerbe*)[4] which had a capital of 100 million florins. It was

[1] The extent of the fluctuations may be seen from the following table which shows the *agio* (exchange premium) payable for converting Austrian paper money into silver:

		%		%
1849	June	24	October	6
1850	February	14	December	31
1851	April	$33\frac{1}{2}$	July	$18\frac{1}{2}$
1852	January	$24\frac{1}{2}$	December	$10\frac{3}{4}$
1853	June	$9\frac{1}{4}$	October	$15\frac{1}{4}$
1854	March	39	August	$14\frac{3}{4}$

See *Deutsche Vierteljahrschrift*, XXII (1859), i, p. 376.

[2] For the Austrian finances in the early 'fifties, see Hanssen, "Einige Data zur Beurteilung der österreichischen Finanzen", in *Zeitschrift für die gesammte Staatswissenschaft*, XIII (Tübingen), pp. 476–89.

[3] See C. S. von Waisenfreund, *Ein Beitrag zur Würdigung der Hypothekar-Credits-Abteilung der österreichischen Nationalbank* (1856).

[4] See M. Hein, *Die österreichische Creditanstalt . . .* (1857). An English translation of the statutes of the Institute was sent by Henry Elliot to Lord Clarendon in an enclosure to his letter of November 21, 1855 (F.O. 7/459, no. 211).

founded by a group of influential Austrian aristocrats and much of the money was raised by the Rothschilds. In August, 1858, the National Bank was authorised to pay cash for paper money[1] and was obliged to hold bullion amounting to at least one-third of the notes issued.

Bruck also encouraged the construction of new railways in the Hapsburg Empire. A number of existing State lines had recently been handed over to private companies as the Government had been unable to run them at a profit and had urgently needed money to pay for the mobilisation of 1854. Bruck continued this policy. By the end of 1858 most of the former State railways were in private hands and there they remained for some twenty years.[2] In 1856 the Austrian tariff was revised. Several duties were reduced, the most important being those on pig-iron and textile yarns. In the following year the free importation of certain textile machines was permitted. At the same time a new special tariff was introduced into Dalmatia (an isolated province separated by a customs frontier from other Hapsburg dominions).

While Bruck was carrying out these reforms in the Hapsburg Empire in the hope of facilitating the future union between Austria and the Zollverein, his old opponent Delbrück was attempting to secure changes in the Zollverein tariff which would render it more difficult for Austria to join such a union. It has been observed that at the General Congresses held between 1854 and 1859 Prussia proposed various reductions in import duties in the hope of widening the gulf between the tariffs of the Zollverein and Austria. These proposals did not, however, meet with much success.

The only negotiations between Austria and the Zollverein to be brought to a successful conclusion at this time were those for the establishment of a German Monetary Union (*Deutscher*

---

[1] See anonymous article, "Die Wiederherstellung einer festen Valuta in Österreich", in *Deutsche Vierteljahrschrift*, XXII (1859), i, pp. 356–89.

[2] See Friedrich Freiherr von Weichs, *Fünfzig Jahre Eisenbahn* (Denkschrift zum fünfzigjährigen Jubiläum der Locomotiv-Eisenbahn in Österreich-Ungarn, 1888), pp. 9–13.

Münzverein).[1] The question had already been discussed at Vienna in 1854 and 1855 but no agreement had been reached since Prussia had refused to agree to Austria's suggestion that gold should take the place of silver as standard money in Germany. Not until Austria gave way on this point in January, 1856, were the negotiations resumed.

It has been seen that in 1838 a fixed relationship had been established—on the basis of the Cologne mark of fine silver—between the thaler currency of Prussia, Hanover and other North German States and the florin currency of the South German States. In 1857 an attempt was made to secure a fixed relationship not merely between these two currencies but also between them and the Austrian monetary system.

This was done not on the basis of the Cologne mark but on that of the metric pound (*Zollpfund*) which weighed 500 grammes. Instead of coining 14 Prussian thalers or 24½ South German florins from a Cologne mark, it was agreed that 30 Prussian thalers,[2] 52½ South German florins[3] or 45 Austrian

---

[1] For German monetary affairs in the middle of the nineteenth century, see A. Soetbeer, *Denkschrift über Hamburgs Münzverhältnis* (1846); H. A. Helferich, "Die Einheit im deutschen Münzwesen", in *Zeitschrift für die gesammte Staatswissenschaft*, VI (Tübingen, 1850), pp. 385–437, and J. F. Hauschild, *Geschichte des deutschen Mass- und Münzwesens in den letzten sechzig Jahren* (1861). For the German Monetary Union of 1857, see anonymous article, "Der deutsche Münzvertrag", in *Deutsche Vierteljahrschrift*, II (1857), pp. 1–85; A. E. F. Schäffle, "Die deutsche Münz-Convention vom 24. Januar 1857...", in *Zeitschrift für die gesammte Staatswissenschaft*, XIII (Tübingen, 1857), pp. 92–141, 264–372; *Papers respecting the Monetary Convention dated January 24, 1857, between the Austrian Government...and the States of the Zollverein* (P.P. 1857–58, LX); M. F. Lakner, *Was für ein Geld werden wir in Zukunft haben?...* (2nd edition, 1858); and Carl T. Helfferich, *Die Folgen des Deutsch-Österreichischen Münz-Vereins von 1857* (1894).

[2] The thaler was the currency of Prussia, Hanover, Oldenburg, Saxony, Hesse-Cassel and various small States. It also circulated freely in Hamburg, Lübeck and Lauenburg (1 thaler = 2½ marks *courant*) and in Schleswig and Holstein (1 thaler = 40 schillings).

[3] The South German florin was the currency of Bavaria, Württemberg, Baden, Hesse-Darmstadt, Nassau, Frankfurt-am-Main and various small States.

florins[1] should be coined from one metric pound of fine silver. This resulted in a reduction of 0·022 per cent in the weight of the thaler and South German florin.

Two new silver coins and two new gold coins were to be issued both in the Zollverein States and in the Hapsburg dominions. The silver coins were the Union thaler (*Vereinsthaler*) and the double Union thaler. The former weighed one-thirtieth of a metric pound and was equal to the new Prussian thaler. The gold coins were the crown (*Krone*) and half-crown. The crown weighed 10 grammes of fine gold. Gold coins hitherto issued by separate States—such as friedrichs d'or, pistoles and ducats—were to be withdrawn from circulation.[2] The four new coins did not secure a very general circulation.

The Monetary Union of 1857 did not establish a single currency in all the Zollverein States and in the Hapsburg Empire.[3] It recognised three main currencies and attempted to fix the relationship between them. It was successful in securing a fixed ratio between the North German thaler and the South German florin. It failed, however, to establish a fixed ratio between these two currencies and the Austrian florin because the Austrian Government broke the Convention of 1857 and retained its fluctuating paper money (except during the short period between September 6, 1858, and April 21, 1859). Reformers argued that the Austro-Zollverein Monetary Convention of 1857 did not go far enough and that a single decimal coinage for the whole of Germany was desirable.[4]

---

[1] The Austrian florin was the currency of the Hapsburg dominions and Liechtenstein. The old Austrian florin had been divided into 60 kreuzers: the new florin was divided into 100 kreuzers. Austria retained the right to continue to issue the Maria Theresa thaler of 1780.

[2] But Austria retained the right to continue to issue gold ducats until the end of 1865.

[3] Luxemburg and the States that were still outside the Zollverein— namely the two Mecklenburgs, the three Hanse towns, Schleswig, Holstein and Lauenburg—did not sign the Austro-Zollverein Monetary Convention of 1857.

[4] See, for example, the proposals made in 1861 by Max Wirth to the fourth Congress of German Economists (*Vierte Versammlung des Con-*

In so far as it applied to Austria the Monetary Union came to an end with the outbreak of the Seven Weeks' War. By the Treaty of Prague it was agreed to open negotiations to wind up the affairs of the Union. These negotiations were successfully concluded in 1867 and the Monetary Union was dissolved at the end of that year. Its provisions remained in force in the Zollverein, however, until they were superseded by the new monetary arrangements of the German Empire.

At the same time that Bruck was pressing forward with internal economic reforms and with discussions for a German Monetary Union he made every effort to secure the opening of negotiations with Prussia for further mutual reductions of duties. In October, 1855, Prussia was asked if she were prepared to begin the discussions contemplated in the February treaty. Prussia asked for a postponement until the Zollverein States had had time to make the necessary preparations. In 1856 both Austria and Prussia prepared for the forthcoming negotiations.[1] It was not, however, until the middle of 1857 that Prussia declared that she was ready for the conference.

Before negotiations actually began both Austria and the Zollverein suffered from the effects of the commercial crisis of

gresses deutscher Volkswirte (Stuttgart, 1861), pp. 87–92), and by A. Soetbeer to the first Congress of representatives of German Chambers of Commerce (Verhandlungen des ersten deutschen Handelstags zu Heidelberg vom 13. bis 18. Mai 1861 (Berlin, 1861), pp. 24–30, 97–100).

[1] See two memoranda of Franz Josef on the proposals which Austria intended to put forward in the negotiations (March 19, 1856, and October 13, 1856), reprinted by A. Beer, pp. 586–8. For the Austrian point of view see also extracts from articles which appeared in the Augsburg Allgemeine Zeitung at the end of December, 1856, reprinted in French translation by É. Worms, L'Allemagne Économique... (1874), pp. 250–3.

[2] Bismarck told Rechberg at this time that "there could...be no question of Austria entering the Zollverein and he regretted that in Berlin the possibility of such a step should have been envisaged". Rechberg to Buol, July 17, 1857 (quoted by A. O. Meyer, Bismarcks Kampf mit Österreich am Bundestag zu Frankfurt (1927), p. 551).

the autumn of 1857. It was difficult enough for comparatively strong German industries to weather the storm but for some branches of Austrian industry and commerce the results of the crisis were catastrophic. Austrian industrialists complained that their losses were due to the abandonment of the old prohibitive tariff and demanded the imposition of higher import duties. Bruck was placed in a difficult position since he wanted a further reduction of the tariff so that Austria might one day form a customs union with the Zollverein.

Negotiations between Austria and the Zollverein began in Vienna in January, 1858, under the shadow of this commercial crisis. Although Austrian statesmen recognised that the industrial depression would make it difficult for them to make many concessions to the Zollverein, they hoped that the recently published Danube Navigation Act (November 7, 1857) would show that Austria fully intended to play her part in facilitating trade in Central Europe. At the Vienna discussions the Zollverein was represented by plenipotentiaries from Prussia, Bavaria and Saxony. Hock, the Austrian representative, suggested that there should be a mutual abolition of transit dues and a mutual reduction of the import duty on wine (in barrels) from six to two thalers per hundredweight. Prussia rejected the abolition of transit dues, and Bavaria—which had an important wine-growing region in the Palatinate—refused to agree to a reduction of duties on wines. The negotiations came to an end in April, 1858, without achieving any result.

Bruck had failed in his new attempt to pave the way for an Austro-Zollverein customs union. He made no progress with his plan in 1858. He hoped that the General Congress, which was to meet at Hanover in that year, would abolish the Zollverein transit dues and so enable negotiations to be resumed with a greater prospect of success. It has been observed that, although Prussia was now prepared to accept abolition, Baden wanted the Rhine shipping dues to be removed at the same time. To this Hesse-Darmstadt and Nassau objected and, in the end, nothing was done. About the same time Bruck sent Professor

Jonák to Germany to ascertain what support could be expected there for Bruck's scheme for an Austro-Zollverein customs union. Jonák reported that, on the whole, German industrialists did not favour the plan, for they had little hope of finding in the Hapsburg dominions a greatly extended market for their manufactured goods. In Prussia, Saxony and the small States on the Rhine there was generally opposition to union with Austria. The North German Press—particularly the *Kölnische Zeitung*—was sharply criticising Bruck's plans. In South Germany Bruck could hope for greater support but there was no readiness to agree to any reduction of import duties on wine.[1]

The disastrous Italian War of 1859 still further weakened Austria's economic position and led to the downfall of Bruck. The financial position of the country became worse and worse.[2] New debts accumulated and new loans had to be raised. The National Bank suspended cash payments in April, 1859,[3] and the sinking fund was abolished in December of the same year. Austria was defeated at Magenta and Solferino and had to give up the province of Lombardy.

Bruck saw that internal reform was more necessary than ever. He laid his programme of reform before the Emperor in a long memorandum that has been described as "one of the greatest State documents ever dedicated to the Hapsburg Monarchy".[4] Bruck himself did not live to see many of the changes he had advocated carried out. One very important reform, however,

[1] Professor Jonák's six reports to Bruck are summarised by E. Franz, pp. 26–7.

[2] For Austrian finances at the end of the 'fifties, see anonymous article, "Zur Finanzlage Österreichs", *Deutsche Vierteljahrschrift*, XXIII (1860), ii, pp. 146–70.

[3] By leaving the silver standard Austria broke the Austro-Zollverein Monetary Convention of 1857. See Carl T. Helfferich, *Die Folgen des Deutsch-Österreichischen Münz-Vereins von* 1857 (1894), p. 21.

[4] R. Charmatz, p. 127. The memorandum was published in 1860 under the title *Die Aufgaben Österreichs*. It has been reprinted by R. Charmatz, pp. 241–81.

was made at the end of 1859—the introduction of a new industrial code.[1]

In 1860 Bruck's career ended in tragedy. Enquiries were made into alleged mismanagement and dishonesty on the part of those engaged in provisioning the army. The Director-General of the Army Provision Department committed suicide after confessing his guilt. Several arrests were made in Triest. The chief director of the Austrian Credit Institute for Commerce and Industry was questioned. On April 20, 1860, Bruck himself was interrogated by an examining magistrate. Two days later he was dismissed from his post. He ended his life with his own hand, but subsequent investigation showed that he was innocent of any dishonesty in his management of the country's finances.

Bruck was one of the greatest Austrian statesmen of the nineteenth century. He combined the efficiency of the successful business man with the breadth of view of the statesman. Before he took office he helped to found the Austrian Lloyd which became one of the leading shipping companies operating in the Mediterranean. Then as Minister of Commerce and as Minister of Finance he carried through far-reaching economic reforms in spite of many difficulties and much opposition. He played a leading part in abolishing the Austro-Hungarian customs frontier and in replacing the prohibitive Hapsburg tariff by protective duties. He fostered railway construction and helped to provide credit facilities for agriculture and industry. He was, in no small measure, responsible for the Austro-Prussian commercial treaty of February, 1853, and the German Monetary Union of 1857. He failed to found a great Central European customs union but he did much to break down economic barriers between Austria and the German States.

[1] For economic conditions in the Hapsburg Empire in the late 'fifties and early 'sixties, see anonymous article. "The Resources and Future of Austria", in *The Quarterly Review*, CXIV (July 1863), pp. 1–42.

(3) COMMERCIAL RELATIONS WITH FOREIGN COUNTRIES, 1854–1859[1]

The most important international negotiations in which Prussia was engaged in this period were those which led to the abolition of the Sound dues.[2] These tolls were levied by Denmark at Helsingör (Elsinore), 22 miles north of Copenhagen. "Stream tolls"—charged upon the same principles as Sound dues—were levied at Nyborg (on Fünen island) on ships passing through the Great Belt and at Fredericia (in Jutland) on ships passing through the Little Belt.

The Sound dues were complicated and preferences were granted to the ships and cargoes of certain States. In the nine years 1842–47 and 1851–53 Denmark secured nearly £250,000 annually from the dues.[3] They formed an important part of the Danish national revenue and had been pledged as security for foreign loans.[4] The three Powers whose ships and cargoes paid

[1] See R. von Delbrück, II, ch. xviii.

[2] See C. F. Wurm, *Der Sundzoll und dessen Verpflanzung auf deutschen Boden* (1838); J. F. V. Schlegel, "The Origin and History of the Sound and Belt Tolls", in *The Merchants' Magazine and Commercial Review*, X (New York, 1844), pp. 218–32 (translated from the Danish); H. Scherer, *Der Sundzoll* (1854); J. R. McCulloch, article on "Elsineur" in *A Dictionary of Commerce*, I (edition of 1847), pp. 544–53; anonymous pamphlets: *On Sound Dues and their Relations with General Commerce* (Stettin, 1854: copy in F.O. 22/244 A), *Letters on the Sound Dues Question* (New York, 1855: copy in F.O. 22/244 A), and *A Few Words on the Sound Dues* (London, 1856); F. P. van der Hoeven, *Bijdrage tot de Geschiednis van den Sonttol...* (1855); *Report from the Select Committee on the Sound Dues* (P.P. 1856, XVI); M. Rubin, "Sundtoldens Afløsning", in *Dansk Historisk Tiddskrift*, VI (1905–6), pp. 172–311; C. E. Hill, *The Danish Sound Dues and the Command of the Baltic* (Duke University Press, 1926), pp. 241–86; and A. Nielsen, *Dänische Wirtschaftsgeschichte* (1933), pp. 451–61. See also seven volumes of documents in F.O. 22/244 A to 22/249, particularly *Memorandum: Sound Dues Treaty* (in F.O. 22/248).

[3] Andrew Buchanan (Copenhagen) to Lord Clarendon, February 2, 1856 (F.O. 22/244 B).

[4] See, for example, *Memorandum: Anglo-Danish Loan of 1825 and Security of Sound Dues* (F.O. 22/244 A).

most dues in 1851–53 were Britain (29 per cent of the total),
Russia (29 per cent) and Prussia (12 per cent).[1]

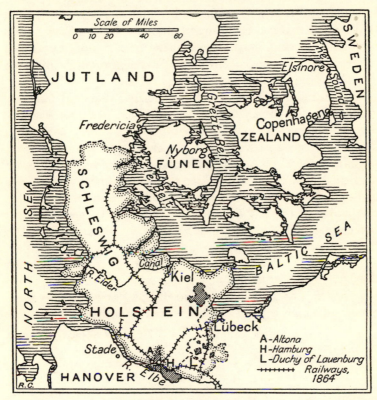

10. Denmark and the Duchies of Schleswig, Holstein and Lauenburg.

Note how Denmark's geographical position enabled her to tax North German
trade by levying dues (a) on the Sound (Elsinore), Great Belt (Nyborg)
and Little Belt (Fredericia), (b) on roads and railways in the Duchies of
Schleswig, Holstein and Lauenburg, (c) on the Eider Canal.

A pamphleteer observed in 1854 that Prussia had "reduced
the fees of her consul at Elsinore in 1845 so that the foreign

[1] See *Tableau montant des quoteparts à payer par les États nommés
ci-dessous...* (F.O. 22/249).

exaction might be less severely felt. Already since 1825 a discount of 2½ per cent has been allowed to Stettin on the import-, export- or transit-dues for all goods passing the Sound to or from that port." In 1845 this concession was extended to all Baltic ports.[1] Baltic traffic was hampered by the Sound dues not merely because tolls were greatly in excess of any service rendered but because much delay and expense might be incurred in making the payment.[2]

The Sound dues were over four hundred years old and were first levied at a time when Denmark held both sides of the Sound. Her right to levy them had been recognised by various treaties. Protests of foreign countries against them, however, were frequent. In the 'forties Denmark reduced the tolls levied on British and Prussian ships and cargoes. The United States had signed a commercial treaty with Denmark in 1826 by which she had agreed to pay Sound dues. Although American ships and cargoes paid only 2 per cent of the total dues collected in the early 'fifties, the United States was interested in the export of raw cotton to Baltic ports and she had often protested against the Sound dues. She claimed that a country which now held only one side of the Sound had no right to levy tolls on vessels passing through it from one open sea to another.[3]

[1] *On Sound Dues and their Relations with General Commerce* (Stettin, 1854), p. 21.

[2] The Hull Chamber of Commerce had complained in 1838 that "the delay at the Sound of a few hours, is often the *cause*, from change of wind, and other circumstances, of a voyage being protracted several days, sometimes of damage, and even of the loss of vessel and cargo..." (*First Annual Report of Hull Chamber of Commerce* (1838), p. 7). Eighteen years later an English parliamentary committee reported that "the Sound dues...as they are levied at present, combine in them what is most objectionable in taxes that fall upon trade; they are unequal in their operation, and they occasion great loss of time and much needless expenditure in the collection of a comparatively small revenue, and, as far as cargoes are concerned, without professing to be raised for any service rendered in return, tend to impede and burden an important branch of trade" (P.P. 1856, xvi, p. 524).

[3] A. P. Upshur (Secretary of State) reported to President Tyler in November, 1843, that "Denmark cannot demand this toll upon any

In April, 1855, the United States denounced her commercial treaty with Denmark and indicated that, when the treaty expired in a year's time, Americans would refuse to pay the tolls. Denmark gained time by securing a prolongation of the commercial treaty with the United States to June, 1857. In June, 1855, the Prussian Government suggested that the Sound dues should be reduced to about a third of the existing level and should be collected at Baltic and North Sea ports (so as to avoid the delay of making payment at Elsinore).[1]

A few months later (October, 1855) Denmark invited all States interested in Baltic trade to a conference to discuss the future of the dues. The United States declined the invitation since the question of Denmark's right to levy tolls on the Sound and Belts was not to be dealt with at the negotiations.[2] The other Powers concerned, however, agreed to confer. The fighting in the Crimea did not prevent the three chief belligerents from co-operating to settle the vexed question of the Sound dues. Negotiations began in January, 1856, and Denmark offered to abolish the dues in return for a payment of 35 million rigsdalers (£3,888,888) which was equal to about fifteen years' purchase of the tolls. This solution of the problem was accepted in principle but it was not until March, 1857, that agreement was finally reached between Denmark and the States mainly interested in Baltic trade. Denmark eventually obtained rather less compensation (about £3,600,000) than she had originally demanded.

Denmark had also hampered North German trade by levying transit dues in Jutland, Schleswig, Holstein and Lauenburg on roads, railways and on the Eider and Stecknitz canals. In

principle of natural or public law nor upon any other ground than ancient usage". See Letters on the Sound Dues Question (New York, 1855), p. 20; C. E. Hill, p. 275.

[1] A copy of the Prussian memorandum on the Sound dues was sent by Lord Bloomfield to Lord Clarendon, June 8, 1855 (F.O. 64/394).

[2] The U.S.A., however, agreed in 1857 to pay Denmark 393,011 dollars if the sound dues were abolished and Denmark continued to light and buoy the sound and the two Belts.

this way she had been able to prevent foreign merchants evading payment of Sound dues by using alternative land routes from the Baltic to the North Sea. In 1838 various Danish transit dues on these routes were converted into a fixed duty of 16 Danish skillings (about $4\frac{1}{2}d$.) per 100 lb. to which a 6 per cent "expedition charge" was added. With the construction of railways in the Duchies some modifications were made. Certain bulky articles were exempted from transit duty on the Hamburg-Lübeck railway and goods carried by the Hamburg-Berlin railway paid only a fifth of the normal duty. (The latter concession assimilated the duties paid on the railway with those charged on traffic on the River Elbe.[1]) It was estimated that the transit dues brought in about 60,000 rigsdalers (£6600) a year to the Danish treasury in the early 'fifties.[2] In 1857 Denmark agreed that the transit duties on all routes connecting the Baltic and the Elbe with the North Sea should be reduced to a uniform rate of 16 Danish skillings per 500 Danish lb.[3] Existing exemptions in favour of goods passing along certain routes were to be extended to all routes. Any future reductions or exemptions were to apply equally to all lines of communication between the Baltic and the North Sea. The abolition of the Sound dues and the substantial reduction of Danish transit dues were of considerable benefit to Zollverein trade.

Other commercial negotiations undertaken by Prussia on behalf of the Zollverein in the 'fifties were of less importance. On January 26, 1856, two treaties were signed with Bremen. By the first, ships of one contracting party entering the harbours of the other were to be treated on the basis of reciprocity. To facilitate trade and to prevent smuggling Bremen agreed that

[1] See *Papers and Correspondence relating to the Danish Transit Dues* (P.P. 1857 (session 2), XLIII, 523) and *Droits de Transit*, a Danish memorandum enclosed in Buchanan to Lord Clarendon, August 30, 1856 (F.O. 22/244 B).

[2] Buchanan to Lord Clarendon, August 11, 1857 (F.O. 22/249).

[3] This was the same rate as that hitherto levied on the Hamburg-Berlin railway except that the slightly heavier Danish lb. replaced the Hamburg lb. as the unit of measurement.

certain portions of her territory should enter the Zollverein and that a Zollverein customs house and warehouse should be established in Bremen. The second treaty with Bremen was signed by Prussia, Hanover and Hesse-Cassel on their own behalf and not on behalf of the Zollverein. It provided for the suspension of the Weser toll and was to come into force when other States interested in the navigation of the river agreed to co-operate. Agreement was soon reached and the toll was suspended on January 1, 1857.[1]

There were negotiations on economic matters with two of the Italian States. First, in 1856 the Kingdom of the two Sicilies agreed to treat all Prussian ships using her harbours in the same way as native vessels. Since 1847 such treatment had been confined to Prussian ships arriving from home ports. Secondly, Prussia was anxious to secure from Sardinia the same reduction in the import duty on spirits that had recently been conceded to France and Austria. Cavour would not agree to this unless Sardinia received some equivalent concession. So in 1856 Prussia proposed to the General Congress that the Zollverein import duty on rice (*geschälter Reis*) should be reduced from 1 thaler to 15 silver groschens per hundredweight. "But Bavaria and Hesse-Darmstadt, who did not export spirits to Italy and were glad of an opportunity of putting a spoke in our wheel, refused to agree to this."[2] Here may be seen a typical example of the petty and selfish economic policy of some of the German States. At the General Congress of 1859, however, Prussia obtained a reduction in the Zollverein import duty on certain silk goods and this enabled her to secure from Sardinia the desired concession regarding the export of Zollverein spirits to that country.

Four commercial treaties were signed with American States. The rise of protectionism in Mexico led that country to de-

---

[1] These treaties of 1856 are printed by F. Houth-Weber, *Der Zollverein seit seiner Erweiterung durch den Steuerverein* (1861), pp. 215–75. Cf. W. Ditmar, *Der deutsche Zollverein*, II, *Die Gesetze, Verordnungen und Verträge* (1868), pp. 263 ff.

[2] R. von Delbrück, II, p. 63.

nounce all her commercial treaties in 1854.[1] A new treaty between Prussia and Mexico was signed in the following year. It
remained in force until 1867 when Mexico denounced all
treaties with States which had recognised Maximilian as Emperor of Mexico. The interest of German States in the economic
development of the La Plata region was increasing at this time
and between 1856 and 1859 Prussia signed commercial treaties
with Uruguay, the Argentine and Paraguay. Attempts to conclude commercial agreements with Venezuela and San Domingo
failed.

The six years 1854–59 had thus been a period of economic
prosperity in Europe in which Germany had shared. But over-
speculation and unwise trading had contributed to the commercial crisis of 1857. The abolition of the Sound dues and the
establishment of the Austro-German Monetary Union had
facilitated German commerce. But the legacy of the first Zollverein crisis of 1849–53 had prevented the reform of the Zollverein tariff. The protectionist South German States had frustrated Prussia's attempts to secure tariff reductions at the
General Congresses. Austria had shared in the prosperity of
the 'fifties to only a limited extent and had suffered severely
from the crisis of 1857 and the Italian War of 1859. Negotiations for an Austro-German customs union were due to begin
in 1860. Bruck was dead but his plan did not die with him. It
was revived by Rechberg in 1862. Prussia, however, was as
hostile as ever to the conclusion of a customs union between the
Zollverein and the Hapsburg Empire. The stage was set for the
second Zollverein crisis of 1860–65.

[1] For Mexico's denunciation of her commercial treaties of 1831 with
Prussia and Saxony, see Lord Augustus Loftus to Lord Clarendon,
October 13, 1854 and enclosure (F.O. 64/376).

Chapter VIII

THE SECOND ZOLLVEREIN CRISIS, 1860–1865[1]

(1) THE PROGRESS OF FREE-TRADE, 1860–1865[2]

The 'sixties, in which Bismarck rose to power in Prussia and challenged Austria, were on the whole a period of prosperity in Germany. The continued production of gold from California

---

[1] The standard work on the second Zollverein crisis, 1860–65, is E. Franz, *Der Entscheidungskampf um die wirtschaftspolitische Führung Deutschlands, 1856–67* (1933). This book contains a useful bibliography (pp. 437–43) which includes references to a number of important articles by Dr Franz himself.

See also "Die Zolleinigung mit Österreich", in *Deutsche Vierteljahrschrift*, xxv, iv, pp. 297–376; *Der Zollverein Deutschlands und die Krisis mit welcher er bedroht ist* (two parts, 1862); F. Wertheim, *Bericht über die österreichischen Vorschläge zur Zolleinigung mit Deutschland* (1862); H. Robolsky, *Der deutsche Zollverein* (1862); A. Emminghaus, *Entwicklung, Krisis und Zukunft des deutschen Zollvereins* (1863); *Bericht der besonderen Kommission des Nieder-Österreichischen Gewerbevereins für Erörterung der handelspolitischen Frage* (1863); K. Hock, "Die Verhandlungen über ein österreichisch-deutsches Zollbündnis, 1849–64", in *Österreichische Revue* (1864), parts i, ii, iii; and "Der Vertrag vom 11. April 1865", in *Österreichische Revue*, v (1867), pp. 1–37; A. Matlekovits, *Die Zollpolitik der österreichisch-ungarischen Monarchie von 1850 bis zur Gegenwart* (1877); K. V. Rieke, "Die Tarifreform im Zollverein", in *Zeitschrift für die gesammte Staatswissenschaft*, xix (Tübingen, 1863), pp. 319–68; J. Frühauf, "Das Projekt einer Zollunion Österreichs mit Deutschland in geschichtlicher Entwicklung", in *Unsere Zeit* (1886), pp. 79–106, 206–25, 376–88; K. Mamroth, *Die Entwicklung der Österreich-Deutschen Handelsbeziehungen...1849–65* (1887); F. Engel-Jánosi, "Die Krise des Jahres 1864 in Österreich", in *Historische Studien A. F. Přibram zum siebzigsten Geburtstag dargebracht* (1929); W. Weber,

---

For the continuation and note 2 see p. 264.

and elsewhere kept up the price level. Credit was plentiful and manufacturers were able to open up new markets. Communications continued to improve. By 1865 there were nearly 8700 miles of railways in Germany. A rapid recovery was made after the crisis of 1857 and some of the lessons of that depression were taken to heart. The Anglo-French commercial treaty of 1860 was the first of an important series of agreements in Western Europe which led to substantial reductions in import duties. Never before or since has commerce had to contend with fewer tariff barriers than in the 'sixties.

German agriculture and industry both shared in the general prosperity. There were excellent harvests in the early 'sixties and large quantities of grain were exported from the Baltic ports. The production of coal, iron and steel increased. Between 1860 and 1864 the production of coal in the Zollverein increased from 12,300,000 to 16,400,000 tons, of lignite from 4,380,000 to 6,200,000 tons, and of iron ore from 1,400,000 to 2,620,000 tons. The consumption of many colonial products rose. The

chs. xxx, xxxi; H. von Festenberg-Packisch, ch. xi; E. Worms, ch. iii; A. Beer, ch. viii and R. von Delbrück, chs. xxvii–xxxv.

The following books contain documents on the Zollverein crisis of 1860–65: L. K. Aegidi and A. Klauhold, *Die Krisis des Zollvereins urkundlich dargestellt* (Beilage zu dem *Staatsarchiv*, Oct.–Nov. Heft, Hamburg, 1862); H. von Poschinger, *Aktenstücke zur Wirtschaftspolitik des Fürsten Bismarck*, vol. I (1890) (see parts i and ii); Bismarck: *Die gesammelten Werke*, vols. III (1925), IV (1927), VI (1929), VIa (1930), VII (1924) and X (1928).

For political and diplomatic events, see, for example, H. von Sybel, *Die Begründung des deutschen Reiches unter Kaiser Wilhelm I* (7 vols. 1889–94 and 1892–95, new editions 1901 and 1913: English translation in 3 vols. 1890–91); H. Friedjung, *Der Kampf um die Vorherrschaft in Deutschland* (1897 and 1916: abridged English translation, 1935); E. Brandenburg, *Die Reichsgründung* (2 vols. 1916).

[2] See the works cited above in Chapter v, sect. (3), p. 179, n. 1 and the following: *Berichte über die Verhandlungen der Kongresse Deutscher Volkswirte* (Berlin, 1864); W. Lotz, *Die Ideen der deutschen Handelspolitik von 1860 bis 1891* (1892), chs. i–iii; O. Schneider, *Bismarck und die preussisch-deutsche Freihandelspolitik*, 1862–76 (1910); and A. Sartorius von Waltershausen, *Deutsche Wirtschaftsgeschichte* (2nd edition, 1923), pp. 208–23.

amount of (cane and beet) sugar used in the Zollverein increased from 7·37 lb. per head of the population in 1860 to 10 lb. in 1863. The woollen industry made progress.[1] The cost of living rose but real wages also increased.[2]

The cotton industry, on the other hand, was temporarily depressed owing to the shortage of the raw material when the southern ports of the United States of America were blockaded by the North during the American Civil War.[3] The crisis had important effects upon the German cotton industry. First, it forced spinners to adapt more of their machinery to Indian cotton. Secondly, it increased the tendency of small firms to disappear: thus in Saxony the change in the 'sixties from small factories using out-of-date machinery run by water-power to large factories containing more modern machinery led to considerable dislocation and caused the number of spindles to decline from 707,000 in 1861 to 472,000 in 1874. Thirdly, the introduction of power for spinning and weaving was encouraged by the drifting of handloom weavers into other industries and by the temporary cheapness of English textile machinery. It was for this reason that in Württemberg the number of spindles increased from 170,800 to 268,700 in the early 'sixties. The crisis thus led to the greater efficiency of the German cotton industry. An official Prussian report stated that the Cotton Famine had "considerably furthered technical improvements, particularly in spinning".[4]

[1] A. Bienengräber, *Statistik des Verkehrs und Verbrauchs im Zollverein für die Jahre* 1842–64 (1868), pp. 33, 259, 265, 267.

[2] J. Kuczynski's cost of living index for Germany (base year 1900, 100) is: 1860, 74; 1869, 82. His index for gross real wages in industry, transport and agriculture (base year 1900, 100) is: 1860, 72; 1869, 76 (*Labour Conditions in Western Europe* (1937), pp. 94–95).

[3] See W. O. Henderson, "The Cotton Famine on the Continent, 1861–1865", in *Ec.H.R.* (April, 1933), pp. 195–207, and P. J. Hutter, "La Famine de Coton en Westphalie, 1861–1865", in *Revue d'Histoire Économique et Sociale* (XXᵉ Année, 1932), pp. 392–405.

[4] *Verwaltungsbericht des Ministers für Handel, Gewerbe und Öffentliche Arbeiten für die Jahre* 1861, 1862 *und* 1863, p. 71.

The persistent propaganda of the German free-traders at last broke down the stubborn opposition of their opponents. The great landowners of East Prussia still favoured moderate tariffs, for they wanted to import manufactured goods as cheaply as possible. The merchants of Hamburg, Bremen and Frankfurt-am-Main were anxious to secure the removal of trade barriers. Prussian statesmen continued to support low import duties since this would make it difficult for the Hapsburg Empire to join the Zollverein. But in the Rhineland and South Germany protectionist feeling remained strong.

German free-traders were faced with three main tasks in 1860. First, they wished to secure the removal of various restrictions on trade within the Zollverein itself. Commerce between Zollverein States was still hampered by internal dues levied to protect local monopolies and local excises. Prussia, for example, levied a duty upon salt imported from Hanover (since she maintained a salt monopoly and Hanover did not) and upon wine imported from Bavaria (since her excise on wine was higher than that of Bavaria). Secondly, free-traders desired to free transit trade from dues levied on roads, railways and rivers. Thirdly, they advocated the reduction or removal of various import duties. They pointed out that at this time imported wine paid 46·6 per cent *ad valorem*, wrought-iron paid from 35·3 to 58·8 per cent, pig-iron paid 18·5, coal paid 12·5 and cotton yarn paid 10·7 per cent.[1] Free-traders argued that there was room for considerable reduction in these (and other) import duties. Further, they advocated the abolition of the general import duty of half a thaler per hundredweight levied upon all articles which were neither on the free list nor specifically subject to duty.

The free-traders gained many successes in the early 'sixties. The Zollverein transit dues were removed and various river tolls were either abolished or drastically reduced. German merchants

[1] W. Lotz, pp. 32–33. The import duties were levied by weight and this estimate of the *ad valorem* rates was based upon prices in Germany between 1853 and 1855.

and shippers also benefited from the removal of the Dutch tolls on the Scheldt. In 1865 the Zollverein tariff was thoroughly reformed, the most important reductions being those made in consequence of the Franco-Prussian commercial treaty of 1862.

The task of freeing transit traffic from vexatious impositions was carried a stage further in the early 'sixties. The problems of the Zollverein transit dues and the Rhine shipping dues had been shelved at the General Congresses of 1858 and 1859. They were at last solved in December, 1860, by special negotiations undertaken at Carlsruhe by States with territory on the Rhine. The joining of the Wilhelm Railway in Luxemburg with Dutch, Belgian and French lines made it possible to send goods cheaply from various North Sea and Channel ports by rail to South Germany and Switzerland. It was seen that Rhine traffic would suffer from this competition and Nassau and Hesse-Darmstadt withdrew their opposition to a reduction in Rhine shipping dues. At the same time the removal of the Zollverein transit dues was obviously desirable if only to placate the French who were on the point of sending a representative to Berlin to negotiate for a Franco-Prussian commercial treaty.

It was agreed at Carlsruhe that in 1861 the dues on goods taken along the German part of the Rhine—between the River Lauter and Emmerich—should be reduced from 120·60 centimes per hundredweight (upstream) and 92·46 centimes (downstream) to a uniform charge of only 20·59 centimes. On March 1, 1861, the Zollverein transit dues—and certain export duties which had replaced such dues—were abolished. These measures were taken at a financial sacrifice of over half a million thalers a year but transit trade benefited considerably. Further, between 1861 and 1863 shipping dues were reduced on the Rivers Neckar, Main, Lippe and Ruhr and on the Main-Danube Canal. They were abolished on the River Mosel.

In 1861 agreement was also reached on the question of the tolls levied by Hanover at the estuary of the River Elbe.[1] Han-

---

[1] See A. Soetbeer, *Des Stader Elbezolles Ursprung, Fortgang und Bestand* (1839); *Report from the Select Committee appointed to inquire into*

over held territory only on the left bank of the river. The dues were usually known as the Stade tolls but were actually levied at Brunshausen (or at Hamburg). They were tolls upon cargoes and not upon ships and were levied upon all traffic proceeding *up* the Elbe. No payment was exacted upon cargoes belonging to Hamburg citizens *and* carried in Hamburg ships. In return for this concession Hamburg kept up the lights and buoys in the Elbe estuary at an annual cost of about £15,000.[1] Since 1850 the Stade tolls had not been levied upon cargoes destined for the Hanoverian port of Harburg. No tolls were levied on traffic going downstream.

The Stade tolls were of very long standing and had last been regulated in 1844 by two agreements—a treaty between States with territory on the Elbe and a commercial treaty between Great Britain and Hanover.[2] The average annual (gross) receipts between 1845–46 and 1859–60 amounted to 220,000 thalers and the average annual administrative expenses of collection were 34,000 thalers.[3]

Great Britain and Hamburg were particularly interested in securing the removal of the tolls. An English parliamentary

---

...*the Stade Tolls*... (P.P. 1857–58, XVII); fifteen volumes of documents in F.O. 34/108 to 34/115 and 34/133; and documents in Mr John Ward's papers in the Perne Library, Peterhouse, Cambridge. Mr Ward was commissioned by Lord Palmerston in 1841 to report on the Stade tolls. He was Consul-General at Leipzig (1845–60) and Hamburg (1860–65) and was Minister-Resident to the Hanse towns in 1865–70. For accounts of his career, see J. Ward to Clarendon, February 15, 1870 (F.O. 33/206) and J. Ward, *Experiences of a Diplomatist*...1840–70 (1872).

[1] Sir J. E. Tennent (Secretary of the Board of Trade) to Lord Wodehouse (Foreign Office), June 12, 1861 (F.O. 34/113).

[2] By these agreements "British vessels, and those belonging to countries having reciprocity treaties with Hanover, are no longer obliged to *heave-to* in passing the guard-ship opposite Brunshausen, but may proceed direct to Hamburg, and pay the duties in the toll-office in that city" (J. R. McCulloch, *A Dictionary of Commerce*, II (edition of 1847), p. 1399).

[3] *Tableau des revenus bruts du droit de Stade dans les exercices du 1 Juillet 1845 au 1 Juillet 1860* (F.O. 34/110). Cf. J. Ward (Leipzig) to the Earl of Clarendon, April 9, 1857 (in J. Ward's papers).

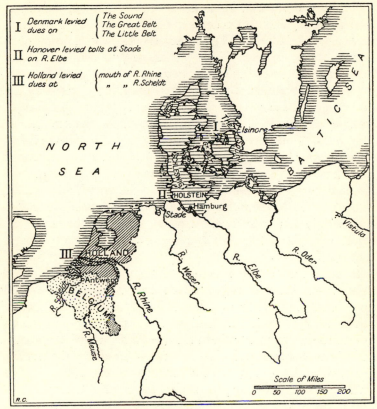

11. Dues on shipping in the North Sea and Baltic Sea.

committee enquired into the matter in 1858.[1] It reported that
the Stade tolls seriously hampered trade and that Hanover per-
formed no service for them whatever.[2] It recommended that

[1] P.P. 1857–58, XVII, pp. 3–4.
[2] Eleven years before this J. R. McCulloch complained that the Stade
tolls "fall heavily on certain descriptions of goods; particularly on some
manufactured articles; and are, at an average, decidedly higher than the
duties charged in Hamburg. They are most objectionable, however, from
their requiring many troublesome regulations to be complied with; all un-
intentional deviation from any one of which exposes the cargo to con-
fiscation, and never fails to occasion a great deal of delay, trouble and
expense" (*A Dictionary of Commerce*, II (edition of 1847), p. 1171).

the Anglo-Hanoverian commercial treaty of 1844 should be denounced so that negotiations could be opened for securing the removal of the dues. The treaty of 1844 was denounced in August, 1858. In 1860 Great Britain made a proposal which formed the basis of a settlement in the following year (June 22, 1861).[1] It was agreed to pay off the capital represented by the Stade tolls on the basis of fifteen and a half years' purchase of 200,000 thalers—that is to say 3,100,000 thalers (about £465,000). One-third of this sum was paid by Great Britain,[2] one-third by Hamburg, and one-third by other States interested in trade on the lower Elbe. About 35 per cent of this last third was paid by various German States, 20 per cent by Denmark, 16 per cent by Holland and the remainder by other countries.[3] Hanover herself contributed a small sum and therefore did not receive the whole of the 3,100,000 thalers; she received 2,875,338⅔ thalers.

Dues levied on the Elbe above Hamburg also hampered trade. It was stated in 1859 that "the amount of the upper Elbe tolls, at all times excessive, has at length become intolerable owing to the competition of the German railroads which threaten to destroy the traffic of the river, and are in turn counter-checked by heavy transit dues on land imposed by the *riverain* States, in order to protect the carriers on the Elbe. In this irrational struggle the interests of commerce are strangled, and so insensible are some of the German Governments to the impolicy of converting the highways of their own trade into a

---

[1] The protocols of the conference which was held at Hanover from June 17 to 22, 1861, to draw up the treaty for the abolition of the Stade tolls are in F.O. 34/144. Cf. *Treaty for the Redemption of the Stade Tolls ...June 22*, 1861 (P.P. 1861, LCV, p. 559). A treaty between Hanover and the U.S.A. for the abolition of the Stade tolls was signed on November 6, 1861 (see Howard to Lord John Russell, November 9, 1861, F.O. 34/115).

[2] Parliament voted £155,000 to cover the British share of the compensation to be paid to Hanover. The requisite number of thalers, however, were purchased for £153,100.

[3] See *Tableau montant des quoteparts que les États nommés ci-dessous auront à contribuer à une somme de* 1,033,333⅓ *thalers...* (F.O. 34/110).

THE PROGRESS OF FREE-TRADE

source of revenue, that whilst some of the States, such as Saxony, Prussia and Anhalt expend more upon the works for navigation than they receive in tolls on the upper river, and others such as Austria and Hamburg refuse to receive any tolls whatsoever, Hanover, Mecklenburg and Denmark derive an annual income far in excess of their expenditure upon the conservancy of the upper stream."[1]

In 1863 an agreement was made by States with territory on the Elbe for the reduction of tolls on the upper part of the river. These tolls were now levied only at Wittenberge. They were collected at two customs houses—one controlled by Austria, Prussia, Hamburg and Saxony, the other by the remaining States with territory on the Elbe. Tolls on the upper Elbe were abolished in 1870.

The Scheldt dues were abolished in 1863.[2] The Dutch held both the north bank of the lower Scheldt and an area of 275 square miles on the south bank. They thus controlled the two main branches of the lower river—the East and the West Scheldt, which were linked by the South Beveland Canal and by the Sloe and Zandkreek channels. Belgium, on the other hand, held the great port of Antwerp, which was some 55 miles from the sea. The time was past when Holland could ruin Antwerp by securing the closing of the Scheldt, but she was still able to take advantage of her geographical position to levy tolls at the mouth of the river. The tax was calculated on shipping tonnage. For one journey upstream and another downstream an inclusive charge of 1½ Dutch florins per shipping ton was

---

[1] Sir J. E. Tennent (Secretary of the Board of Trade) to W. S. Fitzgerald, M.P. (Foreign Office), April 20, 1859 (F.O. 34/109). Cf. *Denkschrift in Betreff des Elbverkehrs und der Elbzölle* (Magdeburg, 1847). This memorandum—drawn up by chambers of commerce and similar bodies in Altona, Berlin, Dresden, Halle-an-der-Saale, Hamburg, Leipzig and Prague—shows that in 1847 dues levied on the upper Elbe were about twice as high as those on the Rhine and more than three times those charged on the Weser (p. 4).

[2] See J. J. G. P. Guillaume, *L'Escaut depuis 1830*, I (2 vols. 1903), ch. iv.

made. By a law of June 5, 1839, the Belgian treasury was empowered to repay the toll on all foreign vessels (except Dutch) using the port of Antwerp. Reimbursement of the Scheldt tolls was usually granted only to ships of countries giving Belgium most favoured nation treatment in commercial matters. This became a heavy charge on the Belgian treasury. It rose from 612,313 francs in 1840 to 1,117,469 francs in 1852.

The recent abolition of the Sound dues and the Stade tolls suggested the method to be adopted for removing the Scheldt dues. In the spring of 1863 Holland signed a treaty with Belgium by which she agreed to abolish the Scheldt tolls in return for compensation which represented their capital value. This was fixed at 36 million francs. In July, 1863, a treaty was signed between Belgium and the chief maritime Powers whose ships used the port of Antwerp. These States agreed to pay two-thirds of the cost of abolishing the Scheldt dues.[1] At the same time Belgium reduced her pilotage dues on the Scheldt.[2]

The radical reform of the Zollverein tariff, so long desired by German free-traders, was secured by the Franco-Prussian commercial treaty of 1862. No fewer than one hundred and sixty-one changes were made in the Zollverein tariff. Many import duties on raw materials and manufactured articles were reduced. Thus duties on cotton yarn were reduced from 3 to 2 thalers per hundredweight; on cotton goods from between 55 and 110 thalers to between 30 and 40 thalers; on woollen goods from between 20 and 50 thalers to between 10 and 30 thalers; and on rough (*grob*) iron articles from 6 thalers to between 1 thaler 10 silver groschens and 2 thalers 20 groschens.[3] Prussia had

[1] See *Treaty and Convention for the Redemption of the Scheldt Toll,* 1863 (P.P. 1864, LXVI, p. 805). In round figures Great Britain paid 9 million francs; the United States of America paid 3½ million francs; France and Prussia paid 1½ million francs each; and Hanover paid ¾ million francs.

[2] The pilot-tax was reduced by 20 per cent for sailing ships, 25 per cent for towed ships and 30 per cent for steamers. It was never to be higher than that charged on the River Meuse at Rotterdam.

[3] See the first three documents printed by L. K. Aegidi and A. Klauhold, *Die Krise des Zollvereins* (1862), pp. 170–205.

considerable difficulty in securing the adhesion of other Zoll-verein States to this treaty but eventually she was successful and it came into force in 1865. The new Zollverein tariff of that year extended to all countries the tariff concessions made to France. Commercial treaties were also signed by Prussia in 1865 with Britain, Belgium[1] and Italy, which further modified the Zoll-verein tariff in the direction of free-trade. The customs law of 1865 included a useful reform—the abolition of the general duty of half a thaler per hundredweight on goods not otherwise dealt with in the tariff.[2] By these means the Zollverein secured a tariff which was based upon free-trade principles.

(2) THE FRANCO-PRUSSIAN COMMERCIAL TREATY OF 1862[3]

It has been seen that at the Zollverein General Congresses held between 1854 and 1859 the opposition of the South German

---

[1] A protocol on commercial affairs, signed in 1863, paved the way for the commercial treaty of 1865 between Prussia and Belgium. See p. 296.

[2] The abolition of this general import duty has a curious history. In 1864 the lower house of the Prussian Landtag was amused at the solemn request of the Government for authorisation to ask the Zollverein Congress to abolish the general import duty upon sea-water for the benefit of the importers of oysters! A deputy thereupon suggested that Prussia should advocate the complete abolition of the general import duty and this was done. See Julius Faucher, *A new Commercial Treaty between Great Britain and Germany* (Cobden Club Essays, Second Series, 1871), p. 280.

[3] For the Franco-Prussian commercial treaty of 1862, see L. K. Aegidi, *Vorwände und Tatsachen. Ein Beitrag zur Kritik der Opposition gegen den Handelsvertrag vom 2. August* 1862 (Berlin, 1862: this pamphlet has been attributed to R. von Delbrück but it is catalogued under L. K. Aegidi in the Prussian State Library); A. D. Hartmann, *Der Zollverein gegenüber dem Handelsvertrag mit Frankreich* (1861); A. E. B. Schäffle, "Der preussisch-französische Handelsvertrag, volkswirtschaftlich und politisch betrachtet", in *Deutsche Vierteljahrschrift*, xxv, iii, pp. 244–378; anonymous articles: "Der Handelsvertrag mit Frankreich", in *Deutsche Vierteljahrschrift*, xxv, iv, pp. 1–85 and "Der deutsch-französische Handelsvertrag", in *Preussische Jahrbücher*, ix (1862), pp. 557–79; W. Lotz, ch. ii; R. von Delbrück, ii, chs. xxvii, xxviii; E. Franz, *Der Entscheidungs-*

protectionists had prevented the adoption of Prussian proposals for reductions in import duties. Prussia recognised that the need for unanimity at the General Congress made it virtually impossible to overcome the protectionist opposition without some sort of coercion.

A reform of the Zollverein tariff was even more necessary in the 'sixties than in the 'fifties. In 1860 the new Anglo-French treaty of commerce provided for considerable reductions in the English and French tariffs. But while Great Britain gave all countries the benefit of the lower duties fixed by this treaty France gave only British goods the benefit of her new "conventional" tariff. The goods of other States continued to pay much higher duties under the old French general tariff. German manufacturers were thus placed at a serious disadvantage in the French market when competing with British rivals. To secure the benefits conferred by France upon England it would clearly be necessary to make substantial tariff concessions to the French. Prussian statesmen saw that if the Zollverein tariff were thoroughly reformed as the result of a commercial treaty with France it would be possible to make acceptance of the French treaty a condition for renewing the Zollverein treaties in 1865. Such a treaty would also place Prussia in a strong position when negotiating with the Hapsburg Empire, for a reduced tariff was a safeguard against the demands of protectionist Austria for admission to the German customs union.

Prussia had for many years desired to place Franco-Zollverein commercial relations upon a more satisfactory footing. Napoleon III's breach with the traditional French policy of high protective duties gave her an opportunity which she could not afford to miss. The French Emperor himself desired the conclusion of a Franco-Zollverein commercial agreement both on economic and political grounds. He regarded the treaty that

kampf um die wirtschaftspolitische Führung Deutschlands, 1856–67 (1933), book 1, and "Die Vorgeschichte des preussisch-französischen Handelsvertrages von 1862", in *V.S.W.* (1932), xxv, pp. 1–37, 105–29.

had just been signed with Britain as a first step towards securing a general reduction of import duties throughout Europe. The Zollverein was, next to Britain, the most important economic region with which France had trading relations. A satisfactory Franco-Zollverein commercial treaty would mark a great advance in the task of breaking down tariff barriers on the Continent. Napoleon III had also a political end in view. He wanted to avert the danger of an anti-French coalition between Prussia and Austria—a coalition which had very nearly been formed in the previous year when Prussia had mobilised at the time of the Italian War. Napoleon III thought that economic co-operation between France and Prussia might pave the way to political understanding and prevent an alliance of the two German Great Powers directed against himself. Franz considers that Napoleon III even hoped to secure by commercial concessions the assent of Prussia to the transfer to France of German territory on the Rhine. But the evidence of any direct connection in Napoleon's mind between an economic bargain and annexation projects is purely circumstantial.[1]

The first move towards the opening of commercial negotiations between France and Prussia was made by Napoleon III himself on January 25, 1860, only two days after the signing of the Anglo-French commercial treaty. The advantages of an economic agreement were obvious, but formidable political and economic obstacles had to be overcome before serious discussions could begin. Prussia hesitated to negotiate with France so long as there was a suspicion that Napoleon III had designs on German territory on the Rhine. She felt, too, that it would be very difficult to secure agreement on the radical reform of the Zollverein and French tariffs which would be necessary to break down the barriers that had so long hampered Franco-German trade.

On July 12, 1860, France officially invited Prussia to enter

[1] Dr Franz admits that his suggestion cannot be proved from Napoleon's cabinet correspondence "since most of the cabinet papers of the Emperor have been destroyed and the remainder are not accessible" (p. 52).

into negotiations for a commercial treaty, a navigation treaty and a copyright convention. For six months preliminary questions were discussed between Prussia and other members of the Zollverein and between Prussia and France. Rechberg reminded Prussia that, by the Austro-Prussian commercial treaty of February, 1853, fresh negotiations between the Hapsburg Empire and the Zollverein were due to begin in 1860. Prussia agreed to such negotiations but she refused to consider the formation of a Central European customs union.

On January 11, 1861, de Clercq arrived in Berlin to begin discussions for a Franco-Prussian commercial agreement. The Prussian representatives were Delbrück, Pommer Esche and Philipsborn. The negotiations lasted from January, 1861, to March, 1862. There were three series of sessions—the first from the middle of January to the middle of March, 1861, the second from the middle of July to the end of August, 1861, and the third from November, 1861 to March 1862.

The French representative put forward three main demands. First, both parties should abolish transit and export duties except those on rags. Secondly, the Zollverein should grant most favoured nation treatment to France. This meant that when the Austro-Prussian commercial treaty of 1853 was renewed Austrian goods would lose the preferential treatment they had enjoyed in the Zollverein market. Thirdly, there should be a "levelling of tariffs" (*nivellement des tarifs*). To secure this levelling de Clercq proposed that where Zollverein import duties were higher than those charged by France they should be reduced to the French rate. This would affect most of the chief French exports to Germany. The change should be brought about by the Zollverein accepting the method of classifying goods adopted in the French tariff. Some Zollverein import duties would have to be altered from specific to *ad valorem* duties. An exception would be made with regard to wines and silks. France levied only a very low duty on wines and she admitted silks duty free. De Clercq recognised that the Zollverein could not be expected to do the same but he hoped to secure very substantial reductions in the Zollverein duties on wines and silks.

The Prussian point of view was stated by Delbrück in a memorandum of April 17, 1861, which was sent to the Governments of all members of the Zollverein.[1] As the Zollverein transit dues had been abolished on March 1, there was no difficulty in accepting de Clercq's first proposition. With regard to the second French demand—the inclusion of a most favoured nation treatment clause—Prussia was willing that the preferential treatment granted to the Hapsburg Empire by the Austro-Prussian commercial treaty of 1853 should end when that agreement expired in 1865. It was on de Clercq's third demand—the "levelling of tariffs"—that there were serious differences of opinion. Prussia argued that the proposed "levelled tariffs" must enable the Zollverein to export goods to France on terms at least as favourable as those granted to Great Britain in 1860. She was, however, unable to accept the suggestion that if France granted this request the Zollverein should be prepared to extend to France all the concessions made to Austria in 1853. There were clearly important differences between the Anglo-French and the Austro-Prussian treaties of commerce. France had made an agreement with the leading industrial State in the world and both parties hoped that its principles might be embodied in treaties with other countries. But the Zollverein had signed a treaty with a country whose manufactures were not nearly as developed as her own and there had been no intention of extending its provisions to other countries.

Prussia declined to accept the French view that the Zollverein should levy *ad valorem* instead of specific import duties. Apart from the general arguments against *ad valorem* duties[2] it was observed that their introduction would be peculiarly dif-

---

[1] Delbrück's memorandum of April 17, 1861, is summarised by E. Franz, pp. 84–8.

[2] For a discussion of this question see, for example, an article on "Die Revision des Zollvereinstarifs" in the *Bremer Handelsblatt* (November 5, 1861, no. 421), pp. 386–7.

ficult in the Zollverein, which was a union of a number of independent States. It would be almost impossible, for example, to secure standardisation in valuing goods in all the States of the customs union. Prussia admitted that there were also serious difficulties in arranging a commercial treaty if one party had specific and the other *ad valorem* import duties. She felt, however, that there was more likelihood of overcoming these difficulties than of arranging for the adoption by the Zollverein of duties levied on value.

A fortnight after the Prussian note was sent to members of the Zollverein a commercial treaty between France and Belgium was signed. This was the first step towards the achievement of Napoleon III's plan for the conclusion of a series of agreements with continental countries which should gradually extend over the whole of Europe the principles of the Anglo-French commercial treaty of 1860. Belgium reduced her duties on French wines, silks and leather goods. In return France agreed to charge Belgian goods under the "conventional" tariff recently established for British imports. There were also special reductions of French import duties on Belgian linens and prepared hides. A most favoured nation clause was included in the treaty. At the same time France and Belgium concluded a navigation treaty and a copyright convention. The Franco-Belgian commercial treaty had an important influence upon the negotiations between France and Prussia. It showed the Prussian negotiators what concessions France was prepared to make to an industrialised continental country. It enabled French goods to enter Belgium on more favourable terms than Zollverein goods. Prussia saw that she must make every effort to enter the new low-tariff group of nations which was being built up in Western Europe.

The replies of the Zollverein Governments showed Prussia that it would be no easy matter to draw up a commercial treaty which would be acceptable both to France and to all the Zollverein States. Favourable replies came from those States which favoured the adoption of a low tariff—Hanover, Oldenburg,

Brunswick, Saxony, the Thuringian States and Frankfurt-am-Main. Nassau and Hesse-Cassel raised no serious objections. Opposition came from the protectionist South German States —Bavaria and Württemberg—and from Baden and Hesse-Darmstadt. Both economic and political factors played their part in influencing the attitude of these States. Two main economic criticisms which they put forward deserve notice. First, there were complaints that the proposed treaty would injure various native interests. The South German wine-growers were alarmed at the proposal to make substantial reductions in the Zollverein import duty on French wines. Secondly, it was pointed out that if the Zollverein came to a commercial agreement with France on the lines indicated by Prussia there would be little chance in the future of fruitful economic co-operation with the Hapsburg Empire. The problem of the renewal of the Austro-Prussian commercial treaty of 1853 would have to be faced.

This criticism of the proposed French treaty was closely linked with political considerations. If Prussia were able to force upon the Zollverein a commercial treaty with France that killed all hope of an Austro-German customs union, Prussia's economic position in Germany would obviously be greatly strengthened. Victory in the economic field might well be the prelude to victory in the political field. It was becoming clear that the Germanic Confederation would soon have to be re-formed. Many Germans felt that whatever changes might be necessary, Austria's position as a member of the Confederation must not be endangered. They considered that the economic links of the commercial treaty of February, 1853, were too important to be weakened for the sake of an agreement with France. Dalwigk, the Hesse-Darmstadt Foreign Minister, was one of the leading opponents of the proposed French treaty.[1] He was alarmed at the growing strength of Prussia in Germany. He believed that the interests of Hesse-Darmstadt could best be

[1] For Dalwigk, see W. Schüssler, *Die Tagebücher des Freiherrn Reinhard von Dalwigk zu Lichtenfels* (1920).

served by fostering close co-operation between the middle States. The spectre of the "third Germany" again raised its head.

Prussia succeeded in preventing opposition to the negotiations with France from coming to a head at the moment. She not merely induced Bavaria to give up the idea of pressing for a special conference of all Zollverein States to consider the matter but even secured her agreement to the postponement of the General Zollverein Congress which was due to meet in Munich in 1861.

Negotiations between de Clercq and the Prussian representatives were resumed in Berlin in the middle of July, 1861. In the second period of the discussions, which lasted until the end of August, there was much hard bargaining. France pressed for further reductions of import duties in the proposed new Zollverein tariff. Prussia demanded the concessions recently made by France to Belgium. The gap between the two parties was narrowed but it was not bridged. It was decided to adjourn the negotiations once more to enable Prussia to obtain the views of other Zollverein States.

While negotiations between France and Prussia were suspended in the autumn of 1861 the situation was influenced by the issue of memoranda by Prussia (September 4) and Austria (September 8) to explain their points of view; the replies of Zollverein Governments to the Prussian memorandum; the holding of an important session of the Congress of German Economists (September 9–12) and of a conference of German industrialists (October 4); the meeting of Napoleon III and the King of Prussia at Compiègne (October 8); and the signing (on October 12 and November 16) of two supplementary conventions to the Anglo-French treaty of commerce of 1860.

A Prussian circular note was sent to the members of the Zollverein on September 4. It has been described as "a masterpiece of Delbrück's political and economic statesmanship".[1] On the one hand, Delbrück endeavoured to show that if the French did

----

[1] E. Franz, p. 109.

not abate their demands (particularly for very low Zollverein import duties on wines and silks) Prussia could break off the negotiations but could still secure the reform of the Zollverein tariff and retain her leading position in the Zollverein. On the other hand, he tried to allay the growing anxiety of the middle States and to secure their support of Prussia's policy. A few days later (September 8) an Austrian note was sent to Prussia, Bavaria and Saxony.[1] Rechberg put forward the Austrian case with moderation. He protested against the inclusion in the proposed Franco-Prussian treaty of terms which might render impossible the renewal of the Austro-Prussian commercial treaty of 1853. He admitted, however, that at the moment "almost insuperable obstacles" stood in the way of the establishment of a customs union between the Hapsburg Empire and the Zollverein.

The answers of the Zollverein Governments to the Prussian circular note of September 7 indicated that little change had occurred in their views since they had replied to the earlier note of April 17. The North German States supported Prussia while Bavaria and Württemberg again expressed doubts with regard to the proposed reductions in duties on wines and silks. But there was fairly general agreement that the Zollverein tariff would have to be reformed whether a commercial treaty with France were signed or not. This was what Prussia wanted, for it enabled her representatives to tell de Clercq that Prussia could, if necessary, do without a French treaty and was not prepared to pay an unreasonable price for it.

The strength of the protectionist feeling in the South German States was indicated by the deliberations of the fourth Congress of German Economists which met at Stuttgart between September 9 and 12, 1861. It has been observed that at former congresses many free-trade resolutions had been passed. On this occasion, however, one-third of the delegates came from Württemberg and a protectionist resolution was passed by a

[1] The note was not sent to Württemberg until March 3, 1862; and it did not go to the other Zollverein States until May 5, 1862.

small majority. Shortly afterwards (October 4) a conference of manufacturers was held in Frankfurt-am-Main and a German Industrial Union (*Verein für deutsche Industrie*) was founded. This was a protectionist body. Prussia drew de Clercq's attention to the activities of these congresses and pointed out that if the proposed new Zollverein tariff were too low it would be very difficult to secure the assent of the South German States to its adoption.

On October 8, 1861, Napoleon III and the King of Prussia met at Compiègne. On the first day of the discussions between the two monarchs economic affairs were discussed while political problems—such as the Schleswig-Holstein question—were left over until the second day. Napoleon III appears to have recognised that, at the moment, there was no hope of gaining political support from Prussia in return for commercial concessions. He felt, too, that he could not afford to allow the negotiations for a commercial treaty to fail. He had welcomed the King of Prussia with ostentatious friendliness and a breakdown of the economic negotiations might create a bad impression.

Two supplementary conventions to the Anglo-French treaty of commerce of 1860 were signed in Paris on October 12 and November 16, 1861. Prussia was interested in these conventions, for she was determined to press for the inclusion in the proposed Franco-Prussian treaty of any new concessions made to Britain.

On November 4, 1861, the Prussian representatives again met de Clercq in Berlin. At first little progress was made. Weber is wrong in supposing that the French were informed that Prussia had decided to come to terms immediately for political reasons. Prussia, in fact, was not prepared to make serious concessions.[1] At last, early in 1862, France showed signs of giving way. She suggested that the levelling of tariffs should be accomplished in stages and not at once.

[1] W. Weber, p. 386. See criticism by R. Delbrück, II, p. 221, and E. Franz, p. 137.

During the last stage of the Franco-Prussian commercial negotiations there was an important development in German political affairs. On December 20, 1861, Prussia suggested that the establishment of a narrower federation without the Hapsburg Empire would contribute to the solution of the German Question. On February 2, 1862, Austria, Bavaria, Württemberg, Saxony and Hanover presented identical notes to Prussia firmly rejecting this proposal. This showed that although the German middle States were divided in their attitude towards the proposed French commercial treaty, they were prepared to join with Austria in presenting a united front against Prussia's political pretensions.

Prussia pressed forward with the negotiations for a commercial treaty with France. On February 22, 1862, Lord Augustus Loftus was able to inform Earl Russell that the negotiations had been brought to a successful termination.[1] On March 29, three treaties were initialled at Berlin by the French and Prussian plenipotentiaries—a commercial treaty, a navigation treaty and a copyright convention.[2]

Both parties agreed to make very considerable tariff reductions which were to be introduced gradually between January 1, 1864, and January 1, 1866. Zollverein goods were, in general, to pay the "conventional" French tariff already granted to Britain and Belgium. There were, of course, modifications to meet the special needs of Franco-Zollverein commerce.

The most significant reductions in the French tariff were those on the importation of iron and textiles. The Zollverein tariff was thoroughly reformed, the chief concessions to France being reductions in the import duties on wines and silks. The

[1] Lord Augustus Loftus to Earl Russell, February 22, 1862 (F.O. 97/336).

[2] It is important to observe that the treaties were not signed but were merely initialled. All that was done on March 29, 1862, was to place "on formal record that the contents of the documents tallied with the results of the negotiations" (*Nationale Zeitung* (August 4, 1862), in F.O. 97/336).

treaty contained a most favoured nation clause.[1] France retained her *ad valorem* duties and the Zollverein continued to levy specific duties.[2] "Whether the commercial treaty be judged from the economic or the political point of view, it was a great achievement."[3]

Prussia now had to undertake four tasks. First, she had to induce the South German States to accept a treaty which they disliked because it reformed the tariff on free-trade lines and because it rendered very difficult further economic co-operation with the Hapsburg Empire. Secondly, she had to induce Austria to accept the situation created by the French treaty. Any new agreement that Prussia made with Austria in 1865— when the Austro-Prussian commercial treaty of 1853 expired— would have to be compatible with the new French treaty. This would involve Austria in the loss of the privileged economic position she had secured in relation to the Zollverein in 1853. Any attempt on the part of Austria to revive the policy of Bruck and Schwarzenberg and to force her way into the Zollverein would have to be repelled. Thirdly, Prussia had to make every effort to secure the wholehearted support of France in bringing pressure to bear upon German States which opposed the commercial treaty of 1862. She possessed one powerful weapon for coercing recalcitrant members of the Zollverein; the Zollverein

[1] Article 31: "Each of the two contracting parties undertakes to grant to the other every concession, privilege or tariff reduction in import or export duties on articles mentioned or not mentioned in the present treaty, which it may in future grant to a third Power. It further undertakes not to establish against the other any import or export prohibition that is not at the same time applicable to other States" (Aegidi and Klauhold, p. 263). For a general discussion of the most favoured nation clause, see L. Glier, *Die Meistbegünstigungsklausel* (1905).

[2] See the Franco-Prussian protocol on the initialling of the commercial and navigation treaties of March 29, 1862; circular note of the Prussian Foreign Minister to the Zollverein Governments, April 3, 1862; the proposed Zollverein tariff of 1862; and the commercial treaty and supplementary conventions as finally signed on August 2, 1862, printed by Aegidi and Klauhold, pp. 170–205, 250–355.

[3] E. Franz, p. 155.

treaties expired in 1865 and she was prepared to refuse to renew them except on the basis of the tariff as reformed by the French treaty.

Fourthly, Prussia desired the renewal of the Zollverein treaties to be accompanied not merely by tariff reductions but also by administrative reforms. Above all she wished to secure the abolition of the *liberum veto* of the General Congress. There was much discussion on this subject in the late 'fifties and early 'sixties. Karl Mathy had advocated the setting up of a customs parliament as early as 1848. It is clear from Bismarck's correspondence between 1858 and 1862 that he favoured the establishment of a customs parliament to control Zollverein affairs.[1]

David Hansemann put forward in 1861 a plan for the reorganisation of the Zollverein. In addition to a Central Authority, he proposed the setting up of two representative bodies, where decisions should be by majority vote. The project was accepted by the first German *Handelstag* which met—under Hansemann's chairmanship—at Heidelberg in 1861.[2] Hansemann laid his plan before the Prussian ministers von der Heydt and Auerswald in June of that year. He also solicited the support of the South German States. He had little success in Bavaria and Württemberg but in Baden the Foreign Minister favoured the establishment of a customs parliament.[3] Austrian

---

[1] See, for example, letters in *Bismarckbriefe*, 1836–72 (edited by Horst Kohl, 6th edition, 1897), pp. 162, 220, 229; and memorandum of December 25, 1862, in H. von Poschinger, *Aktenstücke zur Wirtschaftspolitik des Fürsten Bismarck*, I (1890), nos. 2, 3.

[2] See *Der deutsche Handelstag*, II (1913), pp. 339 ff. The *Handelstag* was a private association of representatives of German and Austrian chambers of commerce. For its establishment, see F. Schupp and K. A. Wettstein, *Entstehungsgeschichte des ersten Allgemeinen Deutschen Handelstages* (1911).

[3] Roggenbach (Baden Foreign Minister) to the Grand Duke Frederick I of Baden, August 10, 1861, in H. Oncken, *Grossherzog Friedrich I von Baden und die deutsche Politik von 1854–71*, I (2 vols. 1927), pp. 274–5.

representatives at German courts watched Hansemann's activities with some misgivings.[1]

If Prussia could preserve the Zollverein intact, secure the adoption of the tariff of 1862, abolish the *liberum veto* of the General Congress, and deprive Austria of the preferences granted in 1853, her leadership in Germany in economic matters would be established more firmly than ever before. The decisive struggle for economic supremacy in Germany was at hand.

(3) THE DECISIVE AUSTRO-PRUSSIAN STRUGGLE FOR ECONOMIC SUPREMACY IN GERMANY, 1862–1865[2]

The conclusion of the Franco-Prussian commercial treaty of March 29, 1862, was the first step in the decisive struggle be-

[1] See the diplomatic correspondence in *Quellen zur deutschen Politik Österreichs*, 1859–66, vol. I (edited by Heinrich Ritter von Srbik, 1934), nos. 465, 474, 485, 498, 502; and A. Bergengrün, *David Hansemann* (1901), pp. 705 ff.

[2] See *Memoirs of Prince Hohenlohe* (edited by F. Curtius and translated by G. W. Chrystal, 2 vols., 1906); *Die Tagebücher des Freiherrn Reinhard von Dalwigk zu Lichtenfels...* 1860–70 (edited by W. Schüssler, 1920); E. Franz, *Der Entscheidungskampf um die wirtschaftspolitische Führung Deutschlands*, 1856–67 (1933), book ii, and works cited at the beginning of this chapter. See also the following articles by E. Franz: "Preussens Kampf mit Hannover um die Anerkennung des preussisch-französischen Handelsvertrages von 1862", in *Historische Vierteljahrschrift*, XXVI (1932), pp. 789–839; "Ludwig Freiherr von der Pfordtens Kampf gegen den preussisch-französischen Handelsvertrag vom 29. März 1862", in *Forschungen zur brandenburgischen und preussischen Geschichte*, XLIV, pp. 130–55; "König Max II von Bayern und seine geheimen politischen Berater", in *Zeitschrift für bayerische Landesgeschichte*, V (1932), pp. 219–42; "Wilhelm von Doenniges und König Max II in der Deutschen Frage", in *Zeitschrift für bayerische Landesgeschichte*, II (1929–30), pp. 445–67; and "Graf Rechbergs deutsche Zollpolitik", in *Mitteilungen des Österreichischen Instituts für Geschichtsforschung*, XLVI (1932), pp. 143–87. In the humorous paper *Münchener Punsch*, XVI (1863), pp. 378–80, there is an amusing criticism (in the form of a play called "Die deutsche Zollvereinsfrage") of the delays in the negotiations. For one important aspect of Austrian economic affairs at this time, see Joseph Neuwirth, *Bank und Valuta in Oesterreich-Ungarn*, 1862–73 (2 vols., 1874).

tween Prussia and Austria for economic supremacy in Germany. Bismarck (who became Minister President six months after the treaty was signed) and the leading Prussian Civil Servants had a definite programme for the future economic reorganisation of Germany. Prussia was the leading manufacturing and commercial State in Germany and her economic strength was growing.

Austria, on the other hand, while strongly objecting to changes in the Zollverein tariff and administration which might injure her economic interests in Germany, had no clear-cut proposals of her own to make. It is true that Rechberg revived Bruck's plan for the establishment of an Austro-Zollverein customs union but he was not prepared to press forward the project with the vigour that Schwarzenberg had shown twelve years before. Austria's economic position was unsatisfactory but was showing signs of improvement.[1] If economic factors alone had influenced the Austro-Prussian struggle of 1862–65 Prussia's task would have been comparatively simple. But political considerations proved to be a serious complication.

Both Prussia and Austria were anxious to secure the support of other German States. The economic interests of Saxony and the Thuringian States were now so closely bound up with those of Prussia that these States gave Prussia their wholehearted co-operation. Franz considers that the services which Saxony rendered to Prussia in the economic struggle against Austria were as important as those which she rendered to the Hapsburgs in the political struggle in Germany in the early 'sixties.[2] Baden, on the whole, supported Prussia but not without reservations. Austria could generally rely on the support of Bavaria, Würt-

[1] The report of the Breslau Chamber of Commerce for 1862 stated that "Austria's efforts to reform her finances and to reduce her deficit by drastically cutting down expenditure on armaments and by regulating the affairs of the National Bank have stabilised her credit and have caused a rise in Austrian shares and in the rate of exchange [of Austrian money]". See Karl Mamroth, *Die Entwicklung der Österreichisch-Deutschen Handelsbeziehungen...1849–65* (1887), p. 162.

[2] E. Franz, p. 30.

temberg[1] and (to a considerable extent) of Nassau. In Bavaria and Württemberg the protectionists strongly opposed the French treaty since it involved the reduction of many import duties. In Hesse-Darmstadt Dalwigk objected to the French treaty on political grounds.

The other German States—particularly Hanover, Oldenburg, Hesse-Cassel and Frankfurt-am-Main[2]—held the balance of power. In general it may be said that they had no serious objections to the commercial treaty with France on economic grounds, for they favoured moderate as opposed to high import duties. But they feared that acceptance of the treaty might lead to a reorganisation of the Zollverein in such a way as to increase unduly the preponderance of Prussia in German economic and political affairs.

Economic particularism was still very strong in Germany and all the States adopted the policy which they thought would be of most benefit to themselves. Although the Zollverein had been in existence for nearly thirty years, its members still thought of their own interests first and of those of the customs union as a whole second. Thus Bavaria's attitude was influenced by the position of the Palatinate. However ready she might be to push her opposition to the French treaty to the point of leaving the Zollverein, she was determined not to accept any scheme of economic reorganisation in Germany that might lead to the erection of a customs frontier between herself and her isolated province on the Rhine. Hanover's policy was influenced by her anxiety to retain her privileged financial position in the Zollverein when the customs union was renewed in 1865. The op-

[1] For Württemberg's point of view, see *Bericht der Centralstelle für Gewerbe und Handel an das K. Ministerium des Innern vom 23. Mai 1862 betreffend des Handelsvertrages zwischen dem Zollverein und Frankreich* (Stuttgart, 1862); *Bericht der volkswirtschaftlichen Kommission der württembergischen Kammer der Abgeordneten über den preussisch-französischen Handelsvertrag...* (Stuttgart, 1863); and A. Rapp, *Die Württemberger und die nationale Frage*, 1863–71 (1910), pp. 45–7, 102–3, 116–18.

[2] For Frankfurt's policy at this time see R. Schwemer, *Geschichte der Freien Stadt Frankfurt-am-Main*, 1814–66, III (1918), part ii, pp. 198–203.

ponents of the French treaty recognised the advantages they had derived from the Zollverein and had no wish to leave it. But they thought that Prussia needed the Zollverein just as much as they did and that she would not go to the length to dissolving the customs union.

It may be observed that Saxony and Hanover played very different parts in the first Zollverein crisis and the second. In 1851 Hanover had agreed to join the Zollverein and so had enabled Prussia to defy Austria and her South German allies. Saxony, on the other hand, had joined the Darmstadt confederacy of 1852 and had supported Austria. But in the second crisis it was Hanover who supported the Hapsburgs and opposed the French commercial treaty while Saxony favoured the acceptance of the treaty and gave valuable support to Prussia. In the early 'fifties Hanover's unsatisfactory financial position made it imperative for her to join the Zollverein, while political considerations drew Saxony to Austria. But in the 'sixties Saxony recognised that her economic interests were too closely bound up with those of Prussia to allow her to leave the Zollverein, while Hanover's fear of the growth of Prussia's political influence in Germany drew her, for a time at least, into the Austrian camp. Hanover, too, hoped to retain her financial privileges by threatening to leave the Zollverein.

The French commercial treaty had only been initialled in March 1862. Its signature was to follow within a month. Prussia was optimistic enough to hope that she could obtain the consent of other members of the Zollverein in this short period. On April 3, 1862, Prussia sent a circular note to the Zollverein Governments explaining the terms of the treaty[1] and a few days later a reply was at last sent to Rechberg's memorandum of September 8, 1861.[2]

Delbrück visited Dresden, Munich and Stuttgart in April in

[1] The Prussian circular note of April 3, 1862, is printed by Aegidi and Klauhold, pp. 174–97.

[2] Bernstorff (Prussian Foreign Minister) to von Werther (Prussian Ambassador in Vienna), April 7, 1862, in Aegidi and Klauhold, pp. 206–9.

the hope of gaining support for the French treaty. He had no difficulty in Saxony but his reception in Munich and Stuttgart showed him that strong opposition was to be expected from Bavaria and Württemberg.

Philipsborn went to Hanover but could obtain no assurance of support there. He told Lord Augustus Loftus "that Count Platen was not indisposed towards the treaty but that there was a very strong feeling towards Austria and a feeling that the treaty both politically and commercially would be highly prejudicial to Austria and to Austrian interests".[1] In Baden there were differences of opinion regarding the French treaty. Vogelmann (the Finance Minister) had his doubts about the economic advantages of the treaty while Roggenbach (the Foreign Minister)[2] favoured it because it might help Prussia in her task of unifying Germany. Baden had a long frontier exposed to French attack and a number of her leaders favoured the establishment of a strong Germany under Prussian leadership.

The opposition of Bavaria, Württemberg and Hanover made it clear that Prussia's attempt to rush members of the Zollverein into accepting the French treaty had failed.

The Austrian Customs Commission discussed the Franco-Prussian commercial treaty on April 18, 1862.[3] It decided that the German middle States should be urged to reject the treaty. Hock, the chairman, regarded this as a tactical move to embarrass Prussia. Other members of the Commission, however, were prepared to carry Austrian opposition to the French treaty to its logical conclusion. This was a revival of Schwarzenberg's policy of trying to enter and to dominate the Zollverein. Only if that attempt failed would Austria endeavour to break up the Zollverein and to secure the adhesion of some of its members to her own customs system. Austrian representatives at German

[1] Lord Augustus Loftus to Earl Russell, April 26, 1862 (F.O. 97/336).
[2] For Roggenbach, see W. Andreas, *Franz Freiherr von Roggenbach* (1933).
[3] See A. Beer, pp. 217–26, for an account of this important meeting of the Austrian Customs Commission.

courts made every effort to strengthen opposition to the French treaty.

In a memorandum of May 7, 1862,[1] Austria stated her case against the Franco-Prussian commercial treaty. It was observed that in September of the previous year, when negotiations between Prussia and France were far from complete, the Austrian Government had urged that her interests should be kept in mind in any treaty which might be concluded. Austria had laid stress on three points. First, Prussia should not grant France unconditional most favoured nation treatment but should reserve the right to make members of the Germanic Confederation concessions not shared by France. Secondly, the Franco-Prussian treaty should not remain in force after 1865 when the Zollverein treaties would have to be renewed. Thirdly, the Zollverein import duties should not be reduced so much that Austria would be forced to raise her "intermediate duties" (*Zwischenzölle*) on Zollverein goods imported into the Hapsburg dominions. Austria now complained that the agreements initialled on March 29, 1862, ran directly counter to her wishes. France did obtain unconditional most favoured nation treatment. The treaty was to last for twelve years. The Zollverein tariff was reduced to such an extent that Austria felt it necessary to increase her "intermediate duties".

The Austrian memorandum declared that Prussia's concessions to France were greater than those obtained in return. It considered that Prussia had concluded the treaty with the object of making "the economic severance of Austria from the rest of Germany an accomplished and enduring fact". The Austrian Government concluded by charging Prussia with breaking the Austro-Zollverein commercial treaty of 1853. It admitted that Prussia might make alterations in individual tariff rates but declared that she had no right to modify the Zollverein tariff so that a policy of protection was dropped in favour of

[1] The Austrian memorandum of May 7, 1862 (enclosure in Rechberg to Count Chotek, May 7, 1862) is, printed by Aegidi and Klauhold, pp. 216–22.

free-trade. Such a change would not only make it impossible to renew the Austro-Zollverein treaty of 1853 but would put an end to the hope expressed in the preamble of that treaty that an Austro-German customs union would one day be established.

Bernstorff replied briefly to this memorandum on May 28, 1862.[1] In effect he told Austria to mind her own business. "I must," he wrote, "with the utmost decision, claim for Prussia and for the Zollverein the full right to act in this respect as they themselves think proper." He denied that Prussia had violated the Austro-Zollverein treaty of 1853. He rejected "any assumption that we have for political reasons given more than we have received". He observed that the Zollverein tariff urgently needed revision and that the Zollverein could not "remain behind when Great Britain and France went before us on the path of great economic reform".

Austria's rejoinder was prompt and unexpected. In July, 1862, Rechberg came forward with a plan for the complete economic reorganisation of Germany. He sent a note to the Prussian Government enclosing the draft of a proposed preliminary treaty for the establishment of an Austro-Zollverein customs union. As soon as this treaty was signed negotiations should begin for drawing up an Austro-Zollverein tariff. Duties were to be levied in silver. Both parties were to retain the customs revenues which they collected except that the income from certain import duties—such as those on yarn, paper, leather, iron, and metal goods—was to be divided between the Zollverein and Austria in the ratio of five to three. To maintain various local monopolies some duties would still have to be levied on the Austro-Zollverein frontier. The proposed customs union was to be established not later than December 31, 1877.[2]

---

[1] Bernstorff to von Werther, May 28, 1862 (Aegidi and Klauhold, pp. 223–5).

[2] A copy of the note was sent to Austrian representatives at foreign courts. See Rechberg to Károlyi (Austrian Ambassador in Berlin), July 10, 1862, in Aegidi and Klauhold, pp. 228–34.

Prussia promptly rejected the Austrian proposal. Bernstorff stated that Prussia was already bound by treaty to France and that the proposed revision of the Austrian and Zollverein tariffs was inadequate for the needs of the Zollverein.[1] Further exchanges of notes between Austria and Prussia did not materially change the situation.[2] Prussia went her own way. The Prussian lower house accepted the French treaty by 264 votes to 12: the upper house accepted it unanimously.[3] On August 2, 1862, the Franco-Prussian commercial treaty (which had only been initialled in March) was signed.[4]

Austria and Prussia had now put forward definite proposals and the middle States had to make up their minds whether to support Rechberg's plan for an Austro-Zollverein customs union or Prussia's policy of reforming the Zollverein tariff on the basis of the French commercial treaty. Bavaria,[5] Württem-

[1] Bernstorff to Károlyi, July 20, 1862, in Aegidi and Klauhold, pp. 235–8.

[2] Rechberg to Károlyi, July 26, 1862; Bernstorff to von Werther, August 6, 1862; Rechberg to Chotek, August 21, 1862, and Bernstorff to von Werther, September 19, 1862, in Aegidi and Klauhold, pp. 238–9, 356–8, 369–70, 396–8.

[3] For the views of the majority of the Prussian legislature, see *Bericht der vereinigten Kommissionen für Handel und Gewerbe und für Finanzen und Zölle über den den beiden Häusern des Landtages zur verfassungsmässigen Genehmigung vorgelegten am 29. März paraphirten Handelsvertrag zwischen dem Zollverein und Frankreich* (1862).

[4] The Franco-Prussian protocol on the signing of the commercial treaty of August 2, 1862, is printed by Aegidi and Klauhold, pp. 242–5.

[5] Von Schrenck to Perponcher, August 8, 1862 (in Aegidi and Klauhold, pp. 358–67). For Prussia's reply, see Bernstorff to Perponcher, August 26, 1862 (*ibid*. pp. 370–83). Reculot, the French Ambassador at Munich, reported on August 14, 1862, that he had been told that the King of Bavaria "was undecided to the last moment as to what he ought to do, and that he agreed to approve the draft of the reply prepared by his ministers only because he was afraid of finding himself in opposition to the Chambers which at this time would not have given their assent to the Berlin Convention" (i.e. to the Franco-Prussia treaty) (quoted by P. Benaerts, p. 206 n.).

berg[1] and Hanover firmly rejected the French treaty and no immediate solution of the difficulty seemed possible.

In September and October, 1862, there was a lull in negotiations on German commercial affairs. Ministerial changes in both Prussia and France at this time had an important influence upon the situation. Bismarck, who became Minister President and Foreign Minister of Prussia, pursued the traditional Prussian policy regarding the Zollverein with far greater determination and ability than his predecessors. Shortly after taking office he frankly informed the Prussian upper house that those Zollverein States which refused to accept the French commercial treaty would have to leave the Zollverein in 1866. He said that "the Government would be glad to be able to renew the Zollverein after the expiration of its present term. Such a boon, however, must be made dependent upon the fulfilment of the programme to which it has adhered in agreeing to the treaty of August 2, and, in so far as her fellow States do not feel themselves in a position to follow this programme, Prussia could not renew the Zollverein with them."[2] Von der Pfordten (the Bavarian representative at Frankfurt) declared in December, 1862, that he had no doubt that Bismarck was "aiming at the dissolution of the Zollverein, the separation of Germany from Austria and, as far as possible, the subjection of German States to Prussia as far as the so-called line of the River Main".[3] Drouyn de Lhuys, who became Foreign Minister of France, was, however, not prepared to support Prussia in her economic struggle with Austria to the same extent as his predecessor Thouvenel had been.

Meanwhile, the rival advocates of the French commercial

[1] Hügel to von der Schulenburg-Priemern, August 11, 1862 (in Aegidi and Klauhold, pp. 367–9). For Prussia's reply, see Bernstorff to von Zschock, August 26, 1862 (*ibid*. pp. 383–5).

[2] Newspaper extract enclosed in W. Lowther to Earl Russell, October 3, 1862 (F.O. 97/336). Cf. Bismarck to von der Schulenburg-Priemern (Stuttgart), November 12, 1862, in Bismarck, *Die gesammelten Werke*, IV, pp. 12–13.

[3] Quoted by E. Franz, p. 258.

treaty and the Austro-Zollverein customs union were doing their best to influence German public opinion. In September the Union of German Economists, at its fifth conference at Weimar, passed a resolution in favour of the French commercial treaty. In October a similar resolution was passed by a small majority (102 votes to 93) at the second German *Handelstag* which met at Munich. On the other hand, leading "Great Germans", who strongly objected to any scheme for a solution of the German Question which would deprive Austria of her place in German affairs, met at Frankfurt-am-Main at the end of October. They passed a resolution approving of the rejection of the French commercial treaty by various German Governments and another which stated that a reform of the Zollverein tariff should be undertaken only in co-operation with Austria. A Great German Reform Union (*Grossdeutscher Reformverein*) was founded at this conference.

On November 7, 1862, Bavaria invited members of the Zollverein to attend the fifteenth General Congress which was to meet at Munich. In the interval between the issuing of the invitation and the opening of the Congress in March, 1863, relations between Prussia and France became somewhat strained. There were fruitless negotiations for a supplementary commercial convention to include those parts of the three treaties already signed which could be brought into force without the consent of other Zollverein States. Further, the Alvensleben Convention of February 8, 1863, by which Prussia agreed to support Russia on the Polish question, alarmed France who now began to consider the possibility of a rapprochement with Austria.

The fifteenth General Congress of the Zollverein began its deliberations at the end of March and lasted until the middle of June, 1863. Much routine business had to be done, since no General Congress had been held since 1859. Bavaria made vigorous but, on the whole, unavailing efforts to unite the middle States in firm opposition to Prussia's policy. Prussia showed her determination to reform the Zollverein tariff by coming to an agreement with Belgium on commercial affairs. On March 28 the representatives of Prussia and Belgium signed three documents—a protocol, a navigation treaty and a copyright convention. The first was the most important. It was agreed that negotiations should be undertaken for a commercial treaty on the basis of most favoured nation treatment. Meantime, Belgium promised to give Prussia the same concessions as those recently made to Great Britain so long as Belgian goods were received in Prussia on most favoured nation terms. Prussia agreed to pay a share of the redemption of the Scheldt dues.

Soon after the close of the General Congress Prussia invited the Zollverein States to a conference to be held in Berlin in November, 1863, to discuss the renewal of the Zollverein treaties. She offered to give up her "transition duties" on wine. She reiterated her demand for a reform of the Zollverein tariff on the basis of the French treaty. She also advocated a change in the method of dividing the Zollverein revenues. This last demand naturally alarmed Hanover which had enjoyed important financial privileges since 1854.

A meeting of the middle States was held in Munich in October to endeavour to agree upon a common policy to be pursued at the forthcoming conference of Zollverein States in Berlin. Representatives were sent by Bavaria, Württemberg, the two Hesses, Nassau and Frankfurt-am-Main. A Hanoverian representative took part in the last three sessions of the meeting. Austria sent an observer. Although all these States opposed Prussia, they were unable to form a united front against her. Hanover, in particular, showed no sign of giving Austria energetic support. Windthorst admitted to Ingelheim that "Hanover is in the unfortunate position of having to sell herself".[1] In other words she would support whichever Power offered her the biggest *Präzipuum*.

The Berlin Conference on the renewal of the Zollverein

[1] Ingelheim (Austrian Minister in Hanover) to Rechberg, October 9, 1863, quoted by E. Franz, p. 327.

treaties was opened on November 5, 1863. Rechberg tried to
secure the support of the discontented middle States by publishing the draft of a new Austrian tariff. He hoped that this
would prove to be a step towards the eventual unification of the
Austrian and Zollverein tariffs. But Prussia's opponents were
still unable to agree upon a united policy and to carry it out
resolutely. Their opposition was still further weakened by the
fact that the Schleswig-Holstein Question was coming to a
head. The King of Denmark died on November 15 and it was
clear that Federal execution against Denmark could be carried
out only if Austria and Prussia worked together. Bismarck
fully recognised the weakness of his opponents. On December
15 he sent a circular note to all Zollverein Governments denouncing the Zollverein treaties.

Rechberg's position at the beginning of 1864 was not an
enviable one. Austria was isolated in Europe. By her attitude
during the Crimean War she had antagonised Russia who was
now (since the Alvensleben Convention) co-operating with
Prussia. There had been no real reconciliation with France after
the Italian War of 1859. If Austria were to take a leading part
in German affairs in the Schleswig-Holstein crisis she could do
so only in alliance with her old rival Prussia. Rechberg attempted the impossible. He tried to co-operate with Prussia
against Denmark, yet at the same time refused to give up completely his attempts at intervention in German economic affairs.
An effort was made to remove Austro-Prussian differences by
direct negotiations at Prague in March, 1864, but no settlement
was reached. It was clear, however, that Rechberg recognised
that there was little hope of establishing an Austro-Zollverein
customs union on the lines suggested in his note of July 10,
1862.

The middle States, too, looked to the future with gloomy
forebodings. German national feeling had been roused on the
Schleswig-Holstein Question, and Bavaria, Württemberg and
Hanover had little choice but to follow the lead of Prussia and
Austria in this matter. Prussia's attitude at the resumed Berlin

conferences of Zollverein States in March, 1864, showed that she was as determined as ever to make no important commercial concessions. Austria's policy was vacillating and the middle States at last began to appreciate the fact that if they wished to remain in the Zollverein they must swallow their pride and accept Prussia's terms.[1]

In the summer of 1864 Rechberg made a last attempt to construct a united front of middle States against Prussia. After preliminary discussions between Austria and Bavaria at Vienna in May[2] a conference of Prussia's opponents was held at Munich in June and July. Heads of proposals (*Punktationen*) for an Austro-Zollverein agreement were drawn up which provided for the gradual assimilation of the tariffs of the two-customs systems.

Prussia, meantime, was coming to terms with various States for the renewal of the Zollverein. In May, 1864, Saxony agreed to renew her Zollverein treaty on the basis of the French treaty. In the following month the Thuringian States, Baden, Frankfurt-am-Main and Hesse-Cassel followed suit. Prussia secured Hesse-Cassel's adhesion by the payment of a sum of money to the Elector. The all-important link between Prussia's eastern and western provinces was thus secured. If the southern States left the Zollverein and formed a customs union of their own,

---

[1] Dalwigk, for example, wrote to Heinrich von Gagern (Hesse-Darmstadt Minister in Vienna) on May 26, 1864: "In the same measure as the settlement of the Schleswig-Holstein question draws nearer so do the problems of tariffs and commerce come to the fore. If Hanover and Hesse-Cassel firmly support what I regard as the German point of view Hesse-Darmstadt will do the same. But if those two States follow the deplorable example of Saxony and go over to the Franco-Prussian camp, then—in view of the opposition of the second chamber and of a populace blinded partly by financial considerations and partly by demagogic 'National Union' (*national-vereinliche*) impulses—it will be very difficult for us to remain true to what we believe to be the only right and patriotic policy" (quoted by E. Vogt, *Die Hessische Politik in der Zeit der Reichsgründung 1863–71* (1914), p. 46 n.).

[2] The results of these deliberations were recorded in a *Registratur* of June 1, 1864, which is printed by A. Beer, pp. 594–5.

they could hardly expect to obtain the adhesion of Hanover which was now isolated in North Germany. In July Hanover and Oldenburg gave up the struggle against Prussia and agreed to renew their Zollverein treaties. Both had to accept a considerable reduction of the *Präzipuum* they had enjoyed since 1854.

For a few months the South German States hesitated before capitulating to Prussia. At last, at the end of September, another conference of Zollverein States met in Berlin. On October 12 all the members of the Zollverein agreed that the customs union should be renewed on the basis of the tariff included in the Franco-Prussian commercial treaty of 1862. The most favoured nation clause remained and the privileged position in German commercial affairs that Austria had enjoyed since 1853 was doomed. A week later (October 18) Franz Josef relieved Rechberg of his office as Austrian Foreign Minister, for he considered that Rechberg had mishandled the Schleswig-Holstein affair.

On May 16, 1865, a treaty was signed for the renewal of the Zollverein for twelve years from January 1, 1866.[1] Many of the reforms so long desired by Prussia were secured. A large number of import duties were reduced. Hanover and Oldenburg lost, to a considerable extent, their financial privileges. Their share of the Zollverein revenue, like that of other members (except Frankfurt-am-Main), was to be calculated on a basis of population but it was to be made up to at least $27\frac{1}{2}$ silver groschens per head. Hanover and Oldenburg also agreed to raise their excise on salt to two thalers per hundredweight so as to discourage the smuggling of cheap salt from these States into neighbouring Zollverein territories. Prussia dropped her "transition duties" on wine and so removed a long standing cause of dispute with the southern States. On the other hand Prussia did not secure a reform of the administrative organs of the Zollverein. The General Congress and its *liberum veto* remained. But it never met again. The Seven Weeks' War of 1866

[1] The treaty of May 16, 1865, is printed in *Verhandlungen und Verträge des Deutschen Zoll- und Handelsvereins*, v (1871), pp. 43 ff.

brought the old Zollverein to an end and the reformed customs union of 1867 had new administrative organs.

Prussia and Austria came to terms on April 11, 1865.[1] The new Austro-Zollverein Treaty, which came into force on July 1 and was to last until the end of 1877, contained many of the provisions of the Austro-Prussian treaty of February, 1853. It was even stated in the preamble that the new treaty was concluded "to prepare the way for a general German customs union", although it must have been recognised that there was now virtually no possibility of such a union being set up.[2] But the preferential duties of the treaty of 1853 were replaced by a most favoured nation clause. Thus Austria had to give up the privileged position in German economic affairs that Bruck and Schwarzenberg had won for her and she was now treated no better and no worse than any other State that was prepared to sign a most favoured nation treaty with the Zollverein. Austrian import duties on Zollverein goods, as fixed by the treaty of 1865, were higher than those levied under the treaty of 1853.

Four months later other disputes between Austria and Prussia were temporarily settled. Serious difficulties had arisen over the disposal of the duchies of Schleswig, Holstein and Lauenburg which had been taken from Denmark in 1864. By the Treaty of Gastein (August 14, 1865)[3] it was agreed that

[1] See K. Hock, "Der Vertrag vom 11. April 1865" (*Österreichische Revue*, v (1867), pp. 1–37); A. Matlekovits, pp. 65–73; K. Mamroth, pp. 172–77; A. Beer, pp. 304–9 and R. Delbrück, II, pp. 332–6.

[2] Bismarck had observed, in a report (*Immediatbericht*) from Biarritz on October 10, 1864, that a reference to a future Austro-Zollverein customs union "would be meaningless so long as Article 31 of the French Treaty were retained, according to which Austria could not be admitted to the Zollverein unless France were treated in the same way" (quoted by A. Beer, p. 596). In 1868, when a new Austro-Zollverein commercial treaty was signed, the pretence that both parties aimed at eventual union was dropped and there was no reference to an Austro-Zollverein customs union.

[3] See Lord Napier to Earl Russell, August 17, 1865, and W. Lowther to Earl Russell, August 26, 1865 (F.O. 64/567).

Schleswig should be administered by Prussia and Holstein by Austria. Prussia received the duchy of Lauenburg—in return for a payment of two million thalers to Austria—and the right to use the naval harbour of Kiel (in Holstein). The fortress of Rendsberg was to have a joint Austro-Prussian garrison.

It was decided that negotiations should be undertaken for the inclusion of Schleswig and Holstein in the Zollverein.[1] Lauenburg—which had a population of fifty thousand—was absorbed into the Prussian customs system at the beginning of 1868. A levy of retrospective duties (*Nachversteuerung*)was made on certain foreign goods imported before January of that year.[2]

The Zollverein and Belgium came to terms on May 22, 1865, on the basis of the protocol of 1863. Some modifications were made. Both parties agreed to drop import duties on coal. This provision benefited the Zollverein whose exports of coal to Belgium were soon far greater than her imports of coal from Belgium.

The three South German States signed a commercial treaty with Switzerland on May 27, but Prussia, Saxony, Hanover and Hesse-Darmstadt refused to agree to it. Eventually the Zollverein and Switzerland agreed to grant to each other the same concessions as those made by recent treaties with other Powers and this provisional arrangement remained in force until 1869.

Negotiations with Italy were complicated by the fact that

---

[1] For the relations between Schleswig-Holstein and the Zollverein see Lorenz von Stein, *Denkschrift über die Zollverhältnisse der Herzogtümer Schleswig und Holstein mit besonderer Berücksichtigung eines Anschlusses derselben an den Zollverein* (1848) (cf. *Zeitschrift des Vereins für deutsche Statistik*, I, 1847 and II, 1848) and W. Seelig, *Schleswig-Holstein und der Zollverein* (1865). The duchies had an area of 6750 square miles and a population of rather less than a million. When they were conquered in 1864 they were separated economically as well as politically from Denmark but the Danish tariff (slightly modified) was allowed to remain in force temporarily. The duchies were annexed by Prussia in 1866 and were absorbed into the Prussian customs system in the following year.

[2] See J. Ward to Lord Stanley, January 7, 1868, and March 6, 1868 (F.O. 33/203).

some German States had not yet recognised the newly established Kingdom of Italy. A most favoured nation treaty was
signed on December 31, 1865, and ratifications were exchanged
in March of the following year.

At the end of 1865 the three Prussian Civil Servants who
exercised so strong an influence upon Zollverein affairs—
Delbrück,[1] Pommer-Esche and Philipsborn—could look back
upon the events of the last few years with some satisfaction.
Prussia had played her part in securing the removal or mitiga-
tion of various irritating impediments to German trade—the
Scheldt and Stade dues, a number of river tolls, and the Zollverein transit dues. She had thoroughly reformed the Zollverein
tariff by reducing many important duties and by abolishing her
own "transition duties" on wine. She had extended the foreign
markets of German manufacturers by concluding with neighbouring States a number of important commercial treaties
which included most favoured nation clauses. She had broken
the opposition of the protectionist Southern States and had
forced both Hanover and Oldenburg to accept a smaller share
of the Zollverein revenues than they had formerly enjoyed.
She had deprived Austria of the preferences granted to her in
1853. She had put an end to Austria's hopes of securing
economic domination in Central Europe.

The economic and financial position of the Hapsburg Empire at this time was deplorable. In the autumn of 1865 Austria
badly needed a new loan. No agreement was reached with the
Rothschilds but eventually, at the end of November, a loan was

---

[1] The extent of Delbrück's influence upon Prussian and German
economic affairs in the 'sixties may be gathered from a statement made by
Bismarck some years later. In a speech to the Reichstag on February 4,
1881—when he was defending himself against charges of inconsistency
with regard to tariff policy—Bismarck declared: "Before I personally
studied tariff problems I had no views (on the subject) myself but accepted
those of my colleague Delbrück whom I regarded as the right man in the
right place." This statement, though an exaggeration, is significant. See
Oswald Schneider, *Bismarck und die preussisch-deutsche Freihandelspolitik*, 1862–76 (1910), pp. 11–12.

raised in Paris by a syndicate whose leading member was Haber. In a report of May 11, 1866, the Austrian State Debt Commission criticised the unfavourable and burdensome conditions on which this loan had been concluded and stated that it had exerted a depressing effect upon Austria's finances.

Prussia's object was now to complete her domination of the Zollverein by replacing the General Congress by an assembly in which decisions should be made not by a unanimous vote but by a majority vote. She also desired to complete the economic unification of Germany by inducing the three Hanse towns, the two Mecklenburgs and Schleswig-Holstein to join the Zollverein.

Chapter IX

THE OLD ZOLLVEREIN AND THE NEW, 1866–1888[1]

(1) THE ESTABLISHMENT OF THE NEW ZOLLVEREIN, 1866–1867[2]

Shortly after the new Zollverein treaties came into force at the beginning of 1866 Germany was threatened with civil war. The commercial classes, whose activities had recently been somewhat hampered by the second Zollverein crisis and by the Cotton Famine, strongly favoured the maintenance of peace.

The executive committee of the Rhenish-Westphalian Chamber of Commerce and Industry, for example, wrote: "The

---

[1] See Bismarck, *Die gesammelten Werke* (*Friedrichsruher Ausgabe*, 15 vols. in 19 parts, 1924–35); W. Weber, ch. 32; H. von Festenberg-Packisch, ch. xii; É. Worms, ch. v; R. von Delbrück, chs. xxxvii–xxxix; A. Sartorius von Waltershausen, part iv, sect. ix; E. Franz, pp. 405–36; H. von Sybel, *Die Begründung des Deutschen Reiches durch Wilhelm I*, vi (ed. of 1913, 7 vols.), book xxii, chs. i, ii, and book xxiii, ch. i; A. Zimmermann, *Die Handelspolitik des Deutschen Reiches*...(1901), pp. 71–125; A. Rapp, *Die Württemberger und die nationale Frage*, 1863–71 (1910); Hans Spielhofer, "Bayerische Parteien und Parteipublizistik in ihrer Stellung zur deutschen Frage, 1866–1870", in *Oberbayerisches Archiv für vaterländische Geschichte*, LXIII (1922), pp. 143–233. See also bibliographies of sections (1) and (2) of this chapter.

[2] See V. Böhmert, "Deutschlands wirtschaftliche Neugestaltung", in *Preussische Jahrbücher*, XVIII (Sept. 1866), pp. 269–304; A. Schneider, *Die Organisation des Zollvereins* (1870); F. Thudichum, *Verfassungsrecht des Norddeutschen Bundes und des deutschen Zollvereins* (1870); *Memoirs of Prince Hohenlohe* (edited by F. Curtius and translated by G. W. Chrystal, 2 vols. 1906); *Die Tagebücher des Freiherrn Reinhard von Dalwigk zu Lichtenfels*...1860–1871 (edited by W. Schüssler, 1920); W. Schüssler, *Bismarcks Kampf um Süddeutschland*, 1867 (1929), part ii, chs. vii, ix; W. Schübelin, *Das Zollparlament und die Politik von Baden, Bayern und Württemberg*, 1866–70 (1935), ch. i; and E. Franz, pp. 405–36.

threatened outbreak of war and the damage which has, in consequence, already been inflicted upon national prosperity have caused conferences, unions and societies of German traders to issue a large number of addresses, resolutions and petitions in

12. The New Zollverein, 1867.

favour of preserving peace. Certainly the commercial and industrial classes are above all called upon to give expression to the desire for peace. But in all expressions of opinion that have been made so far we miss any reference to a matter which should be stressed by the commercial classes—the danger to our German Zollverein of an Austro-Prussian war. Anxiety on this point was first expressed by a resolution of the Chamber of Commerce (*Handelsverein*) of Ulm which observed that 'a war between members of the customs union would shatter the Zollverein treaties which have only recently been renewed at such great sacrifice'. And Chambers at Carlsruhe, Mannheim and Baden have passed the same resolution. It is gratifying that it is just in South Germany that this danger should first be recognised and stressed and, as the executive committee of a Chamber whose membership is almost exclusively Prussian, we gladly associate ourselves with such resolutions. Although the financial and economic disadvantages of commercial isolation would be more serious for the Middle and small States, Prussia has just as great an interest in the preservation of the Zollverein. For us, too, the conditions of production and consumption would be dislocated and the injury caused by a collapse of the Zollverein would be irreparable. We, too, see in a war which would divide members of the Zollverein into hostile camps a civil war in the most lamentable sense of the term. It would destroy the hardly won and most valuable achievement of the last fifty years. It would throw us back into the economic chaos to which the intrigues of Metternich and foreign States combined with our own weakness would have condemned us, and from which only truly wise statesmanship has saved us by carrying out with admirable consistency a policy of sacrificing the interests of separate States. It would break down the strongest and most natural bond that has hitherto united the German States and bound them more firmly together than the fundamental laws of the Germanic Confederation which were inimical to freedom. Just as in 1862 the recognition of this fact victoriously crushed all dynastic and particularist tendencies and kept the Zollverein in being so today it will be able to defeat the same enemies which have sprung up in a new guise. The same problem which the German commercial classes successfully solved in 1862 confronts them again today. We therefore summarise our desire for peace in the practical demand—let us maintain peace between the Zollverein States, for in this way only, we are firmly convinced, can the danger of war between Prussia and Austria be reduced."[1]

Economic interests were, however, not strong enough to

[1] Quoted by H. von Festenberg-Packisch, pp. 410–11.

prevent the outbreak of war between Austria and Prussia. Fortunately the struggle was a brief one and the gloomy forebodings of the German commercial classes were not fulfilled. The losses in men and money were not severe. Trade was, on the whole, not seriously hampered and the customs union itself survived the war. The Zollverein treaties automatically came to an end with the outbreak of hostilities and, from the legal point of view, the customs union was dissolved. Actually the Zollverein remained in being and the belligerents allowed commerce between its members to continue with as little interruption as possible. Prussia merely withdrew her own customs officials who were serving in enemy States. Customs duties continued to be collected. The proceeds were sent to Berlin and were shared between members of the Zollverein as usual. The Zollverein customs receipts in 1866 were 21,346,751 thalers as compared with 23,991,085 in the previous year. The decline in revenue was therefore only 11 per cent.[1] This was a remarkable example of carrying on business as usual between belligerents in time of war.[2]

Prussia's victory at Königgrätz (Sadowa) enabled her to force the Emperor of Austria to agree—by the Treaty of Prague, August 2, 1866—to the dissolution of the "Germanic Confederation as hitherto constituted" and to give "his consent to a new organisation of Germany without the participation of the Austrian Empire".[3] Austria's defeat and exclusion from all political influence in Germany made internal reconstruction

[1] *Report by Mr Lowther...on Trade and Commerce in Prussia and the Zollverein, July 29,* 1867 (P.P. 1867–68, LXIX).

[2] The payment by Britain to Russia of interest on the Russo-Dutch loan during the Crimean War may perhaps be regarded as a precedent. But a convention of May 19, 1815, had provided for the continuance of payments to liquidate the debt even if war should break out between any of the three interested parties. See Pitt Cobbett, *Cases and Opinions in International Law* (3rd edition, 1913), part ii, pp. 38–40.

[3] The peace treaties concluded after the Seven Weeks War are printed by L. Hahn, *Zwei Jahre Preussisch-Deutscher Politik,* 1866–67... (1868), pp. 194–212.

even more essential, and in 1867 the Dual Monarchy was estab-lished as the result of a "Compromise" (*Ausgleich*) between Austria and Hungary.[1] The German Austrians thus suffered a double defeat. On the one hand, they were ejected from Germany and, on the other hand, they now had to share with the Magyars the domination of the motley collection of races that made up the Hapsburg Empire. The expulsion of Austria from Germany put an end, of course, to hopes of an Austro-German customs union.

By the Treaty of Prague Prussia obtained a free hand to do what she pleased north of the River Main except that she promised not to annex the Kingdom of Saxony. Actually Prussia annexed Hanover, Hesse-Cassel, Nassau,[2] Schleswig-Holstein and Frankfurt-am-Main.[3] Bismarck had thus placed Prussia in a very strong position and he could afford to leave the new political and economic organisation of Germany to future negotiations.

. Saxony and the South German States suffered no territorial losses after the Seven Weeks War. Bismarck refused to humiliate them as he wanted their support in the event of war with France. Fear of Napoleon III's designs upon German territory caused the South German States, Saxony and Hesse-Darmstadt to enter into military alliances with Prussia.[4]

[1] From the economic point of view the first years of the Dual Monarchy were a period of prosperity. Between 1867 and 1873 nine hundred com-panies with a nominal capital of over 4000 million florins were founded in Austria-Hungary. But this prosperity soon degenerated into unwise speculation which culminated in a disastrous crash. See Max Wirth, *Geschichte der Handelskrisen* (edition of 1890), p. 466, and Joseph Neu-wirth, *Bank und Valuta in Oesterreich-Ungarn*, 1862–73 (2 vols. 1874).

[2] For a criticism of Nassau's anti-Prussian economic policy in the early 'sixties, see Karl Braun, *Die wirtschaftlichen Verhältnisse des Herzogtums Nassau* (Wiesbaden, 1865) (a speech in the Nassau second chamber).

[3] When the French Ambassador criticised these arrangements Bismarck is reported to have said: "The line of the Main is like a grating across a stream: the grating is fixed but it does not prevent the water from flowing" (*Edinburgh Review*, cxxviii (July, 1868), p. 243).

[4] When the Württemberg lower house and the Bavarian upper house refused to pass the bills necessary to provide for the performance of the

In the autumn of 1866 the South German States agreed that the Zollverein treaty of 1865 should remain in force while negotiations for the reform of customs affairs proceeded. The treaty of 1865, however, could now be denounced by giving six months' notice. This enabled Prussia to threaten the South German States with exclusion from the Zollverein if they refused to accept her terms in subsequent negotiations.

Provision was made in the peace treaties for two important economic reforms. First, Prussia's treaties with Bavaria, Baden and Hesse-Darmstadt provided for the abolition of the Rhine and Main shipping dues on January 1, 1867.[1] The dues levied by Nassau on the Lahn had been abolished in July, 1866, so that the dues payable on the upper Elbe were now the only tolls on river shipping in Germany. They were abolished in 1870. Secondly, the peace treaty between Prussia and Saxony provided for the abolition of the Saxon salt monopoly whenever Prussia should give up her salt monopoly.

The war of 1866 and the treaties that followed it shattered the power of the "third Germany". The middle States had made two fundamental errors. "First, the belief that they could pursue a united policy whereas in practice firm co-operation proved to be impossible. Secondly, the belief in the overwhelming military and economic power of Austria particularly when in association with the middle states."[2]

Negotiations were undertaken for the establishment of a North German Confederation. On the basis of a Prussian proposal, plenipotentiaries of the twenty-two German States north of the River Main drew up a constitution. This was accepted by a Constituent Assembly[3] and by each individual State. The new federation began its career on July 1, 1867. Bismarck desired

military conventions Bismarck threatened to eject Bavaria and Württemberg from the Zollverein. The bills were soon passed! See *Annual Summaries reprinted from "The Times"* (1893), Year 1867, p. 260.

[1] A revised Rhine Navigation Act was signed in October, 1868. Prussia abolished dues on the River Ruhr in 1869.

[2] E. Franz, p. 436.

[3] See *Stenographische Berichte über die Verhandlungen des Reichstages des Norddeutschen Bundes im Jahre* 1867, vol. 1 (Feb. 24–April 17, 1867).

that matters which affected relations with foreign Powers should, as far as possible, be in the hands of the federal Government and that purely local affairs should remain under the control of individual State Governments. This plan was, to a great extent, carried out. The federal Government controlled foreign affairs, the army and navy, postal arrangements, the tariff and commercial matters. The Confederation was a customs union. It regulated the excises on sugar-beet, cognac, salt, beer and tobacco. The federal States retained certain rights such as the power of calling local parliaments and the levying of local taxes.

The two Mecklenburgs and the three Hanse towns, although members of the North German Confederation, did not at first form part of its customs system. Nevertheless representatives from these States sat in the North German Bundesrat and Reichstag and took part in discussions on commercial affairs in which they were not directly interested. The adhesion of the Mecklenburgs[1] was delayed owing to their treaty obligations to France. In June, 1865, Mecklenburg-Schwerin had signed a commercial treaty with France by which she pledged herself not to levy import duties of more than 7½ francs per 100 kg. on French goods. The import duty on French wines was not to be more than 6½ francs per 100 kg. This treaty, to which Mecklenburg-Strelitz adhered, was to last for twelve years. The Mecklenburgs could not adopt the Zollverein tariff, which was higher than their own, without breaking this treaty with France. In January, 1868, however, France released the Mecklenburgs from their treaty obligations and they joined the North German customs system in August of that year. "Retrospective duties" were levied.

Lübeck entered the Zollverein on August 11, 1868, at the same time as the two Mecklenburgs. Retrospective duties were

---

[1] For the relations of the two Mecklenburgs to the Zollverein in the 'fifties and 'sixties, see J. L. Schumacher, "Der Preussische Zollverein und Mecklenburg", in *Rau und Hanssens Archiv der politischen Ökonomie*, VIII (New Series, 1849), p. 33; C. F. W. Prosch, *Betrachtungen über den Beitritt Mecklenburgs zum Deutschen Zollverein* (1853); and M. Wiggers, *Die Mecklenburgische Steuerreform, Preussen und der Zollverein* (1862).

levied on foreign goods found in Lübeck territory at the time of its accession to the Zollverein. Three concessions were made to Lübeck. First, a bonded warehouse was set up in which certain Lübeck merchants might deposit temporarily foreign goods on which no import duty had been paid. Secondly, the erection of certain duty-free private warehouses—such as those for the reception of wine in transit—was permitted. Thirdly, Lübeck merchants were allowed to keep running accounts with the Zollverein customs house in conformity with the practice at the Leipzig fair.[1]

Hamburg and Bremen, on the other hand, retained their economic independence. It has been seen that by a treaty of 1856 certain Bremen territories had been included in the German customs system and a Zollverein customs house and a warehouse had been set up in Bremen. This treaty was renewed (with slight modifications) for twelve years on December 14, 1865.[2] Similar arrangements were made with Hamburg in 1868 when certain Hamburg districts—such as Fuhlsbüttel, Ohlsdorf, Bergedorf, Cuxhaven-Ritzebüttel[3] and the island of Neuwerk —entered the Zollverein. It was agreed that a Zollverein customs house and warehouse should be established in Hamburg. The warehouses were built at the Sternschanze and were opened in April, 1870.[4]

Hamburg and Bremen paid a special contribution to the exchequer of the North German Confederation in lieu of the customs duties and the federal excises which would otherwise have been collected in them. The Prussian town of Altona (in Holstein), which lay so close to Hamburg that it was impracticable to draw a customs frontier between them, was

[1] J. Ward to Lord Stanley, May 25, 1868, and G. Annesley to Lord Stanley, August 12, 1868 (F.O. 33/203).

[2] J. Ward (Hamburg) to the Earl of Clarendon, March 23, 1866 (enclosing printed copy of the Zollverein-Bremen treaty of 1865) (F.O. 33/196) and J. Ward to Clarendon, November 6, 1868 (F.O. 33/203).

[3] But the "outer embankment" (Aussendeich) of Cuxhaven remained outside the Zollverein.

[4] J. Ward to Clarendon, April 22, 1870 (F.O. 33/207).

treated in the same way as Hamburg. "In both cases the merchants complained of the hardship of having to buy a privilege, which, in conformity with long established usage, they fancied

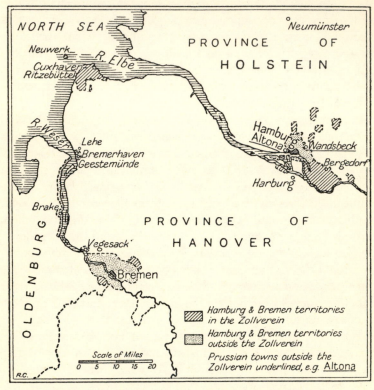

13. Hamburg, Bremen and the Zollverein, 1868, based on
G. Droysen, *Historischer Handatlas* (1886), page 51.

themselves entitled to exercise gratuitously in the interest of the commerce of all nations."[1]

[1] J. Ward, *Experiences of a Diplomatist...* 1840–70 (1872), p. 260. For the relations between Hamburg and the Zollverein in the 'sixties, see V. Böhmert, "Die Stellung der Hansestädte zu Deutschland", in *Vierteljahrschrift für Volkswirtschaft und Kulturgeschichte*, i (1863); J. Hargreaves, *Hamburgs Stellung zum Zollverein...* (Bericht des Freihandelsvereins,

While the North German Confederation was being organised as a customs union, negotiations were taking place for the regulation of commercial affairs between States north and south of the River Main. Bismarck desired the establishment of a new Zollverein in which the General Congress and its *liberum veto* should be replaced by a customs council and a customs parliament in which decisions should be made by majority vote. It has been seen that in the early 'sixties Hansemann and others had agitated in favour of the establishment of a representative assembly to deal with customs affairs.

Both economic and political advantages might be expected from such an arrangement. Commercial legislation could be passed with much less difficulty than before. From the political point of view Bismarck thought that a customs parliament might gradually have its functions enlarged until it would become a general legislative assembly for the whole of Germany. His hopes were shared by others. The Grand Duke of Baden, for example, wrote to Prince Hohenlohe in March, 1867: "Confidential communications from Berlin tell us that the admission of delegates from the South German Governments to the Federal Council, and of South German deputies to the North German Reichstag for tariff matters, and therewith the transformation of the latter body into a Tariff Parliament, may be expected as a possible immediate first step towards a closer union of North and South. Once a beginning were made in

Hamburg, 1865); W. Marr, *Selbstständigkeit und Hoheitsrecht der freien Stadt Hamburg sind ein Anachronismus geworden* (1866); and the following pamphlets: *Neun Gutachten, die künftige handelspolitische Stellung Hamburgs betreffend* (1867); *Hamburg und der Zollverein* (1867); *Beleuchtung der zwanzig Gutachten der Freihafenpartei* (1867); *An ein hohes Zollparlament. Denkschrift des Vereins für Anschluss Hamburgs an den Zollverein* (1868); *Die Stellung der Hansestädte zum Norddeutschen Bunde vom handelspolitischen und volkswirtschaftlichen Standpunkte* (1869); *Der Handel Hamburgs. Sieben Briefe an ein deutsches Zollparlamentsmitglied* (1869). See also Hildegard Budach, *Hamburg und der Norddeutsche Bund* (Hamburg, 1935: Dissertation), but this book should be used with caution.

this way, it would, doubtless, soon be extended to cover other spheres."[1]

The South German States recognised that from the economic point of view it would be in their interests to preserve the Zollverein.[2] They saw, too, that the veto of a single State on customs legislation prevented the smooth working of the Zollverein. But Bavaria and Württemberg were not attracted by Bismarck's proposal to establish a customs parliament. Particularist feeling was still strong in South Germany and it was feared that if a customs parliament were set up Prussia might secure an undue influence in South German affairs.

On June 3, 1867, a conference was opened in Berlin between Prussia, Bavaria, Württemberg, Baden and Hesse-Darmstadt. Bismarck, who presided, put forward a plan (drawn up by Delbrück) for a Zollverein whose legislative organs should be a federal customs council and a customs parliament. The customs council was to be composed of members of the Bundesrat of the North German Confederation with the addition of plenipotentiaries appointed by the South German Governments. The customs parliament was to be composed of members of the North German Reichstag with the addition of South German representatives elected in the same way as their colleagues in the North. Prince Hohenlohe replied that Bavaria "had had quite a different conception of a Tariff Parliament. We had had in mind an assembly to which the North German Parliament and the South German Chambers would make over certain rights (an assembly) which should concern itself with matters relating to the tariff and to trade but which should not be admitted into the North German Parliament."[3] Bismarck threatened to ex-

---

[1] The Grand Duke Frederick of Baden to Prince Hohenlohe, Carlsruhe, March 4, 1867 (*Memoirs of Prince Hohenlohe*, 1 (1906), p. 193).

[2] The industrialists of Offenbach (situated on the left bank of the Main) declared: "Rather than be separated from the North by a customs frontier we would dig a new bed for the river so as to be on the right bank" (quoted by P. Benaerts, p. 649).

[3] See Note by Prince Hohenlohe regarding the conference of ministers in Berlin, June 3, 1867 (*Memoirs of Prince Hohenlohe*, 1, pp. 229–31).

clude Bavaria from the Zollverein if his plan were rejected. So Bavaria gave way on the main issue. Prince Hohenlohe, however, secured two concessions. Bavaria obtained six votes instead of four in the federal customs council and she was to be consulted in Zollverein negotiations with Austria and Switzerland.

Preliminary agreements were signed with Baden and Württemberg on June 4, with Hesse-Darmstadt on June 7, and with Bavaria on June 18. The details were worked out at a customs conference at Berlin a few weeks later. The new Zollverein treaties were signed on July 8, 1867.[1] They came into force on January 1, 1868, and were to last for twelve years. On all important matters the Prussian point of view prevailed. In Baden little difficulty was experienced in securing the approval of the chambers to the new Zollverein agreements. But in Bavaria and Württemberg there was serious opposition.[2] The Bavarian upper house at first refused to accept the Zollverein treaty unless Bavaria were granted the right of vetoing customs legislation. Bismarck would make no concession on this point. Eventually the chambers of both Bavaria and Württemberg accepted the treaty in its original form.[3]

The new Zollverein of 1867 differed in many important respects from the old Zollverein. Between 1834 and 1867 the legal basis of the customs union was a number of treaties between sovereign States. After 1867 the legal position was more complicated. It is necessary to bear in mind both the commercial relations of members of the North German Confederation to each other (which now rested primarily upon the constitution

---

[1] The agreements of June, 1867, are printed by L. Hahn, *Zwei Jahre Preussisch-Deutscher Politik*, 1866–67... (1868), pp. 264–631.

[2] In Württemberg the opposition was led by Moritz Mohl. See his pamphlet, *Mahnruf zur Bewahrung Süddeutschlands vor den äussersten Gefahren. Eine Denkschrift für die süddeutschen Vertreter* (Stuttgart, 1867), particularly pp. 25–42.

[3] For the debates of October 21–23 and 30–31, 1867, in the Bavarian lower house on this question see *Verhandlungen der Kammer der Abgeordneten des bayerischen Landtages...1866–68*, II, pp. 49–126.

of that federation) and the economic links binding the southern States to the North German Confederation (which remained on a treaty basis).

Before 1867 there had been no representative body to deal with customs legislation. The General Congress had been a meeting of official delegates who carried out the instructions of their Governments. A single Government could veto any proposal. Tariff changes could be brought about only by wearisome bargaining between Zollverein Governments.

After 1867 the old General Congress was replaced by a Federal customs council where decisions were by majority vote. There were fifty-eight votes in the customs council. Prussia had seventeen, Bavaria six, Saxony and Württemberg four each, Baden and Hesse-Darmstadt three each, Mecklenburg-Schwerin and Brunswick two each and other States one each. Every member of the Zollverein could send as many delegates to the customs council as it had votes but one delegate could give all the votes of the Government he represented.

But Zollverein affairs were no longer regulated solely by an assembly consisting entirely of delegates appointed by the various State Governments. There was also a popularly elected customs parliament. It was summoned, opened and closed by the Prussian Crown. It was not called together at regular intervals but only when legislative business required or when one-third of the customs council demanded a meeting. The life of each customs parliament was three years.

The customs parliament dealt only with tariff changes, regulations for collecting duties, the conclusion of treaties of commerce and navigation with foreign Powers and the regulation of excises on sugar-beet, salt and tobacco. The powers of the customs parliament were thus strictly limited. It voted certain important sources of revenue but it had no control over the spending of the money it raised. If it quarrelled with the executive it could be dissolved and no new customs parliament could meet unless the Prussian Crown or a third of the customs council desired it. Its members were not paid for their services, so that many possible candidates were unable to offer themselves for election. Bismarck, who was mainly responsible for its constitution, was determined that the customs parliament should not be strong enough to defy him.

In the old Zollverein each member had its own customs administration for collecting duties and there was a system of mutual inspection to secure uniformity of administration. After 1867 the local customs administrations were maintained but uniformity was now secured by the appointment of "customs inspectors" who were Zollverein officials and were not Civil Servants of separate States. Revenue continued to be divided according to population but the financial privileges of Frankfurt-am-Main, Hanover and Oldenburg disappeared. Prussia had absorbed Frankfurt and Hanover and could have claimed the extra revenue formerly accorded to these States but she did not do so. Oldenburg retained her independence and she demanded a continuance of her *Präzipuum*. She had, however, to give it up. By a special agreement, signed on May 8, 1867, the salt monopolies of various German States were abolished and a general Zollverein excise on salt was introduced instead. After 1867 taxes on tobacco also came under the control of the Zollverein. A tax was levied on land on which tobacco was grown. Details were left to future legislation by the customs parliament.

Perhaps the most significant difference between the old Zollverein and the new lay in the position of Prussia. Before 1867 the Zollverein was legally a union of sovereign States with equal rights. At the General Congresses the policy of the customs union was decided by negotiations between partners whose economic resources varied greatly but whose votes were (with few exceptions) equal. Actually Prussia was in a fairly strong position since she was by far the largest and wealthiest State in the customs union and since she distributed annually considerable sums of money to most other members of the Zollverein. She negotiated treaties with foreign Powers and, if she were determined to get her way, she generally succeeded. The threat to break up the Zollverein forced recalcitrant members to accept both the treaty of 1851 with Hanover and the treaty of 1862 with France. But the legal equality of all Zollverein members undoubtedly hampered Prussia's policy. After 1867, on the other hand, Prussia's predominant position in the Zollverein rested upon a legal foundation. She summoned and dissolved the Customs Council. Her representative presided over its deliberations. Nearly a third of its votes were in her hands. She alone might veto any decision which proposed to alter existing customs regulations. She summoned, prorogued and dissolved the customs parliament. She presented for its approval the decisions of the Customs Council. Prussia signed commercial and navigation treaties with foreign Powers on behalf of the Zollverein. Only when treaties were negotiated with Austria or Switzerland was Prussia bound to consult members of the Zollverein who had a common frontier with those States. This legal preponderance of Prussia rested upon solid economic foundations. In the new Zollverein Prussia possessed nine-tenths of the production of the mining and metallurgical industries, half the textile factories and two-thirds of the workers employed in the great German industries. "Such an industrial preponderance was bound to prepare the way for political hegemony."[1]

The new Zollverein had a permanence which its predecessor did not possess. The crises of 1849–53 and 1862–65 showed how near the old Zollverein could come to dissolution. After 1867 the most important part of the Zollverein—the North German Confederation with a population of 29 millions—was firmly united by a permanent constitution. The southern States—with a population of $8\frac{1}{2}$ millions—were, it is true, linked to the North German Confederation by a treaty which could be denounced. But there was very little likelihood of secession on the part of the South. In the report of the committee of the Bundestag of the North German Confederation which examined the Zollverein treaty of 1867 Herr von Liebe declared: "The Zollverein

[1] P. Benaerts, p. 648.

has been given administrative organs which will have a permanent character and their activity will link the Zollverein so closely with the economic and political life of the German people that it is difficult to imagine the dissolution of the customs union. Here lies the great importance of the treaty. It prepares the way for a new future for the union which will have a vitality that it did not possess before. The Zollverein now has a real constitution and although, as far as the South is concerned, this constitution rests upon a treaty which can be denounced, the permanence of a constitution depends not upon the possibility of its dissolution, but upon the necessity for its continuance and upon the strength of the roots which it strikes in practical affairs."[1]

(2) FROM ZOLLVEREIN TO EMPIRE, 1868–1871[2]

After the ratification of the Zollverein treaty of 1867 it was necessary to hold elections in Bavaria, Württemberg and Baden early in 1868 so that South German deputies might meet members of

[1] Quoted by R. von Delbrück, II, p. 398.
[2] For the three sessions of the customs parliament, see *Stenographische Berichte über die Verhandlungen des...deutschen Zollparlaments* (1868–70), cited as *Stenographische Berichte*; Koller and Schneider, *Archiv des Zollvereins. Jahrbuch für Gesetzgebung und Verwaltung des Zollvereins* (2 vols. 1868–69); J. Venedy, *Das Zollparlament* (Freiburg-im-Breisgau, 1868); A. K. Reyscher, *Das Zollparlament und die deutsche Einheit* (1868); anonymous articles: "Die erste Session des deutschen Zollparlaments", in *Deutsche Vierteljahrschrift*, XXXI (1868), i; "Aus dem Berliner Zollparlament", in *Historisch-politische Blätter für das katholische Deutschland*, LXI (Munich, 1868), pp. 803–14, 889–904, 974–88; anonymous pamphlet, *Die erste Session des deutschen Zollparlaments....Aus dem Tagebuch eines süddeutschen Abgeordneten* (1868); W. Wehrenpfennig, "Die erste Session des Zollparlaments", in *Preussische Jahrbücher*, XXI (1868), pp. 698–709; L. Bamberger, *Vertrauliche Briefe aus dem Zollparlament, 1868–70* (1870), and in *Gesammelte Schriften*, IV (1896), pp. 69–217; H. von Poschinger, "Zollparlamentsbriefe", in *Deutsche Revue*, XXIX (1904), ii, pp. 25–8; W. Schübelin, *Das Zollparlament und die Politik von Baden, Bayern und Württemberg, 1866–70* (1935), chs. ii, iii. For other

the North German Reichstag in the customs parliament. It was intended to hold the first session of the customs parliament immediately after the second session of the Reichstag of the North German Confederation.

The South German elections were held in February and March, 1868.[1] They were fought mainly on the question whether the customs parliament should be expanded into a German Reichstag or not. The supporters of the adhesion of the South German States to the North German Confederation were opposed by particularists who desired to defend the sovereign independence of their own States as much as possible. But purely local political, religious and personal factors also played an important part in the election campaign. In Bavaria the opponents of union gained 27 seats and the supporters secured 21. All but one of the opponents of union belonged to the Clerical party. In Catholic Old Bavaria and lower Franconia the Clericals won every seat while in the Protestant parts of middle and upper Franconia the supporters of union were successful. There was a heavy Liberal vote (in favour of union) in the Bavarian Palatinate. In Württemberg opponents of union swept the board. They won all 17 seats. In Baden eight national Liberals (who favoured union) and six Clericals (who opposed union) were elected. In Hesse-Darmstadt, where the elections had taken place at the end of March, 1867, all six

---

aspects of Zollverein affairs between 1868 and 1871, see A. Kessler, *Der Zollverein gegenüber einer neuen Zollvereinsgesetzgebung* (1868); E. Morel, "Commerce du Zollverein de 1868 à 1872", in *L'Economiste français* (August 30, 1873), p. 539; H. von Poschinger, *Fürst Bismarck als Volkswirt*, I (1889), parts i–iv; and *Aktenstücke zur Wirtschaftspolitik des Fürsten Bismarck*, I (1890), parts i, ii; and K. Zuchardt, *Die Finanzpolitik Bismarcks und der Parteien im Norddeutschenbunde* (1910).

[1] For the South German elections to the customs parliament see L. Allmann, *Die Wahlbewegung zum ersten deutschen Zollparlament in der Rheinpfalz* (1913); anonymous article, "Die Badischen Wahlen im Zollparlament", in *Historisch-politische Blätter für das katholische Deutschland*, LXI (Munich, 1868), pp. 760–93; A. Rapp, pp. 266–88; and W. Schübelin, pp. 71–102.

members were in favour of union with the North German Confederation.[1]

The customs parliament met in Berlin on April 27, 1868. It was the first meeting of popularly elected representatives from the whole of Germany since the Frankfurt Assembly of 1848. Bismarck was determined to make full use of the customs parliament to tighten the bonds between North and South Germany. The South German deputies received a warm welcome and were lavishly entertained. Bismarck hoped that they would support, first, a motion declaring the customs parliament to be a suitable organ for the further unification of Germany and, secondly, an extension of the functions of the customs parliament beyond those laid down in the Zollverein treaty of July, 1867. The opposition of the South German particularists, however, led to the failure of these plans.

The King of Prussia formally opened the customs parliament on April 27.[2] The election of officers followed. Dr Simson (chairman of the North German Reichstag) was elected president, Prince Hohenlohe senior vice-president, and Count von Ujest junior vice-president. Next came a discussion on the recent elections in South Germany. There were complaints that both in Bavaria and Württemberg the elections had not been carried out in accordance with the provisions of the Zollverein

[1] Summary of election results:

	In favour of union	Against union	Total
Bavaria	21	27	48
Württemberg	0	17	17
Baden	8	6	14
Hesse-Darmstadt	6	0	6
	35	50	85

See W. Schübelin, pp. 71–102.

[2] The sermon preached on the occasion of the opening of the customs parliament caused offence to some South German representatives since it was on the text: "And other sheep I have which are not of this fold: them also I must bring, and they shall hear my voice; and there shall be one fold and one shepherd" (John x. 16).

treaty of 1867. After heated debates two resolutions were passed. The first requested the chairman of the Federal customs council to approach the Bavarian Government with the object of bringing the Bavarian electoral law into line with that of the North German Confederation. The second requested him to attempt to ensure that future elections to the customs parliament in Württemberg should conform with the provisions of the Württemberg electoral law and with the Zollverein treaty of 1867.

The South German particularists, smarting under this rebuke, were now more determined than ever not to countenance Prussia's political aims in the customs Parliament. Their vigorous opposition secured the defeat of a motion proposed by Dr Metz (a Hesse-Darmstadt deputy) to send to the King of Prussia an address thanking him for his speech at the opening of the customs parliament. The particularists objected to the proposed address because it referred to the strength of national feeling in Germany and to the hope that the country would soon be united. They threatened to leave the customs parliament in a body if the address were carried.[1]

They followed up their success by strong declarations against any attempt to extend the functions of the customs parliament beyond those laid down in the Zollverein treaty of July, 1867. This question was raised on a discussion on the tax on wine levied in Hesse-Darmstadt. Bamberger (a Hesse-Darmstadt national Liberal) complained that the tax did not conform with the Zollverein excise on wine. Moritz Mohl (a Württemberg particularist) replied that the customs parliament had no right to discuss this matter at all. Bismarck refused to accept this point of view. But on the general question of the extension of the customs parliament he declared that the South German States had nothing to fear. Their independence was not in danger and if they ever entered the North German Confederation it

---

[1] For the debate on this question in the customs parliament on May 7, 1868, see *Stenographische Berichte* (April 27–May 3, 1868), pp. 85–108: for the text of the motion see Appendix no. 7.

would be of their own free will.[1] Thus the attempt to expand the customs parliament into a German Reichstag failed. The customs parliament in future devoted itself to commercial affairs.[2]

The political disputes of the first session of the customs parliament did not prevent the passing of important commercial legislation. Commercial treaties with Austria-Hungary, Spain and Rome were accepted. The Austro-Zollverein commercial treaty of 1865 came to an end with the outbreak of the Seven Weeks War. By the Peace of Prague it was agreed to renew the treaty of 1865 but either party might terminate it by giving six months' notice. It was also agreed to open negotiations for the revision of this treaty. Austria-Hungary was now prepared to reduce some of her import duties. She was anxious to secure the benefits of the most favoured nation commercial treaties which had recently been signed by many States in Western Europe. Moreover, after the disastrous war of 1866, the Hapsburgs had to pay greater attention to Hungary's wishes. The Magyars exported agricultural products and imported manufactured goods. They therefore favoured moderate, as opposed to high, import duties on manufactured articles.

A new commercial treaty between the Zollverein and Austria-Hungary was signed on March 9, 1868. It included a most favoured nation clause. Austria-Hungary granted the Zollverein certain special concessions (with regard to the importation of manufactured articles) as well as tariff reductions similar to those recently made to Britain,[3] France and Italy. The Zoll-

[1] See Bismarck's speeches in the customs parliament on May 18, 1868 (*Stenographische Berichte* (April 27–May 23, 1868), pp. 263–6). Cf. Bismarck to Werther, May 1, 1868 (Bismarck, *Die gesammelten Werke*, VIa, no. 1155).

[2] For the question of extending the functions of the customs parliament, see W. Wehrenpfennig, "Das Zollparlament und seine Kompetenzweiterung. Eine Warnung vor falschen Wegen", in *Preussische Jahrbücher*, XXI (1868), pp. 591–600.

[3] By the Anglo-Austrian commercial treaty of December 1865 Austria-Hungary agreed that in 1867 her duties on British imports should not be higher than 25 per cent. *ad valorem*: in 1870 her duties were not to exceed 20 per cent.

verein reduced its duties on various Austro-Hungarian exports to Germany, the most important of which were those on wine and iron.[1]

The Spanish-Zollverein commercial and navigation treaty of 1868 gave the Zollverein most favoured nation treatment in Spain and her colonies.[2] The commercial treaty between the Zollverein and Rome (which was still in Papal hands) also contained a most favoured nation clause.[3]

In addition to approving of the commercial treaties, the customs parliament dealt with the vexed question of the tobacco duties and excise.[4] Hitherto foreign tobacco imported into the Zollverein had paid a duty of 4 thalers per hundredweight. Land on which tobacco was grown in the North German Confederation was taxed at the rate of from 3 to 6 thalers per Prussian morgen. No tobacco land-tax was levied in South Germany but tobacco sent from South to North Germany paid

[1] For the commercial treaty of March, 1868, between the Zollverein and Austria-Hungary, see the anonymous article: "Das Verhältnis von uns zu Österreich", in *Historisch-politische Blätter für das katholische Deutschland*, LXII (Munich, 1868), pp. 78–96; A. Matlekovits, pp. 121–9; A. Beer, pp. 379–83; W. Lotz, pp. 86–90; R. von Delbrück, II, pp. 387–90; and L. Láng, pp. 211–14. There was no reference in this treaty to the possibility of establishing an Austro-Zollverein customs union in the future. It may be added that by an agreement of June 13, 1867, Austria-Hungary had withdrawn from the German Monetary Union of 1857: see Lord Bloomfield to Lord Stanley, October 1, 1867 (Draft, no. 71) (F.O. 356/23).

[2] See *Despatch enclosing copy of a treaty of commerce and navigation between the North German Confederation and Spain, signed at Madrid, 30 March*, 1868 (P.P. 1868–69, LXXIII).

[3] In the following year (1869) the Zollverein signed three important commercial treaties—with Japan, Mexico and Switzerland. The Japanese treaty gained for the Zollverein the concessions already secured by Prussia in 1861: Japan also reduced her import duties on certain German textile goods. For the treaty between the Zollverein and Switzerland, see F. Ruckert, *Die Handelsbeziehungen zwischen Deutschland und der Schweiz...* (1926), pp. 105–8.

[4] Cf. *Denkschrift betreffend Reform der Zucker-Besteuerung (vorgelegt von der Handelskammer in Hamburg im März 1868)* (Hamburg, 1868).

a "transition duty" of 20 silver groschens per hundredweight. The federal customs council now proposed that in future foreign tobacco should pay an import duty of 6 thalers per hundredweight and that a Zollverein land-tax of 12 thalers per morgen should be levied. The "transition duty" would be abolished. The free-traders carried an amendment to this proposal. The Zollverein import duty on foreign tobacco remained at the old rate of 4 thalers per hundredweight and the Zollverein tobacco land-tax was fixed at 3 thalers per morgen. This amendment involved the Zollverein exchequer in loss of revenue.

The first session of the customs parliament lasted for three weeks and came to an end on May 23, 1868. Patriots who had hoped that the customs parliament would be gradually developed into a German Reichstag were disappointed. The South German particularists had made it quite clear that they would not agree to any extension of the powers of the customs parliament. Bismarck saw that the unification of Germany would have to be accomplished by other means. But the first session of the customs parliament was not without significance in the development of German national feeling. For the first time for twenty years popularly elected deputies from all parts of Germany— except from the German provinces of the Hapsburg Empire— had sat in the same assembly. For three weeks representatives from both sides of the Main had debated problems which affected the welfare of the whole of Germany. Co-operation had not been particularly harmonious but it was better than no co-operation at all. Moreover, the approval of the commercial treaties—especially the important agreement with Austria-Hungary—and the settlement of the tobacco import duty and land-tax were solid achievements. The rapidity with which the customs parliament dealt with its business was a gratifying contrast to the prolonged and wearisome negotiations which had characterised the old Zollverein General Congress.

The second session of the customs parliament was held in

June, 1869. Dr Simson was again elected president: Prince Hohenlohe and Count von Ujest were again elected vice-presidents. The import duties on iron and rice were reduced. The duty on the importation of foreign sugar and the excise on home grown beet-sugar were raised. A proposed import duty on petroleum—already rejected in 1868—failed to secure the approval of the customs parliament. The customs parliament met for a third time in April, 1870. The same officers were elected as in 1868 and 1869. The Federal customs council laid before it a revised tariff embodying reductions of various import duties. After heated debates between free-traders and protectionists, a compromise, suggested by von Patow, was accepted by 186 votes to 84. The protectionists were placated by the decision to leave the duties on cotton goods at the existing level. The free-traders were satisfied since the import duties on iron[1] and rice were again reduced. The Zollverein secured fresh revenue from an increased duty on coffee.

No attempt was made, either at the second or at the third session of the Customs Parliament, to extend the legislative authority of the assembly. But, although there seemed no hope of turning it into a German Reichstag, the customs parliament played its part in fostering economic co-operation between Germans north and south of the Main. Prince Hohenlohe told the customs parliament on April 25, 1870: "To the recent sneer of a member of the customs parliament, on his retirement, that it was based on deception and that it adorned itself with the borrowed halo of a German Parliament, I would reply that no deception lies in the common work of German deputies; it is a gain to which we must hold fast. It is the firm ground in which the anchor of our national hope is embedded."[2]

The economic achievements of the customs parliament be-

[1] For the discussions in the customs parliament on the iron duties, see Max Sering, *Geschichte der preussisch-deutschen Eisenzölle...* (1882), ch. iv, sect. vii.

[2] *Stenographische Berichte* (April 21–May 7, 1870), p. 10, and *Memoirs of Prince Hohenlohe*, ii, p. 7 n.

tween 1868 and 1870 were considerable. The Zollverein tariff
had been reformed in accordance with the free-trade doctrines
of the day. Internal freedom of trade in wine, tobacco and salt
had been secured. But the reform of the tariff led to a decline
in the revenue of the Zollverein and the free-traders refused
to raise money by levying an import duty on petroleum[1] or by
raising the tobacco duty and the tobacco land-tax. It was only
with reluctance that they agreed to an increase in the import
duties on sugar and coffee.[2]

The reform of the tariff was carried a step further after the
establishment of the German Empire. In 1873 and 1875 various
import duties were abolished or reduced. Duties on iron—
except upon fine goods—were abolished on January 1, 1877.
The triumph of the free-traders was virtually complete and
Germany had a very liberal tariff. But the protectionist reaction
was at hand.[3]

Some important economic and social reforms carried out in
the North German Confederation in the late 'sixties deserve
notice because they affected a large part of Germany and most
of them were extended over the whole of the country a few
years later. A unified postal administration was established. In
1867 the legal limitation of the rate of interest was abolished.
In 1868 weights and measures were unified by the introduction
of the metric system. The industrial code (*Gewerbeordnung*)
of 1869 gave the worker the freedom to choose what occupation
he pleased (*Gewerbefreiheit*).

The disputes in the customs parliament on political and
economic matters showed how wide was the gulf which still
separated the southern States from the North German Con-

[1] Petroleum was a comparatively new commodity and was not mentioned in the tariff. Owing to the recent abolition of the general import
duty of half a thaler per hundredweight, it could enter the Zollverein duty
free.

[2] The Zollverein tariff of October, 1870 is printed by É. Worms,
L'Allemagne économique... (1874), pp. 587–624.

[3] See, for example, H. von Festenberg-Packisch, *Deutschlands Zoll-
und Handelspolitik*, 1873–77 (1879: collection of Reichstag debates).

federation.[1] The gulf was bridged when France declared war on Prussia in July, 1870. The danger from France brought North and South Germany together. The southern States came into the war as Prussia's allies. The French were defeated and had to give up Alsace-Lorraine.[2] Bavaria, Württemberg, Baden and that part of Hesse-Darmstadt which lay south of the River Main joined the North German Confederation to form the German Empire. With the exception of the German-speaking provinces of the Hapsburg Empire and the tiny States of Luxemburg and Liechtenstein, the German peoples were firmly united under the powerful leadership of Prussia. The Main Line had, indeed, been only "a halting place to take in water and coals".[3]

The German Empire, like the North German Confederation, was a customs union. A separate Zollverein was therefore superfluous. Legislation concerning matters of commerce and navigation was in the hands of the imperial Bundesrat and Reichstag and the Federal customs council and customs parliament were no longer necessary. Duties were collected by officials of the separate States under the supervision of imperial "customs inspectors". Customs revenue was no longer divided among the States but went to the imperial exchequer. Excises were also in the hands of the imperial authorities.

There were still a few anomalies in Germany's economic

---

[1] Bavaria's attitude to the German Question in 1868 may be judged from the fact that Emanuel Geibel lost his royal pension and his honorary professorship at Munich for writing a poem in honour of the King of Prussia which concluded with the lines:

"And may we hope, a last fond wish
    That yet some day thine eye may note
O'er all this Realm, at last made one
    From crag to sea thine Eagle float."

[2] The Franco-Prussian War had important results upon Franco-German economic relations. The Commercial Treaty of 1862 came to an end and was not renewed. By Article 11 of the Treaty of Frankfurt (1871) Germany and France agreed to grant each other permanently any tariff concessions either State might make to Great Britain, Belgium, Holland, Switzerland, Austria-Hungary or Russia.

[3] Miquel, quoted in the *Edinburgh Review*, CXXVIII (July, 1868), p. 240.

structure. Luxemburg, although not a part of the Empire, remained within the German customs system.[1] Hamburg and Bremen continued to pay a special contribution to the German exchequer and did not enter the imperial customs system.[2] Excises, too, were not entirely unified. Alsace-Lorraine levied a different beer-tax from that levied in the rest of the Reich until 1907: Bavaria, Württemberg and Baden retained special beer-taxes until 1919.

The structure of the tariff and the income derived from it at the time when the Zollverein was merged into the new Empire deserve notice. In 1871 the customs revenue of the German Empire amounted to $32\frac{1}{2}$ million thalers. An analysis of the income derived from articles on which more than 50,000 thalers was collected shows that three-quarters of the total customs revenue—nearly 23 million thalers—was derived from dues on popular foods and drinks and on tobacco. By far the most revenue from articles in this group was obtained from coffee on which 10 million thalers was paid in import duties. Textile goods paid $3\frac{1}{3}$ million thalers: iron and iron goods paid over $1\frac{1}{2}$ million thalers. On the remaining dutiable goods 1,800,000 thalers was collected.[3]

With the political unification of Germany in 1871 the economic unification of the country was practically complete. Prussia had taken a leading part in accomplishing both these tasks. It had taken Bismarck less than ten years to eject Austria from Germany, to defeat France and to annex Schleswig-Holstein and Alsace-Lorraine. Economic unification had been brought about more slowly. But the laborious work of Civil Servants such as Motz and Delbrück had at last been brought to a successful conclusion.

[1] The small Austrian districts of Jungholz (in Tirol) and Mittelberg (in Vorarlberg) also formed a part of the German customs system. The former was added to the German customs system in 1868, the latter in 1891.

[2] It may be added that the island of Heligoland, which was acquired from Great Britain in 1890, was outside the German customs system.

[3] F. Perrot, *Die Reform des Zollvereintarifs* (1874), pp. 12–15.

(3) THE ADHESION OF HAMBURG AND BREMEN,
1871–1888 [1]

The establishment of the German Empire in 1871 did not complete the economic unification of the country. Article 34 of the Imperial Constitution provided that Hamburg and Bremen "with such of their own territory and with such adjacent regions as may be necessary for this purpose, shall remain free ports outside the common customs frontier, until they ask to be included within it".[2] The special economic position that Hamburg and Bremen obtained in the German Empire was analogous to the political privileges secured by Bavaria and Württemberg.

[1] See G. Tuch, *Die Sonderstellung der deutschen Freihäfen* (1878); H. von Treitschke, "Der letzte Akt der Zollvereinsgeschichte", in *Preussische Jahrbücher*, XLV (1880), pp. 626–42; reprinted separately in 1880 and 1913; G. F. Beutner, *Der Zollanschluss der Hansestädte Hamburg und Bremen* (1880); T. Barth, *Die handelspolitische Stellung der deutschen Seestädte* (1880); cf. criticism by G. Tuch in *Sammlung wissenschaftlicher und kritischer Schriften aus den Gebieten der Volkswirtschaft und Technologie*, Heft XXXIII (1880); H. Eberstein, *Hamburgs Anschluss an das deutsche Zollgebiet* (Verhandlungen zwischen Senat und Bürgerschaft, I, 1881, and II, 1882); E. Roghé, *Rückblick auf den Anschluss Hamburgs und Bremens an das deutsche Zollgebiet* (1891); H. Blum, *Das deutsche Reich zur Zeit Bismarcks* (1893), pp. 360–72; T. Hansen, *Hamburg und die zollpolitische Entwicklung Deutschlands im neunzehnten Jahrhundert* (1913); Max Oskar Hübner, *Der Zollanschluss Hamburgs vom 15. Oktober 1888, bearbeitet nach den amtlichen Akten der beteiligten Berliner Regierungsstellen und des Staatsarchivs zu Hamburg* (unpublished Dissertation, Hamburg University, 1925); E. Hieke, *Hamburgs Stellung zum deutschen Zollverein, 1879–82. Ein Beitrag zur Wirtschaftspolitik Bismarcks* (Hamburg, 1935: Dissertation); and the following pamphlets: *Handelspolitische Aufsätze...* (1879), *Die Freihafenfrage in ihrer verschiedenen Interessenbeziehung* (1880), *Die Freihafenstellung vom nationalen Standpunkt aus betrachtet* (1880), *Erhaltung der deutschen Freihäfen ein nationales Bedürfnis* (1880), *Zum Zollanschluss Altonas* (Denkschrift des Königlichen Kommerzkollegiums, 1880). See also J. A. Crowe to Lord Odo Russell (June 3 and 9, 1880, in F.O. 64/965); George Annesley to Earl Granville (December 9, 1880 in F.O. 64/971 and February 9, May 1 and June 17, 1881, in F.O. 64/993).

[2] The wording of this clause was the same as that of Article 31 of the Constitution of the North German Confederation except that there was no reference to Lübeck.

The relations of Hamburg and Bremen with the German Empire were much the same as their previous relations with the North German Confederation. The free cities were not included within the German customs system. But the boundaries of the free port areas did not coincide with the political frontiers of Hamburg and Bremen. Altona (in Holstein) belonged to Prussia but was included in the free port region. Various isolated outlying parts of Hamburg and Bremen were included in the German customs area. Both free cities had Imperial customs houses and bonded warehouses. Both paid an annual contribution to the Imperial Exchequer in lieu of the customs duties which would have been collected if they had been within the German customs system.

Many Hamburg and Bremen merchants regarded this as a satisfactory permanent arrangement. They considered that the Imperial Constitution gave the free cities security against attempts to force them into the German customs system against their will. They feared that they might lose some of their entrepôt trade if they accepted the German tariff, which was higher than their own.

There was, however, a growing feeling in Germany that an end must be made of the anomalous situation by which the two chief ports of the Empire were outside its customs administration. It was felt that the existing arrangements could be regarded as only of a temporary nature and that one day Hamburg and Bremen must be included in the German customs system. Bismarck had to deal with many problems in the early years of the Empire and left untouched, for the time being, the economic independence of the two Hanse towns. But he was naturally anxious to complete the economic unification of Germany by including these ports within its customs administration. It is said, too, that he felt that the more closely Hamburg was associated with the Empire the easier would it be to suppress Socialism there.[1]

[1] G. Annesley to Earl Granville, December 9, 1880 (F.O. 64/971). In 1880 a minor state of siege was declared in Hamburg. This conferred special powers on the police.

In the late 'seventies the free-trade era in Germany came to an end. Two main causes led to the return to protection. First, the expenses of the Empire—particularly military expenditure —increased and Bismarck decided to secure the necessary revenue by increasing import duties rather than by raising direct taxes. The proceeds of customs duties were paid directly to the Imperial Exchequer, whereas direct taxes were collected by separate States which subsequently made contributions to the Imperial Exchequer. From the political point of view it was simpler to obtain fresh revenue by raising the tariff than by increasing direct taxation. Secondly, the fall in the prices of agricultural products led the agrarian "interest" which had previously opposed high import duties on manufactured goods, to combine with industrialists to demand a general increase in the tariff.[1]

The return to protection made more difficult the relations between the Empire and the two free cities. It increased the disparity between the tariffs of Germany on the one hand and of Hamburg and Bremen on the other. It necessarily led to a reconsideration of the annual contribution to be paid by Hamburg and Bremen to the Imperial Exchequer in lieu of levying Imperial customs duties. In 1879 it was agreed that this contribution should be raised from 3 to 5 marks per head of the urban population.

Bismarck brought pressure to bear upon Hamburg in two ways. First he threatened to include Altona and St Pauli in the German customs area. A proposal to this effect was made to the Imperial Bundesrat in April, 1880. Since Altona was Prussian territory, a strong case could be made for excluding it from the

---

[1] An account of Germany's change of fiscal policy is given in a despatch of J. A. Crowe to Lord Odo Russell (Berlin, May 28, 1880) in F.O. 64/965. See also H. von Festenberg-Packisch, *Deutschlands Zoll- und Handelspolitik*, 1873–77 (1879; collection of Reichstag debates); Alexander von Matlekovits, *Die Zollpolitik der Österreich-Ungarischen Monarchie und des Deutschen Reiches seit* 1868 (1891), ch. ii; and Max Nitzsche, *Die Handelspolitische Reaktion in Deutschland* (1905).

free-port area. But Altona lay so close to Hamburg that it would be difficult to draw a customs frontier between the two ports unless the Hamburg suburb of St Pauli were also included in the German customs system. Hamburg, however, firmly refused to consent to the removal of St Pauli from the free-port area and this part of the scheme was dropped. As far as Altona was concerned, Bismarck persisted with his plan and, on May 22, 1880, the Bundesrat unanimously agreed that this port should be included in the Imperial customs system. No date, however, was fixed for this change.[1]

Thus Bismarck's first attempt to coerce Hamburg had achieved little success. Hamburg had no serious objection to the inclusion of Altona in the Imperial customs system and she knew that there were almost insuperable obstacles to the construction of a customs frontier between Altona and St Pauli. Her opposition to economic union with Germany remained as firm as ever. On December 9, 1880, George Annesley (the British Consul-General at Hamburg) reported that "it may be clearly stated that there is no question whatever of Hamburg voluntarily joining the Zollverein; such a course at present is hardly discussed".[2]

But Bismarck was determined to break down Hamburg's opposition. He decided to enforce the fourth clause of the Austro-German Elbe Navigation Treaty of 1880 by which customs duties might be levied on goods entering Germany by the Elbe *before* they reached Hamburg. Since the abolition of the Stade tolls in 1861, goods on ships on the lower Elbe were

---

[1] G. Annesley wrote to Earl Granville on December 9, 1880, that "the absorption of Altona into the Customs Union remains solely a question for the Prussian Authorities. The natural difficulties comprised in the position of this township as regards Hamburg are the chief reasons why this matter cannot be readily effected. The actual boundary line passes continuously through houses and other valuable property which would have to be destroyed; roads would require construction, large sums would have to be paid as compensation and an enormous staff of customs officials at a high expense would have to be maintained" (F.O. 64/971).

[2] G. Annesley to Earl Granville, December 9, 1880 (F.O. 64/971).

not liable to pay duty until they were landed. The Elbe below Hamburg was treated as if it were the open sea.[1] Foreign goods could be sent to and from Hamburg by river without paying German import duties. If such duties were now levied on the lower Elbe—at Glückstadt for example—it was feared that Hamburg's entrepôt trade would be seriously hampered. Hamburg therefore protested vigorously against this proposal and claimed that she had ancient rights which guaranteed her free access to the open sea.[2] But the Bundestag accepted Bismarck's point of view.

Owing to this threat Hamburg reluctantly entered into negotiations for adhesion to the German customs system. In the middle of the discussions Bismarck suddenly asked the Bundestag to remove the Imperial customs house and bonded warehouse from Hamburg. This new threat to Hamburg's prosperity showed the Hamburg negotiators that they would have to come to terms with Bismarck. Whatever constitutional rights the free city possessed they were clearly no defence against the power of Prussia to inflict serious hardship upon Hamburg if the free city persisted in its opposition.

A treaty was signed in May, 1881,[3] and was accepted by the legislative assemblies of both the Empire and Hamburg. Hamburg entered the German customs system but secured a free-port area nearly 4 square miles in extent. The Imperial Exchequer was to bear half the cost—up to a maximum of 40 million marks—of constructing the free port. The heavy task of building it was completed in October, 1888. Most of the new free harbour was built opposite Hamburg on the south bank of the northern branch of the Elbe. The total cost was 150 million

[1] On the Elbe *above* Hamburg the special river tolls levied at Wittenberge had been abolished in 1870 but ordinary German import duties were levied at Bergedorf and Schandau.

[2] For Hamburg's point of view, see G. H. Kirchenpauer, *Die Freiheit der Elbschiffahrt* (1880): appeared anonymously.

[3] For an English translation of this agreement, see Enclosure to G. Annesley's Commercial Despatch to Earl Granville (no. 8 of June 17, 1881) in F.O. 64/993.

marks. The lower Elbe was also included in the German customs system but goods on ships proceeding from the open sea direct to the Hamburg free port were exempt from Imperial import duties.

In 1884 Bremen applied for admission to the German customs system. Negotiations were completed in the following year. Bremen, like Hamburg, secured a free-port area. It was built below the old town and bonded warehouses for petroleum were constructed at the outports of Bremerhaven and Geestemünde. The Imperial Government agreed to pay 12 million marks towards the cost of building the free port. The Bremen free port was extended in 1902.

Treitschke had written in 1880 that "the cry of pain of the free inhabitants of Anhalt-Köthen was the cradle-song of German customs unity and by all appearances the last act of the history of the Zollverein—which recently began on the same river, the Elbe—will come to a happy end to the echo of the cries of anguish of the free Hamburgers".[1] The gloomy prophecies of extreme free-traders that the commerce of Hamburg and Bremen would be ruined were not fulfilled. Germany's overseas trade was expanding and the Hanse towns shared in the general prosperity. The free-port areas of Hamburg and Bremen were large enough to cope with an extensive entrepôt trade. When Burgomaster O'Swald retired from his public offices

[1] H. von Treitschke, *Der letzte Akt der Zollvereinsgeschichte* (1880) p. 4. E. Roghé criticises Treitschke's point of view. "It would be difficult (he writes) to fail to recognise the truth more completely or to do a greater injustice to the national feeling of the Hanseatic Towns than to place the 'free Anhalt-Kötheners' of the twenties on the same footing as the 'free Hamburgers' of the eighties. In one case there was an opposition—based upon vain political jealousy—to a measure that was necessary and useful in their own economic interests: in the other there is a defence of important economic interests that affect the two small States as well as Germany as a whole against a blind enforced unification (*Gleichmacherei*) urged upon supposedly 'national' grounds." See Roghé's pamphlet, *Rückblick auf den Anschluss Hamburgs und Bremens an das deutsche Zollgebiet* (Hamburg, 1890), in Holtzendorff and Meyer, *Deutsche Zeit- und Streit-Fragen*... v (New Series, 1891).

in June, 1912, he declared, in a survey of Hamburg's progress since 1870, that "of all the undertakings which have been set on foot the customs union is and remains the most important achievement as far as Hamburg's development is concerned. Without this union Hamburg would never have gained the importance or prosperity upon which we look back today with pride and satisfaction".[1] Few will dispute this judgment.

(4) CONCLUSION

Only sixty-six years separated the first Zollverein treaty from the last. Those who, in 1819, signed the agreement by which the enclaves of Schwarzburg-Sondershausen adhered to the Prussian customs system would have been astonished had they known that this was to be the first of a series of treaties by which practically all the German people of Europe—save those of the Hapsburg dominions—would be united in one great economic system. Those who, in 1885, completed the negotiations for bringing Bremen within the Imperial customs area could see that they were concluding a work of far-reaching importance to Germany and to Europe as a whole.

Germany had witnessed profound political and economic changes in those sixty-six years. A loose confederation of States had been moulded into a powerful federal Empire, under a Hohenzollern Emperor. The Hapsburgs had been ejected from Germany. Several of the middle and small States north of the Main had been absorbed by Prussia. Alsace-Lorraine had been added to the Empire. Since 1871 Germany had been the most powerful State on the Continent. By 1885 the beginnings of naval construction and colonial expansion showed that she was determined to assert herself overseas as well. The economic revolution had been no less striking than the political changes. An agricultural country whose progress was hampered by in-

---

[1] Quoted by T. Hansen, *Hamburg und die zollpolitische Entwicklung Deutschlands im 19. Jahrhundert* (1913), p. 180.

ternal tariffs and poor communications had become the leading
manufacturing State on the Continent and her industrial expansion was causing Britain the most serious alarm.

What share had the Zollverein in bringing about these
changes? It is sometimes assumed that the establishment of the
German Empire was due almost entirely to political forces and
that the rapid rise of her industry and commerce may be dated
from the events of 1870–71. Actually the recognition of the
advantages of economic unity, which had already been secured,
was a factor favourable to the achievement of political unity,
and Germany's industrial successes after 1871 were based upon
the firm foundations of earlier progress. Between 1815 and 1850
the first steps towards industrial expansion were taken by the
founding and extending of the Zollverein and by the improvement of communications. The years 1850 to 1870 saw the rise
of German industries—particularly coal, iron, steel and textiles
—and the development of a capitalist organisation capable of
great expansion in the future.

The development of the Zollverein had thus both an economic and a political significance. It contributed to that expansion of manufactures and commerce in the 'fifties and
'sixties which prepared the way for Germany's rapid rise after
1871 to the position of the chief industrial State on the Continent. It is impossible to estimate the extent to which the Zollverein was responsible for these changes, since many other
factors favourable to industrial development have also to be
considered. It is necessary to guard against the temptation to
lay too much weight upon the part that treaties, laws and administrative decisions play in the economic life of a people.

The Zollverein was established in 1834. Germany's economic
position improved somewhat in the next twenty years. It is
easy to see a connection between the two. But it is a dangerous
half-truth—an over-simplification of a highly complicated
situation—to say that one caused the other. In its early days
the Zollverein was far from complete and its influence was
limited in many ways. The economic progress of the 'forties

and 'fifties was satisfactory but by no means extraordinary. The construction of railways, the enterprise of capitalists, the activity of the great industrialists were probably as important as the customs union in promoting economic welfare. Thus the linking of the agricultural regions east of the Elbe with the manufacturing districts of the Rhineland and Saxony was due at least as much to railway developments as to establishment of the customs union. On the other hand, it is clear that if there had been no Zollverein Germany's economic progress would have been hindered, however strong might have been the other economic forces working in favour of expansion. Prussia—despite the gap between her eastern and western provinces—was probably large enough in area and population and sufficiently rich in natural resources and manufactures to make very considerable economic progress even if trade with other German States were hampered by tariff barriers. But smaller States—except a few with special natural advantages—would probably have found themselves in serious difficulties if they had persisted in retaining their economic independence.

Germany's economic advance in the period 1815–71 may be considered from three angles—first, the gradual economic unification through the Zollverein and other agencies; secondly, the improvement in communications, particularly railways; and, thirdly, advances in manufactures, finance, agriculture and so forth. But such a division is one which should be adopted merely for convenience of discussion. It is essentially an artificial one since there is so much overlapping between the suggested factors. It would be fruitless to enquire which was the most important or which "caused" the others. Actually they are all of great importance and they sprang from similar fundamental causes. The period 1815–71 saw the genesis of the Industrial Revolution in Germany. The great capitalists and financiers and the commercial middle classes who stood to gain most from the industrialisation of the country supported such changes as would promote the progress of manufactures. The growth of the Zollverein and the construction of a railway system were changes of this nature. In this way the German environment was rendered more suitable for industrial advance. The difficulties in the way were due less to economic circumstances than to peculiar political conditions.

The Zollverein contributed to the attainment of German unity. The figure of Bismarck dominates Germany in the 'sixties, and students who investigate the history of the founding of the German Empire are tempted to confine their attention to his diplomacy and to the wars by which unity was attained. But, so far as her economic life was concerned, Germany had achieved a considerable measure of unification under Prussian leadership some time before Bismarck became Minister President in 1862. Only German States were members of the Zollverein. With the single exception of Luxemburg, every State that joined the Zollverein became a member of the Empire. Various suggestions that certain neighbouring non-German countries—such as Holland, Belgium, Denmark and Switzerland—should enter the customs union were not entertained seriously. There might be cogent economic arguments in favour of the expansion of the Zollverein on these lines, but Prussian statesmen felt that the customs union should be a national institution. Above all, the efforts of the Hapsburg dominions to enter the Zollverein were firmly and successfully opposed and here again it was political rather than economic factors that weighed decisively with Prussia. On the other hand, Prussia was prepared to make considerable financial sacrifices to secure the adhesion to the Zollverein of small German States.

Over thirty years of economic unity—even although that unity was not absolutely complete—were bound to have a profound influence upon the German peoples. This influence may easily be underestimated because it is so intangible. Changes which affect the daily lives of ordinary folk, especially when they are introduced piecemeal, sometimes tend to be ignored by those historians whose attention is fixed upon politics, diplomacy and campaigns. It is also easy, in reaction against this attitude, to exaggerate the influence of the customs union

upon German affairs and even to regard the establishment of
the Empire in 1871 as merely the formal completion of a unity
already achieved in the economic sphere.

It is more difficult to steer a middle course between these two
extremes—to claim, on the one hand, that the Zollverein had a
not unimportant share in fostering both economic expansion
and political unity; to admit, on the other hand, that the
economic bonds of the Zollverein were not in themselves
strong enough to bring the German peoples together permanently and that the Zollverein alone could not have brought
about the economic progress that Germany achieved between
1834 and 1871. In any general survey of German history in
these years the significance of the Zollverein should receive
proper attention—but not at the expense of other factors of
equal importance.

The experience which Prussia gained in managing the General
Congresses of the Zollverein was a valuable one. There her
statesmen became thoroughly familiar with the diplomatic
methods they were to practise in their dealings with middle and
small German Federal States between 1871 and 1914. They
learned how to cajole minor allies; how to get their own way
without undue display of force; and how to preserve at least in
form the sacred "sovereign rights" of the smallest Federal
State. How difficult it was to acquire that art may be gathered
from the fact that the Zollverein was twice on the verge of collapse and that it was only after the customs union had been
formally (though not actually) dissolved as a result of the war
of 1866 that Prussia was able to secure the founding of a new
Zollverein with a constitution that embodied many much
needed reforms. It was a disappointment to Prussia that Hanover and the South German States fought against her during
the Seven Weeks War. That struggle—like other civil wars—
showed that political animosities can break the bonds of
material interests. It has been seen that, owing to the division
of customs receipts on a basis of population, most members of
the Zollverein were receiving annually substantial sums of

money from Prussia. It might be argued that a pensioner is likely to become subservient to his patron but that was far from what actually happened. Prussia did occasionally find the financial weapon useful—but it was not nearly so strong a weapon as is imagined by those who believe that economic factors are all-important in political affairs.

Between 1867 and 1870—the period of reconstruction in Germany after the expulsion of Austria—the new Zollverein played a significant part. It was an important link between the German States north and south of the River Main. The Customs Parliament, in which sat popularly elected deputies not only from the North German Confederation but from the southern States as well, was the forerunner of the German Reichstag. Prussia's "customs empire"[1] proved to be the first step towards the establishment of a German Empire under Prussian domination.

A survey of the Zollverein is a study of remarkable contradictions and cross currents. It has been seen how tenaciously individual German States clung to their sovereign rights in the economic sphere. Only very slowly did the wider vision of the economic welfare of the whole people triumph over the supposed interests of separate States. Not until 1867 was it possible to get rid of the old Zollverein Congress with its *liberum veto* by which a single State could block the way to reform. Anxiety at Prussia's growing power, reluctance to endanger their independence, protests of manufacturers and agriculturists who thought their interests might suffer, representations of influential foreign Powers all played their part in making German States reluctant to enter the Zollverein and to co-operate loyally in economic matters. Not infrequently it was simply the hope of securing increased customs revenues that brought States into the Zollverein and subsequently kept them there. Even after 1871 some of the German States continued to judge proposals

[1] The phrase, *das preussische Zollkaisertum*, appears to have been coined by Friedrich Schlegel; see H. von Petersdorff, *Freiherr von Motz...* II (1913), p. 164.

for economic reforms in a parochial spirit. This is shown both by Bismarck's failure in 1876 to unify the various German railways into a single State enterprise[1] and by the strong opposition which he had to break down before he induced Hamburg and Bremen to give up their economic independence in the 'eighties.

In following the chequered course of the Zollverein it has been seen that many cross-currents influenced its progress. The effects on the development of the customs union of the Revolution of 1848, the commercial crisis of 1857, the controversy between free-traders and protectionists, the rivalry between Prussia and Austria, deserve careful study.

There was nothing "inevitable" in the history of the German customs union. Because the Zollverein was founded in the 'thirties and gradually expanded—until by 1871 it included all but two of the States that united to form the German Empire—that does not mean that there was anything in the "logic of history" which favoured that particular line of development as far as Germany's economic evolution in the nineteenth century was concerned. There might never have been a Zollverein at all and —as in Italy—economic unity might have followed and not preceded political unity. The Zollverein might have been founded earlier—say in the 'twenties—on the basis of the nineteenth article of the Federal Act. It might have come later —in 1848 on the basis of the Frankfurt Constitution or in the early 'fifties on the lines suggested by Bruck. There might have been a "Greater Zollverein" embracing the whole of Germany and all the Hapsburg dominions. The customs union that was actually established might not have survived until 1871. To speculate upon these possibilities is to recall the complexity of the factors which influenced the political and economic evolution of Germany in the period covered by the history of the Zollverein.

Through all these confusions the Prussian Civil Servants held their course steadily. They produced no genius for the

---

[1] See Alexander Krueger, *Zur Geschichte des Bismarckschen Reichseisenbahnprojekts vom Jahre 1876* (1909).

hero-worshipper to admire but their greatest representatives—
men like Maassen, Motz, Eichhorn, Kühne, Delbrück, Philipsborn and Pommer-Esche—were men of ability, character and
courage. By their tenacity of purpose they served not only
Prussia but—sometimes without knowing it—a greater Fatherland. They are less well-known than brilliant personalities like
List and Bruck—who both committed suicide, disappointed
and disillusioned—but they built an enduring economic structure. The Zollverein is the contribution of the Prussian Civil
Service to the founding of the German Empire.

Are there any lessons of general significance to be learned
from a study of the Zollverein? Three stand out clearly. In the
first place, the actual establishment of a customs union is only
a first step towards the attainment of the objects for which such
a union is founded. The permanent loyal support of all members
of the union is necessary before real success can be achieved.
If the individual States concerned are always thinking of their
own narrow financial and commercial interests, then the full
benefits of union cannot be secured. Moreover, it is not only
the difficult preliminary negotiations which are of significance
but it is the day to day co-operation of officials and merchants
that actually achieves the practical success of the union.

Secondly, a customs union would generally appear to be a
half-way house. It can seldom be regarded as a permanent
arrangement. Its members must sooner or later decide if they
are to go backwards or forwards. If they go back they revert
to their old position as independent tariff units. If they go forward they unify their economic organisations as far as possible.
Common tariffs are followed by common systems of internal
taxation—the same excises, the same direct taxes, the same
monopolies. They adopt the same weights and measures, the
same coinage, the same railway tariffs, the same code of commercial and maritime law, the same legislation with regard to
the regulation of industry and workers. Some of the early difficulties of the Zollverein were due to the fact that its members
failed to see this clearly. They seem to have hoped to secure the

advantages of economic union and yet to preserve a large measure of economic independence. Only when they recognised that economic unity means more than the establishment of a single tariff were the full benefits of the Zollverein secured. The tendency towards uniformity is seen also in the gradual whittling down and eventual disappearance of the special financial privileges secured by a few States (such as Hanover) when they first entered the Zollverein. This absorption of the middle-sized and small German States into a wider economic system may perhaps—paradoxically enough—be one explanation why Hanover and the South German States went to war with Prussia in 1866. The main reason was obviously a political one. They wanted to preserve a balance between the two German Great Powers and they sided with the weaker against the stronger. But the economic factor should not be ignored. From one point of view the war of 1866 may not unreasonably be regarded as a political revolt of the German middle States against their economic dependence upon Prussia. And when they were decisively defeated, their dependence upon Prussia, both economic and political, was greater than ever.

Thirdly, the history of the Zollverein gives little support to the argument that an approximate equality of economic development and similarity of economic interests in the various regions forming a customs union are essential if such a union is to be a success. It would be difficult to find an area of the same size with greater economic diversity than Germany in the early nineteenth century. Some regions were interested in the trades of the Baltic, the North Sea or the Atlantic; others were almost entirely continental in their economic ties. These differences were neither insuperable difficulties to the founding of the Zollverein nor did they prevent its expansion. Indeed, perhaps the most striking achievement of the customs union was to contribute powerfully to the welding of these divergent areas into a single prosperous economic unit.

APPENDICES

I

Approximate Equivalents of German Money, Weights and Measures at the Time of the Zollverein.

MONEY

German	English Equivalent
Thaler (Prussian)	About 3s.
Florin or Gulden (Austrian)	1s. 8d.
Mark Banco (Hamburg)	1s. 6d.
Mark Current (Hamburg)	1s. 2d.

LENGTH

Meile (league)	About 4⅗ miles.
Fuss (foot)	Varied in different States from 10 in. to 1 ft. 1 in.
Elle	Varied in different States. The Prussian Elle was 2 ft. 2 in.
Klafter	Varied in different States according to the size of the "Fuss". A "Klafter" was six times as long as a "Fuss".
Ruthe	Varied in different States. The commonest was the "Rhine-Ruthe" (4 yd. 6 in.).

VOLUME

Scheffel	Varied in different States. The Prussian Scheffel was 12 gallons.
Eimer	Varied in different States. The Prussian Eimer was 15 gallons; the Württemberg Eimer 65 gallons.

AREA

Prussian Morgen   Rather less than two-thirds of an acre.

WEIGHT

Prussian Zentner (hundredweight)
of 100 Pfund (pounds)   110 lb.
Zollverein Pfund (pound) $1\frac{1}{10}$ lb.

2

PUNCTATION

Reference is made in the text to certain agreements called punctations (*Punktationen*). Their precise significance is not always easy to ascertain. A careful study of the terms and validity of each punctation is necessary. There are various types of punctations.

1. A draft convention, i.e. terms proposed by a Government to lead to a treaty. This is the agreed policy of a single State and not an agreement between States (e.g. the policy of the Bavarian Government regarding a proposed customs union as laid down in the minutes of the Cabinet, May 1, 1820—Eisenhart Rothe and Ritthaler, I, pp. 383–4—and in instructions to Zentner and Stainlein, May 2, 1820—M. Doeberl, p. 60). A punctation may also be a draft convention agreed between statesmen of *different* States before the opening of official conferences (e.g. the agreement between Berstett of Baden and Marschall of Nassau on a proposed South German Customs Union, January 13, 1820—Eisenhart Rothe and Ritthaler, I, p. 371).

2. A statement, at a particular stage of negotiations between States, that agreement has been reached on certain points. The written statement is drawn up simply for the convenience of the plenipotentiaries. It has no binding force on the countries they represent, but would be considered binding upon the plenipotentiaries themselves.

3. A preliminary treaty or *pactum de contrahendo*, i.e. an agreement that a treaty shall in future be made on the basis of the terms agreed upon in the preliminary treaty. Minor details may be left for later discussion. The terms of the treaty do not come into force immediately. The parties have agreed to sign a treaty later on certain terms. So far and so far only are they bound.

For a discussion of the last two types of punctations mentioned see Franz von Holtzendorff, *Rechtslexikon* (Leipzig, 1881), III, pp. 239—40.

INDEX

1. Abbreviations.

Au	Austria(n)	H.C.	Hesse-Cassel
Br	Britain/British	H.D.	Hesse-Darmstadt
d.	died	(n)	note
F a.M.	Frankfurt-am-Main	Pr	Prussia(n)
F.M.	Foreign Minister	R	River
F.O.	Foreign Office	Z	Zollverein
Fr	France/French		

2. Omissions.

General topics, which are very frequently mentioned in the text (such as Germany, Prussia, Zollverein, trade), are omitted from the Index.

3. Titles.

Graf is translated as "Count", *Herzog* as "Duke", *Erzherzog* as "Archduke", and *Grossherzog* as "Grand Duke". *Prinz* and *Fürst* are both translated as "Prince". *Freiherr* has not been translated: the English equivalent is "Baron".

4. Provinces.

Provinces of Austria, Prussia, Bavaria and Hesse-Darmstadt appear in brackets after these States to identify towns—for example: Aachen: Town in Pr (Rhineland).